EVANESCENCE AND FORM

EVANESCENCE AND FORM

AN INTRODUCTION TO JAPANESE CULTURE

Charles Shirō Inouye

Cover image credits: Photo by Hosoe Eikoh, Kamaitachi #8 (Hijikata Tatsumi), Akita Prefecture, 1965.

First published in 2008 by
PALGRAVE MACMILLAN®
in the US—a division of St. Martin's Press LLC,
175 Fifth Avenue, New York, NY 10010.

Where this book is distributed in the UK, Europe and the rest of the world, this is by Palgrave Macmillan, a division of Macmillan Publishers Limited, registered in England, company number 785998, of Houndmills, Basingstoke, Hampshire RG21 6XS.

Palgrave Macmillan is the global academic imprint of the above companies and has companies and representatives throughout the world.

Palgrave® and Macmillan® are registered trademarks in the United States, the United Kingdom, Europe and other countries.

ISBN-13: 978–1–4039–6706–0 (paperback)
ISBN-10: 1–4039–6706–7 (paperback)
ISBN-13: 978–1–4039–6705–3 (hardcover)
ISBN-10: 1–4039–6705–9 (hardcover)

Library of Congress Cataloging-in-Publication Data

Inouye, Charles Shiro.
    Evanescence and form : an introduction to Japanese culture / Charles Shiro Inouye.
        p. cm.
    Includes bibliographical references and index.
    ISBN 1–4039–6705–9
        1. Japan—Civilization—Philosophy. 2. Impermanence (Buddhism)
    3. Aesthetics, Japanese. I. Title.

DS821.I569 2008
952—dc22   2008005344

A catalogue record of the book is available from the British Library.

Design by Newgen Imaging Systems (P) Ltd., Chennai, India.

First edition: October 2008

10 9 8 7 6 5 4 3 2 1

Printed in the United States of America.

In memory of my parents
Bessie Shizuko Murakami
Charles Ichirō Inouye

CONTENTS

LIST OF FIGURES

ACKNOWLEDGMENTS

I wish to acknowledge a number of people who helped with this project. Professors Edwin Cranston, Hosea Hirata, Sumie Jones, and Susan Napier looked over the outline and made helpful suggestions. During the writing of the manuscript, I consulted frequently with Professors Cranston, Rei Inouye, Komatsu Kazuhiko, and Suzuki Sadami. Mie Inouye read an early draft. Edwin Cranston, Rei Inouye, and Gary Leupp critiqued a later draft.

My students at Tufts have also played a vital role. I wish to thank the following undergraduates who read and critiqued the manuscript: Korey Aaronson, Corey Banks, Anthony Basile, Gabriella Bertucci, Peter Browne, Katharine Brush, Ella Carney, Daniel Casey, Yushu Cheng, Elizabeth Chou, Samantha Cohen, Michael Collado, Joanne Duara, Huy Giang, Jason Greene, Chloe Guss, Steven Hanton, Philip Haslett, Patrick Kinsella, Mandy Lee, Patrick Lee, Leon Mandler, Jason Markowitz, Patrick Meyers, Rebecca Mohr, Peter Moore, Alexander Nisetich, Samuel Obey, Danielle Okai, Nathan Paine, Martin Pepeljugoski, Caroline Pronovost, Catherine Richard, Angela Robins, Daniel Sofio, Andrew Sokoloff, Joy Song, Sandy Tang, Ann Tortorella, Alexandra Uden, Stefanie Vermillion, Michael Vitiello, and Jennifer Weiskopf.

I also thank their predecessors who contributed their research to this project: Shigeki Abe, Nicholas Bercovici, Jennifer Chang, Chin Pui Chau, Vivian Cheng, Nicole Cheung, Aditi Dhar, Charlene Engle, Amanda French, Jason Grauer, Nicholas Haslett, Jarred Johnson, Heidi Kim, Michael Kinsella, Lipou Laliemthavisay, John Lee, Charles McClean, Geumbin Park, Kenneth Richstad, Roman Rubinstein, Giancarlo Saldana, Trinh Thach, Lauren Thomas, Ivan Vargas, Anh Tuan Vo, Joel Wertheimer, and Rebecca Wong.

I would also like to thank their predecessors who began this project with me: Austin Blair, Dana Brown, Regan Cerato, Daniel Gaspari, Brody Hale, Brooke Hendrickson, Ray Hsu, John Jordan, Karen Leung, William Matelski, Justin Mercier, Linh Phan, Rishi Sivasiamphai, Miki Stevens, Avantika Taneja, Johnson Thurston, Klementyne Weyman, and Julia Wolfson.

I am grateful to Tufts University for a timely sabbatical, and to the faculty and staff of the International Research Center for Japanese Studies in Kyoto, Japan, where I was a visiting research scholar for one year, 2005–06. I also wish to thank the staff at Tufts University's Tisch Library, and the Harvard

University's Reischauer Institute for making the resources of Harvard-Yenching Library, Widener Library, and the Rubel Asiatic Research Collection available to me. John Solt was instrumental in obtaining permission from Hosoe Eikoh for the cover photo. Nicole Johnson helped with the preparation of the index.

HISTORICAL PERIODS

Jōmon	ca. 4000 BCE	Hunting and gathering, rope-patterned pottery, animism, shamanism, agriculture develops
Yayoi	ca. 500 BCE	Wetland rice cultivation, wheel-turned pottery, metal tools
Kofun	250–538 CE	Horses introduced, powerful clans, huge burial mounds, immigration and cultural influences from the Continent (including writing, Confucian texts)
Asuka	538–710	Yamato clan dominates, Buddhism (538) introduced, land and governmental reform after Chinese model, continued influence of power elites
Nara	710–94	First permanent capital, intense patronage of Buddhism, ritual poetry gives way to lyricism, Japanese writing develops
Heian	794–1185	Capital moves to Heian-kyō, flourishing of sophisticated court culture, romances and diaries written by women, gradual shift of power from court to provincial warrior families, development of popular Buddhism
Kamakura	1185–1333	Ascendance of samurai, feudalism, capital moved east to Kamakura, Zen Buddhism
Muromachi	1333–1568	The Ashikaga move capital back to Kyoto, Zen-inspired Higashiyama refinement, weakening central government, the Ōnin War (1467–77) destroys Kyoto and begins a period of even greater instability

Azuchi-Momoyama	1568–1600	Protracted civil wars among feudal lords, gradual consolidation of land and power, castle building, urbanization, popular uprisings, Jesuits and firearms, invasion of Korea, innovation in the arts
Tokugawa (or Edo)	1600–1868	Peace accomplished by oppressive measures, stability and relative isolation, flourishing of urban bourgeoisie culture, commercial printing of books and woodblock prints, Neo-Confucianism, Nativism, Dutch Studies, tight control of foreign relations gradually erodes as foreigners appear with increasing frequency, Japan "opened" to the world (1854), millenary revolt as Tokugawa government weakens
Meiji	1868–1912	Samurai from Western Japan overthrow the Tokugawa, Japan in a new context of competing nations, survival of the fittest, learning from the West, emperor as symbol of the nation, conservative reaction in the 1890s, Confucianism reasserted, empire building, imperialist wars with China (1895) and Russia (1905), control of Formosa (Taiwan) and Korea
Taishō	1912–26	"Roaring Twenties" prosperity, brief party-led democratic governance, formation of zaibatsu conglomerates, Marxist critique of capitalism and modernity as wealth gap widens and race-relations worsen, Japanese immigrants in the United States resented as economic competitors, Kantō Earthquake (1923)
Shōwa	1926–89	Worldwide depression, patriotic societies and agrarian fascism from bottom up, military takes lead, fascism from top down, State

		Shintō, annexing of Manchuria as military strikes out on its own (1931), invasion of China (1937), spread of Japanese empire to include Southeast Asia and the islands of the South Pacific, Pearl Harbor (1941), carpet bombing of Japan's cities, A-bomb attack on Hiroshima and Nagasaki, end of World War II (1945), U.S. occupation and the Americanization of Japanese culture, pacifism, economic rejuvenation, consumerism
Heisei	1989–present	Collapse of bubble economy, pro-U.S pro-business Liberal Democratic Party survives temporary setback, creeping remilitarization, globalization of Japanese popular culture

PART ONE

THE ORDER OF HERE-AND-NOW: ANCIENT, MEDIEVAL, AND EARLY MODERN JAPAN (TO 1868)

IN SPRING THE CHERRY BLOSSOMS

The university where I teach and do research sits atop a hill that overlooks the city of Boston. From the library roof, you can enjoy the sights of Cambridge and Somerville in the foreground, the urban skyline in the distance, and the Atlantic Ocean far beyond. To the south and west are the hills of Belmont and Arlington, and the neighborhoods of Waltham and Newton. From this spot, I have watched the seasons come and go. In the summer, Medford residents gather to enjoy Independence Day fireworks as they explode above the Charles River. In the fall, it is the maples that flare red and yellow and orange. In winter come the cold snows and the deep magenta sunsets. In spring, the profusion of budding leaves and flowering woods.

Boston's changing seasons remind me of the Zen master Dōgen's (1200–53) famous poem.

Haru wa hana	In spring the cherry blossoms,
Natsu hototogisu	In summer the cuckoo,
Aki wa tsuki	In fall the moon,
Fuyu yuki saete	And in winter
Hiyashikarikeri	The cold snow.[1]

This brief *tanka* is about change, the turning of the seasons. Yet it expresses change by way of a formula. The cuckoo indicates summer. The moon makes us think of fall. Snow is for winter. In spring, cherry blossoms are representative. Clearly, there is a paradox here. While it is true that the seasons are always in a state of change, this change occurs according to a fixed pattern or form.

This book attempts to appreciate this tension between change and form. While the Japanese embrace the notion that life is evanescent—brief, fleeting, ever-changing, unpredictable, and fragile—they also demonstrate a predilection for formality. Certain actions and things are meaningful in an unchanging way. In Japan, formality affirms the potential chaos of evanescence; and coming to understand the interaction of form and flux is our general purpose. In a place that celebrates dreams, ambiguity, and even confusion, why do the trains run on time?

Let us return to Dōgen's poem and to a relevant point that easily gets lost in translation. The first line reads, "*Haru wa hana.*" A more literal translation would be "In spring the *flowers.*" *Hana* can be a generic term that signifies all blossoms—from peonies to lilies. Anyone familiar with the Japanese poetic tradition, however, knows that in poems such as this one, *hana* always means cherry blossoms. Why should this be?

At an early point in Japan's history, *hana* actually referred to plum blossoms, a flower that appears even earlier in spring. But by the tenth century, the term came to signify *sakura*, or cherry blossoms. Since then, this poetic conceit has been remarkably consistent. It is current today. *Hana* still means cherry blossoms, and cherry blossoms still signify the essence of spring: that moment when pale, bright petals scatter from the branch at the height of their beauty. As *hana*, they give form to evanescence.

I turn away from Boston and walk a few hundred yards to the other side of the mall. I am standing in front of Bendetson Hall with its red brick walls and white columns. It is a typical New England academic building. Beyond Bendetson and down the hill to the north lie Medford Center, and the verdant Fells of Winchester and Malden. Still farther beyond, only visible in the imagination, are New Hampshire, Vermont, Maine, and Canada.

I focus my attention on the cherry trees in front the building. It is early May, and I have been coming here once a day for the past week. All signs indicate that tomorrow will be the day my students and I have been waiting for all semester. Last year, we were disappointed. The trees bloomed after classes adjourned. But this year, the timing seems perfect. I will bring my students here tomorrow, and they will experience a Japanese moment for themselves.

Our course of study, An Introduction to Japanese Culture, begins in the dead of winter. On the first day of class, I ask everyone to note the cold and the ice.

> We might not get above freezing for the next two months. But by the end of this class, the world will change dramatically. Spring will arrive. The cold, frozen earth will be warm and alive. Go take a look. Remember what you see. The cherry trees in front of Bendetson are bare and dead-looking now. But by the end of the semester, those same frigid branches will be filled with blossoms. Green grass will be growing. The air will be filled with the scent of new life.

Tomorrow, my students, who have also been checking the trees, will witness the truth of evanescence for themselves. It is a powerful moment. No amount of lecturing or reading and writing about evanescence could substitute for the sight of thousands of delicately pink petals scattering in the spring breeze, dying at the height of their beauty, sadly affirming the fate of us all. Like those blossoms, we, too, will soon be gone. Like those *hana*, we too will become a fleeting memory. The cherry trees—which have read no books, attended no lectures, and have written no essays—will outlast us all. But they too will someday fall.

We sit down on the grass. Bashō's clouds, "the travelers of eternity," move constantly above our heads. They pass before the sun, and momentarily block its warming rays. We remember the white winter we have just survived. But then the sun shines through a gap in the clouds; and we feel the promising warmth of spring and summer again. Having spent a semester studying *hakanasa* and *mujō* (the principal Japanese words for evanescence), our senses are sharpened. The fleeting moment will *not* last. We have learned the sorrowful beauty of change in poems such as Dōgen's. We experience Japanese culture (*bunka*, 文化)—the way that life there has been patterned— by way of this *hanami*, this blossom viewing that includes food, friends, family, and *sake*.

These pages will consider a wide range of responses to the truth of change. Change is fundamental, but its manifestations and the responses it elicits vary. By tracing these, a general profile will emerge. If this study goes well, we will come to understand, for instance, why the corporate section manager, who is admirably hardworking and disciplined at three in the afternoon, is so inebriated by ten o'clock that evening that he needs help getting home. Or why, the next morning, no one remembers the outrageous things that were said or done the night before.

As for how form plays into this analysis, let me illustrate its relevance with a brief story that was told to me by my colleague Anthony Chambers. He was riding the Central Line late one night. In fact, it was the last train leaving Shinjuku Station for the western suburbs of Tokyo. The car was relatively empty. One gentleman, dressed in a white shirt and a dark suit, was standing next to where he was sitting. He was drunk, hardly able to stay on his feet. As the train moved away from the city, stopping at every station, he wavered, like a reed blowing in the wind. His eyes were closed, and his mouth occasionally opened as if he might vomit at any moment. Half-conscious, he continued in this fashion until the train reached Musashi Koganei and suddenly, as if awakening from a dream, he let go of his strap and began stumbling toward the opened door.

Despite his attempts to hurry, he moved slowly. Just as he reached the door, he collapsed. There he was in the doorway, half in and half out—his upper body on the platform, his lower body still in the car. Alarmed, Tony jumped up to help. He was afraid the doors might close on the man's waist and trap him. Would the train take off and drag him along the platform?

Just as he kneeled down at the fallen man's side, a young man dressed in a Japan Railway uniform ran to them from across the platform. Rather than immediately pick up the fallen office worker and drag him out of harm's way, though, he paused. He faced the fallen passenger and bowed politely. Addressing him in formal Japanese, he said, "*Okyaku-sama, orimasu ka? Norimasu ka?*" "Honorable Passenger. Are you getting on? Or are you getting off?"

I have since thought many times about that moment. Of course, the doors would have automatically opened had they pressed in on some obstruction. Of course, the train would not have started off and dragged him to his death. And, yes, it was perfectly logical for the young man to ask the drunken office worker whether he was getting off or getting on. Who would want to be helped back on a train if you were trying to get off, especially if it were the last train of the night?

Those very reasonable considerations aside, it is the formality of that moment that intrigues me. What the incident suggests is that even in times of emergency, form prevails. Does this mean that in Japan, where being polite matters, there is no such thing as chaos and barbarism? The problem with this expectation, of course, is that we know the system actually does break down, and that, precisely because of Japan's formality, phenomena such as panic and chaos and massacre happen in ways that are dramatic and far-reaching, as we shall see.

As with emergencies so with books. In an introductory course on Japanese culture, or for any beginner's text such as this, success becomes largely a matter of which explanations are required, and which are given. Admittedly, I provide only a narrow range of questions and answers, addressing the very form of formality as it emerges as a lasting response to change. And yet, while the following pages present a theoretical and often distanced analysis of Japanese culture, I hope they will also become a practical handbook for cross-cultural learning. My working assumptions going forward are that, first, there is less enjoyable truth in definitions than in moments of defini- tion. While some might hold these to be inscrutable, I believe that they can be shared, as long as we have some appreciation of their cultural context and formal qualities.

Nothing actually beats going to Japan and experiencing that place for oneself. But the ability to reimagine important cultural moments as they have manifested themselves in Japan's long and varied cultural past can, in fact, produce common experience to some degree. All of us are limited by what we have felt and done—and by what we have not felt and not done. No one doubts this. But we are also enabled by our imaginations and our will- ingness to encounter the unencountered. Especially for those who have the ability to translate their experience into another language, or even translate someone else's experience into one's own language, the possibility of even something so complex and demanding of the learner as cross-cultural under- standing is actually real and possible.

To this end, this book is *an* introduction to Japanese culture, not *the* intro- duction. It presents one of many ways a person might begin an exploration of Japan, a place so complicated that any single approach would necessarily be incomplete and, in this sense, misleading. On the other hand, even being in Japan for the thousandth time does not guarantee that one understands what one is encountering. Perhaps the best test of this or any other introduction to Japanese culture is, then, whether or not it profitably leads to other introduc- tions that illuminate still other aspects of life on the archipelago.

Even the cherry trees in front of Bendetson Hall raise the possibility of understanding Japan. By feeling the evanescence of a New England spring, we go from what we know to what we do not know. By way of this willingness to imagine the unknown by way of the known, a meaningful encounter might happen. To this end, this book is a "how to" experiment in "applied humanities." As an intellectual guide to a future *hanami*, it can never substitute for a real cherry blossom party on Mount Yoshino. But at least it is a tree.

CHANGE AND NATURE

The name "Japan" probably evolved from the Portuguese "*Jampon*," which appears for the first time in Tomé Pires's *Suma Oriental* (1512–15). The word is said to have derived from the Malayan *Japun*, or *Japang*, which in turn originated from the Chinese word *Riben*, "日本," which literally means "the sun's 日 origin 本."[2] From the Chinese point of view, Japan was to the east, where the sun comes up. An earlier term, *Cipangu*, was used in Marco Polo's account of his travels to East Asia, naming a place about which he heard but never visited. Nevertheless, the English word "Japan" owes its derivation to the Portuguese, not to Latin or Italian. Just as the English came to know the Middle Kingdom by way of its ceramics (or china), so did they come to know The Land of the Rising Sun by way of its lacquer ware, which they called japan.[3]

Geologically speaking, Japan is a string of islands formed by the movement of huge sections of the earth's surface, a phenomenon known as plate tectonics. Geologists do not know exactly what causes the shifting of our planet's hardened crust, but one theory is that nuclear decay powers this movement. The steady breakdown of radioactive elements is an exothermic reaction. Even though the amount of heat given off at any moment by naturally decaying elements is miniscule, when trapped within the earth's mantle, it builds to tremendous temperatures, hot enough to keep the materials found just beneath the earth's crust fluid. More to the point, the heat also creates up-welling convection currents that move the cooler, hardened portions of the crust in various directions.

Pulled this way and that, the brittle surface fractures and forms into huge pieces or plates. Presently, the Pacific Plate is being moved steadily westward at the rate of a few centimeters per year. It collides with the Eurasian Plate and dives under it along the resulting deep-ocean trench that lies east of Japan. As it is being continuously pulled under, or subducted, this Pacific Plate heats, melts, and then oozes up to the surface in the form of island-creating volcanoes.

Geologically defined, Japan is a string of tectonically produced volcanoes that have accumulated enough mass to protrude from the sea to form dry land. This explains its position on the eastern edge of the Eurasian landmass and also illuminates why there should be so much volcanic activity there. Of Japan's thirty-seven identifiable volcanoes, most have been active in historical time, including Mount Fuji. This beautifully symmetrical cone rises to 12,388 feet above sea level and provides a breathtaking sight for those flying into Tokyo on a clear autumn day. An icon of Japan, Mount Fuji last erupted in 1707–08 and poses a continuing though largely forgotten threat to the 40 million people now living in the Kantō Region.

It is not unlikely that, after having been dormant for centuries, Mount Fuji will erupt again. Other volcanoes have. East of Nagasaki in Kyushu, the dome of Mount Unzen collapsed in 1792 creating an avalanche and tsunami that killed an estimated 14,524 people. After lying dormant for 198 years, the same volcano erupted again on June 3, 1991, when forty-four people died in a suburb of Nagasaki quickly covered by a sudden pyroclastic flow from above. Even massive, seemingly immovable mountains remind the Japanese people of the truth of evanescence—that nothing is permanent.

Earthquakes are another reminder of constant change. Also caused by tectonic activity, tremors occur so frequently in Japan that anyone who has lived there for any length of time is sure to have experienced one. Floors tremble, hanging light fixtures sway. For the most part, the tremors are small and frequent. Bookshelves rarely fall over. Where motionlessness is absolutely required, as in computer chip factories, architects situate buildings on huge rubber washers that absorb and dampen the earth's subtle movements. The colossal steel-frame buildings that create the skyline of Tokyo and other cities are also designed to shift and sway rather than to resist the movement of the earth's crust. Rigidity invites disaster. Flexibility enhances survival.

Like volcanoes, earthquakes are a constant threat. On September 2, 1923, a 7.9 magnitude earthquake struck the Kantō Region and its attending fires destroyed 70–80 percent of Tokyo and Yokohama, killing approximately 142,807 people. More recently, on January 17, 1995, a magnitude 7.2 earthquake struck the Kansai Region to the west, where Kobe and Osaka are located—5,273 people were killed, many trapped by the 164 fires that were ignited by ruptured gas lines and exposed electrical wires.[4] The frequency of such events, as well as the mountainous lay of the land that crowds Japan's population into small areas (only about 12.2 percent of the total land mass is arable) have made the Japanese keenly aware of how the vagaries of nature can take life away in an instant.

Of course, even more obvious are changes in the weather and the cyclical patterns of seasons. Most of Japan is situated within the temperate zone. The climate of the northern island of Hokkaido is like that of Maine, while the southern island of Kyushu is more like South Carolina. Okinawa, even farther south, is tropical. Because the archipelago is also humid, the turning of the seasons is magnified by abundant flora and fauna. As already mentioned, whether by the cherry blossoms of spring or the song of the cuckoo in summer, the four seasons are poetically encoded, expressed by a well-worked-out formula of imagery. Not only do certain seasonal words allow us to identify the (putative) moment of a poem's creation, but the seasons themselves also serve as categories in poetic anthologies.[5]

In one famous early imperial anthology, *The Anthology of Ancient and Present Times*, (*Kokinshū*, ca. 905), 1,111 collected poems are grouped into various categories: poems of lament, poems of travel, and so forth. Poems of longing (*koi*) form the largest group, with 360 poems. Next in abundance are the fall poems, 145, and the spring poems, 134. Interestingly, this number dwarfs the number of summer poems, 34, and winter poems, 28, leading us to wonder why poetic production was so uneven throughout the year.

Perhaps it was not. We know that all fall poems were not actually written in the fall. We might adjust our question, then, and ask why spring and fall are of all seasons most poetic. Are summer and winter inherently less moving? If so, why? What does this tell us about the nature of Japanese poetic practice?

In his *Essays in Idleness* (*Tsurezuregusa*, ca. 1330–32), Yoshida Kenkō (1283–1352) confirmed a general agreement about fall being the most aesthetically pleasing time of year, even as he critiqued the notion.

The changing of the seasons is deeply moving in its every manifestation. People seem to agree that "fall is the time when we most feel the sadness of things (*mono no aware*)." As true as this might be, even more exhilarating are the sights of spring. The songs of the birds take on a particularly spring-like air, and in the peaceful light of the sun, the grasses sprout along the fences. As spring grows deeper, mists spread over the landscape, and just as the cherry blossoms seem about to open, the wind and rain come unabated to restlessly scatter them. Until the green leaves appear on the trees, our hearts are pained by each and every thing.[6]

Why is fall beautiful? It is when change is most obvious—foliage turns colors, and frost brings the death of summer vegetation. Yet if radical change is the essence of beauty, as Kenkō argues, could we not consider spring to be even more beautiful? Is not the transformation that seasonal warming brings—from death back to life—at least as moving as the sadness of fall?

This tendency to codify the seasons is just one aspect of a larger attempt to simplify the complexity of natural phenomena. We see this impulse in the opening passage to Sei Shōnagon's (ca. 966–ca. 1021) celebrated *Pillow Book* (*Makura no sōshi*, ca. 1002).

In spring, the dawn is most beautiful. The first intimations of the sun appear faintly against the outline of the mountains. The sky grows brighter, and a trail of purple clouds floats across the horizon.

In summer, it is night. Moonlit ones are best. On dark nights, the fireflies should be swirling about. Even when it rains, summer nights are so very beautiful! In fall, evening is best. How moving the sight of the gorgeous setting sun as it approaches the mountains, and even of crows flying in small groups as they return to their places of rest.... In winter, I like early morning.[7]

Here, Sei Shōnagon is trying to be clear about important differences. By stressing the best of each season, she pushes toward the essence of each, and, importantly, finds that which is fitting or appropriate to be beautiful and interesting (*okashi*). As made manifest by change, variety heightens the endearing qualities of predictable processes, familiar renewals, repetitions, and so forth.

If we recall Dōgen's poem, we can now see that her sensitivities belong very much to this tradition of codification, or formalism. The rules that gave order to Japanese classical poetic diction were highly restrictive, even formulaic. As mentioned, certain images and words (and therefore certain qualities) were designated to indicate certain seasons. We are already familiar with how snow means winter, and cherry blossoms mean spring. These are not so difficult to appreciate since snow falls when it is cold, and cherry blossoms bloom when things get warmer—depending on location, from late March to about the middle of April.[8]

But there are less clear examples, and reasons to question. For instance, according to classical Japanese poetics the moon is largely reserved for fall poems even though the moon appears throughout the year. Why, then, this special connection with autumn?

A geographic explanation tells us that the humidity suddenly drops after a muggy and oppressive summer, and the harvest moon looms large and clear in the brisk autumn sky. But just as important as this geographic fact is the more arbitrary cultural practice of designating certain meanings to certain things. The moon is also a symbol of Buddhist enlightenment, as in this passage from *As I Crossed a Bridge of Dreams*, a work that is examined more carefully later.

Yume samete	Awake from dreaming,
Nezame no toko no	My bed floats in tears.
Uku bakari	Moon, as you travel West,
Koiki to tsugeyo	Convey my love
Nishi e yuku tsuki	To the one for whom I longed.[9]

To understand this poem, we have to know that the Pure Land, a resting place for the dead, lies to the West, where the moon goes. Thus, the tear-drenched bed, which is the particular place of this poem, is situated within a larger symbolically represented Buddhist universe.

For every rule, there are exceptions. Ironically, the most famous moon poem is not about fall, at all, but about spring. It is attributed to Ariwara no Narihira (825–80).

Tsuki ya aranu	You're not the moon of before.
Haru ya mukashi no	And spring, you're no longer the spring
Haru naranu	we once knew.
Waga mi hitotsu wa	I alone remain
Moto no mi ni shite	the same as ever.[10]

Like Dōgen's, this poem also expresses the tension between that which changes and that which does not. The moon is not the same moon; and the spring is not the one we once shared. Everything has changed, except me.

I continue to exist unchanged, *moto no mi ni shite*. At least that is how it feels; and this feeling of not having gotten over you is painful. The sentimental point of this comparison between myself and spring, then, is my *unnatural* stasis. Everything changes, so why have I not?

How should we understand this tension between an appreciation of the changing seasons and the attempt to express it in such an unchanging, formulaic way? Although a keen awareness of evanescence can be felt in the poems we have considered, it is also clear that the codification of the seasons (and of classical poetic diction generally) indicates a resistance to change and a conformity to certain patterns.

In essence, we are trying to appreciate how and why changing reality is bound by unchanging conventions of form. Consider the phenomenon of *koromo gae*, or the changing of seasonal wardrobes. It was the practice in ancient Japan for those at court to change from a double-layered winter kimono (*awase*) to the single-layer summer kimono (*hitoe*) on the first day of the fourth month, and then back again on the first day of the tenth month. This change was made regardless of actual weather conditions, although peasants and fishermen, who dressed more practically, did not follow the conventions so closely. From the Muromachi period, seasonal wardrobes were changed more frequently than just twice a year. During the Tokugawa period, there were four formal periods when certain clearly specified types of clothes were to be worn. Even today, the formalized practice of choosing clothes to suit the season still exists to some extent, just as the menu of a traditional *kaiseki* restaurant or the artwork in the alcove of a traditional Japanese home also change according to certain turning points of the year.

Surely, wearing seasonally appropriate clothes and eating seasonally appropriate foods makes sense. But my point here is a slightly different one. Sometimes change is, in fact, a formal rather than a practical affair. Some years ago, while I was a graduate student at Kobe University, one of my colleagues would show up dressed in a light jacket or sweatshirt despite a stretch of cold spring weather we were having. He was nearly frozen by the time he completed the walk up the hill to campus from the Hankyū Rokkō Station. Every morning when he entered the common room, he was as stiff as ice, and ready for a hot cup of tea. I finally had to ask, "Why don't you wear a coat when it's this cold." His answer was simply, "Because it's spring."

Perhaps this insistence on a particular idea of spring also explains a perplexing quality of one of Japan's most popular children's songs, which makes itself known with the predictability of, well, cherry blossoms. When spring approaches, one inevitably hears strains of the following tune: lyrics by Takano Tatsuyuki (1876–1947) and music by Okano Sadakazu (1878–1941).[11]

Haru ga kita, haru ga kita.	Spring has come, spring has come.
Doko ni kita?	Where has it come?
Yama ni kita.	To the mountains.
Sato ni kita.	To the village.
No ni mo kita.	To the mores, too!

There are two more verses: one about flowers (i.e., cherry blossoms) blooming, and another about birds singing. Each is similarly insistent in its emphasis on spring coming to the mountains, to the village, and to the moors. Why this near-manic insistence of spring's ubiquity? Is this song saying that when spring comes, it *really* comes—to the mountains, to the village, and to the moors? Or is something else being expressed here?

One possible interpretation is that this song expresses magnitude. Something so encompassing as seasonal change affects a large area. Despite differences of elevation—the mountains being higher and the moors usually lower—spring comes everywhere. Yet the greater source of joy is this: when spring comes, it comes to *all places that can rightly be called Japan*. In other words, the emphasis is not solely on the various elements of spring, cherry blossoms, and birds. Neither is it simply on the spatial extent to which these things appear—the mountains, the village, and the moors. The moment of change captured by this lyrical song is joyous because this change is shared by all similarly formed people. In other words, it is meaningful as an expression of evanescence *and* form. To those who have learned to read the space of Japan in the same way, spring has this overwhelming meaning. In the end, the song is as much a celebration of the Archipelago as it is of spring.

At the quintessential Japanese moment, the cherry blossoms must certainly be falling, as they do in Edward Zwik's film *The Last Samurai* (2003). Zwik tries for cultural authenticity by employing cherry blossoms. But he does so by denying their essence. In the film, the naturally brief season of blossoms lasts a very long time. Long enough for Watanabe Ken to plan and prepare for battle. Long enough to fight heroically and futilely against Gattling-gun-shooting nontraditionalists. Long enough to die in the arms of Tom Cruise while gaining the essential knowledge that those ephemeral blossoms so conveniently surrounding the battlefield "are all perfect." *The Last Samurai* tries to accept, preserve, and propagate this anciently established codification of nature; but in so doing it compromises *hana*. The film's ephemeral beauty is not only long-lasting, but it gives ultimate status to the crazy American. Such is Hollywood's expression of Japan's cultural code. Spring has come! Spring has come! To the mountains, to the village, to a theater near you!

J<small>APANESE</small> P<small>OETICS AND A</small> F<small>IRST</small> C<small>ONSIDERATION OF</small> A<small>NIMISM</small>

Ancient religious practice in Japan was animistic, polytheistic, and shamanistic. Their world was animated by divine powers that were present. Some were benign, others threatening. Some could be influenced by worship. Others could not. Certain behaviors and objects were polluting and avoided, such as anything to do with the bodies of the dead. Yet even the dead became available to the living by way of the shaman, those gifted few, usually women, who could speak on their behalf. In many ways, then, the barriers between human and divine beings were porous, even to the point that the supernatural world *was* the natural world. In Japan, a tree, a waterfall, a rock can be a god (*kami*). This was true anciently. It remains true today.

Japan's world of many gods was hardly exceptional. Polytheism prevailed in many other lands as well, until the advent and spread of monotheism and its attempt to make the Divine similarly omnipresent yet generalized to a single, absolute source. The kinds of abstract thinking (such as theology) required to make the Absolute believable and available eventually paved the way for the development of natural and social science, positivism, and other absolute conceptual formations. Their influence became significant in Japan, too, as we will see. Yet in the beginning there was not the Word but many words, not God but many gods. The Human and Divine shared the same space of mountains, villages, and mores. And the space of Japan itself was awesome and sacred. From ancient times, one's spatial surroundings were meant to be inspiring, a fact clearly reflected in the lyricism of Japanese poetry.

The aura of place makes Japanese poetry happen. Frequent references to notable locales (*meisho*) along with the continuous inclusion of poetic place names and markers (*utamakura*) are two results of this lyrical reading of landscape.[12] The simplicity of *tanka* is a third.

To emphasize the important tie between nature and poetry (and between change and form), I have my students write their own version of a Japanese poem. This happens early in the semester, even before we have had a chance to discuss the early history of this concept of evanescence. The exercise gives them a chance to measure the cultural distance between themselves and Japanese poetic practice; and this allows us to gain a way to assess how much they have learned by the end of the semester.

The assignment to imitate various cultural practices that were already well established by the Heian Period (794–1185) goes like this.

> Over the weekend, try to write a Japanese *tanka* patterned after those we have read in class. Bring it on Tuesday with a plant attached. This can be a sprig or a blossom that inspired your verse. It should be an object that complements and amplifies your poem. Make sure that your verse is handwritten, and that the style of your calligraphy matches the content of your poem. Remember, presentation is as important as content.

As you can imagine, this assignment is not at all helped by January weather in New England. But somehow everyone manages, even if it means bringing in a banana from the cafeteria.

The challenge to my students is to understand the *how* of evanescence by way of *tanka*, which is the fundamental building block of the Japanese narrative tradition. These short poems, which are still written today in great numbers, are an important continuity with the distant past. The centrality of *tanka* to the Japanese civilization explains why they are also called *waka* 和歌, or Japanese songs, and why the emperor today not only composes them but sponsors nationwide contests that recognize notable verses. If my students can manage to write a credible English version of a *tanka*, it means that they are beginning to understand Japanese aesthetic values.

The subtle complications of *tanka* are endless and interesting for this reason. For our purposes, however, we are best served by focusing on a few of the most general properties. First of all, *tanka* are brief. A standard *tanka* is only thirty-one syllables long. It is composed of five lines containing five, seven, five, seven, and seven syllables respectively. Longer panegyric poems (*chōka*, 長歌)—such as those composed by Kakinomoto Hitomaro (active, late seventh century), Yamanoue Okura (660–ca. 733), and other *Man'yōshū* poets—were once an important part of Japan's poetic tradition, but by the beginning of the Heian period they no longer have a major role to play.[13] Their length notwithstanding, even *chōka* are relatively brief when compared to the extended *yukar* (or epic poems) of the indigenous Ainu, who represent one of a number of ethnic contributors to Japan's richly diverse population.[14] As we shall see, haiku are even shorter than *tanka*. As American schoolchildren happily learn, a haiku only has three lines (of five, seven, and five syllables).

This propensity toward brevity raises the question of how meaning can be generated so economically. How do a few words express many things? Certainly, allusion and suggestiveness are important companions to brevity. These can be considered a second quality of Japanese poetics. Associations expand the sparseness of the *tanka* by tying a word or image to a vast realm of related expression, experience, and sentiment. The bridging functions of connotation and association also tie one poem to another, forming a much-valued context of similar times and places. Within such a context, the creativity of Japanese poetry is often a matter of small adjustments to already existing poems (a practice called *honka dori*). This sophisticated form of "plagiarism" follows from an acute awareness of even slight changes.

Third, *tanka* are lyrical They are mostly about emotionally charged moments that elicit an outpouring of feeling. Were these poems more about the way in which time flows inexorably and meaningfully toward some definite point or goal—thus establishing the truth or integrity of this or that epic claim—then the emphasis would surely be more on tracing change over time rather than on the fleeting moment of change itself. While epic qualities exist in the already mentioned Ainu *yukar* and in the narratives of other traditions—*Genesis*, the *Tale of Gilgamesh*, the *Iliad*, or the *Nibelungenlied*, to give just a few examples—in Japan the epic impulse is comparatively weaker than the lyrical, emotive one.

In an epic, a hero or heroine encounters, and usually overcomes, a series of difficulties. By way of these actions, certain beliefs or ideals are proven or disproven. For both these purposes, the narrative epic requires a continuing process rather than disconnected moments. It assumes a definite sense of before and after, and emphasizes the progress and continuity of a heroic figure's intended actions.

To some extent, epic behavior can be found in some early Japanese narratives, such as in the *Record of Ancient Matters* (*Kojiki*, 712). But the lyricism of *tanka* is far more important to the Japanese tradition, as the aesthetic emphasis is on change *in* rather than *over* time. As a consequence, one's sensitivity is articulated more pointedly and vividly by reacting emotionally to a particular discreet moment than by chronicling that moment as a part of a larger process that takes one toward some larger goal. The lyrical *tanka* emphasizes a physical and, therefore, visible and emotional connection with one's environment. By contrast, the epic stresses some invisible notion that allows the hero to prevail and thus *see beyond* the immediate challenge.

Of course, no moments, not even seemingly random encounters, are without a context. And this leads to a fourth characteristic. *Tanka* are situational. Given the *tanka's* function as a lyrical reaction to a particular moment, and given the economy of language that expresses these emotions only partially, these short songs are effective expressions of a moment especially when framed appropriately. Consider, for example, the possible situation that led to the following poem by Ōtomo Yakamochi (716–85). He is one of the poets featured in the first great anthology of Japanese verse, the *Man'yōshū*, which was compiled toward the end of the Nara period or the beginning of the Heian period.

Utsusemi no	I know well
Yo wa tsune nashi to	That in this cicada-husk world
Shiru mono o	there is no permanence:
Akikaze samumi	But the autumn wind is cold,
Shinobitsuru kamo	And makes me long again for you.[15]

The empty, spent shell of a cicada is called *utsusemi*. It is the husk left behind after the insect has crawled from the earth and has metamorphosed into its mature, winged form. Here, *utsusemi* functions as a *makura kotoba* or pillow word—an epithet (or stock descriptive phrase) for *yo,* this world. As an early image of evanescence, *utsusemi* affirms life's brevity and fragility—the active summer that ends with the death of fall. In this instance, its meaning is articulated as "*tsune nashi*" 常無し, "without permanence," a term that in its Chinese reading, *mujō* 無常, later appears as the primary feature of Buddhist reality.

More will be said about the origins of impermanence. For now, let us concentrate on the context of Yakamochi's poem. Did the poet happen upon a cicada shell, which moved him to write this poem? Or was the momentous, situational element of this *tanka* a gust of autumn wind? Perhaps its frigid bite stirred Yakamochi to remember the truth that the warmth of summer had allowed him to forget: that in this world, "*yo,*" the season of growth and life "has no permanence" (*tsune nashi*). Strictly speaking, it is quite possible that there was no actual encounter with either a cicada's shell or the wind. Perhaps Yakamochi simply misses his concubine, and expresses his longing in these spatial terms. Even so, this is a good poem in the sense that we can imagine a situation. We see a space—whether real or imagined—where emotions were stirred. We understand him because we visualize the moment of the poem's creation. This affinity of poet and place is our first glimpse at the lyrical legacy that animism, or the perception of a world animated by spirits, provided.

The *tanka* poet performs the vital function of reacting to what is affecting about the world. He or she expresses this sensitivity in ways that move others. When my students bring their poems to class and read them aloud, our evaluation of their examples begins with the simple question, "Can we *see* the poem? Can we transport ourselves to the lyrical moment and space of its creation?"

Our first attempts to write a Japanese poem illuminate a gap that often separates us from Japanese culture. When we fail, it is usually because we explain things too much. Rather than let images speak for themselves, we feel compelled to elaborate. "Snow" becomes "lonely snow." And "wind" becomes "a bitter gale." Rather than use conventionally established images to establish the brief, passing moment that gives us its power directly, many of my students tend to describe it. In other words, they do not understand the *form* of evanescence. They miss the lyrical immediacy that makes *tanka* effective.

Where does this need to explain and describe things come from? Perhaps it comes from a desire for comprehensiveness. And this, in turn, might be linked to inexperience with the formalized nature of the Japanese lyric. But why expect that they be comfortable with such formality? Why not question the limitations of established meanings? Why not doubt the comprehensiveness or appropriateness of an epithet or image? After all, they have not been trained to know the exact meaning of cherry blossoms. With training, the formalized reach of any image—cicada shells, autumn wind, and so on—can be learned. But the more difficult issue is how these formalities flow from the immediacy of an animistically perceived reality.

Kamo no Chōmei gives this advice to would-be poets.

> Only when many ideas are compressed in one word, when without displaying it you exhaust your mind in all its depth and you imagine the imperceptible, when commonplace things are used to display beauty and in a style of naiveté an idea is developed to the limit, only then, when thinking does not lead any-where and words are inadequate, should you express your feelings by this method, which has the capacity to move heaven and earth and the power to touch the gods and spirits.[16]

To a certain extent, we have supplied a context for Yakamochi's poem. What remains unclear until we read the poem in the context of the anthology itself is that what he longs for, "*shinobitsuru,*" is his dead lover. The object of his longing is simply left out of the poem. Why? By way of this elision the specific comes to be understood as a more general, and in a sense, more powerful statement. Maybe he longs for youth, for the dead generally, for the warmth of summer, and so on. But the point here is that this brevity begs for an explanation precisely because it is situational.

My students' poems provide an effective means to move quickly to the heart of the matter. Implicit in the poetics I have outlined earlier is the rather questionable possibility of agreement as to what this or that image or situation actually means, and whether or not we can understand it *without* explanation. The formalism of Japanese poetics is astounding at first encounter. Could it be possible that all elements of the natural world could be so consistently and so conveniently straightforward as

cicada shell = evanescence = reality?

What kind of cultural patterning encourages such a convention? This is the first difficult conceptual challenge of the semester; and it is one that takes some time to comprehend.

A fifth formal characteristic of *tanka*, made obvious by Yakamochi's example, is the use of imagery as a means of saying a lot without having to say much. Again, the agreement that *utsusemi* should be the epithet for *yo*, this mortal world, is paradoxically part and parcel of an aesthetic formalism that plays strongly to the changeable, momentous occasion of lyrical expression. It seems the embrace of change comes as resistance to it, that the free outpouring of lyrical emotion that creates poetry requires a tremendously wide-ranging cultural consensus and, yes, formal preparation. Although this point might seem counterintuitive at first, this necessary tension between spontaneity and formality should not be so difficult to comprehend as a general phenomenon. Without the tyranny of the four-bar phrase, would we have the brilliance of Mozart? Without a strict and consistent application of countless rules, would a soccer or baseball game be anything but a chaotic and meaningless waste of everyone's time? Truly, without the strictures of form we would perceive no intimations of freedom, nor would we appreciate the possibility of something that transcends the rules.

We know something about the training that might be required to play the violin well or become a skilled baseball player. But how does one prepare to be a classical Japanese poet, and to understand the world as they did? That is more or less the challenge before us. Like fans at an event, we must train ourselves to react spontaneously to developments as they present themselves. And yet, our spontaneity must occur within certain well-prescribed parameters. (The baseball field itself, marked with lines, is one of these. So is a stage.) Time and experience teach us to engage emotionally with the unpredictability of the game or performance; yet we do so always with an awareness of and respect for formal elements. We might not have complete say about the opportunities that come our way. But like baseball, poetry is about learning one's *place*. It trains us to develop in certain directions, which is to say, to learn how to anticipate and enjoy the experience of living in a clearly delineated context, where one's proper relationship with other people and with other things is constantly and dynamically being made into complicated questions with surprisingly simple answers. (So now you know why the Japanese love baseball!)

I tell my students,

> Don't just sit in your dorm room and try to think up a poem. You have to write in response or in reaction to something that moves you. You should be walking around, moving through space. You're on the way to the T stop in Davis Square. Something about the color of the sky, or the sound of the wind blowing through the trees stirs you. Maybe it's the smell of coffee, or the sound of wings as a flock of birds flies to greet the pigeon lady with her bag of bread. Whatever it is, some situation fills you with an emotion that then gets expressed in your poem.

Of course, this is an overcorrection; and my students are quick to point it out. The truth is, with some practice, a poetic moment can be just as easily imagined as encountered. Yoshida Kenkō made just this argument. An imagined situation might be more affecting than a real one: "Are we to see the moon and the cherry blossoms with our eyes only? To experience the spring without leaving our homes, and to dream of the moon from within our rooms is much more rewarding and interesting."[17]

Yet, whether encountered or imagined, the situational premise of *tanka* still holds. Having considered Yakamochi's poem of longing, we should not be surprised to learn that *tanka* have often been framed by prose narratives that actually provide the context of the moment suggested by the poem itself. Consider this example from the *Nihonshoki* (720), one of the two earliest texts of the Japanese tradition, where two poems are linked by prose to tell a simple story.

> In the spring of the eighth year, during the second month, the Emperor traveled to Fujiwara, where he secretly observed the demeanor of Lady Sotōri. She was alone that evening, and yearned for him. Unaware that he had come, she composed this song.

Waga seko ga	This is the night
Kubeki yoi nari	My love will come to me—
Sasagane no	The antics of the
Kumo no okonai	Bamboo crab spider
Koyoi shirushi mo	Tell me tonight's the night!

> Moved by her poem, the Emperor composed one of his own.

Sasaragata	Take off
Nishiki no himo o	That pretty sash
Tokisakete	Of well-woven brocade,
Amata wa nezu ni	And give me, once again,
Tada hitoyo nomi	Just one night of sleepless love.[18]

There you have it—a poetically generated narrative.

This complementary mix of prose and poetry evolved over time. As the prose frames became more extended and involved, the so-called poem tale (*uta monogatari*) was born. The much-appreciated *Tosa Diary* (*Tosa nikki*, mid-Heian) is such a text. Here we have a collection of brief poems connected by a series of narrative frames that collectively add up to something like a loosely plotted story of a woman's loss of a child and her sorrowful journey back to the capital from the provinces. By the time of the lengthy *Tale of Genji* (*Genji monogatari*, ca. 1008), the complementary give-and-take between prose and poem has been worked out to a high degree of sophistication. Murasaki Shikibu, the female author, interspersed numerous *tanka* throughout her tale of romance and court intrigue. Conforming to early precedent, her *tanka* mark particularly important moments of strong emotion that happen along the way.

The brief, suggestive, lyrical, and imagistic nature of *tanka*, along with their situational requirement that calls for an explanatory framework to contextualize them, also explains many distinctive features of Japanese prose: a loose and episodic progression, relatively weak plots, endings that lack closure, and the abundant use of imagery and illustration. It is undeniable that the lyrical quality of Japanese prose became weakened as modernity pushed writing in an increasingly expository and rigorously representational direction. Even so, despite modernity's prosaic emphasis, the poetic and momentary foundation of classic Japanese narrative is still intact today, as we will see. I dwell on this point because without some appreciation for these formal aspects of *tanka*, it is quite impossible to understand the rich and varied works of the Japanese tradition that flow from it.

UTSUSEMI, THE CICADA'S SHELL

Where does this idea of evanescence come from? When did it begin? By posing such a question, we might have already missed the point. Is there such a thing as the beginning of an idea? If so, how would we know it except through the rather unreliable process of imagining our way toward that origin by way of its expression? Perhaps a better way of putting it, then, would be to ask a slightly different question. How did this idea that nothing is permanent, that nothing has a distilled and eternal essence, first gain cultural currency? What were the conditions that allowed the idea to be expressed?

Today, there exists a general understanding that evanescence is essentially a Buddhist notion. The Japanese words *hakanasa* and *mujō* are regularly understood to express an idea that came from India, by way of China and Korea. While this is, in fact, the route that Buddhism took as it made its way to Japan, the story of how evanescence came to be understood by the Japanese in the sixth- and seventh centuries is a far more complicated matter. In truth, a Japanese sensitivity to "all things changing all the time" predates Buddhism's entry into the country in the sixth century, as suggested by an already familiar term, *utsusemi*.

The problem we face is this: to understand the word is to know it before the advent of writing; and this is difficult because we can only know what it was before writing by way of writing. Writing developed contemporaneously with the introduction of Buddhism and other systems of continental thought, notably Confucianism and, a bit later, Daoism. The importation of these three intellectual traditions, like the importation of writing itself, was a part of a larger attempt by members of Japan's elite to embrace the advanced civilization of Sui and Tang China in order to bolster their own power and prestige.

Consider Confucianism, for example. Practical in emphasis, the teachings of Confucianism made good governance a goal.[19] Accordingly, propriety and form were emphasized. Proper human relations were patterned after certain hierarchical relationships—ruler and subject, parent and child, husband and wife, older brother and younger brother. No doubt, the greater intention was for mutual respect to prevail: rulers valuing subjects, and subjects honoring rulers. But the premise of all these pairings is that superiors exist and that their authority is necessary to maintain order.

The practical focus of Confucianism is nowhere more obvious than in the means by which one gains the privileges of rulership. Through diligent study, self-cultivation occurs. But self-cultivation has a practical purpose. It secures one's place in the social order. Consider the examination system in China. It survived for centuries as the principal way to find and promote talented people for positions within the ruling structure. No such examination system developed in Japan. And yet, the advice to "study hard and make something of yourself" exists on the order of common sense, even in contemporary Japan.[20] I know few high school students who consider themselves practicing Confucians. But I do know plenty of young men and women who study hard. The same might be said of Asian Americans who enter colleges and universities at higher than average rates. For East Asians generally, the Confucian impulse to study in order to improve oneself and better one's social status is still present even if no one knows where the motivation came from. Perhaps this shows us how thoroughly Confucian values have become a part of what we might call "good form."

It is not hard to imagine why ancient Japanese found Confucianism appealing. Beyond its demonstrated role in forming the great civilization of the Middle Kingdom, Confucianism's emphasis on order and hierarchy would have been welcomed by the highly stratified clans of the Kofun period (250–538). These early Japanese had no written language of their own. But we can infer from the status of armor-clad rulers grandly buried in their tombs (*kofun*) that their social status was very different from that of the many laborers who would have been needed to dig the moats and heap the earth up to form these massive structures. By providing a rationale for social stability, Confucianism must have resonated with clan leaders (*ujigami*) in their competition for the "peaceful" control of natural and human resources.

The influence of Buddhism was equally profound. It balanced Confucian form with an equally insistent appreciation of change. The idea that all things are always changing is fundamental to Buddhist thought. As for why this idea in particular should have the impact it did, we should consider both the strength of the notion itself and the capacity of the Japanese to receive it. Was there something about ancient Japanese culture that encouraged them to respond so enthusiastically to Buddhism and to evanescence? How else can we explain why the notion of "all things always changing" became more influential than other important Buddhist tenets: such as salvation, or karma (moral cause and effect), or the Way (*michi*) as a practical, hands-on way of gaining enlightenment? How do we account for the dominance of this idea of radical change even when support for Buddhism itself has waxed and waned over the centuries?

Once again, we have little recourse other than to muse about what Japan must have been like before the advent of writing and this influx of continental thought. For this purpose, the *Man'yōshū* is an indispensable text. The last datable poem in this collection was written in 759, with the majority of the poems written after 600. According to the *Kōjien*, the actual range covered is said to be approximately 350 years, reaching back well before the advent of Buddhism and writing. If this is true, then this collection that rendered the oral tradition into written words should provide us with a valuable perspective on the question, "Was there evanescence before Buddhism?"

The existence of the epithet *utsusemi* suggests there was. As already mentioned, this image of the empty cicada shell characterizes the world as perceived by the ancient Japanese. Their cicada-shell world (*utsusemi no yo*) is understood as being empty, frail, and quickly passing. So is cicada-shell life (*utsusemi no inochi*), cicada-shell man (*utsusemi no hito*), and cicada-shell lover (*utsusemi no imo*). This epithet occurs in thirty-nine poems of the *Man'yōshū*, and suggests that even prior to the advent of writing, the Japanese might have already been developing a feel for evanescence as a fundamental quality of reality.

If we look at the poems in which this pillow word (*makura kotoba*) occurs, we see a fairly wide yet coherent range of meaning. By association, the term suggests both the fleeting and fragile qualities of human life and an awareness of life's formal structures. Social mores, powerful hierarchies, unavoidable conflicts, sickness, and other mundane realities add to a mortal sense of disappointment, difficulty, and loss. The generalized truth of life's brevity and fragility only makes our pain more real. In general, the associations of *utsusemi* in these early poems, while not perfectly consistent, coalesce around issues of evanescence and form, with the one amplifying the other.

The cicada-shell world is this immediate world in which men must fight for a mate;[21] it is a sorrowful and pitiful world;[22] the mortal world that gets left behind by the parting dead;[23] the fleeting world that claims me as a mortal;[24] the world of the living that is impermanent and fleeting;[25] the temporary world where one experiences loss;[26] the passing world that makes us remember the dead;[27] the real world of rules that does not cooperate with passionate desire;[28] the real world that requires us to follow orders of superiors;[29] the world of appearances that are not reality;[30] the world that reveals our loneliness;[31] the confusing world of reality;[32] the world of rumors;[33] the mortal world of sickness;[34] the evanescent world that stands in contrast to that of the gods and to heaven;[35] the world of unenduring love;[36] the mundane world where men vie for power.[37]

Figure 1.1 *Utsusemi,* cicada shell, epithet for this changing world (photo by Steven Pinker).

Scholars of the *Man'yōshū* seem to agree that although many of the poets whose work is collected here lived at that time when Buddhism was gaining influence among the ruling elite, the influence of Buddhism on the collection itself was in no way comparable to the profound effect that the new religion had on architecture, sculpture, and painting. Edwin Cranston has identified only two explicitly Buddhist poems in the *Man'yōshū*: nos. 4468 and 4469 by Yakamochi.

Utsusemi wa	Man counts for nothing,
Kazu naki mi nari	A body empty, ephemeral—
Yama kawa no	Let me gaze on beauty
Sayakeki mitsutsu	In clear mountains and rivers
Michi o tazunena	While I search for the Way.
Wataru hi no	Vying with the light
Kage ni kioite	Of the heaven-coursing sun,
Tazunetena	Oh, let me search,
Kiyoki sono michi	That I find it once again—
Mata mo awamu tame	The Way that was so pure.[38]

Note the use of the *utsusemi* epithet in the first poem. Commenting on these poems, Cranston explains,

These two tanka...are that rarity in *Man'yōshū*, poems of Buddhist devotion. The only term used for the faith is *michi*, "the Way," but in conjunction with the implications of ephemerality in *utsusemi* ("mortal man" / "empty locust") and the assumptions of reincarnation in *mata mo awamu* ("to meet it again"), it is enough [to prove their Buddhist meaning]....The evidence in these poems is hardly enough to prove that Yakamochi was a devout Buddhist, though the city and the age in which he lived had seen the sudden rise of the great temples, and the occupants of the throne were ardent believers. The poets of Nara rarely wrote of this side of their lives; Yakamochi here provides a small exception.[39]

Ian Hideo Levy agrees that occurrences of explicitly Buddhist poetry are limited in this collection of early Japanese poetry. He does, however, find unmistakably Buddhist resonances in the work of Yamanoue Okura (660–ca.733) "the Korean-born poet who wrote the only major philosophical and Buddhist verse in the *Man'yōshū*."[40] For his "poem of sorrow and lament over the temporary and quickly-forming-quickly-dissolving (*kegō sokuri*) mortal world" Okura provided a preface, which reads in part as follows:

In this world nothing is permanent. Hills become valleys, and valleys change to hills. The length of a mortal's life is undetermined—thus one lives to a ripe age while another falls to untimely death. In the twinkling of an eye, a hundred years of life are extinguished; in the straightening of an elbow, a thousand years become nothing. In the morning one is the host at a banquet table, in the evening he is a visitor to the Underworld. Even a white steed's gallop cannot match the speed with which death overtakes us. From the green pine over the grave, a sword of loyalty hangs in vain; and over a country grave, the white aspen sways sorrowfully in the wind.[41]

The poem reads as follows:

> Life's changes are as brief as the blink of an eye,
> The passage of human affairs as brief as the straightening of an elbow.
> My emptiness is like the clouds drifting through the great void
> Body and soul are depleted, with nowhere to turn.[42]

Like the two poems mentioned earlier that point to a way (*michi*), these words by Okura clearly show his familiarity with Buddhism, which he claimed to reverence, "foregoing not one day of effort reading the sutras every day and atoning for my sins."[43]

Shall we allow ourselves to be a bit skeptical? Is it really the case that only these few poems are Buddhist inspired? Do not all the *utsusemi* poems briefly summarized earlier also express sentiments that we associate with Buddhism: the trials of mortality, and the world's demanding and harsh yet impermanent and fleeting nature? The presence of this group of poems, all of them containing this epithet, forces us to consider two possibilities. Either scholarly opinion regarding the very limited influence of Buddhism on the *Man'yōshū* is misguided; or the ancient Japanese readily accepted Buddhism's central tenet—that this world in which we live is changeable and fleeting—because they already understood this to be true to their experience, well before the official introduction of Buddhism to Japan from the Korean Paekche court in 538. Regarding *utsusemi*, Abe Manzō and Abe Takeshi suggest that "originally, the term had nothing to do with Buddhism, but as Buddhism spread toward the end of the Nara and beginning of the Heian periods, the emptiness of the cicada's shell came to register deeply, and thus *utsusemi* came to be an epithet for 'this transient world' (*mujō na kono yo*)."[44]

From these thirty-some *utsusemi* poems emerges a general consensus about reality. This world, this mortal span of expectations and frustrations, is both restrictive (because of many rules and obligations) and, at the same time, fleeting and short-lived. It makes us wonder about the fate of the dead, especially those whom we have loved who have gone on before us; and it forces us to ponder our own death. This is reality. This is mortality. The ancient Japanese regard for it, as expressed by these poems, is questioning and critical. Indeed, we might go so far as to say that this often-expressed attitude is even pointed, and this in a collection of poems that supposedly sings of simpler times than those that followed.[45]

As we will see, the ancient force of the term "real" (*utsutsu* 現) is not so dissimilar to that voiced by modern writers, whether Ihara Saikaku of the seventeenth century or Izumi Kyōka (1873–1939) of the twentieth. To both the moderns and the ancients, reality (i.e., this mortal life) was viewed as harsh, disagreeable, and something apart from a more ideal world against which it is measured. Nishida Masayoshi makes the important point that in the early myths, as found in the *Kojiki* and *Nihonshoki*, we find gods that have lasting and even eternal qualities.[46] But the insistence with which the Japanese posit a transcendental realm of eternal beings and values is significantly weakened by the strong pull of the real as inherently changeable.

Japan's early poets linked *utsusemi* and reality (*utsutsu*). *Utsusemi* was closely associated with another similar sounding epithet, *utsusomi*, which served as a modifier for a very similar constellation of nouns: world, person, and life. *Utsusomi* occurs five times in the *Man'yōshū*. It means "this mortal world" or "the present reality." It is written as 宇都曾美 (165, 196, 210, 213, 4214), which is very close to 宇都勢美 (*utsusemi*).[47] In fact, the sounds "*utsusemi*" and "*utsusomi*" were so close that, over time, the one epithet became conflated with the other. As a metamorphic blending of similar metaphors, the cicada's empty shell became nothing less than reality.

Orikuchi Shinobu pointed out the link between these two words.

> Utsusemi means "mortal body" (*utsushiki mi*, 現しき身) and is an epithet for "life," "world," "person," "body," or for "wife," "the *not* lasting (*tsune nashi*)," or "the many."... *Utsusomi* (現身) is a derivation of *utsushimi*. As an epithet, it modifies "person," "life," "world."...Its meaning is this world, the one in which we live.[48]

Also commenting on the closeness of these two terms, Cranston notes, "The meaning may have shifted, as historically it did, from 'actual person' (i.e., human being) to 'empty cicada' (*utsu-semi*, the cast-off husk of a cicada), a prime metaphor for the vacuity of life."[49] In sum, these terms coalesced around two similar senses of the Real. The truth of mortality *is* the truth of evanescence.

In his study of ancient folklore (*Kodai denshō no sekai*), Sakurai Mitsuru quotes an early poem in the *Man'yōshū* and notes its use of the *utsusemi* epithet.

Utsusemi no	Sorrowing over
Inochi wo oshimi	My cicada-husk life
Nami ni nure	Drenched by the waves
Irago no shima no	I gather and eat
Tamamo kari hamu	The jewel-like seaweed of Irago Island.[50]

According to Sakurai, here the term *utsusemi* was still not yet an expression of Buddhist impermanence (*mujōkan*). Rather, it existed prior to Buddhism as an expression of the sorrow (*kanashisa*) and loneliness (*wabishisa*) of life.[51] I have to agree. The evidence suggests that evanescence was already in play by the time Buddhism came to Japan.

But why should constant change become *the* essential quality of (Japanese) reality? Perhaps a clue lies in the nature of the epithet itself. As a literary device, an epithet is understood to be a set phrase that describes or modifies a noun with which it consistently appears. Thus in Homer, "*rosy-fingered* dawn," "*clear-eyed* Athena," "*swift-footed* Achilles," and so on. These set phrases focus on the most important characteristics of the things they modify. In other words, they express essence.

When taking stock of *makura kotoba* as they were used in the *Man'yōshū*, we can note a few salient qualities. First, they are numerous. Konishi Jin'ichi makes the relevant point that without these phrases, many early poems would read as very simple, and very dull, declarative statements.[52]

> Despite the immense amount of research which has been carried out since the Edo period on the subject of the pillow-word and the preface, no one has adequately explained why people of the Ancient Age were moved by expressions produced by pillow-words and prefaces. If people had not been moved by them, ancient poets would not have made regular and frequent use of them over the centuries...
>
> | | |
> |---|---|
> | *Tamamo karu* | Passing by Minume |
> | Minume o sugite | *Where they gather fine sea grass—* |
> | *Natsukusa no* | Our boat draws near to |
> | Noshima ga saki ni | The Cape of Noshimna |
> | Fune chikazukinu | *With its summer growth.* |
>
> If the so-called pillow words "*tamamo karu*" (Where they gather fine sea grass) and "*natsukusa no*" (With its summer growth) are removed from this poem, we are left with, "Passing by Mimune / Our boat draws near to / The Cape of Noshima." There is no scope whatsoever within this statement for the evocation of emotion: thus the reason for this poem being counted among Hitomaro's finer works is to be ascribed entirely to the interfusion of "*tamamo karu*" and "*natsukusa no*." What manner of function, then, is indicated by "*tamamo karu*" and "*natsukusa no*"? Not one satisfactory answer to this question can be found among the superabundance of scholarly theories. None is satisfactory because every theory has heretofore interpreted such expressions as rhetorical techniques.[53]

Konishi's alternative answer to the puzzling nature of these epithets is provocative: they are "guide phrases" in the sense that they guide the *kotodama* into the poem. The *kotodama* is a "word spirit." It had the ability to invest a simple declarative sentence with sacred power. I say this reasoning is provocative because it evokes memories of the twentieth-century ultranationalist position that the *kotodama* was the essence of a uniquely superior Japanese language and, therefore, of a uniquely superior Japanese nation.[54] This is not the place to add more fuel to the fiery discussion of the political status of the *makura kotoba* in contemporary Japan. For our purposes, it is enough to say that these epithets were not merely descriptive or rhythmic devices *in their own day.*

How else do we explain the consistent linking of, for instance, the mortal world (*yo*) to *utsusemi*, the cicada's shell? How do we understand what this linkage means if the epithet does not have a kind of ritual, spiritual, and, in this sense, formal significance? Konishi rejects the interpretation that the epithet is essentially descriptive and, therefore, based on a secular, objective observation of one's environment. His understanding of *utsusemi* requires a world animated by many spirits, constantly changing, and poetically inspiring. In other words, Konishi's point is not that the world of change is irrelevant. Rather, he means to say that the ancient poets were not *describing* that world because they did not place any distance between themselves and it. Without this distance, they were likewise unable to conceive of themselves as beings separated from change. Thus, the mortal world (*yo*) and the people (*hito*) who had life (*inochi*) while experiencing it were all similarly cicada-like (*utsusemi*) in essence.

Separating the human out from this mono-dimensional reality was both difficult and unintended. Speaking of the clumsiness with which the personification of characters is handled in the *Nihonshoki* (720), a Chinese-inspired history of ancient Japan commissioned by Emperor Tenmu, Konishi explains,

> The lack of clarity with which human characters were described here follows from an insufficiently objectified spiritual subjectivity. This is a reflection of how in ancient Japan the spiritual aspect of humanity and the material aspect of nature were not mutually separated but, rather, intimately fused. In the early songs, a pure love of nature prevails, and objective descriptions of nature are hard to find. In short, from the beginning, spirit and nature did not exist in opposition.[55]

As briefly mentioned, the world of the ancient Japanese was animistic. Once again we turn to Konishi,

> When other creatures besides human beings have the power of speech, and react to human language, the workings of the *kotodama* will bring about various phenomena and situations. Rocks, grasses, and trees become conscious beings capable of speech for the simple reason that they possess spiritual natures akin to those of humans. Once it had been established that, "in the Land in the Midst of the Reed Plains, bases of boulders, tree trunks, and leaves of plants also have the power of speech," all natural phenomena were presumed to possess spiritual natures as well.[56]

From our present vantage point, now that modernity has played itself out, there is some room once again to begin considering the possibility of a world where human beings consider themselves a part of world that is more than an unfeeling resource. Even so, having sympathy for a possible alternative to environmental collapse is not necessarily the same as grasping what an animistic regard for the world actually was.

Konishi's argument that there is no such thing as observation and description in ancient Japan helps us understand not only why, as Nakanishi Susumu puts it, "the perception of the ancient Japanese was persistently concrete and immediately visual,"[57] but also why the concrete and the visual still exist as salient aspects of Japan's expressive tradition even today, whether we are talking about baseball, *manga* (comic books), or *matsuri* (festivals). The possibility that the utterance of the epithet was a sacred speech act also helps to explain the tendency toward brevity in Japanese poetry and prose. As noted by Konishi, verbosity would only weaken the impact of ritual language. "Wordiness is...taboo to animistic beauty."[58] To name the world simply it is to recognize its power.

Over time, the sacred nature of the epithet becomes largely forgotten, but brevity prevails. Why? Probably because the formality of form can continue even when the meaning of a form is lost. To use Ian Levy's words, Japan's formal tendency is a type of "absolute propriety" that is, a "stylistic inheritance" from the animistic tradition.[59] Perhaps ritualistic expression devolved toward brevity because it had to be both timely and to the point. Poetry had a social function. To survive politically, especially when clarifying lines of political and economic power, was to know how to be poetically relevant. In a constantly changing world, an epithet such as *utsusemi* was necessarily formulaic because it had to be both immediate and perfectly appropriate.[60]

HAKANASA AND MUJŌ

To identify with a constantly changing world is to admit that our influence on events around us is necessarily limited. The term *"hakanai"* expresses this changing reality. It is an adjective that shares a root, *haka* (はか), with the verbs *hakaru*—"to measure, to plan"—and *hakadoru*—"to advance, to make progress." Anciently, a *haka* was a unit of cultivated land that represented a division and rationalization of space for agricultural purposes. The negative form of this adjective, *hakanai*, indicates a denial of all that which *haka* try to establish. Think of *hakanai*, then, as the futility of measuring, or as the inability to make progress, whether in agriculture or in the constant struggle for power and romance that seemed to preoccupy the Heian courtiers.[61] In an evanescent world, we must struggle in order to accomplish anything long-term. Constant change works against our desires to make reality comply with our need to rationalize and control its processes. Unless we know how to work harmoniously with that reality, our lives become nothing but disappointment and frustration. Nothing adds up—*hakadoranai*.

The related term *hakanai* occurs infrequently in the *Man'yōshū*, but it occurs with great frequency in the romances and diaries of the following Heian period. In works such as *The Gossamer Years* (*Kagerō nikki*, after 974), *The Diary of Izumi Shikibu* (*Izumi Shikibu nikki*, 1003) *The Tale of Genji* and *As I Crossed the Bridge of Dreams* (*Sarashina no nikki*, ca. 1059), the general focus on the wider cicada-shell world (*utsusemi no yo*) comes to be replaced by an interest in a narrower, more specific realm: the world of human relations (*yo no naka*) and, in particular, the sensitive feelings that exist between male and female lovers.

What could be more changeable than matters of the heart? When we consider the Heian-period classics, many of them written by women, we are struck by the fluidity and formality that combine to make matters of love infinitely complicated and delicate. The simpler world of conjugal love that was once so inspiring to the *Man'yō* poets comes to be replaced by involved and intricate scheming. Love becomes a game that is no more stable despite its many rules. To be sure, the evanescent context in which the rules of courting were deployed produces at least as many losers as winners. It is *un*requited longing (*koi*) that prevails in the inwardly focused world of the Heian court, where love is, generally speaking, *hakanai*—changeable and fleeting.

To be sure, these romances and diaries express the emotional life of a small privileged elite. We do not know what love was like for the unlettered populace, nor can we blithely assume that life as it was lived by the wealthy courtiers in the capital necessarily followed the romances that were left behind. Scholars have tried to piece together a picture of what the realities of romance, courting, and marriage might have been. With regard to life in Heian-kyō, what we can say is that love and sex were made complex by the social realities of polygamy, polyandry, and a woman's continuing ability to inherit family wealth and to remain in her own home even after marriage.[62] The women of these romances are often depicted as propertied flowers rooted in their mansions, with men visiting with bee-like attentiveness, or the lack thereof. Because they possessed their own space, had their own sources of economic power, and similarly dwelt within the hierarchical structures of social power, women were to be approached, encountered, and, yes, left behind in carefully prescribed ways.

We have already considered how an exchange of poems might lead to a possible assignation. In the well-known preface to the *Kokinshū*, we are told that poetry "softens relations between men and women."[63] The utility of well-chosen words lies here. But words alone are not enough. In addition to the quality of the poem itself, handwriting and the choice of paper on which it is written were also aspects of good form. In Sei Shōnagon's *Pillow Book* (*Makura no sōshi*, ca. 1000) we find a list of "hateful things" that gives us some idea of still other expectations.

> A good lover will behave as elegantly at dawn as at any other time. He drags himself out of bed with a look of dismay on his face. The lady urges him on: "Come, my friend, it's getting light. You don't want anyone to find you here." He gives a deep sigh, as if to say that the night has not been nearly long enough and that it is agony to leave. Once up, he does not instantly pull on his trousers. Instead he comes close to the lady and whispers whatever was left unsaid during the night. Even when he is dressed, he still lingers, vaguely pretending to be fastening his sash.[64]

It is difficult to know where Sei Shōnagon's personal preferences end and where her society's commonly held expectations begin. Surely, one influenced the other. As described here, a would-be lover must attend to the balance between directness and indirectness, presence and absence. Longing, or *koi*, distinguishes itself as a kind of evanescent presence that is absence. "You are here, and already I miss you." Conversely, *koi* similarly nurtures and even requires an attitude that renders a state of being elsewhere as being here, always on the mind, as if in a dream. Thus we understand the famous opening lines of Izumi Shikibu's diary: "Frailer than a dream had been those mortal ties for which she mourned, passing her days and nights with sighs of melancholy. And now the tenth of the fourth month had come and gone, and the shade beneath the trees grew ever deeper."[65]

Koi plays with the possibility that love is nothing more than a dream, thus accentuating the difficulty (and maybe even the impossibility) of ever finding a fulfilling relationship. In the world of amorous dealings, things go rarely as planned. Among human endeavors, the act of finding love is certainly one of the most *hakanai*. Evanescence teaches that nothing lasts. And yet the heart wants otherwise. It strives. More often than not, it fails.

Earl Miner articulated the inherently sorrowful link between love (as dreaming) and evanescence.

> In the West there rose the identification of love with death, which is treated in versions as different as *Tristan and Iseult, Anthony and Cleopatra,* and Freud's association of Eros and Thanatos. In Japan, love was associated with dream; the Buddhist implication is clear. At its simplest, or most explicit, we get the bewilderment of the Ise Shrine Priestess after her night with Narihira, asking, "Was our night a dream? Reality? / Was I sleeping? Or was I awake?" Far more profoundly we get Narihira's reply, with its concluding challenge: "You who know the world of love, decide: / Is my love reality or dream?" But the challenge acknowledges his own wandering in "the darkness of the heart," an attachment to a human being which is as ill-advised as it is natural.... Later poets heighten the illusory quality of love by making the dream a dream one sees on a spring night, which was proverbially brief, or by making the sleep no more than a short dozing.... So charged is this motif of dream that when the *renga* [linked verse] poets codified into their rules the implicit practice of the court poets, they decided that "dream" might be used only once in a hundred stanzas.
>
> What gave such strength to the image is the Buddhist conception of the transience of experience, the lack of stay (*hakanasa*) in human affairs. Of course such transience was thought to underlie all worldly existence, but the poets grounded much of their understanding of it in their treatment of love.[66]

Love comes as a change of heart, often like a dream that hints and suggests unpredictable developments, some too good to be true, others promising only disappointment. In the spirit of Tsurayuki's preface, this combination of love and dreaming makes warriors into poets and opens all to new questions and vulnerabilities. In support of Buddhist truths about this tawdry, dusty world of *samsara*, or the endless cycles of life that we must endure if we do not awaken to the reality of *maya*, or illusion, dreams do us the favor of helping us question the realness of the real. But is illusion about illusion the same thing as truth?

Here we are prepared to grasp the thrust of Ono no Komachi's oft-quoted poems about love and dreaming.

Omoitsutsu	Was it because
Nureba ya hito no	I fell asleep thinking of love

Mietsuramu	That he appeared to me?
Yume to shiriseba	Had I known it was a dream
Samezaramashi wo	I would never have awakened.[67]

As with the exchange between the Ise Priestess and Narihira, here the questions fly, and the hard distinction between the real and the dreamlike becomes blurred. If the emotionally heightened moment of love is hard to contain, so are other lyrical experiences, such as spontaneously responding to the scattering of cherry blossoms or wanting to share the sight of the moon with someone else. In the end, it becomes difficult to chose (or even distinguish) between a dreamlike reality and a dream. One seems as real as the other, even though the poetess admits elsewhere that there still *is* a difference.

Yumeji ni wa	Though I ceaselessly walk
Ashi mo yasumezu	The path of dreams
Kayoedomo	In search of you,
Utsutsu ni hitome	Those many times are nothing
Mishi goto wa arazu	Like seeing you once in reality.[68]

Dreams raise questions. But they also provide answers. Dreaming can become a way to truth. This is the mystical thrust of *As I Crossed the Bridge of Dreams* written by another female writer of the Heian court.[69] We know her only as the Daughter of Sugawara no Takasue (1008–?), a woman who at age fifty-three composed this influential work by loosely linking notes, jottings, and previously composed poems.

She took her dreams seriously. The short text mentions eleven; and nine are presented as the narrator's own. Interestingly, most are visits by religious figures—handsome priests and even Amida—who provide guidance, warning, instruction, and comfort. In fact, the tension that moves the narrative forward places these kinds of useful dreams against useless ones of a more romantic sort. She explains.

> I lived forever in an insubstantial [*hakanaki*] world. Though I made occasional pilgrimages to various temples, I could never bring myself to pray sincerely to become like other people. I knew of those who read the sutras and practiced religious devotions from about the age of seventeen; but I had no interest in such things. If I wanted anything, it was that a well born gentleman like the Shining Prince Genji, perfect in looks and manners, would visit me once a year in the mountain village where he would have hidden me away like Lady Ukifune. There I should live a dreamy existence, my thoughts turned to the blossoms, the autumn leaves, the moon, and the snow as I waited for an occasional word from him, for his splendid letters. These were my continuous thoughts, a dream that I came to feel might actually come true.[70]

Gradually, her obsession with romance and romances gives way to more sober dreams of religious import. When she realizes that her health is declining, and that she has "wandered through life without realizing any of [her] hopes," her attention shifts from dreams of love to dreams of salvation.[71]

> We continue on despite life's unpleasantries. Being worried that my dreams for the next world would also be disappointed, my only hope was a dream I remembered from the thirteenth night of the Tenth Month of the third year of Tenki. In that dream I saw Amida Buddha standing in our garden. I couldn't see him clearly, for there was a layer of mist between us. But I kept looking his way; and when the mist cleared, I saw that the lotus pedestal on which he stood was about three or four feet off the ground, and that he was about six feet tall. He glowed with a golden light. One of his hands was stretched out toward me, and the other formed a sign. No one could see him but me. To my eyes, it was exquisite yet also terrifying. I didn't have the courage to move away from my blinds and draw nearer to him. And so he said, "I shall leave now, but I will come for you later." I was the only one who heard his voice. When I determined that no one else had noticed, it was already the morning of the fourteenth. After this vision, it was on this dream alone that I pinned my hopes.[72]

Dreaming is a response to evanescence, as much as it is an evanescent response. Some kinds of dreams do not last. Some, such as dreams of impossible love, are never fulfilled. But one wonders, "Can't there be life-long *koi*?" Is a lifetime of unrequited yearning not possible?[73] Perhaps this is why we institutionalize dreaming. We give it credence and permanence. By pursuing dreams, we create reality, even as we try to distinguish the Real from the Ideal, and even as we deny the hardness of toil and the possibilities of failure that follow the ease of dreaming. Some dreams last long enough to create and sustain nations. Some build houses, cities, fields, and factories. Others lead to friendship and marriage. In their role of establishing meaningfulness and purpose, are our dreams yet another pathetic delusion? Or are they a noble response to what the Buddhists call "this world of dust"?

As the narrator of *As I Crossed the Bridge of Dreams* reasons, in this world that passes as quickly as a dream, "We continue to live despite all our suffering." Such is *hakanasa*, the evanescence of a world (*yo no naka*) grown smaller and more sophisticated than the broader, more rural cicada-shell world (*utsusemi no yo*) of the previous era. As Miner suggests, the complications of human affairs are illuminated by a Buddhist moon and adumbrated by ideas from the continent about the dangers of attachment to anything in this world of dust and sorrow. Yet Karaki Junzō would adjust this statement to highlight two important points. First, the influence of Buddhism came on gradually. And second, there is a recognizable difference between *hakanasa* (the nominal form of *hakanai*) and *mujō*, which is the unmistakably Buddhist term for evanescence (Chinese, *wuchang* 無常).[74]

The evolution of the relevant terminology, then, shifts from *utsusemi* to *hakanasa* to *mujō*. As expressed by the magical epithet *utsusemi*, the generative notion of the animist's ephemeral cicada-shell world (*yo*) was gradually amplified by the rhetoric of *hakanasa*—or the unreliability of Heian-period human relations (*yo no naka*)—on its way to becoming the central tenet of a stark Buddhist worldview: *shogyō mujō*, "all things are impermanent." As William LaFleur suggests, the thoroughness with which Buddhist symbols eventually came to be deployed was impressive, even definitive of what we generally think of as Japan's medieval period.[75] But this Buddhist notion did not dominate from the moment of its introduction. As mentioned, *mujō* (無常) never appears in the *Man'yōshū* even though its Japanese reading, *tsune nashi* (常なし、the lack of anything lasting) occasionally does.

Japan's symbolic understanding of Buddhist symbols was no doubt modulated by what Joseph Kitagawa has called a "nonsymbolic understanding of symbols"[76] that characterized the earlier age. This was an animistic affirmation of a world not only filled with spirits but inherently meaningful. There was a disinclination to look beyond present space, since that space was sufficiently alive and powerful and, yes, constantly changing. An awareness of change, then, preceded Buddhism, which would profoundly affirm it, making a sense of evanescence doubly important and increasingly powerful as a cultural value.

ANITYA IN A WORLD OF SPONTANEITY

What exactly is the Buddhist understanding of evanescence? In the *Nirvana Sutra* (*Daihatsu nehangyō*) the already mentioned statement that all things are evanescent is linked to deliverance.

Shogyō mujō	諸行無常
Kore shōmetsu no hō nari	是生滅法
Shōmetsu metsu wo owarite,	生滅滅已
Jakumetsu naru wo raku to nasu.	寂滅為楽

All things are evanescent—
This is the way of rising and falling.
When life is fully extinguished,
In extinction there is rest.[77]

In classical Buddhism, *anitya*, the notion of impermanence, was considered to be one of three fundamental marks of existence. The other two were *duhka* (suffering) and *anatman* (no-self).[78] *Anitya* is the idea that both the phenomenal world and our perceptions of it are constantly changing. That is, it is *not* simply that all things change, since our understanding of change is also changing. This is an important distinction because it helps us understand how the ontological truth of *anitya* can serve a spiritual purpose. The Buddhist emphasis on change, in other words, is a matter of the *mind in relationship to the world*. There is an emotional and devotional intention for thinking that nothing in this world is permanent.

That intent is this: pondering *anitya* heals *duhka*. Suffering results from desiring mutable things that we misperceive to be immutable, things that are falsely real in this sense. We suffer because we desire the impossible and the unobtainable. We want that which does not exist, and, therefore, live in a state of endless frustration. The solution is not to insist that things are good because they are hard to get—we do not necessarily enjoy "no-pain-no-gain" perfection in this sense. The way, rather, is to become more accepting and appreciative of simplicity, not to reject what we do know in order to pursue what we do not (and cannot).

An understanding of change is also necessary if we are to grasp the third mark of Buddhist existence. The truth of *anatman* is that we are a part of this world and are, therefore, also changeable and conditional. Many of us would like to think that even in a world of change, the self, or the soul, is lasting, and that it can stand on its own. We might wish to believe that identity is stable. In modern secular societies, there were those who wished to believe that the self was a permanent and reliable thing in an otherwise changeable world. Thus, the seminal modern thinker René Descartes famously came to his assertion—*cogito ergo sum*, "I think, therefore, I am"—upon considering a changing ball of wax that he held before a warm fire. The wax's unstable form stimulated his quest for something more permanent and reliable than the phenomenal world. As a result, the notion of the stable, centrally important self was reinforced, and its gradual separation from the physical, natural world was greatly accelerated. Indeed, the secular notion of the unchanging, critically minded self as "the measure of all things" continued well into the twentieth century in the West, until the emergence of a deconstructive critique that came to question this stubborn fundament of modern thought.

Emerging as it did from the highly sophisticated philosophical traditions of India, classical Buddhism anticipated this deconstructive critique by thousands of years. One result was that the cultures influenced by its comparatively more intricate and sophisticated theories of knowledge viewed the nature of the self, and its relationship to the world, in ways that did not necessarily lock the self into opposition with nature. Some interpretations of *anatman* led to asceticism, monasticism, or what we might call a mystical retreat into nature that flowed from an acceptance of the mutability of all things.

Again, of these three qualities of existence—*anitya, duhka, and anatman*—*anitya* is foundational. It is the truth from which the others flow. As already stated, when this idea came to Japan, it entered a spiritual realm where perceptions of reality were polytheistic, animistic, and shamanistic. Such a world encouraged the interaction of the human and the divine, of people and their environment, and of the living and the dead. To the extent that such a worldview encouraged an *available* kind of sacred experience, it discouraged speculation about the relatively unavailable God of monotheism. Man was not set against an ideal realm of God or Nature, but coexisted with numerous gods—clan gods, gods of the mountains and seas, the gods that the dead had become, and so on. No doubt, a relative lack of idealism in Japan followed from an acceptance of evanescence as reinforced by a voluminous Buddhist literature that kept flowing to Japan from the continent.[79]

Perhaps I belabor the point, but it is one that we cannot afford to ignore or misunderstand. The religious world of early Japan was a world of gods, not of God. *Kami* were multiple rather than single (and exclusive). They were available and plentiful, rather than transcendent and rare. We can understand neither ancient nor present-day Japan without knowing this. Unlike God, *kami* are normally visible and spatially coexistent with human beings. Their worship encouraged precisely the sort of idolatry that monotheism strenuously tried to eradicate. In Japan, if you visit a shrine and encounter a tree that has been marked off by a special rope (*shimenawa*) draped with paper streamers (*gohei*), what you are seeing is a space recognized as sacred, as *kami*. A sumo master wears a similar marking, a "horizontal rope" (*yokozuna*) that indicates his godlike status among those who participate in a sport that anciently was a life-and-death, stay-situated-in-space ritual performed to propitiate the gods. Importantly, these markers of the Divine point to something that is present and visible, rather than to something that is transcendent and glorious in its abstract invisibility. Understanding the fundamental difference between the function of a *shimenawa* (as it points to something that is here) and, for instance, a cross (as it points to something that is higher and not here), will help us grasp the nature of two very different types of form that have developed in Japan to give meaning to an ever-flowing, ever-changing world.

Figure 1.2 Sumo champion Asashōryū. His status is indicated by the *yokozuna*, or "horizontal rope," he wears (photo by Reuters).

Certainly, the close relationship maintained by Japan's ancient clans (*uji*) with their immediate environment partially explains the importance of natural imagery in the poetic tradition. As we have already seen, aspects of nature were ritually invoked by the sacred language of the *Man'yōshū* poets. Later, as articulated in Ki no Tsurayuki's (ca. 868–ca. 945) preface to the *Kokinshū*, the close ties between human beings and their surroundings continued to be an important source of meaning even though the ritual significance of utterance was gradually being lost.

Here is a partial quotation of Tsurayuki's famous preface. Notice the abundance of natural imagery used to describe poetry's true character.

> Rooted in the human heart, Japanese song finds expression in a myriad of leaves. Making their way through this tangled world, men and women use what they have seen and heard to give voice to the feelings of their hearts. The singing warbler among the blossoms, the croaking frog in the pond—is there any living thing not given to song? Without exertion, poetry moves heaven and earth. It stirs the feelings of the gods and the spirits of the dead. It softens relations between men and women, and calms the hearts of fierce warriors.[80]

As described by Tsurayuki, human beings are poetically equal to (rather than the masters of) warblers and frogs. Written words are like leaves (*koto no ha*), and spoken words are like the songs of birds. Although the expressive mode became more lyrical than ritual, as it once was for the earliest *Man'yōshū* poets, language still connected human beings with the gods and spirits, and with each other. This is the legacy of animism. Poetry helps people remember a world where neither God nor Man dominates as master.

What are we to make of this claim that poetic communication occurs "without exertion"? The reality of such a natural response to one's environment actually lies buried deeply in the grammatical structure of the Japanese language itself. Consider the so-called spontaneous form of verbs. Known as *jihatsu* (自発), it is employed when a particular situation is so powerful or evocative that it elicits an immediate response on the part of the agent of the verb. In other words, something about a certain place or situation makes us feel or react in a certain way. We cannot help it. The beauty of a forest, or the sadness of a fall day, induces certain irrepressible thoughts that "just come to us" spontaneously.

By the Heian period, a formalized way of expressing just this *jihatsu* situation had developed grammatically. For example, in the Evening Faces (*yugao*) chapter of *The Tale of Genji* we find this expression of closeness between agent and context. The handsome Prince Genji is having an affair with a young woman. She does not know his name, and he knows her simply as Yugao, after the flower blooming outside her home. One evening, bothered by the noise of her neighborhood, he takes her away to another villa.

> In a hurry to get away before the moonlight found them there, he quickly lifted Yugao into his carriage. Her servant Ukon climbed in after them. They reached a certain villa; and as they waited for the caretaker to be summoned, *Genji's eyes*

could not help but be drawn to the inexpressible darkness of the rotting gate and the lush ferns that grew on it. The morning dew was heavy. When he raised the blinds of his carriage, his sleeves became drenched.[81] (My emphasis)

If you are a fan of Japanese horror movies, you must read this passage in *The Tale of Genji*. In its courtly way, it marks the beginning of many J moments to come. Genji senses danger. But he has to take Yugao into that house with its sinister, darkly growing ferns.

He cannot help seeing them. The verb, to look up, is normally *miageru*. But here it is *miageraretaru*, a passive construction of this special *jihatsu* type.[82] As a spontaneous expression, *miageraretaru* highlights Genji's sensitivity to each and every nuance of his environment. The space of the soon-to-be-haunted house fills him with foreboding. What might have been "he looked up" becomes "his eyes could not help but be drawn to" as evanescence and form resonate portentously. In sum, Genji's reaction is passive, automatic, and natural, where "natural" means having a formal response to an evanescent situation.

My point here reinforces an earlier one. The willingness to accept the Buddhist notion of *anitya* might also lie here in this sort of close identification with the natural world, in this lyrical yet patterned response that was a cornerstone of Heian-period (710–94) poetics as it had gradually developed in earlier Nara-period texts. To the extent that the natural world is one of change, we might even say that Genji identifies with change itself. In other words, this tendency is not merely an observation and a noting of things evanescent, but something more direct and heartfelt. By Tsurayuki's day, such lyricism yielded a highly formalized reality. To state the point more mechanically, the algorithm is this: a change of environment or situation results in a corresponding change of emotion. In sum, the changing world makes me feel this and that emotion.

Is there a simpler way to understand Tsurayuki's rhetorical question: "Is there any living thing not given to song?" Poetry comes lyrically, or "without exertion," because people were not yet supposed to be separated from the animistic roots of the world that animated them. As we will see, the twentieth-century painter Higashiyama Kaii will eventually rephrase Tsurayuki's point about our poetic passivity with pointed clarity. We do not live. Rather, we are made to live. Our environment causes us to move, to feel, to respond. This is a Japanese emphasis, an awareness of the need to accept things beyond our control. This includes an acceptance of the space in which we exist. We live because the world makes us respond continuously, spontaneously, and emotionally to change. Change is everywhere evident in the spatial context in which we live.

Building upon the already existing sensibilities of *utsusemi* and *tsune nashi*, Buddhism helped to mold spontaneity into a foundational cultural premise, even as the ancient roots of this predilection were being compromised by the vast and impressive metaphysical apparatus that eventually undermined the immediate power of the *makura kotoba* as a vessel for the *kotodama*. As Buddhism continued to grow in influence, evanescence became understood more symbolically as *mujō*—a truthful sense of mutability and fleeting mortality; and the world of frogs and blossoms became an *ukiyo* (憂き世)—a lamentable realm of fleeting sensations. If the Buddhists insisted on painting reality as deceptive and troubling, Japan's animistic legacy required that realm to remain awesome. Thus, a complex mix of sometimes-conflicting sentiments was captured in the term *aware*, an exclamation-turned-noun—*Ah! Hare!*—that expresses the existence of something both remarkable and sad. The world makes us respond spontaneously. We cry out "Awesome!" We do so in joy and trembling.

LIFE AS IT SEEMS, NAGARJUNA'S EMPTINESS

My students are usually uncomfortable with the possibility that the self does not exist; yet they are not strangers to the idea that all things change. Change is everywhere. Even the least observant among us can see that things move and develop. A moment's reflection should reveal alteration and variety as preconditions of pattern and structure. I ask my students to hold their hands in front of their eyes, and to try to remember what their fingers looked like a year ago, or five years ago, or ten years ago, or fifteen years ago (when most of them were still young children). Then we try to imagine ourselves into the future. What will that hand look like five years from now, or ten, or fifteen? What will our hands look like at the moment of our death? And what will they be ten years after our deaths?

Buddhist texts such as the *Vimilakirti Sutra* make a certain point plain: the contemplation of the changing body was an important spiritual technique. On the one hand, the relative permanence of our bodies helps us formulate a sense of who we are. I am that person who is muscular or slight, dark or fair, short or tall, and so on. On the other hand, nothing teaches us the truth of change as effectively as our bodies. Up to a point, we grow stronger and more capable. After a point, our hair goes gray or falls out, our teeth decay, our vision weakens, our memory loses its sharpness.[83] Thus it is that the layman Vimilakirti (and many other Buddhist teachers) focused on the body in the attempt to teach us to accept evanescence. He tells us that our physical frame is "transient, weak, impotent, frail and mortal; never trustworthy, because it suffers when attacked by disease."[84]

Physical changes, especially illness, point us to the future. The future, in turn, directs our attention toward death. Standing before my students, I profess with unwanted questions.

Who will you be ten, twenty, thirty, or forty years from now? How do any of you even know you'll even be around for forty more years? How do you know you'll be around tomorrow for that matter? Isn't it possible that you'll walk out of class today and get hit by the shuttle bus? *Wham*, just like that! It's all over.

Not that I want the bus to run over my students, but thinking about change inevitably leads to many important questions, including the big issues of illness and death. As Yoshida Kenkō put it, "A man should firmly plant the threat of death in his mind, and never forget it even for a moment. If he does this, how could the weight of the world not grow lighter, and how could one's desire to follow the Way of Buddha not grow stronger?"[85]

We wonder. How can we live without a self? What of the soul? But to ask about the existence of such things is to risk missing the point entirely. When we look at a photograph or portrait of a loved one who has passed on, who can help but wonder if that person who meant so much to us in the past has been utterly obliterated by death? Has *something* about that person continued? Is the real test of the soul ashes and dust? Or memory and influence?

Regardless of whether or not my students have thought much about the meaning of death, it is not hard to convince them that they are more than their transcript. "You are not solely student X, majoring in Japanese, with a 3.75 grade point average, heading toward magna cum laude and a well-compensated job someday as an executive for Toyota Corporation. There is more to you than an academic record." Even so, few would deny that our academic accomplishments are a lasting part of who we are, that our performance now will have consequences for the future, that knowledge somehow remains with us to inform our decisions and maybe even give us wisdom, skills, and the ability to get along with others, and to make a living. Does the narrative of college—work hard, get a degree, go on to graduate school, get a good job—not assume a permanence of some sort? Does learning not also presuppose a self that learns? And what of enlightenment? What is the "who" of enlightenment? And how can the Buddhist idea of karma, or moral cause and effect, make sense if there is nothing that lasts long enough to be affected by the past? Does cause and effect not presuppose a continuing (and maybe even consistent) means by which the ties between our actions and their effects become measurable or knowable?

Indian Buddhists in the centuries following Siddharta's death came to take such questions seriously. By the time of Nagarjuna (ca. 150–250 AD), "the second Buddha" who became a central figure of the Mahayana tradition, various metaphysical and epistemological theories were created in order to posit a continuing essence. The historical Buddha warned people to stay away from metaphysics. They are a waste of time; and Nagarjuna agreed. He himself was not a metaphysician by intent. But in order to return to the original pre-theoretical teachings of Buddhism, he had to fight fire with fire. Using theory to challenge theory, he exposed the fallacious and ineffective nature of philosophical speculation. His purpose was to return to the simple practice of faithful life based on the principle of *sunyata*: emptiness, mutual dependency, lack of essence, zero-ness.

What many consider to be Nagarjuna's thorough and groundbreaking deconstruction led, in other words, not to a denial of truth but to the pursuit of a truthful life that depends upon the foundational admission that change, especially change of heart, is not to be avoided. Such change is necessary, and should be cultivated. By using logic against the Logicians, he pushed critical methods as far as they could go in order to expose the inability of intellect alone to save us.

His refutation of fixed essences, for example, goes something like this.

> For if one really examines change, one finds that, according to the *catuskoti*, change cannot produce itself, nor can it be introduced by an extrinsic influence, nor can it result from both itself and an extrinsic influence, nor from no influence at all. All the logical alternatives of a given position are tested and flunked by the four error method. There are basic logical reasons why all these positions fail. It would first of all be incoherent (*no papadyate*) to assume that anything with a fixed nature or essence (*svabhava*) could change, for that change would violate its fixed nature and so destroy the original premise. In addition, we do not experience anything empirically which does not change, and so never know of (*na vidyate*) fixed essences in the world about us.[86]

Nagurjuna's critical method, the so-called four-step refutation or *catuskoti*, was a logical tool meant to give method to doubt and lead to another *kind* of thought, one that embraced change by realizing that form, which provisionally exists, is capable of becoming something very different. Even the provisionally permanent entity is, in other words, still capable of being influenced. If so, then *all* things are changeable; and this is the case because of something called "mutual determinacy" (*sunyata*) that permeates everything.

Because of this thorough dependency, all things have "emptiness," which is another possible translation of the crucial term *sunyata*. It is not that things do not exist because they are empty, but just the opposite. Everything exists *because they are empty*. Emptiness is not nihil, but something closer to the ancient notion of ether. But the crucial point, of course, is not an ontological truth but a spiritual one. A thing, including the self, does not exist as an immutable essence, separated from all other things. It is contingent upon another. Therefore, concern about the fixed essences of Braminic (or Platonic) idealism tend to get in the way of practice which is, in the end, the only real way to change how we live. It is a way to get us to move from where we are (in our delusional state) to a point nearer nirvana, or enlightenment.

If only in passing, I mention Nagarjuna in this study of Japanese culture because of his influence on most schools of Buddhism that eventually became popular in Japan. This is not the place to sort out the various sects. Suffice it to say that Buddhism in Japan evolved from the Mahayana tradition (the so-called greater vehicle), with its emphasis on enlightenment and the ability of people to progress beyond the entrapments of delusion. More specifically, what we must appreciate is the simple idea that this emptiness of which Nagarjuna taught is shared by all. It makes possible our ability to relate to each other and to all other things. It is commonality. The reason it is called emptiness rather than fullness is because it speaks to what is potentially the case rather than to what is actually manifest. It is "nothing" because it prompts us to rid ourselves of our obsessive attachment to everything that we do not have in common: personal possessions, prestige, power, self-concern, and so on.

In a word, a focus on emptiness teaches us the dangers of a false sense of permanence. In a world of radical and constant change, something cannot be exactly what we think it is at any given moment. Thus, the intermediate challenge is to grasp the possibility of a good kind of nothingness. Nancy McCagney sums it up this way. Sunyata is "synonymous with space, the perfection of wisdom, free, having no own-nature, unproduced, unconditioned, boundless, immeasurable, signless, wishless, unthinkable, incomparable, equal to the unequalled, ungraspable, providing no basis for support, etc., in sum, the summum bonum of Buddhist practice."[87]

The problem with selfishness is not that hard to grasp. Yet most of us spend our lives pursuing ideals that prevent us from understanding the real and subtle complications of our experiences. By clinging to something, including our critical intelligence, we become blind to the ways we are both thoroughly compromised and possibly saved. Only because of our interdependence with everyone and everything can we become thoroughly condemned and, therefore, endlessly compassionate and moved. Anything that does not allow this change to happen must be abandoned for the reality of evanescence.

SHUKKE: LEAVING THE WORLD

The English mathematician and philosopher Alfred North Whitehead criticized Buddhism for being "a neat little system of thought which oversimplifies its expression of the world."[88] I personally doubt Whitehead understood the object of his derision. True, "Life is suffering" is an elegant elocution. And perhaps the goal of release from *samsara* is less positively rewarding than the more "developed" goal of worshiping God, a situation that Whitehead preferred. But to call Buddhism negative and lacking in feelings of worship is to ignore both the meaning of enlightenment and the pietistic turn that the worship of Amida took once Buddhism became a faith for the masses from the late Heian period on.

I admit that the pronouncement that "Life is suffering" is, in fact, a negative assessment of what we are up against. It condemns the illusory nature of our pre-enlightened reality, and is necessarily blunt in order to make us recognize our delusions. We need "the whole truth and nothing but the truth." And yet, even telling it straight does not always work. We often need a less direct means of coming to humility.

The third chapter of *The Lotus Sutra* (*Myōhō renge kyō*) presents us with a famous analogy. This mortal life is like a burning house. We are children playing in it, unaware of the danger. If we were told the truth—"Quick. Get out! Your house is on fire!"—we would never believe it. We are, after all, doing passably well, even in our deluded state. Short of presenting us with something even more interesting or amusing than the world we have come to know, we will never leave our dangerous situation. We must be coaxed away from danger by *hōben* (Sanskrit, *upaya*) or "expedient means."

The evanescent world calls to us with its enticements. It gives us ways to measure our success and security, however illusory they might be. Society supplies distractions, entertainments, inducements, prizes. When it comes to the tawdry game of life, some of us play it pretty well—so well that it comes to seem like an opportunity for triumph. We forget that the world is a fleeting dream from which we must awaken, that ours is a cicada-shell existence. In short, we do not see the fire. And so we need the promises that the wise Sariputra concocts in order to save his children.

As already noted, the Japanese term for this world of *samsara* is "the disagreeable world" or *ukiyo* 憂き世. To emphasize its lack of true substance, the Japanese also wrote the word with the homonym, 浮世, or "floating world," a term that, as we will see, came to have a contrary meaning as time passed. At this point, both readings similarly refer to a world that is undesirable in the sense that it is impermanent, unmoored, and without substance. The world floats. We float. To seek security and permanence by attaching ourselves to that which is unpleasant and floating is to be deluded. If we knew what was good for us, we would leave such a place right away.

In Heian Japan, the idea of leaving the world behind became formalized. You could shave your head, don simple robes, and make vows to live differently, even ascetically, within a community of Buddhist believers or, in some cases, in relative isolation. This process was called *shukke* (出家), or "leaving home." In *As I Crossed the Bridge of Dreams*, the narrator's mother, for example, exercised her option to abandon the world and became a Buddhist nun. The literature of the period gives us this and many other examples of both women and men saying farewell to the burning house of sorrows and taking up a life of resignation.

In some cases, this abandonment was an abdication by those who held considerable political power. In some of these instances, *shukke* was actually a way to remain in control by removing oneself from the limelight to work behind the scenes. Although the capital had ostensibly been moved from Nara in 794 AD to escape the growing Buddhist influence there, Heian-kyō also became temple bound, hemmed in by Buddhist interests for at least two reasons. First, the ties between powerful families, such as the Soga or the Fujiwara, and the various temples that lent their patrons prestige and peace of mind continued to exist. Second, like the Fujiwara clan who rose to power by marrying their daughters into the imperial family, the Buddhist institutions also continued to enjoy significant landowning and tax advantages that had carried over from the preceding period. This was not simply a matter of not having to pay less tax. They could increase the size of their manors by incorporating surrounding non-protected cultivators. To put it bluntly, Buddhist properties grew as farmers gave their land to the temples in return for the double salvation of lower tax rates in this world and peace in the world to come.

It was only toward the end of the Heian period in the twelfth century that an enduring triumvirate of power—the Buddhist institutions, the nobles, and the imperial house—started to come undone. This was the result of the emergence of a fourth group: the samurai, who began to be a political factor from the 930s. Some of these men were descendants of polygamist aristocratic families that sent their superfluous sons away from the capital and into the countryside, where they established their own bases of power. Given their lineage, they understandably harbored both aristocratic pretensions and considerable ambition. At first, in concert with provincial strong men, they did the bidding of the wealthy families that employed them. They protected and managed the courtiers' landholdings. But they gradually evolved from "those who serve"—which is the literal meaning of "samurai"—to become the new ruling class.[89]

Even as rulers, they continued to serve. Instead of serving aristocratic landowning families, however, their masters became, at least nominally, the Imperial family itself. In reality, these warriors struggled to dominate each other in their desire to become more powerful in relationship to all other centers of power. There was much in fighting, and the usurpation of property and privilege. Rather than displace the imperial institution altogether, however, the samurai practiced an enduring principle of Japanese politics that is valid even today: whoever controls the emperor controls Japan. Few ever considered doing away with the emperor altogether, probably because of widely held respect for the form that he (or she) represents.

The samurai used this form to their advantage. Their revolutionary challenge to the vested interests of the Heian aristocracy and the jockeying for power that ensued among competing warrior families from about 1150 on led to violent, even cataclysmic social change. For those who witnessed the destructive battles between the Taira and the Minamoto that occurred during the 1170s and 1180s, the killing seemed only to reinforce the notion that life is fragile and brief. Political upheaval also added a sense of urgency to the practice of *shukke*, which remained formalized as a way to try to avoid implication and (sometimes) slaughter.

One famous recluse, Kamo no Chōmei (1155–1216), lived to tell the tale of destruction that accompanied this shift of power from the courtiers to the samurai. He himself had been a part of the inner circle of power in the capital. But he left privilege to live a simple secluded life, first in Ōhara and then in the hills east of the nearly destroyed capital. There he penned his brief elegy, *An Account of My Hut* (*Hōjōki*, 1212), which remains a powerful statement about the truth of evanescence.

The work begins with a few lines that Japanese schoolchildren still learn by heart.

> The river flows without ceasing; yet its water is never the same. Foam appears in the eddies, disappearing and reforming, never attempting to linger for even a moment. In this world, equally evanescent are men and their dwellings.[90]

Chōmei was the son of a prominent senior prelate, Kamo no Nagatsugu, who controlled one of the most important shrines in the capital. He was given a court rank at the age of six and learned how to take his place in a world in which etiquette (*reigi*) and political advancements were intricately connected. With his father's strong connections and assuming his own probable promotion to a similarly high post, Chōmei seems to have put his best efforts into music and poetry, which he later claimed to be his only connection with (and usefulness to) the court.

As we can infer from his *Anonymous Writings* (*Mumyōshō*, ca. 1211), which deals with poetic theory and aesthetic life in the capital, his future was both helped and hindered by his artistic ability.[91] On the one hand, he was honored by the inclusion of his poems in the imperial anthology *Senzai wakashū*, (ca. 1180) when he was just thirty-two; moreover, he was selected to be a member of an elite group of poets, the so-called *waka dokoro*. On the other hand, his lack of tactfulness and moments of improper behavior put him at odds with others at court and eventually led to his decision to leave the world.

More specifically, he offended and received a rebuke from the cloistered Emperor Gotoba when he and his friends, caught up in the moment, played the piece "Takuboku" at a music party. This was a special number secretly passed down from master to pupil, not to be played at public gatherings without special permission. Chōmei ignored the rules, and paid a price for his digression. On another occasion, which similarly demonstrates the great importance placed on proper etiquette and tact, he embarrassed a powerful relative, Kamo no Sukekane, with a poem he entered in an official poetry contest. His *tanka* was dismissed by the judges for including a reference to a river that did not exist, "*ishikawa ya / semi no ogawa*," "The Rock-strewn River, the Cicada Brook." But he made an appeal, and a second judgment was made. When this judgment led to a consultation with Chōmei himself, he explained to the referee that the expression "*ishikawa*" was a well-known reference to the Kamo River, an epithet that anyone who knew anything about the history of the Kamo Shrine should know.

The poem was not only accepted, but later became anthologized in the prestigious tanka collection, the *Shinkokinshū* (1205).

Ishikawa ya	The Rock-strewn River,
Semi no ogawa no	The Cicada Brook,
Kiyokereba	Was so clear
Tsuki no nagare wo	That the moon came to dwell
Tazunete zo sumu	In its transparent flow.[92]

Humiliated by this incident, Kamo no Sukekane, who was the prelate of the Kamo Shrine, later stood in the way of Chōmei's promotion to become the head of another major shrine in the Kamo complex, the *Tadasu no yashiro*. The post would have been a stepping-stone to advancement to his father's post, but it was not to be.[93] Another person was appointed in his place; and although Emperor Gotoba was willing to install him in another equally prestigious position, Chōmei himself lost interest in advancement and later abandoned the world for life as a recluse.

We know that the *Mumyōshō* was written at roughly the same period as *An Account of My Hut*, thus raising questions about why these interests should be on the writer's mind at the same time—caring about the formalities of poetry while urging abandonment of the world. If he truly was embracing the notion that life is fleeting and that court life is unworthy of his most sincere attention, then why this continuing concern with poetic form and aesthetic protocol? Would walking away from civilization not tempt one to forget manners rather than become preoccupied with their importance? Needless to say, Chōmei's bold assertion about the vanity of life also harbors a lingering desire to dwell poetically. As suggested earlier by Levy, to be poetic is to be appropriate. Perhaps there is a quota of doubt to be granted any strong assertion of this sort. But in Chōmei's famous treatise on disaster and the futility of attachment to this floating world, we detect a very human patina of formal nuance and social dog-eat-dog complication.

His contemplation of froth on a stream might be summed up in this way: if we understand the impermanence of life on this planet, then we will see that the houses we work so hard to build and adorn might be contributing to our unhappiness. Indeed, they might even collapse on us someday. For reasons already mentioned, Chōmei's metaphor of the house was particularly apt. Beyond unmistakable resonances with the Buddhist burning house, homes are also an eloquent statement of how successful we think our lives have been. Chōmei's treatise thus gains narrative force as he recounts his life of progress toward smaller not grander places of abode. In his sixties, he finally takes refuge in a pieced-together hut in the woods, "one last old cocoon"[94] that to him indicates "no claim to the land" since "a beautiful place has no owner."[95] It is the simplest of structures, "ten by ten, and no taller than seven."[96] It is an appropriately temporary hut. As a shelter, it provides no more than what is absolutely necessary. "Caught inside, a house might crush you."[97]

Why should we need anything more than this? The reasons flow to the enlightened, not as a choice "to live deliberately," as Henry David Thoreau would have it, but as a resignation to the lack of choices this floating world actually offers.

> Our life in this world is difficult.
> We and our houses are fleeting and hollow.
> From position and rank flow many problems.
> A lowly man who lives beside a man of power
> Cannot openly rejoice even when he is happy.
> Yet when his sorrow becomes unbearable,
> Neither can he cry out.
> His anxious air and constant fear
> Are like those of a sparrow living near a hawk.
> A poor man who lives near a rich man is shamed by his shabbiness.
> He goes in and out, day and night, maintaining a self-effacing air.
> He knows the envy of his wife, children, and servants.
> He also knows that the rich man despises them all.

And his heart is troubled.
He will never find peace.[98]

Chōmei's statements about conformity and evanescence are baldly general, a critique of the power structures of his day; yet, especially in light of his *Mumyōshō*, they are also intensely personal. Indeed, *An Account of My Hut* is so self-concerned that it seems nearly modern in places. Consider, for example, the emergence of what is perhaps the first modern description to be found in all of Japanese letters.

> On the east side, a three-foot awning. . . . By the south wall, a bamboo mat. On the north, a screen of Amida. . . . On the south, a bed of dry brackens. To the southwest, a bamboo shelf holding three leather-lined baskets for poetry and music. . . . Next to the shelf, against the wall, a koto and a biwa.[99]

This description of his hut is modern in essence. The point of view is unusually clear, fixed, and self-producing of the writer.[100] It makes a claim on reality by way of a personal investment in a larger encompassing system—as represented by orderly references to north, east, south, and west. It also flirts with a confusion of the general and the particular, or with the personal as general. In other words, our vision of his abode emerges by way of a fixed point of view, in which everything in Chōmei's small hut is seen in relationship to both the cardinal directions and to the author's place at the very center of this universally valid orientation. He is the resident, the seer, the self-concerned man who is, paradoxically, trying to be selfless. In the end, his self-consciousness leads to an astonishingly frank admission that will be repeated ad nauseum in the more consciously modern era that is already beginning to dawn.

> "Has your discerning mind done anything more
> Than drive you mad?"
> To these questions of mind,
> There is no answer.
> And so all I can do is use my impure tongue
> To pray futilely to Amida—
> Once, twice, once again.[101]

Clearly, both success and failure propped up this self-discovery. As mentioned, Chōmei's private victories and disappointments in court prompted him to retire to the woods. Yet the truth of vanity is more than one man's statement of personal fortune or misfortune. What gives *An Account of My Hut* its expansive power are the observations he is able to make about life in the capital. They apply to everyone, not just for one well-connected but politically unsuccessful poet and musician. While in the capital, Chōmei witnessed fire, political instability, and a disastrously unsuccessful attempt to relocate the capital. He experienced drought, crop failure, starvation, plague, and earthquakes. All these catastrophes, whether natural or manmade, visited the grand capital of Heian and mocked its sophistication and finery. These events reinforced the notion that we are nothing but foam upon a stream.

> I was surprised to see painted boards mixed in with the firewood,
> And bits of gold leaf.
> I inquired to learn that the desperate
> Had broken into the temples,
> Stolen the Buddhist statues,
> And had reduced the woodwork of the halls
> To kindling.
> What sinful times![102]

This striking moment of truth brings Chōmei to the inescapable conclusion that even the most opulent building will someday become nothing more than firewood. The house of this world is indeed on fire. Both men and their dwellings are like bubbles of an ever-changing stream.

In this floating world, great success leads to great failure. If we understood the world for what it really is, we would flee its complications and live simpler lives, ones that do not center themselves on possessions and foolish attachments. The problem for us is that, whether working until exhaustion or endlessly distracting ourselves before pixels, whether giving ourselves to gluttony or starving ourselves to be slender, we hardly notice the heat and flames closing in around us.

SUCCESS AND FAILURE

Life is brief, fragile, ever-changing. Nothing lasts. As with bullets shot into the sky, so with careers, marriages, and the stock market: having gone up, they will come down. Certainly, the Japanese have not cornered the market on vulnerability and failure. Neither is ephemerality solely a Buddhist lesson. "Lord, make me to know mine end, and the measure of my days, what it is; that I may know how frail I am" (Psalms 39:4). That said, one significant cultural nuance to consider is how consistently the Japanese aestheticize sorrow. They chose to see frailty as an unavoidable and potentially beautiful part of life. As Ivan Morris put it, there is "the nobility of failure" in an evanescent, even declining world.[103]

These days, most of us do not often associate Japan with failure. Living in an area only as large as California (and with significantly less arable land), Japan's population, which is roughly half that of the United States, has created the second largest economy in the world. Agriculture, fishing, manufacturing, education, finance, government, service—practically all areas of human endeavor are highly developed if not always effective. Crime is low.[104] Longevity is high.[105] Literacy rates and general levels of education are impressive.[106] Japan's mass transportation system is the envy of the world: taxis are fuel-efficient and clean; buses and trains are well maintained and dependable; the Bullet Train is a wonder. Whether traditional or cutting edge,

Japan's cultural accomplishments are noteworthy and influential. We must wonder. How does all this come from a culture that appreciates failure?

The answer to this question can be found in another of the Japanese classics. Like Chōmei's *An Account of My Hut*, *The Tale of the Heike* (*Heike monogatari*, ca. 1219–43) recounts the cataclysmic social changes that accompanied the final ascendance of the samurai to power toward the end of the twelfth century. It is a massive collection of orally transmitted tales that were gathered, redacted, and written down by clerics, storytellers, and former courtiers who found each other in the great Buddhist monasteries of the day. These stories recount in dramatic fashion the major battles and personalities of the transition from court- to samurai-dominated society. The text begins with a clear affirmation of evanescence, announcing the theme that will give coherence to the entire work: "The sound of the Gion Shōja bells echoes the impermanence of all things; the color of the *śāla* flowers reveals the truth that the prosperous must decline. The proud do not endure, they are like a dream on a spring night; the mighty fall at last, they are as dust before the wind."[107] Those who prosper *must* decline. Failure *must* follow success. The proud will not last. In this floating world of illusion and misguided attachments, our moments of victory and accomplishment are like a dream. We ourselves are like dust in the wind.

The Tale of the Heike focuses on the Heike clan, who were also called the Taira. Their fate is embodied in the person of Taira no Kiyomori, the leader of this family and its associates, whose brilliant yet brutal maneuvering allowed him to become the new ruler of Japan and, therefore, the nominal protector of the emperor and a partaker of all the grandeur, elegance, and tradition that the imperial house continued to express. In becoming the principal "servants" of the imperial house, Kiyomori challenged not only the vested interests of the courtiers but also the supremacy of the Buddhist institutions. He formed alliances with those noble families who would support him and destroyed those who would not. A man of great ambition, he would not be stopped.

As told by this tale, even in his final decline, as Kiyomori was suffering from a disease that left him burning with a fever so hot that "people could hardly bear to remain within twenty-five or thirty feet of the bed,"[108] his last wish was not to be forgiven or memorialized. He wanted only the head of his enemy Minamoto no Yoritomo.

> "I have seen my prosperity extend to my offspring. There is nothing left for me to desire in this life. My sole concern is that I have not seen the severed head of the Izu Exile Yoritomo. Build no halls or pagodas after I die; dedicate no pious works. Dispatch the punitive force immediately, decapitate Yoritomo, and hang the head in front of my grave. That will be all the dedication I require." Those were deeply sinful words indeed.[109]

Kiyomori's "prosperity" is fated. The Taira had gained position and wealth. But an insurrection against them had already begun by the time of

Kiyomori's passing. As he feared, his rival Minamoto no Yoritomo led a revolt against them. The Taira fled the capital and, after three major defeats at Ichi no tani, Yashima, and Dan no ura, they were eventually routed. In the concluding chapter of *The Tale of the Heike* we read:

> The [Heike] men captured at Dan-no-ura had either been paraded through the avenues and beheaded or else sent into distant exile, far from their wives and children.... It was all the fault of the Chancellor-Novice Kiyomori, the man who had held the whole country in the palm of his hand and executed and banished as he pleased, disrespectful of the Emperor above and oblivious to the myriad folk below, with no concern either for society or for individuals. Who could doubt that the evil deeds of a father must be visited upon his offspring?[110]

There are different ways to understand the Heike family's fall from power. We could say it is simply a matter of evanescence: everything eventually changes for everyone, even the powerful. But a second, conflicting explanation would flow from a different principle. Moral cause-and-effect requires that both failure and success follow irrevocably from bad or good deeds. While change prevails, a countering force reinforces unchanging principles. Certainly, this tension comes from the contradictions we have already noted in early Buddhist thought. If all things are in flux, and if what we perceive (including the self) is an illusion, and if reality is hardly distinguishable from our dreams, then how is it that attempts to find meaning (and by extension, the curses or blessings that pass from yesterday to today, or from ancestors to their posterity) are possible? As we asked earlier, without some semblance of permanence, how can anything be measured or meaningful?

In the specific case of Taira no Kiyomori, one type of permanence does predictably flow from the Buddhist principle of karma. But two other types of form are perhaps even more important. They are propriety and tact. According to the *Tale of the Heike*, Kiyomori's downfall is his arrogance. He cannot stay within the bounds of acceptable behavior. He fails because he is unrefined. Thus, the many people who had a hand in creating this text have made sure to portray Kiyomori as a barbaric man, especially in contrast to his oldest son, Shigemori, who is presented sympathetically as a thoughtful and careful Confucian gentleman.

When Kiyomori expresses his distrust of the Retired Emperor Go-Shirakawa, whom he suspects of plotting to get rid of the Heike clan, Shigemori gives this father a word of advice.

> You must never show the slightest hint of any such attitude in your manner or speech. It would be unfortunate if people were to notice that you felt that way. As long as you obey the Retired Emperor and treat others with consideration, you will enjoy the protection of the gods and Buddhas. And what is there to fear if you have that?[111]

Such is the case for propriety. When Shigemori leaves the room after demonstrating more maturity and thoughtfulness than his father,

Kiyomori dismisses him, "Shigemori is a remarkably phlegmatic man."[112] As the story is told, the father fails to appreciate the son's wisdom, even though any Confucian knows that a Gentleman should be careful with words, and that proper behavior is essential for one's advancement in society. Say nothing, then, about the advancement of society itself. To Kiyomori, formalities mean little or nothing. He is all desire and ambition. Denying the kinds of form that might have saved him, he is soon crushed by evanescence.

In the Japanese world of nuance and constant change, formality (including the formality of nuance) provides a provisional way to assign meaning to actions and to guarantee that things move forward as they should. Thus Shigemori's advice to his father—"As long as you obey the Retired Emperor and treat others with consideration"—appeals to both the imperial center of society and the members of the various social circles that radiate from it. Unfortunately, Kiyomori sees himself as too good to be bound by the usual strictures of acceptable behavior. He is driven by wrath, hubris, and greed. Ignoring his son's wisdom, he offends, the former emperor, Go-Shirakawa. And for this, he pays a price.

In the fog of war, we might expect that formalities and rules of decency should count for little; but that is not the message *The Tale of Heike* delivers. Even the engagement of warriors at the height of battle is controlled and, therefore, given meaning by numerous formalities: the calling out of names, pre-battle exchanges of poetry, and so on. The identification of contestants is important, if only because a warrior would seek engagement with someone of equal or higher status, and avoid fighting or be killed by someone of lower status.

This need to know the position of one's enemy accounts for the many lengthy descriptions of armor we find in a text such as *The Tale of Heike*.

> Tonō was attired in an olive-gray *hitatare* and a suit of armor with a design of small cherry blossoms, redyed in yellow, on the lacing. At his waist, he wore a sword with blue-black alloy fittings; on his back, there rode a quiver containing arrows fledged with white feathers. His rattan-wrapped bow was at his side; his helmet was tied to his shoulder-cord.[113]

The many common elements in these frequent descriptions, such as the "rattan-wrapped bow," signifying that all warriors belong to a generic group, much as the dark suit and white shirt is common to salaried workers in Tokyo today. Within this realm of formality, subtle differences in color and quality establish finer, important distinctions.

Helmets and masks are more formal than faces; and so comes the agony that the Minamoto warrior Kumagae no Naozane must experience at the Battle of Ichi no tani. He closes with a well-attired Heike enemy, rips off his helmet, only to find a beautiful young boy. Because of his formal role as a samurai, Naozane must behead the young man even though Atsumori reminds him of his own son, and his first impulse is to let him escape.

Kumagae's heart would let his enemy live. But some of his own men are closing in from behind, and he must meet their (formal) expectations of him. Even if he were to let the boy live, his comrades would jump at the chance to take the head and win the reward. Knowing his fate, Atsumori tells Kumagae to do it quickly. With no options remaining, the older man kills the younger one, and suffers the spiritual consequences.

Moral consequences make sense to us. We can understand the failure and decline of people who *deserve* what they get. But what of evanescence? According to the inexorable law of all things changing all the time, consequences do not always seem to flow from understandable causes. Having proven himself a brilliant tactician and a faithful supporter of his older brother Yoritomo, another hero of the *Heike*, Minamoto no Yoshitsune finds himself unfairly accused of being a traitor, and is hunted down by his brother's men. None of this is deserved. Ethically speaking, it does not make sense. Yoshitsune's persecution should not happen. It is the result of the deceit and capriciousness of lesser men. Nevertheless, the greatest military hero of the Genpei Wars must end his life with his own sword, committing *seppuku* as Yoritomo's men close in on the burning house where he breathes his last. The undeniable message here is that the pull of evanescence claims everyone—good or bad, justified or not, Heike or Genji.[114]

Another truth of this important text is that success does not last. By the end of *The Tale of the Heike*, Kiyomori is long dead; and the theme of *mujō* is driven home by way of his daughter, Kenreimon'in. Like the Fujiwara leaders who ruled before him, Kiyomori similarly pursued a strategy of marrying his daughters to the male members of the imperial line. This is how Kenreimon'in became mother to Emperor Antoku, a sure sign of their prestige and glory. Yet at the battle of Dan no ura, Kenreimon'in must witness the death of her son, who drowns in the waves as the Minamoto warriors draw near. Seeing no reason to live, she tries to follow him in death. She jumps into the sea, but is unceremoniously dragged back into a boat by her long black hair.

Her plight is at once depressing and moving. Having enjoyed a life of luxury, she is sent to live in a "shockingly dilapidated abode, separated from all her kinsmen."[115] Despondent and lonely, she is like a "fish on land, or a bird torn from the nest."[116] She shaves off her hair and leaves the world. Like Kamo no Chōmei, she seeks solitude, a place "where she might remain while the dew of her life must await the wind."[117] Her final resting place is the lonely Jakkōin in the hills of Ōhara, north of the capital.

> The ephemerality of worldly things is like springtime blossoms scattering in the breeze; the brevity of man's existence is like the autumn moon disappearing behind a cloud. On mornings when the lady had enjoyed blossoms at the Chengyang Hall, the wind had come and scattered their beauty; on evenings when she had composed poems about the moon at the Zhangqui Palace, clouds had covered the moon's face and hidden its radiance. Once she had dwelt in a magnificent abode with jeweled towers, golden halls, and brocade

cushions; now her brushwood hermitage drew tears even from the eyes of strangers.[118]

Having begun with the melancholy sound of bells, this saga of the Taira also ends with somber tones and with this reference to the ephemerality of spring blossoms (*mujō no haru no hana*). Keireimon'in's time finally comes. "She recited the *nenbutsu*, clasping the five-colored cord attached to the hand of the central image. 'Hail, Amida, Lord of the Western Paradise! Please allow me to enter the Pure Land.'"[119] She prays to escape from this transient world of dust, where pain follows every pleasure and failure follows every victory. Only in death is peace possible.

According to the law of failure-follows-success, it is not even the case that bad things *might* happen. Evanescence requires that they *will* happen. Do not bother, then, to question whether it is our fault or someone else's. Either way, the fall will come, and it might come with a vengeance. The import of *The Tale of the Heike* is, simply, that if it happened to the Taira clan, it could happen to us, our associates, our friends, our family members. We may be doing well today, but misfortune will strike tomorrow.

What a bleak picture! How does anyone not get bogged down in despair? It might be a truism that only darkness allows us to see the light. Still, "bad things happen to good people" is not especially comforting. We might go into denial and ignore the inevitable. We might try to swim against the current of evanescence. But to do so would be senseless.

Is there no way out? My students are quick to see one. Because they grasp the logic of salvation as it exists in an evanescent reality, they also understand that our prospects are justifiably hopeful. Why? Simply because if it is the case that failure follows success, then the converse of this statement must also be true. Success follows failure. You cannot have one without the other.

So the *good* news is that we are all going to fail, since success follows. Here, many Japanese sayings come to mind. "Failure is the foundation of success" (*Shippai wa seikō no moto*). Or how about, "Fall down seven times, get up eight?" (*Nana korobi, ya oki*).[120] I try to explain these homilies, probably dated to the Edo period. "Anytime something bad happens to you, tell yourself it is not permanent. Things will turn themselves around sooner or later. Just keep playing the game and you will have your share of victories."

On the other side of the coin, I suppose we should not forget that anytime something good happens, failure is just around the corner. Knowing this might take a little luster off our victories. But sensing our vulnerability, even in times of success, might save us from arrogance and hubris. The failure implicit in success might even make us gracious, just as the success implicit in failure might help us to be hopeful. The point here, of course, is that being able to see our outcomes as both success *and* failure—all rolled into one—follows from an acute awareness of change. Nothing gives the mind stability like an awareness of the world's radical instability.

THE TRANSCENDENTAL ORDER / THE ORDER OF HERE-AND-NOW

Up to this point, we have not been talking about an undifferentiated chaos but about cycles of change, such as the four seasons, or the coming in and out of a dreamlike state, or the intelligible changes in a person's luck. In other words, the assertion that all things change does not preclude continuity. The literary expressions of change that we have examined so far have presupposed *some* type of continuity and, therefore, *some* kind of pattern or structure. But what exactly is the nature of this form within change?

Let us go back to our original question of evanescence and form as they exist in tension with each other. For the sake of analysis, let us try to establish a fundamental pattern for this tension by diagramming evanescence as a continuous and continuing line that forms an endless number of circles. These circles might represent the constant alteration of day and night, or the seasons. They might also represent the daily cycles of *samsara*, a state of endless illusion that has us going around and around until we gain the clarity that allows us to break from it.

In such a context of constant change, enlightenment comes when we see the world for what it is. We are enlightened when we are no longer delusional, when we no longer think we can have pattern without change, and change without pattern. In other words, living in *samsara* is a meaningful activity in its own right. But enlightenment is strikingly so. Why? Because *satori* represents a clear break from this kind of circularity, a moment when

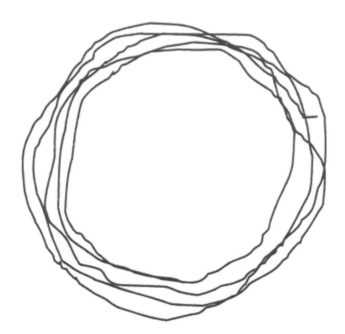

Figure 1.3 *Samsara*, this evanescent world.

we think that absolute newness is possible. This moment of enlightenment signifies a movement toward something else, even if that something else is nothing more than seeing an old thing in a new way.

The rhetoric of enlightenment is encouraging. We progress. We escape. We come to see things clearly. Spiritual clarity helps us avoid attaching ourselves to meaningless fantasies. Through a training of our perceptions, we control our desires until we reach a point where we are able to leave the continuously vexing cycle of rebirth to enter what we might generally call "the other world," a reality that is beyond and above the physical one in which we live. It is a realm that only our spiritual eyes can see. It exists above and beyond *samsara*. In the idiom of those popularized forms of Buddhism that proliferated in Japan from the second half of the Heian period through the Kamakura period (1185–1333), this other world was often called the Pure Land, or Western Paradise. It is a heavenly state of glory marked by peacefulness and a presumed slowing of change.

Buddhism teaches us to seek an end to life's cycles of vanity by resisting attachment to this world. At the same time, the Enlightened who are able to leave choose *not* to go on to Paradise but to return to the world of change. These are the so-called Bodhisattva, people whose great understanding also gives them great compassion. These two qualities come as a pair, and never separately. You cannot be understanding without becoming loving. Having gained the ability to leave, the enlightened few turn back to help those who

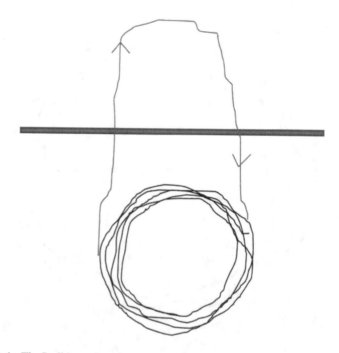

Figure 1.4 The Bodhisattva's path, a return to evanescence.

are still struggling. In other words, the Bodhisattva has learned how to love the world by overcoming it—to not be of it, but to be in it. If escape from the world of change is meaningful, then return is even more so.

Although often misunderstood, this same pattern of return is central to other religious traditions as well. As Abraham learns, only by turning away from God, as expressed by his bargaining with the destroying angels, does a believer finally come to be oriented like God: not faced away from Sodom and Gomorrah but attentive to their needs. Surely, the presence of Lot and his family were not the only reason Abraham sought to save those cities. Too bad, then, that in our desire for heaven we become blind to the world's suffering, and to its sorrowful beauty. Wanting to get away, we become trapped in a state of judgment. Being judgmental, we do not progress to compassion. We praise justice, never feeling the need for mercy.

Turning from God is the only way to be like God, just as the rejection of reprieve is the only way to know good and evil. Unless we go back to *samsara*—like a bodhisattva or a saint—our orientation remains focused on abstractions: justice, rights, retribution, and so on. This is the linearity that our thirst for meaning has generated, and it is what the more cyclical discourse of change seems to challenge and, perhaps, correct.

We will take up this question of compassion again. For now it is enough to see that the development of popular Buddhism in Heian- and Kamakura-period Japan established a few powerfully motivating concepts—such as *gō* or karmic retribution, and the light-like mercy of Amida. It also posited a few powerfully motivating imaginary spaces, such as Western Paradise or the numerous hells that await the wicked. Through copying, translating, and studying the sutras and the commentaries that were written about them, through the production and worship of religious images, through rituals that gave symbolic form to life, a transcendental realm was established as an ideal world that existed *apart* from this floating world. That other, higher world serves as a pattern for life here. That is its usefulness, its function, its importance.

Belief in non-changing, metaphysical form encourages us to live a meaningful life because it allows us to reference our lived experiences against the forms of unchanging Truth. We might be living on earth, but we are actually living for heaven—or, perhaps, for hell. Images of eternal punishment that circulated among the masses made the importance of living a good life graphically clear. Such works of life after death were dramatically depicted, establishing an unmistakable symbolic connection between mortality and the six realms of being (*rokudō*) that gave form to evanescent life. One could progress to a higher level or regress to a lower one depending on how well one's behavior conformed to established standards. Thus, hierarchies of being and orthodoxies of belief developed as the faithful endeavored to seek the ideal world that awaited the righteous after death. This was preferable to the horrible hell that awaited the wicked. In sum, thinking of another world of predictable, unchanging laws and principles was one way that the Japanese formally countered the even more inescapable truth of evanescence: that life is brief, fragile, and ever-changing.

To our diagram of *samsara* let us add, then, a grid that represents the order of the metaphysical world as it exists above the chaos of the physical one, which we actually inhabit. Let us call this higher form the transcendental order.

Whether complex or simple, ideological formations give to their subscribers a sense of meaning. By way of certain ideas, we have purpose, we are motivated, we have a way to determine whether we are living well or poorly. The manner by which societies form in relation to abstract values—such as the elevated status of the imperial family, or the prestige of one's lord, or the compassion of Amida—flows from a constant and pressing need to link what we do and feel to a *higher* source that justifies our behavior. Most often, this link is made through symbols—whether words, sculptures, paintings, buildings, and so forth—that represent the transcendental Truth. They express such abstractions by way of their concreteness and materiality. But they do so by claiming to be less important and attractive than the things to which they point. A holy book or a statue is supposed to be less important than the God it affirms, for example.

One notable aspect of Japanese religious practice is a relative lack of what we might call scriptural habit. To be sure, there have been, and are, many

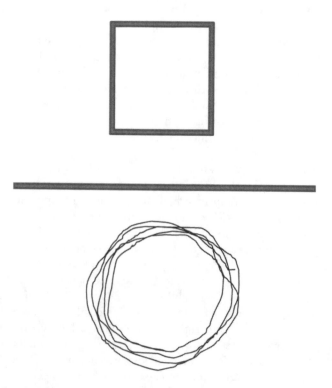

Figure 1.5   The transcendental order as it exists above the world of change.

Figure 1.6 The Kiyomizu Temple, referencing the transcendental order.

Japanese books. Literacy rates in Japan have consistently been among the highest in the world. There have also been numerous sacred texts, such as *The Heart Sutra* (*Hannya shingyo*) and other commentaries by important Buddhist thinkers, just as there have been many people who have devotedly recited and studied these works.[121] And yet, this textual activity notwithstanding, in Japan there has not been a widespread, commonly shared practice of daily reference to a particular holy book (or books) as you might find in China or India, in the Middle East, Europe, or in the Americas. As we shall see, the closest the Japanese ever came to a widely practiced scriptural habit was during the late modern period, when the Rescript on Education became this holy text for an entire nation. So if you ask, "What is Japan's Bible?" The answer is, "There isn't one."

The twentieth-century anthropologist Yanagita Kunio (1875–1962) explains,

> It is only through familiarity with the ceremonial observances known as *matsuri*, "festivals" that an understanding of the religious beliefs peculiar to Japan is to be gained, in terms of their original forms, and the alterations that have been made through the years. When compared with such organized religions as Buddhism and Christianity, the most immediately obvious characteristic is that they are not derived from or based on a canon of sacred writings. Nor have there ever been preachers, or evangelism apart from the ceremonies and observances themselves.[122]

Yanagita is speaking here about Shintō, a general rubric for the attempt to organize indigenous animistic beliefs into a system. Shintō's festival- and ritual orientation resisted the more scriptural emphasis of other faiths as they entered Japan from the continent. This would include Buddhism, of course, with its many sutras and commentaries. It would also include the *Analects* and the *Dao de Jing*. The Japanese reception of foreign traditions, like the practice of indigenous ones, have tended not to be scriptural in the way that, for instance, Christians have emphasized the study of the Bible, Moslems have revered the Qur'an, or Jews have venerated the Torah.[123]

How do we understand this non-textual orientation, and how is this relevant to evanescence and form? Once again, an animistic understanding of the immediate world as filled with visible and spatially available gods did not simply go away once conceptual systems of thought entered the country. Indeed, the visual reception of many gods greatly influenced the way Buddhism, in particular, was understood in Japan. Despite the massiveness of the Buddhist cannon, more important to its popular transmission than the assiduous study of texts were its temples, paintings, sculptures, and rituals. These visual forms pointed the believer to a metaphysical world beyond the physical one in which he resided. For instance, the great Buddha at Kamakura, which has outlasted the building that once housed it, symbolically refers to a transcendental realm that is *not* here, and *not* now. Representing a higher realm, it symbolizes *permanence*. It points to a world that is neither this realm of constant change, nor partakes of its essence.

At the same time, forms of indigenous worship that sometimes blended with Buddhism often resisted the representational nature of its symbols. In contrast to this religion from India, various animistic practices continued to emphasize the closeness (or the literal proximity) of the Sacred, not the distance between the physical Real and the immaterial Ideal. The indications of holiness that we find at a place such as the Fushimi Inari Shrine—the gate, the *shimenawa*, the laver, the dance floor—function not as pointers to a higher, unchanging reality but as enclosures of the Changeable yet Sacred. This lower world is spatial, visible, and available as a part of the present world. What it is not is necessarily mundane. As markers of sacred space, the "nonsymbolic" symbols of the shrine are there to help us make the proper worshipful approach. This movement is called "*mairi*," which literally means, "going humbly." To move through space humbly is to worship, to experience the sacred. By moving ahead, we are bound visually with that which is holy; and by doing so, space itself is allowed to reveal an essentially worshipful premise: that we ourselves are a part of this sacred world into which we have entered or are approaching. The ancient game of *sumo* shares this same simple logic: leave the designated circle (of sacred space) and you lose. Sometimes you lose even your life.

The act of *physically* approaching the *physically* present sacred realm provides us with a non-textual way of defining our relationship to holiness. It allows us to define the Sacred immediately and without symbols.[124] In other words, more than texts and other representations of a transcendental order,

Figure 1.7 Encountering the sacred within the here-and-now. The Fushimi Inari Shrine, Kyoto (photo by Mie Inouye).

it is the grounded and spatial context of Japan itself that tells the Japanese who they are. The formal structuring of present space—whether that of the Shintō shrine or the sitting room in one's home—provides the possibility of propriety, which is a fundamental form of the sacred and of meaningfulness. This is a key to understanding evanescence and form. The Japanese confirm their identity by moving through inherently Japanese space in certain formalized ways. They confirm their status by affirming the visual field properly and appropriately. Space is a cultural constant that is, nevertheless, constantly changing. Thus, a continuing affirmation of space, maintained even to the point of losing awareness of the fundamental religiosity of one's cultured movements, defines one. This kind of spatial orientation devolves toward the inclusion of *every* act as an expression of meaning and identification. It explains Japanese lyricism, which is an expression of the closeness of person and context. It also explains formality. Do not bite into an apple or wear a baseball cap to class. Take a gift when you visit someone. And so on and so forth.

We will come back to explore the far-ranging consequences of this non-textual emphasis on the physical, spatial, and visible ground of being. For now, we might look to how the richly textual Buddhist tradition was received in order to see just how powerful the enduring pull of this non-textual approach was. In a word, the spread of Buddhism to the masses was accomplished only upon rendering abstract, scriptural practice into concrete ritual practice.

Consider the emphasis placed on the *nenbutsu* in Japan. The *nenbutsu* literally means praying (*nen*, 念) to Buddha (*butsu*, 佛). In his *Exposition of the Meditation Sutra* (*Kammuryoju-kyo sho*) the Chinese Pure Land master Shandao (613–81) found in the Buddha's advice to the illiterate and lowly the very essence of all Buddhist practice: they were simply to think always about Buddha. Shandao departed from the established interpretation of "praying to Buddha" by insisting that the *nenbutsu* was not simply a visualization of Amida in his Western Paradise. He pushed for something more palpable. He sought an *action*: not just thinking, but chanting. A person of faith was to repeat the words "I find refuge in Buddha," *Namu Amida Butsu*. This was something that all could do: men and women, young and old, educated and ignorant, healthy and infirm. Of course, the crucial point is that this formalized action could be done often, and done correctly. In short, the saying of "*Namu Amida Butsu*" was a chance to act appropriately, and to let appropriateness deliver its blessings. In a minimalist way, the utterance of these few words brought them as close as they cared to come to a scriptural habit.

In Japan, Kūya (903–72) pioneered the popularization of Buddhism by way of the *nenbutsu*. A monk on Mt. Hiei, he came down into the capital and mingled with the people, dancing and striking a bell hung around his neck. He exhorted all to chant the *nenbutsu*; and, in times of crisis, he encouraged them to construct their own images of Amida, just as the wealthy had done. Why should anyone be excluded from the saving powers of Amida? By calling out "*Namu Amida Butsu*," they, too, could be saved.

The Japanese priest Genshin (942–1017) similarly stressed a popular approach to salvation. Calling himself an "ignoramus," he found in Kūya a spiritual ally. He also saw that Shandao had been driven by a similar motivation to identify with the lowly masses. Although he himself was also an accomplished scholar, Genshin became keenly aware of his own failings, convinced that the easily corruptible *hoi polloi*, especially in the dispensation of *mappō* (or the Decline of the Law), needed a simpler means than study to gain the blessings of Buddhism. Genshin's reading of Shandao's *Exposition of the Meditation Sutra* yielded his own confirmation of the importance of the simple act of chanting the *nenbutsu*. He went on to write *Essentials of Birth in the Pure Land* (*Ōjō yōshū*, 985), a vivid and highly influential account of the six realms of existence (*rokudō*) and the glorious rewards or horrific punishments that await the dead. Especially in its illustrated form, the text was a sort of *Salvation for Dummies* that boiled various metaphysical principles down to graphic depictions of the afterlife and suggested certain well-defined practices for those who would take advantage of Amida's vow to save all sentient beings. *Essentials of Birth in the Pure Land* had an immense impact on Buddhist thought and practice in Japan. It inspired numerous paintings of the afterlife that allowed the masses to gain an understanding of abstract concepts without having to master difficult languages and spend their lives in arduous study.

Here again, salvation was not simply a matter of looking beyond the vagaries of this floating world to contemplate something more permanent and meaningful. One needed to act on one's faith, to move through space in ways that displayed it. The chanting of the *nenbutsu* became this appropriate act. Despite its metaphysical complexities, the Buddhist Law was reduced to this simple action that required a demonstrable level of sincerity and exactitude. At the moment of one's death, it was important for a believer to be chanting the *nenbutsu* properly. Others could not do it for you. Neither was there a religious authority present to endow this blessing of passage. How is one saved? By acting properly, even unto death.

To facilitate a successful transition to the next world, Genshin formed believers into groups of twenty-five who would gather together, especially when one of their number was in decline, to make sure that the necessary act was accomplished. As we saw in Kenreimon'in's passing, physical props were made available in order to help the required action happen correctly. An image of Amida riding down on purple clouds was placed in the room, and a cord actually connected the hand of Amida to the hand of the dying. In this way, the metaphysical world and this physical world of pain and sorrow were linked visually and spatially.

By forming these groups of twenty-five, Genshin is said to have initiated a broad popular movement that was eventually given new impetus by the Tendai priest Hōnen (1133–1212). Inspired by Genshin's *Essentials of Birth in the Pure Land* and by Shandao's *Exposition of the Meditation Sutra*, Hōnen also reaffirmed the importance of chanting the *nenbutsu*. In a move that came to have profound consequences for the development of Buddhism in Japan, Hōnen broke from the orthodox interpretation on Mt. Hiei that both Amida and the Pure Land were places in one's consciousness. While the prevailing view was that visualizing Buddhist metaphysical concepts was the goal of meditation, Hōnen, who asserted action over thought and favored concreteness over abstraction, attempted to pull the metaphysical world into the physical one. He claimed that Amida actually did exist and really did come to greet the dead on purple clouds. One's successful passage to Western Paradise actually was marked by a "marvelous fragrance" and "the sound of music."[125] In other words, the Pure Land was not a metaphysical dream. To the contrary, this world, this life of dust and sorrows, was the dream; and only chanting the *nenbutsu* made one's brief, fragile, and illusory existence bearable.

While Hōnen and his disciple Shinran (1173–1263) insisted upon the relevance of certain enduring abstractions, such as the blessed state of salvation in the Pure Land, the *nenbutsu* was itself radically formulaic, practical, and contextual in its orientation. It bears the influence of Japanese poetics, being brief, momentous, suggestive, highly emotional, spontaneous, and responsive to context. Like classical poetic diction, the words of the *nenbutsu* establish an order that is inherently contextual and, therefore, non-scriptural in this limited sense. In other words, the rules that govern the *how* of the *nenbutsu* indicate that the action of utterance is utterly and patently common.

It was also made visual. Taking things another step, the itinerant priest Ippen (1234–89) made the *nenbutsu* even more obviously of the moment. He established what was called the *nenbutsu odori* (or the dancing *nenbutsu*), a raucous performance that took place in quickly constructed, open-walled rooms with floors of thick wooden planks. A number of adherents would begin their chanting and dancing on this rumbling floor, and huge crowds would gather to participate. This frenzied dance was the forerunner of the *obon odori*, or Lantern Festival dance, which is still widely performed throughout Japan in the month of August. Some even trace the origins of the kabuki theater to this same *nenbutsu odori*.

What does this development of the *nenbutsu* mean for our analysis? What do we make of this emphasis away from reading and toward exclaiming and dancing the Word? Let me try to provide a simple rendering of the problem at hand. If it is possible to assert orderliness by virtue of a metaphysical world that exists above and beyond this physical world of ever-changing situations and circumstances, then perhaps it is also possible to assert a different order that exists *within* the physical world. In other words, perhaps it is possible to establish an order that has only tenuous ties to a specifically definable metaphysical reality yet still performs the important function of giving form, and therefore meaning, to life in an ever-changing world.

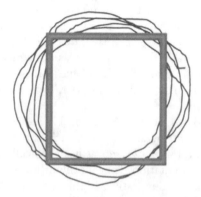

Figure 1.8 The order of here-and-now, form within the changing world.

To our earlier diagram of the world of change as set beneath the transcendental realm of unchanging metaphysical form, let us add an altogether new kind of form, one that exists in the realm of change itself.

Let us call this second system of meaning formality, or the order of the here-and-now. Unlike the metaphysical or ideological order, formality institutes actions that are accepted as appropriate and woven into the social fabric so carefully and completely that they tend to lose, or at least obfuscate, their symbolic connection to ideology. They tend, in other words, to become what we normally call custom and habit. We might be tempted to dismiss custom as the residue of forgotten metaphysical systems. To our distanced understanding, they are simply "the way things are done" (*shikitari*). But in Japan these ways are a well worked out remembrance and confirmation of meaning.

Figure 1.9   Formality: Empress Michiko moving properly through space (photo by Reuters).

Flowing from a complicated blending of both a sense of sacred space and the ideological order, they provide a counterbalance to radical change by asserting clear ways to do things properly.

For example, the act of bowing is commonly practiced in Japan. It is a pervasive custom that, even today, is learned correctly—from the hips, with one's back straight. Lowering one's head is not only an act of deference, but is a concrete, measurable sign of respect. Thus, an exchange of name cards often takes place when people meet for the first time in order to allow the parties involved to know who should bow lower than whom. Needless to say, the meaning of a bow is highly dependent on context and on the particular intentions of the moment. A structural analysis might link bowing to the exposure of one's neck, as an intentional show of one's vulnerability (to the sword). An aesthetic analysis might link bowing to the fact that in Japan the nape of a woman's neck was once considered to be an erogenous zone. Although no one usually thinks of it in this way now, could it be that the erotic value of this spot owes something to it also being the place of decapitation?

It would be unreasonable to insist that bowing, as it is commonly practiced today, immediately fills anyone with thoughts of beheading or seduction. But this does not mean that the action was not at some point a very explicit show of vulnerability, and that its nuance of humility persists for this near-forgotten reason. What but the long life of a custom allows such an act to become distanced from its original idea? Admittedly, it is possible to be clueless about the prescribed meaning of an act and still sense that it is appropriate. Is taking your shoes off when you enter a Japanese home simply a matter of good housekeeping? Or is it an indication of significant space? When you go to the public bath and notice people scrubbing themselves with amazing thoroughness, are they just practicing good hygiene? Or is there still something spiritually important about being clean even if no one gives conscious thought to the matter?

For the purposes of our analysis, we must consider the meaning of seemingly meaningless habitual behavior. Such acts are not obviously symbolic since we cannot tie them to this or that ideological principle. But does this very meaningless not mean something important? I am suggesting, of course, the weight of formality, and the function of form that is at once trivial and specific to context. We must not forget that while formality tends to lose its connection with explanation it is also more immediately binding and relevant than explanation. As etiquette or protocol, formality determines the faux pas and the dignified gesture. As an expression of the hegemonic order, formality has the power to encourage acceptable actions quite apart from our ability to elucidate the ethical or rational basis for why we do what we do. Truly, the linkage to meaning grows surprisingly weak and even unthinkable. When asked for an explanation, all we can say is, "That's just the way it's done."

Formality is conventional in this sense. As a highly conservative force, it honors precedent. It asserts the appropriateness of certain behaviors, all of them formally acted out in space. Epistemologically speaking, the order of here-and-now pays attention to the shape of space, and tends to distill many possible configurations into a few essential ones. Thus, all *hana* in Heian-period poetry become cherry blossoms rather than plum blossoms, all rice bowls are to be held in the left hand, with the thumb on the rim and the base of the bowl resting elegantly on the ring and middle fingers.[126] Hold your rice bowl the wrong way, and you might lose your promotion. Why? Because something so seemingly trivial as good form is, within the spatial order of here-and-now, a defining, meaningful act.

We can now understand rules of etiquette—how to hold one's chop-sticks, which towel to use when—as conventions as to how one should move through space properly, that is, in ways that enhance one's proper definition. Being visible and spatial, movements of the body are rarely hidden. They are not a matter of the invisible soul or the inner mind, but are in a state of constant display. They are, therefore, consistently and constantly being checked by habit in a way "the thoughts of one's heart" are not. This is why, as Joy Hendry points out, wrapping can be as important as content.[127]

Needless to say, this emphasis on lyrical, situation-based meaning does not fit comfortably with the realm of exposing assumptions, clarifying definitions, affirming laws and principles, and discoursing upon the unchanging essences of the metaphysical world. Indeed, to a certain point of view, the obtuse and situational qualities of formality can seem only false and deadening, a poor substitute for genuine feeling and real meaning. Does not protocol and engrained habit impede the search for new possibilities? Is it not superficial? At its worst, formality might even block the path to originality, articulateness, and learning. Some might even argue that the order of the here-and-now tends to deny rather than encourage creativity and critical thought. Why? Because the formal life that appropriateness supports generates meaning not by insight but by sight. We progress not by way of reference to hidden principles that only the brilliant and the spiritually gifted can perceive, but by way of context, precedent, and adage—things that any decent person should understand. In other words, the realm of here-and-now is not the world of "Seek ye first the kingdom of God." Rather, it aligns with the truth of "If a dog walks, it finds a stick." *Inu mo arukeba, bō in ataru.*[128]

Formality and etiquette are the often unspoken rules that establish how a person moves through space in ways that define us. Such rules are too common to be written down and studied as scripture. But they do get expressed: as highly codified poetry, as bowing, as visiting a shrine once a year even though one is not aware of actually believing in anything. Lacking the exalted status of scripture, good form nevertheless defines a person as effectively as any Holy Book. Within the Japanese cultural sphere, having good manners is not simply a matter of being polite. It is nothing less than a matter of being. How we move through space determines our purpose and existence; and this is because propriety belongs more easily to the concrete reality of animistic space than to the abstract idea of heavenly (or hellish) space. There is no distance between us and the actual world we live in; just as there are no excuses for doing things the wrong way, or for dressing or speaking inappropriately.

The here-and-now is meaningful by nature. And it is this nature that explains why the Japanese garden is so artificial. Consider the Moon-Viewing Platform at the Silver Pavilion (Ginkakuji) in Kyoto, an exemplary expression of evanescence and form in tension with each other. The cone is astonishingly precise. It seems out of place in an ever-changing environment of trees, moss, and water. But then we realize that this solid geometric shape is made of sand, the most shapeless of materials. It is neither a pyramid made of stone blocks, nor an obelisk cut from marble. It is nothing but sand, an ever-changing shapelessness that must be constantly formed.

By grasping this tendency to identity with space—and to be identified by space—we have another way to understand Joseph Kitagawa's claim that "to the early Japanese, the natural world (Japan)...was essentially the religious universe, a world in which all facets of daily living were considered religious acts."[129] To a certain extent, this still holds true today. Even the natural world is formal—where *utsusemi* always means "world," "life," "person;" and the moon indicates autumn. Japan is a constantly appropriate realm, a world where cherry blossoms obediently express the beautiful sorrow of change. Could anything less than this constant reaffirmation of form within the here-and-now—a tightly interwoven complex of aesthetic, moral,

Figure 1.10 The Kōgetsudai (Moon-Viewing Platform), Silver Pavilion, Kyoto (photo by Rei Inouye).

religious, *and* practical values—counterbalance the equally persistent truth that all things are changing all the time?

ZEN, *KATA*, AND THE NOH THEATER

Like Pure Land Buddhism, which became a faith for both commoner and samurai, Zen Buddhism similarly de-emphasized scholasticism and metaphysical speculation. Patronized by the samurai leaders of Japan, Zen came to emphasize a disciplined and highly formalized Way (or *dō*, 道) that would apply to all activities: how to drink tea (*sadō*), to how to write (*shodō*), to how to fight (*budō*), and so on. In each case, emphasis was placed on the mastery of certain set methods, or *kata*. By way of these kinetic forms, one could establish a meaningful place for oneself in the fleeting, cherry-blossom world where defending one's master was a matter of life or death.

Indeed, it would be difficult to overemphasize the importance of *kata* in the various arts that flourished during Japan's medieval period. The term has a wide meaning: "model," "pattern," "prototype," or "that which distinguishes one tradition or school from another." More generally, *kata* can also mean "style," "that which is characteristic," "that which allows us to distinguish one thing from another." When written with the character 形, as in the word *ningyō* 人形 or doll, *kata* can mean "shape," "form," "manifestation," "trace," "print," "sign," "copy." By extension, *kata* can mean the "security" for a loan, that is, a "sign" of one's intention to repay borrowed money. In the various Zen-inspired arts that came to flourish during the Kamakura and Muromachi (1333–1568) periods, *kata* specifically meant set patterns of movement, or the way that certain fundamental actions are always done—if done properly.

By virtue of their conservative force, *kata* become a counterbalance to evanescence. They constitute never-changing prototypes to be repeated in exacting ways. As such, they define the teachings that are transmitted from teacher to student, and from one generation to the next. When learning calligraphy, for instance, there is a proper way to sit, to hold the brush, to grind one's charcoal stick with water to make the proper consistency of ink. There is also a proper way to make a basic horizontal stroke. And so the beginner starts out by repeating the character for one, 一, over and over, until it is perfected. The fluidity and individualistic style that marks the work of accomplished calligraphers is built upon a mastery of such fundamental strokes. Whether the art to be learned is calligraphy, painting, or *karate*, one becomes a master by first patiently learning established patterns of movement until they become second nature.

In the often-violent world of the samurai, strict discipline and steady focus on fundamentals enhanced a fighting man's chances of survival. From our vantage today, we might be tempted to see this exactness as a spillover of military technique into nonmilitary pursuits. Yet we should also remember that a larger context of formality had already asserted itself prior to the rise of the samurai class during the late Heian period. Through the medieval era, we see a deepening appreciation of form, heightened perhaps because the ephemeral nature of life under samurai rule was only more evident. With the division of the land into numerous fiefdoms, there occurred a multiplication of clans, schools, and styles—all of them situated in a more or less competitive relationship with each other. The effect of this decentralization and competitiveness seems to have forced the transmission of knowledge to become increasingly personal, practical (i.e., a matter of learning by doing), and secretive—all tendencies that support the practice of *kata*, or following the example of one's master with exactness.

Teachings and techniques were also reserved in the form of secret documents that were carefully protected and passed from one master to the next. But the primary "texts" of feudal transmission were not written. They were the *kata* themselves: carefully practiced patterns that were personally taught to one generation by another. They were living documents of essential knowledge. In a world where philosophy was lived, and thought was merged with action, devotion to a master was absolutely necessary. The famous Noh playwright Zeami Motokiyo (ca. 1363–ca. 1443) expressed this sentiment in the secret text "The True Path to the Flower," (*Shikadō*, 1420). "A beginning actor must follow his teacher and study dancing and chanting as thoroughly as possible."[130]

To say that this kind of learning was done "by heart" is to raise many questions about the effectiveness of repetition and memorization. Present notions of creativity and critical thinking, for instance, often criticize as deadening learning by rote—memorizing facts without thinking about what facts are, or accepting the reality of events without understanding how events come about. In defense of *kata*, we might say that only by mastery of the fundamentals does one progress to a more fluid state of creativity. No one becomes a great mathematician without memorizing the times tables first. No one becomes an accomplished martial arts expert without first learning basic fundamentals of blocking and striking. Constant repetition leads to the ability to adapt. The fixed leads to the brilliance of the fluid.

The Noh stage itself is highly formal: a sparsely decorated square connected with a walkway to offstage. We can easily understand why the samurai would have been interested in such a space; for on this spare yet colorfully elegant stage of meditative movement, the dead come back to visit the living, and the conflict between one's formal place in life and one's ability to imagine oneself more broadly is worked out in a highly ordered way that yields spiritual resolution, fluidity, and wholeness.

There are various categories of Noh plays. But, generally speaking, the typical play follows a pattern of gradual revelation that solves a mystery closely associated with a particular place. By way of five acts and a kyōgen interlude, we are led through a process of questions and answers, a chain of clarifications that build to the eventual fullness of a highly lyrical and kinetically vigorous encounter with pure knowledge and spiritual reconciliation. This aesthetic expression of Buddhist enlightenment turns divisiveness into unity and makes the moment of singularity an eternally reverberating one.

By this I mean only to say that although the end of a play is a quickly passing moment, it is one where talent, which is the literal meaning of the word "Noh," flowers into a statement of beauty that resolves all issues for the time being.

Zeami's play, *Atsumori*, exemplifies this progression. It begins with a familiar warning about the dangers of attachment to the things of this world.

> Life is a lying dream, he only wakes
> Who casts the World aside.[131]

The *waki* (or dueteragonist) is the monk Rensei, formerly the Minamoto warrior Kumagai no Naozane, who we encountered in our discussion of *The Tale of Heike*. True to form, he brings us to a place, Ichi-no-tani, the sight of the great battle where the Minamoto routed the Taira. This is, of course, the very spot where Kumagai killed Taira no Atsumori, the young Heike warrior who reminded him of his son.

This narrow strip of beach is associated with unresolved issues. As mentioned, Kumagai's initial impulse was to let Atsumori go, but he knew that his fellow warriors were watching and that his duty as a warrior required him to behead his enemy. As recounted in *The Tale of the Heike*, Kumagai obeyed form and killed the boy. In this play that revisits the incident, we learn that Kumagai's grief has caused him to renounce the world and become a monk. "I have left my home and call myself the priest Rensei; this I have done because of my grief at the death of Atsumori, who fell in battle by my hand."[132] He has come to the very beach where the death occurred in order to "pray for the salvation of Atsumori's soul."[133]

In Act Two, he encounters the *maejite* (or the protagonist), a youth whose lot in life is to eke out a living by evaporating seawater to make salt. By way of the obligatory question-and-answer period that follows, Kumagai learns that the rustic salt maker knows a lot about the famous battle where the Heike were routed. He even knows the details of Atsumori's death because he is, in reality, Atsumori himself. This true identity is revealed in the fourth act.

In less decorous and concentrated language, the kyōgen interlude supplies the general story of Kumagai and Atsumori to anyone who might not already know it. It prepares us for the final, fifth act, where the transformed protagonist, now the *shite* (or second, true form of the protagonist), is moved by lingering feelings of revenge and animosity to attack Rensei.

> "There is my enemy," he cries, and would strike,
> But the other is grown gentle
> And calling on Buddha's name
> Has obtained salvation for his foe;
> So that they shall be re-born together
> On one lotus-seat.
> "No, Rensei is not my enemy.
> Pray for me again, oh pray for me again."[134]

In the end, Atsumori's anger is quelled by the *nenbutsu*.

Calling the Buddha's name would not be as moving as it is without the stark formality of this dramatic form, which preserves the ancient force of drama as a sacred doing. Like the *nenbutsu*, Noh is also true to what we have learned so far about Japanese poetics. The dense polysemy of the terse libretto pushes the connotative powers of language and imagery to their limit, establishing many overlapping layers of meaning and numerous connections with other texts. The sparseness of the stage and the splendor of the costumed actors that move so purposefully over it create an otherworldly atmosphere where the logic of the moment prevails. Here the single instance becomes an expansive and inclusive mystery, a moment of *yūgen*. As with *tanka*, brevity—practiced to the point of stillness and silence—speaks volumes. According to Zeami, the sign of a truly accomplished actor is his ability to hold his audience spellbound during those moments when he himself is completely motionless.

For some, Noh is formal to the point of being static. The naturalist play-wright George Bernhard Shaw was unable to see the point and famously pronounced, "Noh drama is no drama." In stark contrast, William Butler Yeats found inspiration in Noh's aristocratic slowness. Finding in the Noh theater's indirect qualities a much-needed antidote to the prevailing realism of his age, he tried to create something similar in *The Only Jealousy of Emer* and other "plays for dancers." Yeats sought to free drama from realism by moving closer to decoration and dance. He discovered this breath of new life in the (less than accurate) translations of Noh texts that came to him by way of Ernest Fenollosa and Ezra Pound.

Yeats had a Japanese vision of theatrical possibility. From Noh he learned a sense of the sacredness of place. He did not shy away from the supernatural nor from subtlety or even from stillness. He preferred portraying states of mind, or conditions of being, rather than developing well-rounded human characters. In other words, while the symbolic and the decorative are semi-otically at odds with each other—since the former connects us with meta-physical depth while the latter is meant to keep us on the surface—the aesthetics of *yūgen* obliterated this distinction by collapsing metaphorical tenor and vehicle so that the one does not simply refer to the other but actu-ally becomes the other.

Stated otherwise, Noh's emptiness is that quality of form that allows the possibility of all other forms to come to mind. The Zen goal of achieving nothingness, or *mu*, is to create emptiness in a way that is radically receptive. Thomas Merton explained the dangers of not doing this. "When one is in possession of something, that something will keep all other somethings from coming in."[135] As reflected in the sparseness of the Noh stage, this "empty-mindedness" was consonant with the way of the warrior, whose path (at least until the Tokugawa period) was disciplined by battle and death. Paradoxically, only more form overcomes the difficulties of formal life. Only by way of practice, do things flow together without coercion.

We are talking, then, about the fluid state that the rigidity of *kata* makes possible. To give an example from the world of calligraphy, Sengai Gibon's

(1750–1837) well-known image of the cosmos—a circle, a square, and a triangle—seems to approach symbolism; but its simple, sparse form invites a reading that is nonsymbolic—a nothingness that is everything. In the creation of such an image, the process is supposedly more important than the product, which is of value only to the extent that it reminds us of the movement and moment of its creation. The practiced yet lyrical affirmation of *jihatsu* (spontaneity) that so naturally produces a *tanka* or a haiku also produces a lively display of flowers, the perfect cup of tea, or the simple yet endless complications of a garden of gravel, rocks, and moss.

HEDONISM

Just at this point in the semester when we are beginning to understand the nature of evanescence and form, we encounter a significant twist. As we have seen, one response to the truth of life's brevity and mutability is to be more exacting, to be more purely single-minded, even to be, as we have just considered, no minded. Yamamoto Tsunetomo's (1659–1719) *Hidden Leaves*, (*Hagakure*, 1716), encouraged thoughts about the radical change that death brings as a way to achieve equanimity.

> Contemplate death daily. Every morning, calm your body and mind; and think of being torn apart by the bow, by the rifle, by spears, and by swords. Imagine yourself being struck down by a great wave, thrown into a roaring fire, struck by lightning, knocked down by an earthquake. Feel yourself falling from a thousand foot cliff, or dying of sickness. Know how you'll feel upon following your lord into death. Prepare to live each day by dying each morning.[136]

A similar text, *The Book of Five Rings* (*Go rin no sho*), said to have been written by Miyamoto Musashi (1584–1645), gives similar advice.[137] Go to the "self-improvement" section of your neighborhood bookstore, and you will likely find these volumes there. The athlete, the executive, anyone who wishes to succeed. seems to glean much from the suggestion that we ought to step only in the direction of our goals. Life is short. There is no time to waste. Focus. Work hard. Let nothing stop you.[138]

But let us reconsider. Are better discipline and more effort the only reasonable responses to evanescence? Is not dedicated effort only one of many? If we know we might die tomorrow, rather than training ourselves to accomplish some difficult goal, rather than working ourselves to the bone only to face inevitable failure and defeat, why not just relax and enjoy life? Maybe the rat race really is for rats. Is it not the case that the wisest among us know when it is time to kick back and relax?

Some say that work should come first. But is this really so? Why not spend our limited time pursuing those things that give us the most pleasure? If work is not fulfilling, why take it so seriously? If the end could come at any time, why not have as much fun as we can while we can? What could be a more sensible proposition? Why postpone that vacation? Why not buy that car? Why stay on that diet? If we know certain things that give us satisfaction, why waste precious time in the pursuit of anything else?

As we are beginning to see, the Japanese have responded in many ways to this idea of evanescence. If believing in dreams, forsaking the world, having faith in the *nenbutsu*, living with a constant awareness of death, and giving oneself to strict discipline are some of these, hedonism is yet another. Just as an awareness of life's fragile and brief nature seemed to sharpen and accentuate these other responses, so too does it add a sense of urgency to the pursuit of pleasure. Strict discipline and hedonistic abandon might not seem at first like close cousins, but we can understand their common link to evanescence by considering the change that the Buddhist term for mortality, *ukiyo*, experienced over time.

A bloody sixteenth century saw the consolidation of numerous fiefs into a unified political unit ruled by the Tokugawa. Their rule was long (1600–1868), and relatively peaceful. In this period of peace that followed war, a great flourishing of bourgeois culture occurred; and with it came a new understanding of evanescence. By the Genroku era (1688–1703), the term *ukiyo* came to have an emphasis quite unlike the Buddhist- and bushidō-inspired force that we have considered to this point. It no longer meant the illusory world to avoid, but the illusive world of fleeting pleasures that one ought to pursue with abandon. Howard Hibbett explains,

> In Genroku the *ukiyo* itself—the world of pleasure, of the pursuit of money necessary to enjoy it, and of the instability that underlay all—was still an exciting discovery. Only since the beginning of the seventeenth century had the term *ukiyo* become more than a reminder of the brevity and uncertainly of life. By mid-century it had acquired such meanings as "modern," "up to date," "fashionable," or even "fast." It was prefixed to the names of all sorts of novelties, from dolls to dumplings. "*Ukiyo*-madness" was an addiction to visiting the pleasure quarter; piquant gossip was called "*ukiyo*-talk"; popular songs, of the sort sung by courtesans, were known as "*ukiyo*-tunes." Above all, *ukiyo* meant the life of pleasure, accepted without thinking about what might lie ahead. In Asai Ryōi's *Tales of the Floating World* (*Ukiyo monogatari*, c. 1661) it is defined as living for the moment, gazing at the moon, snow, blossoms, and autumn leaves, enjoying wine, women, and song, and, in general, drifting with the current of life "like a gourd floating downstream." Still, *ukiyo* retained the overtones of its earlier Buddhist usage to suggest the sad impermanence of all earthly things.... But *ukiyo* usually suggests the buoyant exhilaration of the Genroku spirit, rather than its underlying awareness that life is fleeting. Zest for the current fashions made it hard to think that another season, possibly not so brilliant, would overthrow them.[139]

Does this changing nuance of the term *ukiyo* suggest an evolving attempt to make something good of a bad situation: that life is short and unpredictable? Not the temple and shrine but the kabuki theater and the brothel formed the center of this new realm of pleasure and impulse. For us today, commercial advertisements do their best to persuade us in a similar direction—"Just do it!" "Obey your thirst!" This is the logic of *ukiyo* as newly understood: an awareness of limitation that leads to action and enjoyment, even if that pleasure comes with an awareness of the temporary or even false nature of what is done.

The pursuit of pleasure in Japan today takes many forms, none more brash than the so-called soap lands that dot the landscape. These were once called "Toruko buro," or Turkish baths. But an objection voiced by the government of Turkey resulted in a nationwide campaign to "Name that Institution." After much consideration, it was decided that these places of ill-repute would be called Soap Land (*sōpu rando*). While this might seem arbitrary, it is not a misnomer. At a Soap Land, men pay to get lathered up and rinsed down. They might as well be standing on the banks of Chōmei's ever-flowing river. What could be more fleeting than the purchase of such slippery pleasures?

Whether then or now, the buoyant exhilaration of the pleasure industry is hard to separate from the melancholy pull of *anitya*, the impermanence of all things. Perhaps no writer of the Genroku period expressed this subtle and engaging mix of joy and sorrow more eloquently than Ihara Saikaku (1642–93) whose "*ukiyo*-books" chronicled the evanescent lives of both merchants and their haughty samurai superiors. As a prolific poet who responded to the modern turn to prose, Saikaku rode the early waves of mass production to become, after Asai Ryōi (ca. 1612–91) who coined this new nuance of *ukiyo*, Japan's second professional author. With a verve and mastery of detail that we can still appreciate today, he made a career of delving headlong into the quintessentially modern topics of power, money, and sex.

His *Woman Who Loved Love* (*Kōshoku ichidai onna*, 1686) is a parody of an established literary form, the Buddhist confessional, or *zange*. In other parts of the world, many other men also wrote about "bad women" at similar junctures in modernity's march toward individualism—Tolstoy about Anna Karenina, Flaubert about Madame Bovary, Defoe about Moll Flanders, Hawthorne about Hester Pryne, and so on. Like these other writers, Saikaku found in this subject of the sensuous woman the germ of a developing self. Sold as a commodity and given a new name and identity, made to exist as an integral part of a larger commercial enterprise, made to learn a standardized language (*arinsu no kotoba*) in order to speak with customers from various regions of Japan, constantly exposed to strangers who demanded intimacy, she was thus forced to ask the modern question, "Who am I?" In short, she was a pioneer of a modern, fast-moving present marked from page one by the enduring relevance of cherry blossoms.

To quote the ancients, "A beautiful woman is an axe that chops off life." The blossoms of the heart are scattered; by evening the tree itself has turned into firewood. Who can escape? As for those who wander out into an unseasonable morning tempest, drown in lust, and die young—how very stupid of them! Yet their kind is by no means rare.[140]

As we have seen other Japanese writers do, Saikaku similarly begins with a customary bow to evanescence. His particular rendering of the usual trees and blossoms, however, comes with a new piquant twist. In this burlesque treatment of the Buddhist truth that "all is vanity," Saikaku's scattering blossoms express the fleeting pleasures of sensuality (*iro*).

Saikaku's heroine is promiscuous by nature. She is defined by her sexuality, a notion that is openly discussed in this age of the dawning self. We first encounter her as an old woman living out the remainder of her days in a hermitage. She is visited by two young men who, having noted the "endless variety of this changing world," are of different minds regarding the question of whether love is ultimately a good thing or not.[141] One of them simply cannot get enough sensual pleasure, while the other has already had more than his fill. They seek the wisdom of the older woman, who is by experience an expert on the topic. As they drink together, she begins to reveal the scandalous story of her past—how she began as a proper young woman and ended up a penniless streetwalker.

Step by step, episode by episode, her slide into depravity seems both inevitable and irreversible. She is seduced by a court noble at the tender age of thirteen. When the two of them get caught, he is executed and she gets sent home. Endowed with good looks, grace, and talent, she then becomes a professional dancer under her mother's watchful eye. She is the embodiment of cherry-blossom beauty: light pink in complexion and ready "to come into full bloom upon being moistened by a single shower."[142] She is adopted by an older couple—a handsome husband and not-so-attractive wife. She allows herself to become overly familiar with the former, and is booted out by the latter. Still considered a respectable young woman, she is next chosen over many other blossom-like beauties to become a daimyō's consort. But this, too, ends poorly, with his inappropriate advances. Although he is not up to the challenge, not even when fortified with his "*jiō* pills," she gets sent home yet again.[143]

While still enjoying the privileges of her birth, she happens to overhear the sorrowful song of a beggar, a woman who once enjoyed a higher rank in the world of love.

> How cruel the floating world,
> Its solaces too few—
> For soon my soon forgotten life
> Will vanish with the dew.[144]

She laughs at the woman's poverty, unaware of the turn in fortunes that will soon strike home. One of her father's careless financial dealings brings disaster; and he is forced to sell her to a brothel. She experiences life in the pleasure quarters as a *tayu* or high-ranking courtesan; but she quickly and steadily descends through the ranks, getting an increasingly thinner mattress to sleep upon and simpler clothes to wear. As time passes, she begins to lose her looks. She is like a cherry blossom, her beauty short-lived. She comes to realize for herself that "there is nothing more fragile than a woman. It's a cruel world!"[145]

> Every now and then I got sick of selling my love, but when I was hard up I went back to the same old line. . . . Sometimes I had clerks and artisans, sometimes even priests, or actors. Still, though I frisked with all sorts of guests, I wasn't particularly happy. When I thought how innumerable were my intimate friendships, and how brief, it seemed to me that my feelings towards a man—no matter if I liked him or disliked him—were those you might have towards a fellow-passenger on a ferry-boat before it reached the opposite bank. I talked with the men I found attractive, but even then it wasn't heart-to-heart talk. As for the others, I turned my head away, let my thoughts wander, and counted the cross-pieces in the ceiling as I waited for them to get it over with. Thus I lived, drifting down the muddy stream of the floating world.[146]

By and by, she becomes "a rather wilted blossom."[147] She has a nightmare in which she sees her ninety-one children, all victims of abortion. But her amorous nature prevails over remorse; and she keeps doing what she does best until she can no longer interest a man of any kind. Only then does she abandon hope. Like Kamo no Chōmei, like Kenreimon'in, like Kumagae, she finally accepts the teachings of Buddhism and abandons the world.

To the very end, Saikaku keeps the images of trees and blossoms in play. In the final chapter, he cannot resist the dark comparison that allots to mortals a lack of seasonal cycles. "The mountain forests are asleep and the cherry branches are buried in snow tonight...but soon they will awaken with the spring dawn. Only man has nothing pleasant to look forward to as he grows old."[148] Where is faith in the next life? Where is the possibility of salvation and paradise? Where is the reconciliation of nothingness and the oneness of the moment that is to tie her to all other moments? Appropriately enough, the amorous woman's last confession is about a visit to a temple. With unalloyed irreverence, Saikaku's heroine closely inspects the faces of the many statues placed on display, and finds something strangely familiar about them all.

> Of all these five hundred figures, which I calmly inspected at my leisure, not a single one failed to remind me of a former lover. . . . "How wretched and shameful of me to enjoy such a long life," I thought, "when I've spent it giving my body to more than ten thousand men!" At this, my heart began to pound like the rumbling of the fiery car of Hell, and my tears were scattered like bubbles of boiling water. Instantly I went into a delirium. Unaware even that I was in a temple, I fell writhing on the ground.[149]

In addition to blossoms, Saikaku repeats other descriptors of evanescence. The bubbles on the water that began *An Account of My Hut* become boiling tears, and the somber bells that both began and ended *The Tale of the Heike* are heard here with the insistence of a wakeup call. Will she awaken to Amida's compassion or to a sense of who she is as a worldly, modern person of desire and agency? Surely, Saikaku plays the Buddhist card with the impure facility of one who speaks for the floating world in its *new* meaning as a realm of worldly pleasures. Unlike Zeami's, his mission is to pique and to satisfy voyeuristic desire rather than to lead souls to enlightenment. With Saikaku, we have turned a corner.

MATSUO BASHŌ, PERMANENCE AND CHANGE

The Genroku era produced still other modern perspectives on change. Matsuo Bashō (1644–94), a contemporary of Saikaku, delved deeply into the tension inherent in evanescence and form. In *The Narrow Road to the Deep North* (*Oku no hosomichi*, 1694), we find this passage.

> There was a mountain temple called Ryūshakuji in the province of Yamagata...known for the absolute tranquility of its compound....When I reached it, the sun was still in the sky. After arranging to stay with the priests at the foot of the mountain, I climbed to the temple situated near the summit. The whole mountain was made of massive rocks thrown together, and covered with age-old pines and oaks. The stony ground was ancient and covered with velvety moss. The doors of the shrines built upon the rocks were firmly barred, and not a sound was to be heard. As I moved around the cliffs and crawled up the boulders, bowing reverently to each shrine, I felt the quiet loneliness of the magnificent scene pervade my whole being.

Shizukasa ya	How still!
Iwa ni shimiiru	Piercing into the boulders,
Semi no koe.	The cry of the cicada.[150]

Bashō's traveling companion, Sora, took notes; so we know that much artifice went into the writing of this work that seems to flow as naturally as a series of lyrical encounters.[151] It seems that Bashō did not actually write the *Narrow Road* haiku in the order in which they are presently found, nor did their creation necessarily happen as noted in this famous work. Understanding this, we can appreciate all the more just how carefully he attempted to balance the ephemeral with the lasting in this account of Ryūshaku Temple.

We already know that the cicada (*semi*) was an important metaphor of evanescence. Its empty shell (*utsusemi*) reminds us that life is brief and quickly passing. In this poem, it is the ephemerality of the cicada's *song* that is contrasted with the solidity of rocks, the insect's shrillness measured against the stillness of the temple grounds. At the same time, while these contrasts are being established, a lyrical blending of the poet's emotions with all elements of this context occurs. One thing mixes with another—as the poet enters this holy space, as the sound of cicadas penetrates (*shimiiru*) the boulders, as the eternal "silence" pervades the poet's being.

Bashō's thoughts about poetic composition centered on evanescence and form. His term for these values was *fueki ryūkō*, 不易流行, "the unchanging and the ever-changing." *Fueki* is the eternal, unchanging foundation of poetry. *Ryūkō* is its manifestation, newly renewed moment by moment. Both are said to come from the sincerity of a refined heart (*makoto*).[152] Such a heart perceives evanescence; such a heart perceives form: a moving sky and seemingly immovable cliffs, moss growing on ancient pines, the sound of cicadas penetrating boulders.

In a treatise called *The Three Booklets* (*Sanzōshi*, 1702) written by one of Bashō's students, Hattori Dohō (1657–1730), we read the following passage about change and form.

> We find in Bashō's poetry both the eternal unchanging and the momentary ever-changing. These are two extremes, but their source is one and the same: the sincerity of poetry. How can we say we have truly understood the Master's *haikai*, if we do not understand this unchanging element? The unchanging depends neither on the new or on the old, and has nothing to do with change or fashion. It firmly stands implanted in sincerity.
>
> When we study the work of past generations, we can see that poetry has changed with each generation. Yet there are many poems that transcend the old and the new. They appear now as they appeared in the past. They are deeply moving. We should understand such poems as unchanging.
>
> The law of nature is that all things change. If we so not seek change, art cannot be renewed. When we do not seek change, we become content with the current fashion, and do not pursue the truth [*makoto*] of *haikai*. If we do not seek the truth or devote ourselves to it, we cannot know sincerity and its changes. Such people only imitate others. By contrast, those who pursue truth will naturally move ahead, never content to keep treading on the same ground. No matter how much *haikai* may change in the future, if it changes sincerely, it will be the kind of *haikai* advocated by Bashō.
>
> Bashō said, "One should never, even for a moment, lick the slobber of the ancients. Like the seasons in their due course, things must be renewed. This is true of all things."[153]

Here, Dohō is trying to justify Bashō's style of *haikai* and its attempt to expand the range of poetic topics beyond the strictly limited codifications of classical *tanka* and *renga*. To be inclusive of places and things not already in the established lexicon was to "move ahead" and to be "ever-changing." A good poem, when produced this way, would be unchanging, like excellent poems of the past. Stated otherwise, Bashō's *haikai* expanded the rigid codes of nature and poetic diction while respecting the established classical aesthetic that we noted in Dōgen. His haiku were meant to be inclusive without being vulgar, and modern without being dismissive of tradition. They express both change as truth and truth as change.

As pointed out by Haruo Shirane, the need to keep *ryūkō* (the ever-changing) in balance is reflected in the Genroku landscape style (*keiki*) that became popular during Bashō's time. Here the attempt was to depict an external landscape (*kei*) and infuse it with human emotion (*jō*). While this relationship between the artist and his surroundings is itself traditional, a carryover from the medieval *tanka* tradition and its non-dualistic emphasis, the naturalistic impulse that can already be felt at this point, toward the end of the seventeenth century, was in fact new and potentially destabilizing in a modern way. As informed by the empirical thrust of Neo-Confucianism, it represents an early "discovery of landscape" that occurs in the Edo period, well before the nineteenth-century phenomenon that the contemporary critic Karatani Kōjin (1941–) found central to the emergence of the interiorized self in Meiji-period writers, such as Kunikida Doppō (1871–1908).[154] This earlier realistic interest necessarily widened (and challenged) the established poetic order and the well-codified relationship between one and one's surroundings. It led to the creation of new poetic associations with place (*haimakura*) and new poetic resonances. So doing, it also led to the conceptualization of a new countering form of permanence, namely, the self, as it began to establish itself as a nexus of sincerity, and against the flux of its perceived surroundings. Thus we understand Bashō's felt need for travel, for prose, and for the beginnings of a more descriptive and prosaic view of reality that balanced the brevity of *haikai*.

In speaking of *fueki*, Dohō's practical emphasis does not posit a philosophical ideal so much as a lasting sentiment or aesthetic quality that can be discerned throughout time, no matter the era.

> Since ancient times, there have been many masters of Chinese and Japanese poetry. They have all emerged from *makoto*, poetic sincerity, and have followed the path of the same. Our Master gave *makoto* to verse that had never possessed sincerity, thus becoming a guide for endless generations to come.[155]

But the truth of the matter is that this sentiment had changed significantly by Bashō's time, and would continue to do so with ever more rapidity as the Tokugawa period wore on. On the one hand, Bashō's lyrical relationship with landscape furthered a well-established reading of space, as codified by assigned poetic associations—places and images that mean this and not that. This formal perception of space was the point of the earlier mentioned *uta-makura*—poetically inspiring places in traditional poetic practice. At the same time, the modern expansion of what counts as being seriously and sincerely poetic begins to alter significantly how space is being understood.

With Bashō we find a theorization of the traditional impulse to identify with one's surroundings. This self-conscious regard for space becomes articulated as *butsuga ichinyo* (object and self as one). Again, we rely on Dohō's commentary for clarification.

> When the Master said, "As for the pine, learn from the pine; as for the bamboo, learn from the bamboo," he meant to cast aside personal desire or intention [*shii*]. Those who interpret this "learning" in their own way never learn anything.
>
> The phrase "learn" means to enter into the thing, to be emotionally moved by the essence that emerges from the object, and to let your feeling become verse. Even if you clearly express the object, if the feeling doesn't come naturally, then you will not be one with it, and your verse will not have poetic truth [*makoto*]. The effect will be an artifice that results from personal desire.[156]

This unity of thing (*butsu*) and self (*ga*) follows from both animistic and Buddhist notions of non-duality and is a radical development of landscape *haikai* that tends to obliterate the clear distinction between the artist and what he is seeing. Clearly, to identify oneself with one's surroundings was already understood as a form of selflessness, a lack of "personal desire" or *shii*. But to say that "this self... is not the modern notion of the 'self' but a selfless state free of personal desire (*shii*)" is perhaps to exaggerate the contrast, and to miss the subtle point of Bashō's early modern, and intensely personal, desire to establish his identity by aligning himself with what he held to be a lasting truth about reality.[157]

Makoto Ueda would agree with Haruo Shirane and many others who have commented on Bashō's selflessness. Ueda's reading emphasizes the "impersonal" nature of Bashō's poetry.[158] Explaining the quality of *sabi* in Bashō's *haikai*, he makes the important point that there is a difference between sorrow and loneliness, the latter being a more generalized and, thus, a less personal emotion.

Sabishisaya	Loneliness—
Hana no atari no	Standing amid the blossoms,
Asunarau	A cypress tree.

Commenting on this poem, Ueda writes.

> It is spring, and cherry blossoms are in full bloom. But in the middle of them there is something that does not harmonize with the loveliness and gaiety of the scene: a green cypress tree. Because of that cypress, the scene somehow yields the atmosphere of loneliness. In this poem, then, loneliness is not referring to a man's personal emotion; it is describing an impersonal atmosphere, a mood created by a natural landscape. Sabi, derived from sabishi, seems to connote this sort of objective, nonemotional loneliness.[159]

Ueda sees "objective, nonemotional loneliness" as a form of impersonal selflessness. But I wonder whether something important is not getting lost in this interpretation. Is it not the case that the modern self, in its accommodation to larger systems of thought, eventually discovers itself in either ideological purity or in discomfort with and alienation from this or that ideological position? In other words, what we usually understand as the modern self actually forms *by way of* the objective, the nonemotional, and the lonely—all values present in this poem about the cypress.

To put it simply, Bashō was a self-concerned poet even as he advocated selflessness. At this point in time, selfish intention (*shii*) is a handy explanation for a bad poem, or for the lack of becoming one with the pine tree. And yet, we cannot say that there is no self-awareness here, even as the verse reflects a traditional (and even anciently formed) passivity in relation to one's environment. "The gods seemed to possess my soul and breathe madness into my heart, and the images along the roadside seemed to invite me from every corner, so that I was beside myself with anticipation."[160] Shirane, too, is right to say that Bashō's calling was to "explore the relationship" between the world of the road and his inner world of imaginings and memories.[161] But to attempt the fusion of *butsuga ichinyo* was necessarily to consider, and to gain a sharpened awareness of, both their commonality *and* their separation. The faint undercurrents of loneliness and alienation that are everywhere in the travel journals are both moving and memorable. They presuppose the tenuous possibility of finding one's way even in the midst of contingency. For the first time, contingency itself is starting to be negotiated.

To speak of a *way* is to recall Zen practice and already mentioned ties to Daoism and the nameless nominality of the world. For Bashō, *michi* was a movement through space that was, at the same time, a progression toward enlightenment, made possible by places that still yielded up their rejuvenating powers. I agree with Earl Miner when he speaks about the power of place. "This view holds that places—or, more properly the divinities of places—impart spiritual power to the visitor. Behind this view...is a Shinto, animist belief in a spiritual presence to every location."[162] As we discussed earlier, it is this close relationship between human beings and space that underlies the lasting impact of evanescence. Just as *butsu* is in a steady state of change, so is *ga*. Both find their ultimate relationship in oneness (*ichinyo*) as made possible by tapping into the creative source of both.

Here, then, is one possible way to understand the tremendous contradiction that Bashō represents: this self that is trying to not be a self, poised at the dawn of modernity. This merging is both a self-construction and a selflessness: the former because it requires consciousness of difference, and the latter because it still tries to minimize the same. We know that this is true because this union of landscape and self does not become a monistic stability. Stasis will not occur as long as the unifying principle that makes such a coming together possible is change itself. The term *zōka* has been translated in various ways: as Nature, as the Creative, and so on. Literally, Bashō's injunction to "follow the creative" *(zōka zuijun)* means to comply sympathetically (*zuijun*) with the ever-changing process of creativity (*zōka*) or making.

Let us revisit an earlier passage.

> Saigyō's poetry, Sōgi's linked verse, Sesshū's painting, Rikyū's tea ceremony— all possess one thing in common. In their art, these artists follow Creativity and are friends to the four seasons. Whatever they see is a flower, and whatever they think is the moon. Only the barbarous see something other than flowers; and only an animal mind thinks of something other than the moon. The first lesson for the artist is, therefore, to leave barbarity and follow Creativity, to return to Creativity.[163]

As articulated here, the essence of Creativity is change. Thus, those who are creators are "one with the four seasons." Seasons change, and so do we. Change is also our essence. By this admission, we are capable of establishing an equation with Creativity, so that the creative principle that exists within us is able to harmonize and meld with the same principle of becoming that

is the essence of cherry blossoms, the moon, and so on. Within this understanding of reality, to say that there is one and only one Creator is heresy. At
this juncture, the developing modern self does not yet aspire to the late modern delusion of becoming the One, the Genius, the Author, the Dictator.
Rather, what is beautiful about cherry blossom and the moon is that they are
neither no more nor no less created than anything else, and that their beauty
is what teaches us that we, too, are like them. We are both made and makers,
alive to our truest nature (as agents of and for change) by virtue of our sameness with all that surrounds. Realizing this sameness, we become poets, realizing that "the changes of heaven and earth are the seeds of poetry."[164]

Bashō's contribution to the development of Japanese culture was to create
a "secular" aesthetics based on his understanding of various religious and
philosophical traditions. I bracket this term because, by his own admission,
Bashō was a liminal figure. Although he wore a priest's robes, he was "neither
a priest nor an ordinary man of the world."[165] He was well versed in Buddhist
metaphysics and understood the notion of *mujō*. He was also fond of the
Taoist text *Chuang-tzu* and knew of its principle of the *zōbutsusha*, or "that
which makes things, a creative force that gave birth to and governs the movement of all things in the universe."[166] And from Neo-Confucianism, he also
understood the notion of the "Ultimate" or *taikyoku*, (太極), that which
guides all things with its balancing principles of material force (*ki*, 気), that
which "gives life to and creates all things." He also knew theory (*ri*, 理), the
metaphysical notion that regulates the movement of the vital force and
"causes constant motion or change."[167] His was a synthetic eclecticism.

In sum, from these various influences Bashō established a poetics that had
change at its foundation. As Hosea Hirata puts it, " … this deep understanding of the impermanence of the world constituted the core of his haiku."[168]
For Bashō, an ever-changing reality lended itself to the obliteration of difference that, in turn, created a poetic consciousness, or a creative self in this
limited sense. As such, Bashō's understanding of himself is both dynamic
and beautiful in its contingency. It is both passive and active in its appreciation of the permanence of sensibility that emerged by way of radical change
and an equally radical sense of order. What could be more constricting than
the various rules and conventions of *haikai*? Yet what could be more generalizing and vast than the imagery of these tiny poems? To quote Hirata again,
"The raison d'être of haiku seems to reside in its paradoxical imagistic structure, in which the sublime is released from a gap between the miniature and
the immense, between mutability and permanence."[169]

Reflecting the Bodhisattva ideal, Bashō's poetic *michi* is also a *return*.
This need to return to the down-to-earth follows from a devotion to something higher. Following the crea*tive* (*zōka zuijun*) requires discipline and
cultivation. It encourages us to become something other than "barbaric"
and "animal." We aspire. We wish to be something higher. Yet this is precisely why we must eventually return to the low. For only by grounding
ourselves in the low, or what Kamo no Chōmei called the "commonplace,"
is *haikai* legitimized as a form of poetic activity. Only then does it take us

beyond the already existing order of conventional poetics to something that possesses lightness (*karumi*) even when driven by such seriousness of intent. Poetry comes from a heart "possessed by the desire to see the full moon rising over the mountains of Kashima."[170] Once again, this particular kind of novelty results in part from an empirically driven development toward realism and toward a gradual expansion of what the self was permitted to see, whether landscape or pornography.[171] But in its returning to the here-and-now, rather than ascending to the assertion of a new transcendental alignment, we can still feel the pull of the poetic tradition or *fueki*. In these early stages of Japan's modern era, here-and-now continues to be a more prevalent form of order than the kinds of ideology that will eventually break the intimate relationship between the poet and the physical world. For now, it is still possible to find oneself in nature.

The term for this trajectory of rise and return is *kōgō kizoku*, "awakening to the high and returning to the low." "The Master taught, 'You should awaken to the high and return to the low.' 'You should constantly seek out the truth of poetry and with that high spirit return to the *haikai* that you are practicing now.' "[172]

In sum, Bashō's poetics are still well grounded in the sensible, visible, concrete, and humble context of what we are calling the here-and-now. As such, this return to the concrete and to the spontaneous moment of understanding helps us realize another important aspect of evanescence. Form reveals change; just as change gives meaning to form. Bashō's poetic wanderings teach us that radical form reveals radical evanescence; and that even radical evanescence is capable of finding resolution in a state of inclusive nothingness—as it brings the immense truths of the world above to the particular level of frogs, and bamboo, and the cry of cicadas. Such things are formal manifestations of transcendental values as they make themselves felt as nonsymbolic symbols. To care about why a frog is only a frog is joy.

MONO NO AWARE: THE SADNESS OF THINGS

Lest we get the impression that the long Tokugawa tranquility was a natural state of endless harmony, we should be aware of the numerous measures that were taken to keep the peace. One was a hostage system, by which feudal lords were required to spend half their time in the capital, Edo, and leave their families behind whenever they returned to their respective provinces. This policy of "alternate attendance" (*sankin kōtai*) minimized challenges to the center of power; for if a lord began to foment rebellion in the outlying areas, his family could be immediately exterminated. A second policy was to restrict the use of firearms, a measure taken after these deadly tools had proven themselves instrumental in unifying the country during the many wars of the last decades of the sixteenth century. A third was to limit contact with foreigners by restricting travel and trade. And a fourth was to suppress Christianity in the attempt to rid Japan of the dangerously destabilizing idea that all people were equal in the sight of God.

The Tokugawa leaders wanted stability, not equality. They looked to Confucianism to establish a hierarchy of four main social classes. At the top were the samurai, who served the emperor and protected the people. Below them were the peasants, who produced the food that all required. Beneath them were the craftsmen, who were also productive but nonagricultural. And at the bottom were the merchants, who enjoyed only low status because they handled money and were not by nature productive.

I hasten to add that this was the nominal social order. In reality, the samurai eventually became indebted to the merchants, who provided the financial services that commerce and travel between the provinces and Edo made necessary. Even with their mounting debts, the samurai class did not hasten to relax their continued suppression of merchants' political rights, however. In reaction, the merchants and wealthy agricultural families channeled their energies away from the political process and toward the pursuit of wealth, pleasure, and the arts. Thus, the hedonistic turn.

The emergent bourgeoisie had few places to turn in order to seek political fulfillment. The already described pleasure seeking kept the disenfranchised distracted but not necessarily hopeful. Consequently, over the two-and-a-half centuries of Tokugawa rule, a sense of fated acceptance settled in as the need to find one's place *within* the parameters of the established order was both strongly felt and strictly enforced. Through an ever-developing elaboration of protocol (*girei*) and regulation—one should step aside when a samurai approached, one should always speak humbly of one's own, one should not build an elaborate home or wear costly clothing, and so on—life under the Tokugawa became remarkably formal. An oppressive political order asserted itself even in play and distraction, as the townsmen of Edo, Osaka, and Kyoto gave themselves to the floating world with what we might call regulated or licensed abandon.

Momokawa Takahito finds this state of sorrowful gaiety central to Japanese identity as a whole. In the wake of Zen's focus on enlightenment and Pure Land Buddhism's affirmation of the self as a recipient of Amida's grace, the oppressive environment of Tokugawa Japan choked a developing individualism and led to an acceptance of a general state of what the mid-Tokugawa-period scholar Motoori Norinaga (1730–1801) called *mono no aware*, or "the sadness of things."

I describe this term to my students in this way:

> The limitations placed on my rights as a person leads me to accept my inferiority as inevitable. I am no good. I am powerless. Now, if these two statements are true, then it follows that, in a strictly demarcated class society, another member of my class is in the same boat. I am no good and powerless. But so is next person, and the next, and the next. In fact, all my peers (who are the ones who matter to me) are similarly no good. We may be unlike our samurai superiors who are by nature privileged. But what our oppression means in actuality is that by accepting our lowly status and generalizing everyone else in our class into the same miserable situation, we establish a point of lowest common expectation that then allows us to seal away our discontent and to indulge in a

"self-conscious schizophrenia," a playful and *harmlessly* rebellious mode of life that allows us to accept our sorrow and powerlessness in as painless a way as possible.[173] We become the denizens of a floating world of pleasure tinged with sorrow, temporarily finding reprieve. We come to live in a world of manners and make believe, a realm that in accepting falseness shows little pretense for forcing social change.

Life might be bad. But so what? You're no good. I'm no good. Everybody's no good. What else is new? Why not let the spirit of *mono no aware* lead us, therefore, to fatal attractions and false moments of gaiety, and, while we're at it, why not have it guide us to an appreciation of all things pleasurable, however fleeting and ridiculous? Once again, we cannot escape the enduring relevance of cherry blossoms. The fall from the branch might be sad; but at the same time it is also beautiful in a self-pitying yet assertive way.

In short, *mono no aware* is the aesthetics of the sullied and the weak. According to Momokawa, it is "the sentiment of sadness which has formed the core of the identity of the Japanese since the Edo period."[174] Perhaps the potential for a Japanese version of the renaissance was impeded by this coincidence of hegemony and the fundamental "difficulty in setting a viewpoint based on a fixed set of ideas with regard to social reality."[175] In short, in Tokugawa Japan we have the development of various modern systems (of transportation, communication, trade, and so on); but we do not witness an equally robust emergence of individualism since the cultural field came to be utterly formalized by the order of here-and-now, which Momokawa articulates as a problematic melding of interiority and exteriority or the tendency to project oneself into one's environment (which we saw as a virtue in Bashō). Formality tended to preserve class and regionalism. Etiquette continued to place emphasis on appearances, on visual, space-oriented identity. Conformity hampered the imagination's grasp of the higher ideological order that would eventually make citizens out of folks, as happens in the following Meiji period.

But, of course, "*mono no aware*" was itself an ideology, a general theory of *aware*—the impressive poignancy of all things. As first articulated by Motoori no Norinaga, a founding scholar of the national learning (*kokugaku*) movement, it expressed a native essence that could be held up in opposition to existing schools of continental thought. Norinaga sought to locate a local (i.e., non-Neo-Confucian, non-Buddhist, non-Chinese) sense of identity for the Japanese, or a "private realm" of "individual experience" not vitiated by "objectified, 'rational' principles."[176] He found such pure experience in the earliest of Japanese texts—the *Kojiki* and *Nihonshoki*—which by that time had been largely forgotten. He also praised *The Tale of Genji* for being particularly expressive of a kind of lyrical and true emotional response to life that various continental discourses had vitiated. Being antiquarian and nativist, he was naturally critical of both the modern and the "foreign." Yet, his analysis of *mono no aware* seems to reveal an attitude that made the paradoxical acceptance of both Confucian propriety and Buddhist nothingness both possible and even necessary.

Makoto Ueda explains,

> According to Norinaga, *aware* consists of two interjections, *a* and *hare*, both of which are used when one's heart is greatly moved. One cries out, for example, "*A*, how beautiful the moon is!" or "*A*, what a pitiful thing this is!" or "*Hare*, how lovely the flowers are!" or "*Hare*, what a good child you are!" *Aware*, which combines these two interjections, is primarily a word describing a deeply moved heart, a heart filled with intense emotions.[177]

This lyrical response directly connects a person with one's context and is, in this sense, true. It is neither reasoned nor ethically driven. It is simply one's uncompromised reading of and spontaneous reaction to ever-changing reality.

The "*mono*" of *mono no aware*, means "things," and serves to generalize the relevance of *aware*. *Mono no aware* is, then, a deep feeling about all things. This emotion is not necessarily sad, but *aware* has come to be understood this way because, according to Norinaga, of all emotions, grief is the most universal. It is also the most intense. We have many opportunities to feel sorrow and disappointment, to lament and regret. We experience sickness, death, and failure. Thus, the samurai code of thinking lightly of death is, for Norinaga, yet another distorting conceptualization of reality. Who does not feel sad about dying? What is to be gained by conditioning ourselves not to feel what the moment requires? Is that not delusion?

In short, Norinaga's understanding of emotion and lyricism is notable because it produces a strong theory of Japanese identity. As a modern writer, his desire to define all things native as superior to all things foreign yielded not only *mono no aware* but an essential understanding of Japan itself. Not surprisingly, this search for Japan leads us back to evanescence and cherry blossoms.

Shikishima no	Should someone ask,
Yamatogokoro wo	"What is the soul
Hito towaba	Of Yamato, our ancient land?"
Asahi ni niou	It is the scent of mountain cherry blossoms
Yamazakurabana.	In the morning sun.

Remember this poem, because it will provide many of the key cultural terms and concepts for nationalist thinkers who follow. In the twentieth-century, many will refer to these lyrical lines in their attempt to explain Japanese identity and to make their claims of exceptionalism and superiority. That said, it is also true that the "antinationalist" Sakaguchi Ango will also sympathize with Norinaga's dismissal of bushidō, the way of the warrior, as a great distortion. Ango had no stomach for the samurai's commitment to vengeance, whereas Norinaga disliked the warrior's suppression of death's sadness. At this juncture, what is particularly relevant to our analysis about essences is the claim that emotion, not reason, is the better measure of reality.

This surprising assumption follows from what we have come to understand about propriety as a formal response to evanescence. The order of here-and-now requires there to be an emotional response that is both lyrical and predictable at the same time.

According to Norinaga, a person of understanding will always experience things similarly. He will *always* feel what the occasion calls for. This happens not by intention, but spontaneously, because there is no appreciable separation between poet and context. Those who do not know how to respond to things in general (*mono*) predictably lack the proper sensitivity. In this way, then, Norinaga assumes a rigid formality, an appropriateness imposed upon something that normally resists form. For what could be more changeable and *hakanai* than emotion? And what is more varied than everyday experience and its constant mutations of place and time—these situations that supposedly engender this and that proper response? These difficulties notwithstanding, Norinaga's attempt to theorize form within evanescence yields this formal claim that Situation A yields Emotion A.

Surely, this echo of Tsurayuki's preface to the *Kokinshū* is an appeal to the order of here-and-now, to the rules about space that define those who occupy, move, and feel. This is a clear articulation of the tie between evanescence and form that we first noted in Dōgen's poem about the seasons. It is also an affirmation of Kamo no Chōmei's poetics, as well as an echo of the Tsurayuki's paradoxical certainty about certain things engendering a predictably spontaneous poetic response.

The lyrical thrust of Japanese aesthetics points us to a breakdown of the barriers between the self and its surroundings, between the inner and the outer. And yet, this emotionalism is also strangely and strictly formal and predictable. No doubt, this predisposition to become one with the moment prepared the Japanese to accept Buddhism, even though Norinaga claimed that the two are incompatible. Perhaps he thought that the possibility of nothingness—or becoming one with everything—that is presupposed in the lyrical apprehension of one's context is neither chaotic nor nihilistic since even a spontaneous (*jihatsu*) response to one's context must stay within the parameters of form. After all, the assertion that a person of understanding always experiences what the occasion calls for is nothing if not an appeal to propriety. Thus, like Ki no Tsurayuki's thoughts about poets and frogs, Norinaga's theory of the sadness of things is quite clearly yet another attempt to give radical form to radical change.

After Norinaga, *mono no aware* came to express a beautiful resignation, "a sadness that is constantly evolving toward gaiety,"[178] a sentiment already anticipated in Saikaku's floating-world stories of the ebullient Genroku era. Looking ahead, this sense of generalized inferiority will eventually aid a violent nationalist reaction in the Meiji, Taishō, and early Shōwa periods. With the devastation brought on by World War II, the feeling will actually be revived as an element of a postmodern "return" to a Tokugawa-like order of here-and-now, with its appreciation of gaiety and style as a fatalistic response to the profound sorrow of the human condition.

Resigning oneself to the sadness of reality has its own rewards. The syllogism that brings evanescence and sorrow together to yield something more "positive" would go something like this.

> A: Life is evanescent and, as a result, sorrowful.
> B: Sorrow heightens the beauty of things.
> C: Therefore, evanescent life is beautiful.

This same cluster of values helps us to understand two often-discussed aesthetic values: *wabi* and *sabi*. *Wabi* is the beauty found in sparse, simple things, such as an undecorated and uncomplicated tea bowl. *Sabi* is the beauty of age and decay, such as we might find in the patina of moss on an earthen wall, or the look of unpainted, weathered wood. Such values stand in stark contrast to the gaudy and colorful, which are also undeniable elements of Japanese aesthetics. This contrast might be confusing, but now we have a way to understand it. Garish elements are an exuberant reaction to evanescence, while the more somber tones of *wabi* and *sabi* express a more modulated acceptance of the same. Either way, gaiety and sorrow are linked by way of evanescence.

What would happen if we substituted "evanescent" with "oppressive" in the aforementioned syllogism? We would approach an even stronger, more arresting definition of Norinaga's *mono no aware*: oppressive life that is beautiful. With this bold step, we finally arrive at a paradox that formal life both presents and resolves. The beauty of sorrow is an extension of the floating-world mentality of making the most of a bad situation: we are more inclined to accept our unfortunate lot in life if we know that *temporary* relief is not only available but worthy of sincere pursuit. I explain it to my students this way, "A person might be politically powerless and even socially despised, but at least he can taste the beauty of his own sorrow; and also know, by the way, how to have a good time!"

This substitution of distraction for true happiness is a kind of inversion, and maybe even a perversion (to an ideological, ethical point of view). But, perversion or not, a sense of a sad-yet-vibrant hedonism was a prevailing attitude of the floating world—as expressed by the worldly exaggerations of *gesaku* (playful texts of popular literature), the tearful yet erotic music and dance of the demimonde, the pornographic force of wood block prints, the sentimental fandom of the kabuki theater, and so on.

At its most confidently aggressive, this seeking of pleasure became articulated as *iki*, or chic, a spirited, perhaps proto-revolutionary, attitude of exalting the low. This attitude lent itself to a pathetic glorification of prostitutes, those unfortunate women who were sold into sexual slavery yet were able in some cases to gain considerable status as paragons of an inverted kind of virtue. Given the details of her mercantilist circumstances, we should feel the sharp edge of her sadly vibrant beauty as portrayed in the floating-world prints of, for example, Kitagawa Utamaro (ca. 1753–1808). In truth, the courtesan was a victim of circumstance. As mentioned in our discussion of

Saikaku's "woman who loved love," she was a slave, a commodity of sexual desire who had been sold once by her parents so she might be rented out again and again and again. Of all Edo-period souls, she was best qualified to put on the required act—the clothes, the hairdo, the makeup—in order to personify the erotic drama that the sorrowful yet pleasure-seeking customer both paid for and participated in. It was this sublimated lie, this enjoyably floating state of affairs, that temporarily liberated the townsmen (and even samurai) as they endured the "peaceful" Tokugawan hegemony.

A complicated spirit of *iki* held for both supplier and consumer. It was a rebellion with no political place to go. At its best, losing oneself momentarily in the elegant Yoshiwara, this "purveyor of romance and...manufacturer of dreams," was a *tasteful* admission of one's powerlessness.[179] It was a way to cultivate a tea-ceremony-like appreciation of *ichigo ichie* (一期一会), "one moment, one meeting." Each moment in our lives never happens again; and so we must learn how to make the most of each. If we can do this, the joy of the part will speak to the whole. Serving and drinking tea is not unlike giving and receiving sexual pleasure. Both are ways to recover, if temporarily, from the sorrow of evanescence. The many rules of etiquette that govern both are, therefore, not felt to be onerous. They allow us to feel enlightened, awakened, and enlivened. By giving ourselves enthusiastically to formality, we deceive ourselves as experts, learning how to meet everyone as if for the first time. Because of evanescence, the first time is also the last time. Knowing this, there is joy. And knowing joy is to appreciate sorrow.

PROTOCOL AND LOYAL RETAINERS

As the long Tokugawa peace wore on, the function of the samurai warrior became increasingly formalized and bureaucratic. A rule of rules gradually came to replace the rule of swords; and the samurai's twofold path of *bu* 武 —military prowess—and *bun* 文—literary accomplishment—shifted to emphasize the latter. As this happened, the identity and function of the warrior became increasingly formalized, so that compliance with protocol became an all-important foundation of a social order that kept the various classes in place.

The importance of protocol to the samurai spirit was underscored by an incident that shocked the developing nation.[180] On April 21, 1701, a daimyō named Asano Naganori met with another high-ranking official, Kira Yoshinaka, who had been assigned to be his tutor in the needed formalities. Asano was to receive an imperial envoy from Kyoto, and had to know the proper protocol for doing so. When Kira refused to give him the necessary information (because he had not received the expected bribe), Asano lost his temper, and drew his sword. Kira survived the assault; but the drawing of swords in the Edo palace was strictly forbidden, and the Shōgun Tsunayoshi, outraged at such a breach of the rules, ordered Asano to commit suicide by *seppuku*, or ritual disembowelment.

No doubt, Asano followed proper procedures in effecting his death: wrapping a sheet of white paper around the blade of his dagger, then thrusting its point into the belly on the right side, cutting across to the left side, turning ninety degrees and pulling upward so the razor-sharp edge left an L-shaped opening from which his entrails gushed out. How far did he manage to get through this painful ritual of death? Protocol required that the blade be withdrawn from the ruptured body and held with the point up, so that the dying samurai could fall forward on it and pierce his throat as he collapsed. But there are real limits to both human strength and courage, and a second man usually stood behind the dying one, his long sword raised to deliver a *coup de grâce* should the condemned fail to finish himself off.

When the self-executed Asano perished, he left behind family, property, and over a hundred retainers. According to well-established tradition, they were expected to avenge their master's death. If they were true samurai, they would kill Kira. To do anything less would be dishonorable. And yet the anticipated vendetta did *not* happen. Asano's head retainer Ōishi Kuranosuke and his subordinates disgraced their master and themselves by not attacking Kira's residence. They became masterless samurai, or *rōnin*, literally "wave people," or drifters, the same title given today to high school seniors who have failed college entrance examinations and take an extra year or two to study for reexamination. Living in a state of nonaffiliation, these hapless *rōnin* suddenly became outsiders to the protocol that had been giving their lives meaning.

In disgrace, Asano's men went their separate ways. But a year later, on January 30, 1703, a portion of them secretly gathered. Having tricked Kira's men into thinking they were cowards who had turned their back on social expectation, they attacked the Kira mansion by night, and avenged their lord by cutting off Kira's head and carrying it to the Sengaku Temple, where they awaited judgment as to their future. By killing their lord's enemy, they restored their honor. They strictly followed the samurai code at a time when people thought the days of such behavior were over.

In fact, by the eighteenth century it was actually illegal to avenge a master's death in this way. So by being obedient to a more ancient way of the samurai, they had to break the rules of the land that forbade such violence. In response to this dilemma, a vigorous debate ensued. Should these loyal wave men be forgiven, having shown their loyalty to their master and their honor as samurai? Or should they be executed as criminals, having broken the law? Positions on both sides were articulated. In the end, they were sentenced to death, albeit a respectable death. Like their lord, they were allowed to die honorably by committing *seppuku*.

Today the graves of these retainers can be found at Tokyo's Sengaku Temple, a place of pilgrimage for those who still honor their loyalty. Their courageous deed was also memorialized by a number of plays that were written soon after the event. The most famous of these is the puppet play, *A Treasury of Loyal Retainers* (*Kanadehon chūshingura*, 1748), by Takeda Izumo (1691–1756), Miyoshi Shōraku, and Namiki Senryū. Soon adapted for the kabuki theater, this play has become a perennial favorite of the "distorted" stage. Indeed, it would be hard to find an adult in Japan who does not know at least the rough outlines of this story, and, more to our point, does not understand the values that led to this mass killing. For the sake of dramatic effect, the plot necessarily elaborates upon the details of the actual event. Nevertheless, *A Treasury of Loyal Retainers* retains a traceable correspondence to what actually happened. Asano becomes En'ya Hangan in the play. Kira is Kō no Moronao. Ōishi Kuranosuke is Ōboshi Yuranosuke, and so on.

From this event and from the play, we learn a few things. One is the obvious importance placed on protocol. Knowing what to do at this or that time was considered to be a matter of utmost importance. A second point is that the dramatic power of the play comes from its movement either toward or away from fulfilling various social expectations. *Chūshingura* gives meaning to both action and nonaction as Yuranosuke takes us with him on an emotional roller coaster. He knows he must avenge his master's death. But will he act or not? On the face of it, he appears to have lost all sense of duty and propriety. He seems a coward, an irresolute floater, a useless wave man. He is despised for shirking his responsibilities. But *he* knows he is loyal; and so we rejoice when, in the end, he rallies his men to fulfill their responsibilities. Needless to say, this is a joy that could only exist because of certain obligations, *giri*, as they collide with *ninjō*, human emotions.

Although formalized as a literary trope in Chikamatsu Monzaemon's (1653–1725) plays, a similar *giri-ninjō* tension had already appeared centuries earlier in *The Tale of the Heike* and in the Noh play *Atsumori*. Certainly, all these instances of obligation-versus-feeling flowed from the basic tension between evanescence and form. Just as Kumagai was torn between the formal expectation to kill Atsumori, on the one hand, and his merciful feelings as a father, on the other, so, too, are many of the characters that appear in the Genroku-period works of Saikaku and Chikamatsu. Coming a bit later, *A Treasury of Loyal Retainers* is another variation of this so-called *giri-ninjō* conflict.

The relevance of these points is simply this: the dramatic tension of this play flows from a core paradigm of change versus form, one that we have identified as central to so many other Japanese cultural phenomena. For En'ya Hangan, his world is an unchanging and unyielding realm of protocol, as it has been placed in tension with changeable emotions of venality, resentment, hatred, and so on. As for En'ya's head retainer Yuranosuke, he must live out his fate between the same poles of social expectation and his perceived inability to remain emotionally true to his deceased lord. In the case of Kanpei, who was flirting with his lover when he should have been helping En'ya, the world of change manifests itself through the vicissitudes of sexual attraction, while stasis appears as his samurai responsibilities. Become unanchored from protocol and all is lost. In a world of incessant change, formality is vitally important.

When Asano committed this breach of etiquette, his world suddenly collapsed, bringing along with him all those who had tied their fates to his own. The cataclysmic consequences of his mistake required a violent reassertion of form. His men had to avenge their lord; and honor had to prevail at all costs. At a time when the continuing peace of the Tokugawa rule had weakened the original raison d'etre of the samurai—these blossom-like warriors ready to fall from the branch at a moment's notice—the events of Asano's suicide and the vendetta that eventually followed stirred the Japanese imagination. Donald Keene explains,

> The boldness of the vendetta caught the imagination of the people of every class. At a time when the samurai ideals of loyalty and resolute action seemed to have been forgotten, thanks to the peace of almost a hundred years, this sudden dramatic gesture came as a heartening reminder of what being a samurai had once meant. Even the Confucian scholars, normally pacific men, were moved to admiration, remembering the old teaching that a man should not permit his father's enemy to live under the same sky as himself. They further declared that the forty-six loyal retainers perfectly embodied the highest ideal of the virtuous man. Numerous poems and essays, mainly in Chinese, were composed to commemorate and glorify the forty-six heroes.

> But not all the Confucianists approved of the vendetta. Ogyū Sorai, the greatest philosopher of the time, expressed his reservations soon after the events: "By righteousness we mean the path of keeping oneself free from any taint, and by law we mean the measuring rod for the entire country. A man controls his heart with decorum and his actions with righteousness. For the forty-six samurai to have avenged their master on this occasion shows that they are aware of shame, as becomes men who are samurai; and since they have followed the path of keeping themselves free from taint, their deed is righteous. However, this deed is appropriate only to their particular group; it amounts therefore to a special exception to the rules. . . . This is not to be tolerated under the law. If the forty-six samurai are pronounced guilty and condemned to commit seppuku, in keeping with the traditions of the samurai, the claim of the Uesugi family will be satisfied, and the loyalty of the men will not have been disparaged. This must therefore be considered as a general principle. If general principles are impaired by special exceptions, there will no longer be any respect for the law in this country."[181]

To a Confucian scholar such as Ogyū Sorai (1666–1728), change must be checked by the unchanging: "A man controls his heart with decorum and his actions with righteousness." As in Bashō's *fueki ryūkō*, resolution is found in the balance between the eternal and the ever-changing. In the case of these loyal retainers who reinvigorated the already romanticized way of the warrior, the interplay between the constancy of principles and matters of the heart finds a just compromise in self-immolation.

In Japan, it is not the bosom but the gut (the *hara*) that harbors the spirit. That is why the samurai cut there: to spill one's entrails, to pass from life to death in a way that maintains decorum despite the gore of the spurting, spilling, foul moment. What is *seppuku*, or *hara-kiri*, if not a formally perfected affirmation of evanescence? It is the chaos of change as it exists within a context of well-developed formalities and principles, the display of protocol in its most dramatic form. It is the visible moment of life becoming death. As the natural barrier between inside and outside, skin is split open so that the inside becomes the outside, and vice versa. Structurally speaking, this too is lyricism and non-duality.

INNER AND OUTER, AND THE EXPANDING CONTEXT OF MODERNITY

Despite the Regime's policy of *sakoku*, or isolationism, Japan was never completely sealed off from the influence of other countries. In 1636, the Tokugawa Shōgunate ordered the construction of an artificial island in Nagasaki Bay. It was intended to be a place where Portuguese merchants could reside. They (along with small populations of Chinese and Dutch) had been allowed to remain in Japan. But by the time the island was completed, the Portuguese had been expelled because of their proselyting activities; and in their place, the Dutch were moved in. For centuries thereafter, these Europeans were accepted as a marginal part of Japan's population, enjoying the status of permanent outsiders, as clearly expressed by the configuration of the island itself: located offshore, and connected to the mainland by only the narrowest of land bridges. Called Dejima, or the"island that sticks out," this space was not considered to be Japanese space per se.

As reflected in this spatial distinction, conceptual categories of inner (*uchi* 内) and outer (*soto* 外) were kept sharp. One's circle of family and associates constituted *uchi*, and others were *soto*. Thus from the Muromachi period onward, the celebration of the coming of spring has been marked by the rites of Setsubun, usually held on February 2 or 3, when one opens the windows and doors of one's house, and throws ritual beans into the air while shouting, "Prosperity in, ogres out" (*Fuku wa uchi, oni wa soto*). Simply put, one identifies with *uchi*, and not with *soto*. This binary split survives even today as a "shoes-on/shoes-off" phenomenon, where the space of shoes-off, such as one's home, is kept clean and orderly, while the space of shoes-on, such as public streets or beaches, can sometimes be surprisingly unkempt.

What the Shogunate's xenophobic policies toward non-Japanese did not prevent was the sort of change that came by way of the continued development of what Edwin Reischauer called Japan's "incipient capitalism." Cities grew and roads were built. Increasingly frequent encounters with strangers forced the modern quest to find identity among difference. An example of urbanization (as a centripetal way of encountering difference) and of the struggle to formulate a new definition of the self is found in Shikitei Sanba's (1776–1822) *Bathhouse of the Floating World* (*Ukiyoburo*, 1809–13) and *Barbershop of the Floating World* (*Ukiyodoko*, 1813–14). These humorous texts (*kokkeibon*) replicated urban spaces where people (including strangers) came together and interacted for a meaningful moment. For the most part, the stories that narrate their relationships are discrete and only loosely connected. As such, they are less powerfully creative of self-identity than vigorously emplotted narratives that channel the process of change toward purposeful developments. Nevertheless, Sanba's loosely formed narratives are still able to reveal modern identity in oblique fashion by showing the ways all people are different and yet the same.

With tongue-in-cheek humor, Sanba delivers his theory of the bath-house.

> There is, one realizes on careful reflection, no shortcut to moral learning like the public bath. It is, after all, the way of Nature, and of Heaven and Earth, that all are naked when they bathe—the wise and the foolish, the crooked and the straight, the poor and the rich, the high and the low. The nakedness of infancy purges them all of sorrow and desire, and renders them selfless, be they Sakyamuni or Confucius, Gonsuke or Osan. Off with the wash water come the grime of greed and the passions of the flesh; a master and his servant are equally naked when they rinse themselves. As surely as an evening's red-faced drunkard is ashen and sober in the morning bath, the only thing separating the new-born baby's first bath from the cleansing of the corpse is life, fragile as a paper screen.[182]

To live is to bathe. And to be aware of life as a series of baths is to know that the interval between one's first and last soak is rather short. In Sanba's affirmation of evanescence, life is as thin as paper, as lasting as a haircut.

We can understand the Tokugawa-period bathhouse as a developing "public" space of modern life. As such, it had a mass-producing, leveling effect. Once naked and stripped of our packaging, we can concentrate on what we have in common. In the tub, all are men are brothers and all women sisters, even "a master and his servant." So into Sanba's bathhouse come the old and young, male and female, rich and poor, the high and the low.

Most of the patrons Sanba describes are familiar with each other. But the experience of a certain traveler "from the western provinces, on his first visit to Edo" underscores the way in which life in nineteenth-century Japan had not yet become fully standardized and predictable. Upon entering the Edo bathhouse, this outsider becomes confused. He does not know how things are done in the East. His reading of the space and its particular forms of here-and-now falls short. Consequently, his encounter with difference is comically unpleasant. Sanba expresses this discomfort as a mistaking of one man's loincloth for another man's wash towel.

> "Hey! What's going on?" he said. "What happened to the loincloth I left here a little while ago to soak? It doesn't make any sense for something you haven't even washed yet to disappear! It's got to be somewhere, for Heaven's sake!" Spotting the man from the western provinces using the loincloth as a towel to wash his face with, he said angrily, "What the hell! That's not your towel, is it?"
>
> "No, of course not," said the man. "I found it in this bucket. I hung up my own over there."
>
> "Good grief!" cried the man from the Kamigata. "What a damned idiot! That's not a towel! It's my loincloth! Washing your face with a loincloth, indeed—how can you be so stupid? Have you been bewitched by a fox? Or are you just crazy?"[183]

The scene is exaggerated. Yet the point about inner and outer is valid. Ignorance of, and nonconformity to, the norm is to be treated as *in*human. Take your pick. The poor outsider from western Japan is either stupid, bewitched, or crazy. No doubt, over time, the increasing frequency of this sort of conflict yielded a common understanding of bathhouse protocol for all places, which then produced a common understanding of the *normal* human being (rather than the Westerner or the Easterner). Thus, from a myriad of particular examples comes a generalized definition of modern man and woman.

A second, centrifugal way of encountering the changing world can be found in Jippensha Ikku's (1765–1831) *Shanks Mare* (*Tōkaidōchū hizagurige*, 1802–14), a travel novel that seems to have stood the test of time far better than other works of the early nineteenth century. To say the obvious, what made Ikku's depiction of early modern life on the road possible was the creation of roads themselves. When the Tokugawa Shōgunate established the requirement for daimyō to spend half their year in Edo, an extensive system of routes was developed in order to connect the outlying provinces with the capital.

The five main circuits, the so-called Gokaidō, radiated out from Edo's Nihonbashi, the epicenter of this system. They provided a structure that facilitated Japan's coalescence as a unified space of common imagination and culture. Taking to the road that led from Edo to Kyoto, Ikku's two comic heroes Yajirōbei and Kitahachi encounter one adventure after another. This is the same road, by the way, that was made famous by Ando Hiroshige's (1797–1858) *ukiyoe* (literally, floating-world picture) series, *Fifty-Three Stations on the Tōkaidō Road* (*Tōkaidō gojūsan tsugi*, 1834–42), which visually documents both the space of the corridor and the people moving through it.

Like Hiroshige's series, *Shank's Mare* was also a great commercial success. The fictional trip taken by Ikku's two heroes was enjoyed by many contemporary readers who paid to discover new regions vicariously. By way of these pages, they met new people, observed different ways of life, consumed different cuisines, and tried to enter into as many sexual dalliances as possible. The various ploys that Ikku used to keep the reader's interest are important to our analysis; for they indicate the standard (and standardizing) forms by which the dynamism of modern life was being structured around the turn of the nineteenth century. In a word, what Japan's gradually developing modernity comes to suggest is that, in this evanescent world, a certain kind of change is inherently more interesting and important than all others. It is the kind of change that will later be called "progress."

A rigorous discussion of modernity will have to wait. For now, it is enough to note some general trends of modern development and their effects on Japanese culture. Needless to say, they had a profound effect on the understanding of both evanescence and form.[184] Note how Ikku's modern engagement with the floating world focuses upon money and consumption in particular. Kita and Yaji are always on the brink of poverty, always asking about prices, and always counting their change. So why, then, do they never run out of funds? If we identify with their impecuniousness, we also appreciate the nearly miraculous way they maintain purchasing power from beginning to end, as if they have a credit card that never requires payment. Surely, as they make their way down the Tōkaidō, they hold our interest precisely because they possess this incredible buying power that makes (modern) dealings with others possible.

Originally conceived as a "how to" book, *Shank's Mare* propped up the possibility of the modern self by maintaining Kita and Yaji's place within a developing capitalist realm. In this sense, we might say that this irreverent and bawdy novel is essentially accomplishing a rationalization of Japanese space and culture, pushing harder and farther than Saikaku's earlier attempts. It is a story about change as exchange, a series of transactions that happens along the Tōkaidō to allow certain developments to occur: the purchase of food, transportation, entertainment, and even companionship.

These purchases have the larger purpose of establishing the identity of Ikku's two comic heroes. Notice how often Kita and Yaji try to use their anonymity and oft-repeated encounters with strangers to pass themselves off as people they really are not. For this modern development to happen, fiction (as initiated by Ryōi and Saikaku) is of the utmost importance. In one instance, Ikku's heroes pretend that Yaji is the head clerk of a well-established shop. In another, they indulge in role-playing, where one is the master and the other is the servant. In yet another surprising turn of events, Yaji even claims to be Jippensha Ikku, himself.

> "May I ask your pen name?" continued the stranger.
> "I'm Jippensha Ikku," said Yaji.
> "A most celebrated name, indeed. So you're Master Jippensha."[185]

By way of such fictitious imaginings, identity is born—whether of writer, reader, or of an objectified third-person character. Paradoxically, the imagination is both stimulated and limited by a general template that produces individuality, which then becomes an impossible (and, therefore, fictitious) uniqueness of view that nevertheless claims universality.

Unlike the earlier traveler Matsuo Bashō, Ikku himself is not on the road as a first-person presence, tossing off this and that poem in response to what he discovers along the way. If anything, his third-person narrative even more powerfully constructs the author's persona—"that's a very celebrated name"—than Bashō's mix of poetry and prose. In short, a more obviously fictional authorial stance gives Ikku the ability to ponder an infinitely greater variety of life along the East Sea Road. There are getting to be fewer and fewer limitations of real space and real experience to worry about. More easily than Bashō, Ikku can assume a position of authority. He can become the "objective" interlocutor of truth, the one we call an author. It is this market-worthy exercise of the developing modern imagination that both furthered and limited the possibilities of change by making them increasingly far-ranging yet also increasingly linear and supportive of certain clearly defined ideals and themes.

To reiterate, fictional works such as these by Sanba and Ikku helped to conceptualize Japaneseness by way of an increasingly linear form of change that came to emphasize the self itself as an emerging, and even lasting, existential identity. Such stories established selfhood as a stability that perceived continuity in a permanent, defining kind of way, allowing the author and his readers to respond vicariously to an ever-expanding range of discoverable spaces and seeable experiences. As the imaginable expanded by way of this developing modern consciousness, the porous barriers that once existed between Inner and Outer (as praised by Norinaga and lamented by Momokawa) began to become impermeable. The earlier lyricism, the emotive blending of an artist with his context, came to be increasingly difficult and, eventually, even problematic. In order to assert its existence more vigorously, the self began to pull away from the spatial context that once lyrically contained it; and an inside and an outside were born, framing encounters with the Other by way of an ideological, transcendental point of interpretation. In other words, as modern subjectivity began to form, even the floating world of consumeristic pleasures was rendered an object of contemplation. Although not articulated quite so philosophically, Ikku's authorial self was like Descarte's *cogito* in structure. They both resisted the chaos of random change by asserting an impervious essence called the self.[186]

We have reached another important milestone in our study of Japanese culture. In contrast to the nothingness that is everything (the *mu* that we have been considering), a new kind of nothingness is now starting to form. As created by this more representational view of reality, this new nothingness will eventually become nihil, a state where *soto* comes to be so objectified that one's distance from it becomes absolute and unbridgeable. In the process of this development, Bashō's land of poetic conceits and lyrical identifications has already yielded to Ikku's more prosaic field of observable and describable commercial phenomena: no longer a lonely road to the deep north but a busy thoroughfare that connects Japan's two major urban areas. Of course, the space-hungry wanderings of Kita and Yaji still only anticipate the creation of Japan as an ideologically unified (and in this new sense, unchanging) nation, one that will come to generate individual identity by way of the citizen's atomization within a larger and larger ideological system that, by virtue of its attempt to be consistent and universal, will also become imperialistic and, even, genocidal.

Put simply, just as ritual earlier gave way to lyricism when the principal feature of poetics changed from the magical epithet to the metaphor, so, too, will the lyrical realm of sympathy for the changeful cicada eventually yield to the descriptive, prosaic world of increasingly ideological (and in this sense changeless) expression. As this occurs, the lyrical cherry blossom that supplanted the husk of the cicada as the most common expression of evanescent reality will transform itself into a lasting *symbol* of the imagined Japanese nation. Once such a symbol ties the space of Japan firmly to a represented transcendental order, lyricism will come to be patriotism, or a love of nation (*kokka*) rather than a love of village (*sato*); and evanescence will be channeled into increasingly linear paths of development so that all change becomes either progress or regression.

MONSTROSITY

One way to understand the magnitude of this shift from the order of here-and-now toward the transcendental order is to compare the look of the one against that of the other. For example, we might compare the famous garden at the Katsura Detached Palace in Kyoto with the equally well-known one at the Versailles Palace in France. I make this an intercultural comparison not because there are no examples of the latter in Japan, but because Versailles is both a well-known and an easily understood point of comparison.

At Katsura, we enter through a modest gate, and follow a stone-lined path that leads us through the space. It changes direction. It turns abruptly. It rises. It falls. It makes us look down at the ground. Every now and then we pause. We view the garden as it engulfs us. Seeing it requires us to have a moveable point of view, as we become a part of the space itself. Moving through it, we tend to notice details at least as much as we see the larger picture. Occasionally, we do see a vista. But our vision of the garden is more

Figure 1.11 The Sumiyoshi Pine at Katsura, Kyoto. Preventing the large view (photo by Rei Inouye).

often limited, and made beautiful because it is incomplete. Trees and hills limit our perspective. At one spot, we find a hedge-lined corridor that draws our eyes into its depth. But instead of seeing a view of the pond beyond, we see a tree, the Sumiyoshi Pine, that has been planted there to block our view. It is there to *prevent* us from seeing the whole garden at one time.

Compare this to how we normally experience the gardens at Versailles. Standing on the veranda just below the Hall of Mirrors, we look out over a vast area that unfolds in a single glance.

Although there are paths that lead us on, we are tempted to pause where we are standing, high above the seemingly endless vista. The space we see seems to conform to *us*, to our point of view. We do not conform to it. Everything has been carefully arranged to please our eyes, to affirm our fixed point of view. The space is vast; and if our relationship to it is less intimate than in the Japanese garden, here it is more heroic. Even the rectangular pond in the far distance has been altered in order to draw our attention toward a distant vanishing point and to an imagined world beyond the one that we actually see. We think the edges of that water run parallel to each other. But, in fact, they have been skewed to make the pond, and therefore the garden, seem even longer and more impressive. The magnificent view suggests an unalterable, true order. It affirms the spacious garden as a reflection of a transcendental realm that justifies such a concentration of wealth, power, and design. Like the sun images inside the palace, this garden also

Figure 1.12 Versailles, France. Facilitating the large view (photo by Rei Inouye).

symbolizes the glory of Louis XIV, the sun king, and his developing France.

By the twentieth century, Japan will come to envision space in this second, symbolic way. It, too, will be structured by a transcendental, ideological order. As this occurs, Japan will come to look more familiar to Western eyes. And yet, many vestiges of the ancient order of here-and-now will remain. For example, if we consider the house in Kyoto where I am writing this book, we can detect a mixing of these two different kinds of space. As I look out the front window, I see a small garden and a pine tree that leans gracefully over the gate. This tree greets the members of my family as we come home from the world beyond the garden wall. It is a visual marker of a particular kind of space called "home" (*uchi*). Like the sacred *shimenawa* rope that marks off sacred territory, the pine points to what is here, not to what is absent. In fact, the pine is so utterly grounded in space that its assigned role is simply to wait. (The noun for "pine" is *matsu*, and the verb, "to wait," is also *matsu*).

This tree is echoed by another one inside the house. The *tokobashira* is a special, unhewn pillar that marks the most important space in a traditional Japanese home. In the case of this house in Kawashima Chōshi-chō, an unblemished length of crytomeria stands next to the alcove in the sitting room. By well-established convention, it marks meaningful space. When guests come over, I have them sit close to the unhewn tree, and it honors them. Like a shrine gate, it marks importance by delimiting present space. It provides form without referring to a higher symbolic reality.

The alcove next to the *tokobashira* is another important visual marker that forms space by marking importance. It is simply an indentation in the wall. But in this special space the passing of seasons is noted by ever-changing displays of flowers, painting, and calligraphy. Along with the waiting pine and the unhewn pillar, the alcove is also being lost as urban spaces become ever more crowded and costly. That they have survived at all, however, is a notable indication of how deeply rooted the visual order of the here-and-now actually is.

To realize the blended nature of Japanese space is to understand a particularly striking feature of Japanese culture as it made itself manifest during the Tokugawa period. During the centuries-long negotiation between the ancient here-and now and the evolving modern transcendental order, a visual discourse of monstrosity appeared as a resistance to the developing regime of rationalized space. We cannot do justice to this phenomenon in such limited space; but the importance of monsters to Japanese culture needs to be mentioned. For one thing, the rise of monstrosity in the mid- to late Tokugawa period shows us that Japan's own path toward modernization and the birth of realism was not so unlike what had happened in Europe. Urbanization and the consolidation of political power led to the creation of ordering systems of various kinds, including the systems of visuality that we call perspectivalism and realism. But due to its deeply rooted animistic past, Japan saw considerably more resistance to what Edwin Panofsky called perspective's rationalization or conceptualization of space.

The slowness with which the Japanese embraced perspective is well known. Consider this example of a hand-colored woodblock print by Okumura Masanobu (1686–1764). This is an *uki-e*, not an *ukiyoe*. It was inspired by Western perspectival models, and was meant to show volumetric space. Notice how the straight lines of the brothel's interior are brought into alignment in a way that suggests depth. The awkwardness with which the background and the bridge to the left are rendered, however, suggests the difficulty the artist had in trying his hand at this "natural" way of seeing the world. Because the background does not conform to the same visual system as the foreground, we get the impression that the buildings in the distance are located on a steeply rising hill, which then works against the illusion of vastness and unfolding space that Masanobu might have wished to convey. His handling of the bridge also breaks up the visual field into a third plane, which spoils the sense of a single system of realistic, rational vision.

By comparison, Shiba Kōkan's (1747–1818) efforts were more successful. By actually copying Western images, he managed to create a single visual field that expressed the required illusion of depth. By doing so, he accomplished a more systematic and unified way of seeing the world, one that had the effect of giving a new form to evanescence. While *ukiyoe* honored the flatness and availability of the here-and-now, *ukie* employed the kind of symbolic, depth-giving perspective that was found in the Dutch *vedute* or

Figure 1.13 An early attempt at perspective: *Enjoying the Cool at Ryōgoku Bridge* by Okumura Masanobu (courtesy Museum of Fine Arts, Boston, William S. and John T. Spaulding Collection).

single-sheet prints of accentuated perspectival views that were "probably the single largest body of Western visual data arriving in Japan."[187] The vastness of what we see in Kōkan's Westernized views of stilled life create a Versailles-like space, along with its symbolically suggested and infinitely huge metaphysical order. It tempts our eye toward what is beyond the distant, barely visible horizon. Even to images of people, he adds mountains in order to stimulate the viewer to imagine vastness and to consider what might lie beyond the limits of sight. Most importantly, by doing this, he also begins to suggest the thoughtful interiority of the people who are capable of understanding the expanded exteriority of landscape. Here together, then, we have different types of visuality: sight that sees what is present; insight that perceives what is hidden; and foresight that imagines what is possible.

Perspectivalism did not become dominant until after the collapse of the Tokugawa Regime in 1868. For those Europeans who believed in an omniscient, all-seeing God, the usurpation of Divine Vision by the developing modern human imagination seems to have been much easier to accomplish. Iconophobic injunctions against idolatry had already rendered the material world into a representation of a more important immaterial and invisible one; and so it was only a matter of time before all matter came to be seen as the expression of various laws and principles of a higher nature—whether divine, scientific, or humanistic. By contrast, in Tokugawa Japan such cautions against graven images were rare because of the lingering importance of significant space and the affirmation of here-and-now.

The logic of idolatry could not prevail in a world of inherently meaningful space where, as Kitagawa put it, a "nonsymbolic reading of symbols" prevailed. This world did not point to or express a transcendent God or Creator. Rather, it was filled with many gods that were, if anything, all too available. Komatsu Kazuhiko has studied Japan's uncommonly wide range of available beings, and has proposed that those that could be influenced by ritual were considered *kami* (gods) while those that could not were monsters (*yōkai*).[188] The latter were the uncontrollable ones, particularly frightening for this reason. They existed anciently. However, I hasten to repeat that the golden age of these uncontrolled *yōkai* was the mid- to late Tokugawa period rather than an earlier, more devoutly religious era. This suggests that their nature as changing things (*bakemono*) came to be of great interest precisely because their metamorphic aspect did *not* square with a gradually strengthening emphasis on fixed realities—whether the scientific principles of Dutch Studies, Motoori Norinaga's general theory of *mono no aware*, or the positivistic thrust of Neo-Confucianism and natural history (*hakubutsugaku*).

In other words, Japan's fabulous panoply of monsters flourished in the eighteenth- and nineteenth centuries more because of their rationalized status as objects of *expression* than as objects of belief. Their time on the stage was early modern, not premodern, coming at a time of creeping doubt rather than of spreading faith. We can understand such flights of monstrous imagination as increasingly marginalized reactions to the formal strictures of realism. The birth of science brought skepticism to the fore and the reality of *yōkai* into question: there can be no monsters in a rational world. Yet in this increasingly rational environment, the pictocentric Japanese artist could find no better way to account for the ill-fitting bits and pieces of modern life that did not easily conform to this rational or otherwise ideal view of the world.[189]

As time passed, the *yōkai's* lack of actual physical reality came to be rationalized as an imaginative expression of an emotional or psychological state. By the time of Ueda Akinari's (1734–1809) haunting tales of the supernatural—*Tales of Moonlight and Rain* (*Ugetsu monogatari*, 1776) and *Tales of the Spring Rain* (*Harusame monogatari*, 1808–09)—the metaphoric mode of lyricism that had been the mainstay of Japanese poetics since at least the time of Ariwara no Narihira was giving way to a more prosaic realm of realism, as we saw in Ikku's travel novel. Even by the time of Santō Kyōden's (1761–1816) secular versions of monstrous sexuality, the first (and not very convincing) experiments with perspectivalism had already begun.

Of course, the gulf that separates Katsura Detached Palace in Kyoto from the gardens at Versailles should not be exaggerated. As I have already suggested, the propensity to show a small, non-perspectival picture does not mean that the Japanese could not deal with the ideologically structured big picture. Their reception of Buddhism certainly demonstrated an ability to reference this world of constant change against a higher one of unchanging values. But understanding Buddhism was a relatively more manageable task than accepting the viewpoint of perspectival space, partly because Buddhism (as *xiangjiao* or "image teaching" as the Chinese called it) was a figurally rich tradition to begin with, and also because its epistemology required that more space meant more change, not less. In comparison, a more positivistic view of reality favored vastness, or that state of more space as justified by (and expressive of) less change. In short, the big picture has as its source an unchanging, absolute, singular perspective of universal truth.

Over time, detailed observation and description came to require nothing less than both a dramatic disciplining of the visual field and an increasingly one-dimensional understanding of evanescence. As a consequence of both, Japan's famous monsters come to all but disappear for a season. They become rationalized into nonexistence by people such as Inoue Enryō (1858–1919) who ground them into the flour of psychology, in much the way that Sigmund Freud relied on dreams to establish his interpretative discourse of psychological states. Within the march of modernity, monsters become phantasms, manifestations of illness and psychosis. They also come to be tagged as belonging to a disappearing regime of traditional and, therefore, backward sentiment.

The fate of these changelings as reactions to the onset of modernity is highly significant for our study of Japanese culture, because their eventual demise will signal nothing less than a thorough melding of the order of here-and-now with the transcendental order. What we are about to see, as the Tokugawa period ends and the Meiji period (1868–1912) begins, is a linking of these two realms in a way that brings together etiquette and ideology. As propriety joins hands with patriotism, Japan will become one of the most cohesive, coherent, and, yes, brutally violent societies the world has ever known.

PART TWO

CHANGE UNDER THE TRANSCENDENTAL ORDER: LATE MODERN JAPAN (1868–1970)

THE COLONIAL CONTEXT: ADAPT OR DIE

For most of my students, Japan begins to seem more familiar from this point forward. This is because a great influx of Western culture flooded the country in the wake of the Meiji Restoration (1868). The era thought of itself as a time of reform (*kaikaku*) and of "civilization and enlightenment" (*bunmei kaika*). Importantly, both of these values were seen as inspired by the Western examples. Yet, as profound as these influences were, Japan did not simply and completely become Western. For one thing, its ability to respond positively to outside influence was largely a result of its own well-established base of modern institutions, which would include a sense of itself as a viable cultural community. During the Tokugawa period, bureaucracies had formed, transportation systems had developed, standardized language and standardized markets had emerged, capital formation had begun, positivism had started to make itself felt, wide-reaching educational institutions had developed, and, importantly, various forms of mass media had been deployed, thus giving impetus to the establishment of mass society. A second, more general reason to avoid conflating modern and Western is that the process of absorbing foreign influences characterized *all* cultures that were modernizing at this point in time, including Western ones. Sharing was important, because modern conscious developed in response to conceptions of the Other—regardless of whether those reactions were sympathetic or hostile. Finally, a third point to consider is that, despite the scale of change that occurred in these modernizing countries, many of the things that made them culturally different from each other remained influential. This is clear in the case of Japan, as we shall see.

Having said this, I will also admit that the nearly complete colonization of Asia by the West suggests that Westernization occurred far more forcefully than I have just expressed. Even when taking the march of colonialism into account, however, we must recognize that Japan (along with Thailand) was able to resist becoming a colony of a Western foreign power partly because it was able to maintain important connections with its cultural past. Why was this possible? Why was Japan able to modernize yet resist colonization when larger, wealthier, more powerful countries such as China were unable to do so?

A great amount of work has been done on this question. Some point to Japan's geographic isolation, to its being off the beaten path of imperialism, a path that ran directly to China's great wealth. Some have also considered the value of its martial traditions, or the institution of Dutch Learning that taught the Japanese how to respect Western power and respond to it with care and speed. One other possible explanation that speaks directly to our analysis of evanescence and form is that Japan's appreciation of change actually helped it embrace necessary reforms. Did sensitivity to the truth of evanescence encourage the Japanese to make the difficult choices that other cultural systems failed to accommodate in a timely fashion? Does this responsiveness to change explain why the new leaders of Meiji Japan distanced themselves from their earlier, clearly xenophobic position of shunning the Western world, a policy that helped them rise to power in the first place? As mentioned, the anti-Tokugawa rebels first promised to "Cast Out the Barbarians." Once in power, however, they decided to "Learn from the West." This abrupt change in policy seems to have made a decisive difference in Japan's survivability.

The utter convenience and hypocrisy of this about-face did not escape the critical eye of the comic writer Kanagaki Robun (1829–94), who in his *Sitting around the Boiling Pot* (*Agura nabe*, 1871) pointed out the ways in which his fellow countrymen were, if anything, too quick to change.

> We really should be grateful that people like us can eat beef now, thanks to the fact that Japan is fast become a truly civilized country. Of course, there are always those boors who cling to barbaric superstitions and say that eating meat makes you unworthy to pray to the Buddha or to the gods. But that just shows they don't know a thing about natural philosophy. Savages like that should be forced to read Fukuzawa Yukichi's essay on the virtues of eating beef. In the West they're free of superstitions. They do everything scientifically, and that's why they've invented such amazing machines as the steamship and the locomotive.[1]

Here, Robun makes fun of Japan's accommodation of the West as faddish and superficial. But we must wonder just how well he understood earlier, similar moments of cross-cultural learning. We have only to recall the great importation of Confucianism or Buddhism. For all their influence, they do not seem to have overwhelmed what we have been calling a native regard for the here-and-now. As for Japan's ability to be quick to adapt, we might note Oda Nobunaga's fondness for Portuguese clothing or Izumo no Okuni's wearing of the crucifix. In short, the Meiji-period adoption of new influences was not exactly new.

As it had done earlier, Japan once again allowed itself to adapt quickly to new ideas and to new objects. What might actually be singularly true about cultural borrowing during the Meiji and Taishō (1912–25) periods, however, is the duress that marked this newest wave of influence from abroad—whether from Europe or America. Described dramatically, life in the nineteenth century became a matter of adapt or die, colonize or be colonized.

One result of this threatening atmosphere was that Japan's understanding of change became considerably more linear and goal oriented. In other words, change became dominated by a progressive vector that asserted a focused and at times even monomaniacal orientation. Offering something that was, by its own definition, better than before, modernity ensured a brighter future than what the benighted or traditional past had offered. Indeed, modern progress needed to establish a foil—namely, the backwardness of Tokugawa culture—in order to press ahead.

As already suggested, progress is one of many kinds of change. Unlike evanescence in general, it has a specific direction. It expresses intention. It is pointed. It would seem, therefore, to be antithetical to *utsusemi*, dismissive of *hakanasa*, and unappreciative of *mujō*. Rather than focus on bubbles drifting haphazardly upon the river of change, the rhetoric of progress comes to fixate upon the current itself. Nationalism, colonialism, and imperialism, therefore, emerge with a built-in metric and an eagerness to refer to it constantly. Their progress measures reality so that progress becomes reality. Rather than simply dream about this or that, progressive vision accomplishes this or that. Of course, whether random or structured in this linear way, both kinds of dreaming flow from the same assumption of change.

What has, in fact, changed about change, however, is that modernity came to affirm it massively. Modern culture is mass culture. Consequently, for those living in Meiji Japan, a general consensus needed to form around many issues. Economic development had to happen. Japan needed to become a nation of loyal citizens. The countryside needed to contribute to the development of the cities. The samurai class had to be abolished, and their privilege of bearing arms had to be given to large citizen armies. As modernity entered a more mature phase, the nation had to agree to fight costly wars of expansion. Everyone needed to share an identity and to send the same message to the rest of the world: Japan was no longer an impoverished string of islands in the Pacific but an empire that deserved colonies of its own.

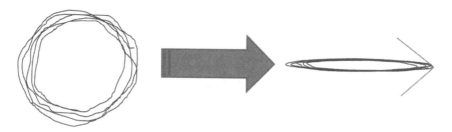

Figure 2.1   A consequence of modernity: from *samsara* to progress.

Even if the Japanese could not foretell the nightmarish consequences of modernity's full development, from at least as early as the final decades of the Tokugawa period, they could not avoid becoming aware of the assertive nature of progress. The appearance of Russians from the north, Americans from the east, and Western Europeans from the south could no longer be ignored nor prevented. Their encroachment forced a comparison and, therefore, a moment of true cultural crisis: for now the world beyond Japan mattered in a way that required the Japanese to change their conception of space itself. This new way of thinking would eventually render Japanese space, along with the order of here-and-now, a relative rather than absolute source of meaning and identity. In short, Japan would become a part of (world) space rather than the definition of space itself.

As this change occurred, spatial form gradually came to be nearly supplanted by discursive forms of explanation and theory. Identity-giving space—what we have been calling the order of here-and-now—could no longer supply a fully satisfying answer to "Who am I?" The era of isolation was over, and the age of positioning Japan in a more abstract, conceptual, and contextual way began. Like other developing nations, Japan needed to make its position within the suddenly and greatly expanded context of competing nations viable and current. In addition to the many customs that had once shown a person how to be defined by Japanese space, something more— such as the famous journalist Fukuzawa Yūkichi's reasons for eating of beef— became necessary. In sum, Japan now needed a rationale, a complement of expository language to give it a place within a largely expanded world. For this to happen, reference not to this or that tree or stone but to this or that concept or principle was required.

Here, then, begins what we might call Japan's Age of the Transcendental Order, a period that starts in the so-called *bakumatsu* era (or the end of the Regime) and continues through to the end of World War II. The final decades of the Tokugawa period were marked by turbulent and even millenarian revolt. Weakened by natural disaster, the period was also one of numerous social disasters. That the Tokugawa order experienced significant decline is indicated by the increasing frequency of popular rebellions (*ikki*). Whether we agree with Hattori Shisō, who argues that the many outbreaks of violence and disorder that occurred from 1852 to 1867 were the result of a forming class consciousness, or with Motoyama Yukiko, who explains the unrest as a less politically conscious fiscal collapse caused by increased expenditures for defense that the coming of the foreigners made necessary, we must agree that the final years of Tokugawa rule were unstable and even apocalyptic.[2]

The end of Japan's putative isolation came decisively in 1854, with the (second) arrival of America's Commodore Matthew Perry. His fleet entered the bay near Edo and forcefully advanced straight into the wind. In essence, this steam-powered intrusion forced the Japanese to connect the domestic order of here-and-now with a larger, abstract "world order." In this process, Japan became a small part of a larger whole that was so vast and varied that its entirety could not be seen without a stretching of the imagination. Within this necessarily more abstractly understood world, Japan itself needed to be rendered into a compatibly conceptual form, into a theoretical essence or *genri*. Its values and cultural practices had to be defined and translated in a way that would yield comparative value: in a manner that would make international exchange possible, and that would allow the nation to survive in a context of many competing nations. In short, Japan suddenly had to make sense to foreigners who did not intuitively and lyrically understand Japanese space.

Spain, England, France, Russia, the United States, Germany, Holland—at this same time there were other rapidly modernizing nations in the world, all of them potentially threatening to any space that did not own a clear and defensible concept of itself as a coherent political unity. Stirred by this new vulnerability, the late Tokugawa intellectual, Aizawa Seishisai (1782–1863), came up with the secret that allowed Europeans to both form into nations and to take control of other peoples' lands. Ostensibly, they came to trade. But what they really wanted was to occupy and to possess. What made it possible for them to do so? "Does their wisdom and courage exceed that of ordinary men? Is their government so benevolent that they win popular support? Are their rites, music, laws, and political institutions superb in all respects? Do they possess some superhuman, divine powers? Hardly. Christianity is the sole key to their success."[3]

Aizawa saw Christianity as a religion founded upon the principle that all people are equal in the eyes of God. To him, this notion was both a clever deceit and a highly effective weapon. It posed no small threat to Japan because of its irresistible appeal to the lower classes. It taught them the seductive fiction that all people universally deserve God's love, and that this love is a power greater than the authority of a local samurai, a daimyō, a shōgun, or even an emperor. "Its main doctrines are simple to grasp and well-contrived; they can easily deceive stupid commoners with it."[4]

When had there ever been such an emphasis on equality in Tokugawa Japan? Had the inherently unequal status of people not been the solid Confucian bedrock of the Tokugawa regime? Corrosive to the hierarchical Neo-Confucian order and oblivious to the identity-giving manners of Japan's very orderly, civilized, and polite society, Christianity was a barbaric poison. It dangerously turned thoughts to heaven, rather than keeping them earthbound and focused upon Japan's "beautiful customs." "The barbarians believe it their god's will that they seduce other peoples into subverting their respective homelands; they borrow the slogan 'universal love' to achieve their desired ends. Barbarian armies seek only plunder, but do so in the name of their god."[5] When placed within a larger context of powerful nations and the Spencerian process of the survival of the fittest, it was precisely this abstract way of considering the world that gave Europeans and Americans the intellectual justification to subjugate one Asian civilization after another.

As Aizawa pondered Japan's dangerous new context, he formed an arresting analogy. The world was like the human body. Its head was Japan. And its ass? "The country they call America is located at the rear end of the world, so its inhabitants are stupid and incompetent."[6] Why are Americans the butt of all? According to Aizawa, the inferiority of both Europeans and Americans followed from how they violated the order of space. They were "the thighs, legs, and feet of the universe" because they did not know how to stay put.[7] In other words, they did not know their place, which is to say, they had no appreciation of the order of here-and-now. They were not, therefore, properly defined. Their world was not the teahouse nor the alcove, but something more vast and conceptual: the ocean, the territories. Appealing to abstract, textually transmitted notions rather than to the humble experience of identity-giving space, they traveled the world over, taking their books, their ideas, and their identity with them.

Aizawa's second argument for Japan's superiority was also spatial and concrete. Japan was better than other nations of the world because it grew the best rice. "Amaterasu obtained the best rice seeds, and desired to nurture Her people with them, so she planted them in Her august rice field."[8] While this point might seem laughably provincial, now that we appreciate the Japanese understanding of space, the assertion is actually meaningful.

Emiko Ohnuki-Tierney has studied the role of rice in the formation of Japanese identity.[9] Rice grown in paddies has been Japan's staple crop since before the beginning of historical time. As sustenance and as a traditional measure of wealth, rice still has heightened importance today. Consider the heated negotiations that took place during the late 1970s when California's rice growers pressed to have their crop exported to Japan. The Japanese put forward various objections, but the one most relevant to our discussion was the sacredness of the homegrown crop. Understandably, this argument carried little weight with Californian growers; yet from a cultural point of view, the sentiment is not ridiculous. Even today, the emperor performs a rice-planting ceremony each spring as a part of his sacred duties. *Sake* is still used in weddings and other important ritual moments, and is considered to be *the* Japanese wine, *Nihon shu* (日本酒). Cakes made of pounded rice are still important to New Year's ritual decorations, and mounds of freshly cooked rice are still one of the principal offerings that Buddhist families place before their ancestors' tablets in the family altar. Changing this rice offering was a family ritual that my grandmother taught me when I was a young boy.

This rice-versus-Christianity comparison reveals two very different ways that cultural identity accrues. One forms concretely and visibly. The other forms abstractly and invisibly. Indeed, one way to explain the cultural crisis that occurred toward the end of the Tokugawa period is to say that the more concrete mode of space-based identity was suddenly rendered "backward" by the "progressive" conceptualizations that brought the West knocking on Japan's door. What once passed as a cultivated person's proper context in real space became abstracted and contextualized by a larger, ideological framework. Consequently, life became atomized within a suddenly expanded world that gave all things structure and meaning by way of various systems of unchanging principles. As modernity continued to develop, these abstract systems came to dominate the concrete truth of rice. So what we can say about Japanese rice in the 1970s might be said about Japan in the 1860s: when Japan suddenly entered the wider context of world markets, much of what was once sacred quickly lost its ritual value. Rice took on a commercial, comparative meaning within the metrics of capitalism. As it did, the order of here-and-now became destabilized by the wide reach of portable ideologies, not just the Christianity that Aizawa feared, but also capitalism, nationalism, imperialism, socialism, and so on.

One place where these two modes of identification came together to produce something that had never been a part of Japanese culture before was the twelve-storey Ryōunkaku, or "Cloud Scraper" that was built in the Asakusa district of Tokyo in 1890. Designed by the Scottish engineer, William Kinninmond Burton, this towering building rose 225 feet into the air and, now that the Edo Castle tower had been destroyed in the fighting that attended the Meiji Restoration, was far taller than any other building in the capital. Designed to be a showcase of world space, the tower introduced the Japanese masses to a larger, international context. It did this by way of representative objects, and by way of the new perspective on Japanese space that the exaggerated height of the structure allowed.

On the first floor was the entrance. The second through seventh floors housed forty-six shops that sold goods from all over the world. On the eighth floor was a lounge, a place to rest before continuing the journey upward. The ninth was an exhibition space, where paintings, photographs, and other objects were displayed. Finally, the tenth through twelfth floors were observation decks that afforded visitors a panoramic perspective of the city of Tokyo (no longer called Edo) and beyond. In short, the Ryōunkaku was a new kind of Japanese space that challenged the traditional limits of concrete, identity-giving space by drawing a visitor's attention to, first, foreign countries and their representative objects then, second, to the space of Japan that now included the sprawling city and more. From atop the Ryōunkaku, one could even begin to imagine a third kind of "imperial" space, beyond the distant horizon of one's actual vision.

The tower was not only emblematic of a fixed yet expansive modern point of view, but it also established just such a view. It allowed one to see all that there is to see, and then enticed them to see more. It afforded a fixed and uniting perspective, such as the one we considered in our earlier discussion of Versailles. As the one structure that could be seen from every quarter of the city, the tower became a singularly obvious, even symbolic, landmark; but it was also the one place from which it was possible to see everything else. In short, the Ryōunkaku was an enticement to explore and to expand. It was an attempt to redefine space by way of a projection of cultural essences that, being abstract and unchangeable, were the appropriate means to force modern change upon the rest of the world. By learning how to share this expanded view of space, and, along with it, an even more willful, linear understanding of change that had been slowly developing since at least as early as the failed invasions of Korea by Hideyoshi's troops toward the end of the sixteenth century, Japan adapted enough to survive.

EXPLAINING JAPAN: LINKING HERE-AND-NOW WITH THE NEW WORLD ORDER

As was happening in other parts of the modernizing world, the space of various locales (*kuni* 郡) became atomized parts of larger concept units, such as nations (*kokka*, 国家) and empires (*teikoku*, 帝国). If designing and building architectural structures such as the Ryōunkaku was one way to accomplish this transition, another was the use of slogans, which similarly encouraged the Japanese to imagine a new kind of world by way of a few powerful concepts. Easily remembered and repeated, words such as "Civilization and Enlightenment" (*bunmei kaika*) and "Rich Country, Strong Army" (*fukoku kyōhei*) became a ubiquitous part of Meiji-period life. These four-character sayings rendered a vision of Japan into a few easily remembered and repeatable words. They were one of many steps taken to textualize the Japanese experience, or, stated otherwise, to tie all thoughts and feelings to a particular ideological order that had as its goal the construction of Japan as a credible modern nation.[10] To this end, nothing less than the forging of a new relationship between the order of here-and-now and the transcendental order of Truth was required.

The new Japan became a space in which a massive, systematic, and thorough correspondence between etiquette and ideology took place. Like other modern nations, Japan too would have to be imagined into existence. Its folk would also have to become citizens by way of certain commonly held notions that made everyone think they belonged to each other even if their experiences in different provinces of the islands were considerably different.[11] Those common modernizing notions were nation, empire, race, and so on. All these "spaces" were conceived conceptually. Yet all were packaged as aspects of Japanese custom, old acts newly employed to take on this more abstract, symbolic meaning.

The single most important symbol of Japan was the Meiji Emperor himself. Past emperors had not played an active political role for centuries. But Mutsuhito actually became an integral part of the new political system. To understand the process by which he came to be the very embodiment of the constructed nation is to grasp the general outlines of Japan's late modern culture and the nature of evanescence and form in their new, "enlightened" manifestation.

At the dawn of this new era, the emperor was largely invisible to the common people. His residence was removed from theirs. Only a small portion of the population interacted with him. Yet because he was an obvious source of here-and-now identity, his usefulness to the Meiji oligarchs was too obvious to be left alone. In order to establish his utility as a unifying symbol of the new nation, he was sent out on a number of excursions to meet the

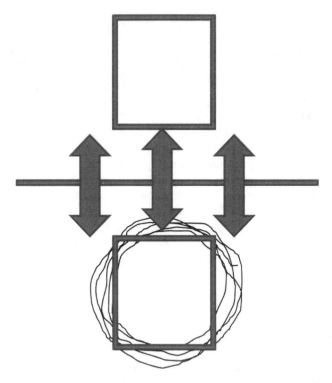

Figure 2.2 Joining the order of here-and-now with the transcendental order.

people. Upon seeing him in the flesh, they were able to identify him as their leader, a point of commonality. Once this relationship was established, he again retreated from the public eye; and in his place was created a more abstract version of imperial power. Photographs were taken of his portrait, and these images were mass produced and sent to every corner of the land. Japanese schoolchildren grew up learning to honor and adore the nation by honoring and adoring this image.[12] On ceremonial occasions, the usually veiled photograph would be uncovered, and those present would shout in unison, "Long Live the Emperor!" (*Tenno Heika, Banzai*). Needless to say, ten thousand years, "banzai," was hardly meant to be an affirmation of evanescence.

Largely by way of this apotheosis of the emperor as an *unchanging* and *lasting* essence of the nation, Japanese political culture gained a stable, authoritative point of view and, therefore, a perspective on the world by which the struggling nation could systematically express and extend the unified and unifying truth of its own culturally correct version of modernity. Couched in semiotic terms, the emperor became the head signifier, or the sign by which all other subjects of the nation took their orientation. As the point of view from which the vastness of the Japanese nation could be seen, he was not so unlike the Ryōunkaku that towered over the capital.

Another way that the space of here-and-now became linked with the transcendental, abstract order was through the creation of a scripture-like text and by the establishment of a scriptural habit. By the 1880s, the initial enthusiasm for all things Western began to cool; and a revival of Confucianism occurred. Largely through the efforts of the emperor's tutor, Motoda Eifu (1818–91), an Imperial Rescript on Education was issued in 1890. With it, a massive text-based protocol was born, perhaps for the first time in Japan's history. To be sure, other texts had been studied, just as other words had been copied and printed. Still other words had also been chanted, leading to the popularization of Buddhism in Japan, as we have seen. In late modern Japan, however, no single text so powerfully and intentionally bestowed identity upon its readers as this Confucian statement about the officially recognized purpose of learning. All schoolchildren memorized and routinely recited its words. From it, they learned truthful connections between themselves and the State. They imbibed the principles that would justify Japan's rightful place within the newly expanded context of competing nations.

Here is an English translation of this modern scripture.

Know ye, Our subjects:

Our Imperial Ancestors have founded Our Empire on a basis broad and ever-lasting and have deeply and firmly implanted virtue; Our subjects ever united in loyalty and filial piety have from generation to generation illustrated the beauty thereof. This is the glory of the fundamental character of Our Nation, and herein also lies the source of Our education.

Ye, Our subjects, be filial to your parents, affectionate to your brothers and sisters; as husbands and wives be harmonious, as friends true; bear yourselves in modesty and moderation; extend your benevolence to all; pursue learning and cultivate its application, and thereby develop intellectual ability and per-fect moral powers; furthermore, advance public good and promote common interests; always respect the Constitution and observe the law; should emer-gency arise, offer yourselves courageously to the State; and thus guard and maintain the prosperity of Our Imperial Throne coeval with heaven and earth. So shall ye not only be Our good and faithful subjects, but shall also render illustrious the best traditions of your forefathers.

The Way here set forth is indeed the teaching bequeathed by Our Imperial Ancestors, to be observed together with Our Descendants and Subjects, with-out fail in all ages, whether at home or abroad. It is Our wish to lay it to heart in all reverence, in common with you, Our subjects, that we may thus attain to the same virtue.

The 30th day of the 10th month of the 23rd year of Meiji. (October 30, 1890)[13]

What has become of evanescence? Could an emphasis on permanence be any clearer? With the propagation of such a text, the sacred was clearly meant to be that which does *not* change, and never had. The basis of the modern empire is "everlasting"; and its virtue is "deeply and firmly implanted." Japan's citizens are "ever united" and beautiful "from generation to generation."

We also cannot help but notice how the private is wedded to the public. Love of parents, siblings, and spouses becomes the "public good" and the nation's "common interests." Similarly, the physical and metaphysical are joined together by way of the Imperial Throne that links "heaven and earth." Again, this linkage of practice and ideal occurred because Japan was no longer able to be a space unto itself. From this point forward, the nation was to become thoroughly conceptualized, so the "Way" of the Japanese people could become "infallible for all ages and true in all places." Finally, in this more abstract form, Japaneseness could travel undiminished beyond the borders of Japanese space, a necessary condition if Japan was to have its own empire.

It was this Imperial Rescript that my grandfather recited as a schoolboy in the mountains of northern Kyushu in the 1890s. These words taught him to be loyal to the emperor and, by extension, to the nation of Japan even after moving to the United States. In turn, my father attended a Japanese language school in northern California in the 1920s in order to learn the same loyalty. He stood before a similar Imperial image, and recited portions of the passage quoted earlier. He was educated to be Japanese "in all places." Because of their portability, both the emperor's portrait and the Rescript on Education allowed Japanese identity (which was now as mobile as Christian, Jewish, or Moslem identity) to travel beyond the actual space of the divine nation for the first time. On the other hand, precisely because loyalty to an imagined place far away had become possible, my grandfather and father were eventually relocated from their home in Menlo Park, California, and sent to a concentration camp in Wyoming following the bombing of Pearl Harbor in 1941. There in Heart Mountain they were asked to declare their loyalty, either to Japan or to the United States. It had to be one or the other, since more than one modernity could not be true and universal at the same time. If someone was right, someone else had to be wrong. This was the aggressive, even deadly logic of modernity.

At a meeting held prior to their declarations of loyalty, my father addressed his fellow prisoners. "All our lives, we've been told to be loyal to the Emperor. But can any one here name one specific thing the Emperor has ever done for us?" As the story goes, there were people lying in wait for my father as he returned from the meeting that night. They were ready to kill him for the blasphemous things he had said against the emperor. Fortunately, there were also those who were willing to protect him, and so he made it safely back to his barrack. My grandfather, who had already heard reports about what had happened, was waiting for him. He delivered strong words to his son. "What do you think you're doing? How could you say such things? If you ever speak out against the Emperor again, I'll cut my belly open and die." ("*Hara wo kitte, shinu zo.*") Such was the tremendous cultural force of the here-and-now, as bound to the universe of abstract ideals.

JAPAN AS BUSHIDŌ

Nine years after the Rescript on Education was issued, Nitobe Inazō (1862–1933)—a broadly educated, well-traveled, cosmopolitan intellectual of the kind that the Meiji Enlightenment with its injunction to learn from the West had produced—published a book on Japanese culture that became an international "runaway best-seller."[14] Written in English for the purpose of answering his non-Japanese friends' many questions about enigmatic Japanese life, *Bushido, the Soul of Japan: An Exposition of Japanese Thought* (1890) began with a familiar image: "Chivalry is a flower no less indigenous to the soil of Japan than its emblem, the cherry blossom."[15]

Nitobe defined chivalry to be the principal quality of bushidō, literally, the way (*dō*) of the warrior (*bushi*), that by extension came to be considered by many at the time to be "an authoritative description of the Japanese character."[16] Interestingly, in essentializing the Japanese, Nitobe did not emphasize the fleeting and fragile nature of cherry blossoms, but the durability of samurai values and practice: just as cherry blossoms have always been around, so has the spirit of bushidō. Not only this, but he presented bushidō as an "unformulated...animating spirit, the motor force of our country"[17] that is "an ethical *system*."[18] In denying the evanescence of this blossom-like virtue, Nitobe also felt the need to deny its spatial ties to the here-and-now. Under his authorship, it becomes an abstract system that exists unquestionably and undeniably as an ideal.

Nitobe claims that the defining code of Japanese identity had not yet been written down.[19] It was not yet a text, not yet an ideology, not yet rendered into scripture. He would make it all of these things. That was his job as a world intellectual: to textualize practice, and to provide a systematic conceptualization of Japanese life in order to explain (and to describe) Japan to the foreign Other. In so doing, he would also be explaining Japan to itself, a task made necessary by its having been so recently and vulnerably opened to the rest of the world. In short, Nitobe responded to how the new context of Japan's identity required Nihon to become a homeland rather than just a home. In order to be imagined correctly, Japan required the perspective and authority of the *author*, who might comprehend the brave, new world as a system, a community given reason and order by way of clearly knowable and fixed (that is to say, realistic and true) principles.

Still, a tension between traditional and modern, or between Japan the unique and Japan the universal, is apparent in Nitobe's treatment of the samurai code. For while he tries to explain bushidō as a general system, he insists that the warrior's spirit is utterly particular and local, grounded like a cherry tree in the soil of Japan.

> Yes, the *sakura* has for ages been the favourite of our people and the emblem of our character.... The Yamato spirit is not a tame, tender plant, but a wild—in the sense of natural—growth; it is indigenous to the soil; its accidental qualities it may share with the flowers of other lands, but in its essence it remains the original, spontaneous outgrowth of our clime. But its nativity is not its sole claim to our affection. The refinement and grace of its beauty appeal to *our* aesthetic sense as no other flower can [Nitobe's emphasis]. We cannot share the admiration of the Europeans for their roses, which lack the simplicity of our flower. Then, too, the thorns that are hidden beneath the sweetness of the rose, the tenacity with

which she clings to life, as though loath or afraid to die rather than drop untimely, preferring to rot on her stem; her showy colours and heavy odours—all these are traits so unlike our flower, which carries no dagger or poison under its beauty, which is ever ready to depart life at the call of nature, whose colours are never gorgeous, and whose light fragrance never palls....When the delicious perfume of the sakura quickens the morning air, as the sun in its course rises to illumine first the isles of the Far East, few sensations are more serenely exhilarating than to inhale, as it were, the very breath of beauteous day.[20]

Like *sakura*, bushidō is also one of a kind, "a teaching so circumscribed and unique, engendering a cast of mind and character so peculiar, so local, [that it] must wear the badge of its singularity on its face...."[21] How then, we must ask, can it serve as a viable system for anyone except those living within Japan itself?

Trapped by this simultaneous pull toward both universality and particularity, Nitobe concludes that bushidō—with its emphasis on justice, courage, benevolence, politeness, sincerity, honor, loyalty, practical education, and self-control—will die as a system *even in Japan* (now that is has been swallowed by a larger world context), but will nevertheless survive as a part of some larger moral force. It will become subsumed within larger evolutionary forces that, he hopes, will continue to move Japan from Confucian benevolence, on to Buddhist compassion, and finally to Christian love, which he holds to be the apex of human morality. (Needless to say, in his converting to Christianity, Nitobe imbibed the very foreign poisons that Aizawa Seishisai so feared.) When placed within the larger global context of competing international cultures—"Christianity versus materialism," as Nitobe finally puts it—bushidō's lack of a textual basis guarantees its demise. This was an age when far-reaching textual cultures overwhelmed local, non-textual ones.

Are we to understand this as the end of Japan itself? Could Japan only become what the wider world's way of generalizing essences required it to be? In the way of conclusion, Nitobe ends with a touch of fatalism, suggesting a poignant frost and the winter to come.

Having no set dogma or formula to defend, [bushidō] can afford to disappear as an entity; like the cherry blossom, it is willing to die at the first gust of the morning breeze, it is dead as a system, but alive as a virtue.[22]

Like its symbolic flower, after it is blown to the four winds, it will still bless mankind with the perfume with which it will enrich life...its odours will come floating in the air as from a far-off, unseen hill...[23]

The last line is an obvious reference to Motoori Norinaga's poem about the cherry blossom essence of the Japanese spirit.

Shikishima no	Should someone ask,
Yamatogokoro wo	"What is the soul
Hito towaba	Of Yamato, our ancient land?"
Asahi ni niou	It is scent of mountain cherry blossoms
Yamazakurabana.[24]	In the morning sun.

In fact, Nitobe provides his own translation of this poem, along with an explication of the special status of cherry blossoms.

> Isles of blest Japan!
> Should your Yamato spirit
> Strangers seek to scan,
> Say—scenting morn's sunlit air,
> Blows the cherry wild and fair!

> Yes, the sakura has for ages been the favourite of our people and the emblem of our character. Mark particularly the terms of definition which the poet uses, the words *the wild cherry flower scenting the morning sun.* [Nitobe's emphasis]
> The Yamato spirit is not a tame, tender plant, but a wild—in the sense of natural—growth; it is indigenous to the soil; its accidental qualities it may share with the flowers of other lands, but in its essence it remains original, spontaneous outgrowth of our clime.[25]

Here Nitobe is emphasizing particularity—the uniqueness of the cherry blossom and Japan. But note how he also tries to give this particularity a universal validity, striving to have it both ways at the same time. Thus, as *symbolized* by the cherry blossom, bushidō is evanescent yet universal, a fleeting fragrance that will somehow return, as from "a far-off, unseen hill."

   Why has this source of Japanese fragrance become unseen and far away? Is this not the result of Nitobe's perspectival vision—his literary version of what the Cloud Scrapers taught to anyone who climbed its steps? Notice how Nitobe takes the eye far beyond what is merely local and concretely present to imagine much more. With this assertion of an authoritative, far-seeing point of view come vanishing points and marginal areas, aspects of the vastness that have come to include Japan and its abstracted culture of blossoms and warriors. In this new contextual way of seeing, Japan's particular cultural traits become transformed into universal principles; and ethnicity becomes aestheticized as a truthful perfume that enriches life *for all.* At the same time, that which does not naturally fit within this world in which the particular has become universal—as bushidō becomes a truthful way of life in general—becomes dismissed as marginal or gets lost in the vastness altogether.

   Nitobe would probably have been alarmed to see that his cultural critique of the warrior spirit generated the principles by which genocidal conflicts were later justified. In his own day, he probably had little conception of what Walter Benjamin later formulated as the essence of fascist thought and behavior: when art informs politics with an aesthetic of purity and the beautifully ideal, resulting in the fury that insists violently on making the entire world uniformly good and beautiful.[26] In this process of beautification, impurities must be eliminated. Yet Nitobe confidently quotes Burke in speaking of the necessary atomization of the (fictive) subject in modern society—"that proud submission, that dignified obedience, that subordination of heart which kept alive, even in servitude itself, the spirit of exalted freedom."[27] In his enthusiasm for "proud submission," could Nitobe have predicted that the fleeting cherry blossom would, in fact, become part of a political system of aestheticized politics that posited Japan's emperor as "the bodily representative of heaven on earth"?[28] Could he have anticipated that "the universal politeness of the Japanese people"[29] and the gestures that are similarly the "bodying forth"[30] of thoughtful feelings, these elements of the form of here-and-now, would lock hands with ideology in a way that eventually would create the concept of *kokutai* (the body of the nation, 国体). With this formation, the concrete organization of Japan became an abstract truth of divine superiority.

Especially for the sons of farmers who joined the Imperial Army, bushidō represented an important cluster of values. The privilege of wielding weapons, once limited to the samurai class, was justified by it. Bushidō also eased the dangers of putting themselves in harm's way for the sake of the nation. As for families who once belonged to the samurai class, Nitobe's words must have been an equally valued reminder of past glories. My grandfather occasionally spoke of the days before the Restoration when he saw his grandfather dressed in a formal kimono, wearing his long and short swords. Even after moving to America, he often told stories of Minamoto no Yoshitsune, who thus became a family hero, an example of the principles of loyalty and sacrifice that he wanted to pass on to his children, and to his children's children.

Surely, general feelings of belonging mattered just as much as any of the particulars of samurai behavior. Living in a city that celebrates the "Red Sox Nation," my students do not have a hard time grasping the attractions of surrendering oneself to a larger cause. I ask them,

> Who doesn't like to win? And who hasn't felt the thrill of belonging to a group that takes us in and accepts our "proud submission"? Isn't this what fraternities do? Isn't this what universities do in selecting a student body? You might say that it's one thing to be loyal to a sports team and quite another to be loyal to a country; and you would be right, of course. But isn't the basic emotion pretty much the same?

What Nitobe said of the Japanese person as an individual would later be said of the Japanese people as a whole. They became the "bodying forth" of the military spirit that led to the disasters of the 1930s and 1940s: "...by constant exercise in correct manners, one brings all the parts and faculties of his body into perfect order and into such harmony with itself and its environment as to express the mastery of spirit over the flesh."[31]

Although the context has changed considerably, this is yet another articulation of being in the moment, being at one with all—which now means being one in a profoundly political, ideological way. Thus united, the modern Japanese citizen would consider no sacrifice too onerous. Bushidō placed the sons of peasants squarely on the modern grid. It empowered them so that no goal would be impossible, no sacrifice too great, no lack of resources too dire, no destruction of the enemy too cruel. For in the widened context of the modern world, the fragrance of cherry blossoms now came not from the tree planted deeply in Japanese soil but from beyond the hill, just beyond the horizon of the ever-expanding Japanese empire.

This had been the case from at least as early as 1895, when Japan fought and won its first war of expansion against China. To celebrate the victory, a national celebration was held in Ueno Park. Four hundred thousand people gathered to celebrate. It was here that the *symbolic* linking of cherry blossoms with empire was made clear. The foreign correspondent James Creelman describes this turning point:

> The scene in Uyeno Park was one of strange and never-to-be-forgotten beauty.... Fantastic maskers danced under the shadows of gnarled and twisted pines; thrilling sounds of singing filled the air, and from a thick grove came the long, sweet booming of a hidden bell.
>
> Old Japan, with her top-knotted men and her child-women—graceful, poetic, innocent Japan—rustled and glided about in waves of color and life; and high above the heads of the joyous multitudes were the mimic heads of Chinamen swinging from poles—ghastly reminders of the scenes I had left behind me.
>
> The crown prince was there, and the nobles of Japan, and as the vast processions moved along they sang the new ode written by the Japanese poet, Fukushi:—
>
>> Across the rolling waves of the ocean to a far distant land.
>> Confronted by the Imperial intelligence of our great lord, by the invincible hosts of our warriors,—who can hope to conquer?
>> *Refrain:*
>> Teikoku banzai! banbanzai!
>> Flag of the morning sun;
>> Flag of the morning sun;
>> By thy favor we have multiplied the glory of our land; we have pressed forward with speed.
>> The strongholds of the enemy have fallen continuously; the ships of the enemy have been ground to powder. The war has been victory upon victory. To our sunland there is no parallel in the world.
>> We have but one spirit of loyalty. Even to boys and maidens, if for thy [the Emperor's] sake, we are ready to die; for the sake of our country we grudge not our bodies.
>> O Mountain Cherry! send out thy perfume in the morning sun.[32]

With emphasis now on its invisible fragrance, cherry blossoms are no longer simply and concretely grounded in the soil of "old Japan." They become a boundless symbol of a newly expanding Japanese empire.

Japan as Tea-Ism

As Japan continued to struggle to find a place in the wider world of competing nations, the need for other explanations and for other essential Japanese traits continued. Like Nitobe Inazō, Okakura Kakuzō (1862–1913), another cosmopolitan intellectual who attempted to explain Japan to the West, also struggled to see Japan as both particularly respectable and universally valid. His widely admired *Book of Tea* (1906), like Nitobe's popular *Bushido*, was also published in English; and it also focused strategically on what he deemed to be the essence of Japanese culture. Finding such a focus was easy for Okakura, who determined that there really was only one oriental custom that the occident had taken seriously to that point: "Strangely enough humanity has so far met in the tea-cup. It is the only Asiatic ceremonial which commands universal esteem. The white man has scoffed at our religion and our morals, but has accepted the brown beverage without hesitation."[33]

Compared to Nitobe's flowery style, Okakura's is direct, even pugnacious. To be sure, there is the matter of personalities to consider; but the less obtuse tone also reflects a different time. Since the writing of *Bushido* in 1899, Japan had made considerable progress in climbing the ladder of nationhood. Having learned how to build battleships and cannons, having won its war with China, Japan then went on to distinguish itself as the only Asian country to fight and win a war against a European nation. Victory over Russia in 1905 sent a strong message to Japan's heretofore mentors of modern warfare: their brilliant protégé had learned the lessons of modern warfare only too well, and would require an empire of its own.

Somehow, Japan had adapted too quickly and too completely to the lessons that Western technocrats had to offer. From this point forward, Japan's space would have to be Japan and something more. Reflecting the ideological orientation of Japan in its expanding context of competing empires, Okakura wrote not of tea but of tea-*ism*: not about tea as a formality performed within a certain confined space, but tea as an ideology, as a way of life, a worldview, something capable of being generalized from "the sordid facts of everyday existence." It was a particular essence that traveled well "[Tea]…inculcates purity and harmony, the mystery of mutual charity, the romanticism of the social order. It is essentially a worship of the Imperfect, as it is a tender attempt to accomplish something possible in this impossible thing we know as life."[34]

According to Okakura, life at the turn of the twentieth century had become "impossible." In the face of worldwide tensions and contradictions, he chose to emphasize tea's small, ordinary, and humble aspects. Sitting down with someone over a cup of "the brown beverage" was a way to gain a modicum of peace in a less than peaceful world. Tea-ism was a way to retreat, to take a break from the rush of modernity.

By locating tea in a past, isolated time, he, like Nitobe, found an interpretation of pre-Enlightenment Japan to be crucial to his understanding of Japanese culture: "He [the Westerner] was wont to regard Japan as barbarous while she indulged in the gentle arts of peace: he calls her civilized since she began to commit wholesale slaughter on Manchurian battlefields."[35]

Speaking as a pacifist, Okakura echoed the xenophobic Aizawa when he suggested the crucial difference distinguishing the stationary, tea-drinking

East from the ever-moving, war-mongering West. But the deeper point is, of course, that Japan had compromised itself by learning "wholesale slaughter"; and he wished to take his country back to an innocent past: "You have gained expansion at the cost of restlessness; we have created a harmony which is weak against aggression. Will you believe it?—the East is better off in some respects than the West!"[36]

Drinking tea is a way to understand (and to be contained within) one's limitations in space. Even so, by Okakura's own admission, this reaffirmation of evanescence and form had already become a much larger "romanticism of the social order."

This is nostalgia. Like Nitobe, Okakura looks back to the Tokugawa period, considering it that time when Japan formed its true identity: a time of relative isolation from Western influences that was still "conducive to introspection."[37] Of course, looking back to the past was something that modernity actually stimulated. With its emphasis on the present, modern thinking needed a past to define itself against. By marking what went before as "traditional," Okakura was actually laying the groundwork for the ultranationalists of the 1930s, who would claim the superiority of Eastern morals over Western technology in their attempt to assert a position as the chosen race and the rightful rulers of Asia. No doubt, what helped make the smallness of tea the only thing worth doing in Okakura's eyes was a sense of being trapped within the expanded context of competing nations.

Moving between Japan and America, Okakura saw the difficulties that lie ahead for both.

> The heaven of modern humanity is indeed shattered in the Cyclopean struggle for wealth and power. The world is groping in the shadow of egotism and vulgarity. Knowledge is bought through a bad conscience, benevolence practiced for the sake of utility. The East and West, like two dragons tossed in a sea of ferment, in vain strive to regain the jewel of life. . . . Meanwhile, let us have a sip of tea. The afternoon glow is brightening the bamboos, the fountains are bubbling with delight, the soughing of the pines is heard in our kettle. Let us dream of evanescence, and linger in the beautiful foolishness of things.[38]

We have reached another important milestone in our study of Japanese culture. Evanescence is no longer a reality but something to dream about. It belongs to a lost age of "foolishness" that has been rendered forgettable by the aggressive grip of expanding empires and the universal truths that enable and justify such "utility." The world of tea is a forgotten world of politeness, a failed realm of aristocratic pleasure. By turning his back to the late modern perspective of wealth and power that has made life self-obsessed and vulgar, Okakura, in a decidedly backward-looking move, points us nostalgically to the details of a lost here-and-now: the light falling through a bamboo grove, the sound of a boiling kettle. The year 1906 is a vanished moment of *jihatsu* and enlightenment. Living and writing at this moment in history, Okakura could only hope to recall a lyricism and unity of presence now once removed, now romantically beyond the reach of even the foolish who realize the need to reestablish what has disappeared.

Precisely because he is faced with this separation from true experience, Okakura tries to elevate the momentary act of drinking tea to be something restorative and of the utmost importance.

> The Philosophy of Tea is not mere aestheticism in the ordinary acceptance of the term, for it expresses conjointly with ethics and religion our whole point of view about man and nature. It is hygiene, for it enforces cleanliness; it is economics, for it shows comfort in simplicity rather than in the complex and costly; it is moral geometry, inasmuch as it defines our sense of proportion to the universe. It represents the true spirit of Eastern democracy by making all its votaries aristocrats in taste.[39]

Despite this attempt to make tea-ism a multidisciplinary force of ethics, religion, hygiene, and economics, the ongoing tension between particular and universal brings the author back to struggle romantically, and helplessly, with the concrete space of Japan itself.

Ultimately, the truth lies in the *practice* of ideas. Okakura's tea-ism is not so much a matter of grand thoughts but of small practices and formalities, what we once identified as the form of here-and-now. Like Nitobe, he, too, is a defender of politeness—that knowledge of what to do where and when, a knowing "naturally" expressed by the trained actions of the body: "Perhaps we reveal ourselves too much in small things because we have so little of the great to conceal. The tiny incidents of daily routine are as much a commentary of racial ideals as the highest flight of philosophy or poetry."[40]

This retreat to "small things" is a free fall toward a lost moment of particularity and inwardness, an appeal to the truth of one person's emotions rather than to the grid of modern consensus. Of course, Okakura reflects a very modern concern with self. Yet, a new site of truth is posited as an adjustment of the Cartesian subject/object split. In this new site, space and time merge fluidly together: "It is in us that God meets with Nature, and yesterday parts from tomorrow. The Present is the moving Infinity, the legitimate sphere of the Relative. Relativity seeks Adjustment; Adjustment is Art. The art of life lies in constant readjustment to our surroundings."[41]

Here, Okakura tries to recapture the lost "Present," "the *moving* Infinity" [my emphasis], "the legitimate sphere of the Relative." But the moment of this present is not evanescent. It is, rather, a *re*captured evanescence, the *re*presented Present that must now make apologies for its relativity and its limited "sphere." The perspective of objective truth must doubt: How can there be Truth if all that matters is the particularity of each person's singular moment of truth? Since its veracity must also be systematic and universal, how can modernity allow more than one truth? Thus, Okakura's mollifying suggestion is that we look to art as a means of survival, since art is "adjustment" to relativity and to the harried space in which the modern soul finds itself. In short, here-and-now has become the sought-for *idea* of here-and-now, a small-scale practice of aesthetic retreat into a distant past.

Finally, we should note that what Okakura calls "our surroundings" is no longer the isolated space of Japan but the space of a modern nation surrounded by competing national modernities. As a result, Okakura's attempt to aestheticize the moment does not really lead him out of the fatalistic loop that has been created. By his own suggestion, everything can become art, just as art can become spiritual culture. But the precise meaning of spiritual culture is no longer as obvious as flowers falling dutifully from their branch. "When we consider how small after all the cup of human enjoyment is, how soon overflowed with tears, how easily drained to the dregs in our quenchless thirst for infinity, we shall not blame ourselves for making so much of the tea-cup."[42] The moment of falling flowers is over. It has been nullified by progress, and needs to be recreated nostalgically. Lyricism has become patriotism.

JAPAN AS EROTIC STYLE

In imperial Japan, the geisha, or professional entertainer, was also made a modern stereotype of Japanese-ness. This resulted in part from strict travel restrictions placed on Western photographers who had earlier made their way to Japan in the last decades of the nineteenth century. They could not wander in an age of aggressive wandering. Filled with desire to see the discovered Other, they staged scenes of Japanese life as they wished to see them. Such people as women, samurai, and umbrella makers were brought into their studios and photographed. The resulting images were then sold as souvenirs to travelers, or shipped overseas as foreign exotica. Japanese photographers also seized upon this commercial opportunity. By propagating certain images of Japan, they aided in establishing the mysterious land of Mikado, the sexualized universe of Madame Butterfly, and the endlessly fascinating realm of the geisha.

The idealization of the geisha was not so unlike the romantic regard Japan came to have for samurai and tea. It, too, began in the Tokugawa period but was further distilled and codified in the Age of the Transcendental Order. The French-trained philosopher Kuki Shūzō (1888–1941) analyzed their essence in *The Structure of Style* (*"Iki" no kōzō*, 1930). Along with Nitobe's *Bushido* and Okakura's *Book of Tea*, this book is another important marker of the continuing, though now severely compromised, influence of evanescence as a cultural force. With these other writers, Kuki shared both an awareness of and discomfort with Japan's place within the expanded context of competing nations. Like them, he struggled to find ways to situate Japan anew and to make sense of its behavior within this larger world. But by 1930, the sense that Japan could not comfortably follow in the ways of Western universalism had become increasingly widespread; and one expression of this unease is this famous essay that looks nostalgically back at the past, in a decidedly modern way that is, at the same time, critical of modernity.

On one level, discomfort with modernity resulted from factors common to other rapidly developing nations: the alienation caused by increased mechanization and specialization, the anonymity of urban life, awareness of the gap between the wealthy and the poor. In an earlier essay, Kuki had already drawn attention to what he regarded as the dangers of capitalist ideology, and the need to place Japan outside of its realm.

> In all good will, we cannot fathom the kind of mentality that acts and speaks by the law of the dollar weight alone, that mental necessity to level everything to the horizon of money. To our taste, there could be no uglier proverb imaginable than "time is money." And yet, at the moment I write, this proverb is being adopted and adored all over the world. Born in the new world, it has successfully invaded the old world as well. Under such compelling circumstances, shall we also join in and announce our intention to take the same path? No, our logic is different. We, at least, shall take a different path.[43]

Discomfort with the leveling of all things to "the horizon of money" came from two sets of parallel contradictions: first, the *particular* attributes of Western culture were being propagated as *universal* truths; and second, Japan's own ways were also held to be universal and, therefore, allowing of expansion and empire. Again, this need to assert one's cultural values as being "true" in a comparative sense had Japanese intellectuals looking back to the Tokugawa period to rediscover a beleaguered Japanese essence. As a Eurocentric Japanese intellectual who had finally returned to his cultural homeland after many years abroad, Kuki agreed with Nitobe in affirming bushidō as a particularly Japanese response to the Buddhist truth of *anitya*. He also tried to reconstitute the vanishing order of here-and-now, not by way of the tea ceremony as explained by Okakura, but through the complex of playful rituals that informed another moment of extreme service: the taking and giving of sexual pleasure.

As with Saikaku, so with Kuki. In the existence of the prostitute, he found a paradigm of modern reality, a resigned and (because of this) possibly enlightened self. As the late Edo-period novelist Tamenaga Shunsui (1790–1843) had earlier explained, the prostitute had a profound understanding of life's evanescent nature because her indentured servitude taught her that nothing lasts and that the world is full of pain: "Not nine, but ten years, decked out in flowery robes they do their time in a world of grief; once you reach enlightenment, how delightful, this transient world of pleasure, where all the beauties are gathered together in a single district, in this long-flourishing town of Yoshiwara."[44]

Ten years was the usual length of a young woman's bondage. Here Shunsui compares this term with the nine years that Daruma meditated on the transience of life before reaching enlightenment. His suggestion is that the sexual prisoner of Yoshiwara knows, even better than the enlightened One, the truth of evanescence. No doubt, this is one reason why Kuki focused upon these captured flowers of the erotic moment.

In order to better understand the lost world of Edo's floating world, Kuki collected and analyzed the *nagauta* or parlor songs that geisha routinely performed. Not surprisingly, the songs he quotes in *The Structure of Style* frequently employ water imagery, which, as we have seen, express values of danger, sorrow, and yes, change.

> A man's heart changes like the Asuka River, that's what you learn the hard way in this line of work.
>
> Unable to keep my head above water, I float away in the current. (*Ukami mo yaranu, nagare no ukimi*)[45]

Trapped in this flowing world, geisha were forced to become resilient and wise. At best, they came to have *iki*, defined by Kuki as a combination of coquettishness, pluck, and resignation.

Kuki came to a detailed understanding of the pleasure quarters, although he might not have had a wide enough perspective to see the full force of its already developing modernity. He misunderstood the *kuruwa* as a premodern phenomenon, isolated from the influences of modern life. While he thought it was capable of becoming an antidote to its modern poisons, in truth, the prostitute's modernity is exactly what Kuki responded to so enthusiastically. Such was his antiquarian and modern*ist* bent. In other words, the courtesan that he discovered was not behind, but actually ahead, of her time. Hers was a spirit of rebellion that made itself evident as a heightened and even arch sensuality, as an abandonment, and a playfulness. A prostitute with *iki* was enlivened by the strictures placed upon her, especially the capitalist captivity against which Kuki railed. She presented, for Kuki, the entrapped who understood one way out of the trap.

For him, the universalism of (Western) modernity presented a threatening backdrop against which the virtues of evanescence needed to be rediscovered. Like bushidō and tea, *iki* was another example of a nostalgic regard for constant change. Paradoxically, the process of recovery also rendered evanescence into yet another competing universality. That is to say, by Kuki's time, *iki* had become an erotic practice of history itself, one that drew a person closer and closer to real experience without allowing arrival to occur. But this, of course, was only fitting. As with modern historical processes, so too with seduction: "The essence of erotic allure is to continuously decrease the distance while never allowing that distance to be completely annihilated."[46]

Explained in this way, Kuki's *iki* stands a step back from nothingness. Those with pluck are able to come seductively close without ever getting there. In other words, *iki* denotes a kind of intimate interaction that is not intimate. It is essentially pornographic—the disingenuous control of being out of control—a perfect metaphor for Japan as it began spinning toward its fascistic fate. This was not the tea ceremony, not the freshness of meeting everyone as if for the first (and last) time. Surely, the naïvete of belief in such a genuine encounter in the licensed quarters had been seriously cast into doubt by Kuki's day. Sexual encounter was more like a performance than a real experience. As such, it was very close to fiction—the insistently imagined possibility of the untrue as true—a perversion of the sort that makes style all the more important for its being consciously close but never arriving at a fullness of the lost lyrical moment. By the 1930s, that intuited moment of truth was largely forgotten even while it was made impossible by a kind of Cartesian subjectivity that had formed by way of the (Japanese) subject's dominance over its (non-Japanese) object. It was in this fated and pathetic, secondhand heroism of *hara-kiri*, tea-ism, and sexual dalliance that the Jap was allowed to feel at home within a wider and dangerous world of *gaijin* who, like Puccini's Pinkerton, wanted nothing more than to make the whole of Japan his sexual object. Just as the paying customer would make the prostitute his, so too would the Western world have Japan.

In Kuki's late modern context, the actual (physical) site of *iki* had disappeared into the vanishing point of global perspective. Along with nursing one's baby in public, or bathing with the opposite sex, the brothels came to be condemned by a puritanical realism that was as concerned about what could not be seen as with what could. The writing was on the teahouse wall. Advanced nations frowned on prostitution.

Especially for those disenchanted with the West, the gradual decline of the courtesan's status suggested nothing less than the end of cultured and meaningful life. Kuki was not alone in lamentation. Lost Edo was grieved by other antiquarians, writers such as Izumi Kyōka and Nagai Kafū (1879–1959), who saw in the culture of the geisha a means, now increasingly fictive and fantastic, to preserve what little remained of Japan's cultural authenticity. Painters, such as Yokoyama Taikan (1868–1958), Hishida Shunsō (1874–1911), Tomioka Tessai (1837–1924), and, Kawai Gyokudō (1873–1957) similarly reacted to the building hegemony of realistic Western painting (*yōga*) by establishing a consciously traditional school of Japanese painting (*Nihonga*). Like Kuki, they tried to "overcome modernity" even as they could not avoid being influenced by it.

For Kuki, Edo (not Tokyo) was a haven that lay outside the reach of the universal (*fuhen*). As a "landscape of the spirit,"[47] it was a Bashōesque antidote to the dominance of the modern novel with its descriptive landscapes and psychological interiors. Like the work of Nitobe and Okakura, his was an affirmation of non-textual space as a source of identity; yet it was at the same time a vision of reality that needed to be thoroughly textualized if it was to have a chance of surviving at all. Like the folklorist Yanagita Kunio's (1875–1962) *Tales of Tōno* (*Tōno monogatari*, 1910–13), or the philologist Orikuchi Shinobu's (1887–1953) *Book of the Dead* (*Shisha no sho*, 1939), *The Structure of Style* was a textual bottle for a vaporous reality that was all too quickly evaporating into thin air. This tension is nowhere more apparent than in the awkward title of Kuki's treatise, "*Iki*" *no kōzō*, where the intellectual's jargonesque *kōzō* (structure) meets an evanescent *iki* trapped tightly between quotations marks, as if a mayfly of the Japanese spirit ready to escape the scholar's determined approach.

We might as well admit it. This text is not concerned with lived conditions, or with reality at all. Rather, it sadly elucidates the style of the here-and-now from the point of view that "here" and "now" no longer exist. By this point in the development of Japan's modernity, resignation has already become one part Buddhist truth and nine parts alienation. Living in a world that did not fit, perhaps all that Japanese intellectuals of this period could reasonably do was to fall back to nostalgic fantasies about the way things once were.

By writing about something as ephemeral as fashion, Kuki tried to resist the steady slide of all expression into the clutches of the symbolic order, where the concrete must be slavishly expressive of the abstract truths of modern life. To the modern view, the surface conceals depth, and is an ephemeral wrapping put into the service of lasting content. But for Kuki, who no doubt sensed the approaching tragedy of modern life devolving toward another world war, the superficial needed once again to be meaningful if Japan was to be saved. If style was no longer considered depth, neither could he allow it to be dismissed as meaningless. At the very least, style had to bring to light a kind of order that, heightened in poignancy by the tension between evanescence and form, was actually mastered by the denizens of the floating world. Truly, explaining Japan in terms of Style rather than Truth signaled a resignation, yet another manifestation of a lingering *mono no aware*.

And yet, we get the impression that Kuki meant the well-practiced pursuit of sexual pleasure to lead to plentitude rather than to despair. In fact, we are tempted to think of *iki* as the truth of ephemerality, the intuitive moment of connection to everything. At the same time, we cannot be fully convinced, because we see that this enlightenment is reconstituted from within a late modern perspective, and is weighed down with a considerable ideological load. Let us give him credit. Kuki attempted to separate *iki* from an objective reality that flows from the straight lines of the urban block, the printed page, the marching battalion, and the prison cell. And yet, the author is strangely blind to the fact that *iki*, too, is also compromised. It appears as Kuki's own admiration for the vertical stripes of the late Edo kimono: "Parallel lines are the purest visual objectification of duality, extended on forever, eternally equidistant. It is no coincidence that stripe designs are considered to be *iki*."[48] In the end, his vision of style too enthusiastically agreed with the latticed walls of the brothel as they advertised the prisoners who could give the customer his paid-for moment of erotic freedom. Ironically, Kuki, in his archival passion, did not see these straight lines as an inchoate perspective, and the very source of his deepest anguish. He failed to see them as signs of an already well-developed modern captivity of the sort that Norinaga had earlier explained.

Did Kuki's anthropological nostalgia cause this blindness? In his *Structure of Style*, he wished to isolate Japan once again, to go back to an earlier time when the space of Japan was still *the* context of identity, when the islands of Japan were still home (*uchi*) and easily distinguishable from the world beyond its shores (*soto*). Like Nagai Kafū and many other Japanese intellectuals of the generation that followed Nitobe and Okakura, he also left home in order to return to it. Admittedly, Kuki studied in Europe for a longer period than most, and came to know a wider world in its variety and difference. Yet if his extended stay abroad heightened his appreciation of Japan, like Nitobe and Okakura, he, too, tried to see his country as both a particular space *and* a universal concept.

If Kuki was tortured as a Taishō-period (1912–35) intellectual, it was because he was held back by the ancient pull of space in an era of the concept. In the preface to a short piece he penned while still living in Paris, he wrote: "Just as their sky is different and their rivers have a different nature from those in other countries, the Japanese are the complete opposite of the Europeans in their customs and habits."[49]

Situated within the tension of spatial context and conceptual text—the mannered and stylish realm of the demimonde on the one hand and the world of his extensive reading in Western philosophy on the other—Kuki came to honor the gravity of space even upon entering the orbit of higher concepts. He thus admitted, "The place one lives will naturally be reflected in his philosophy."[50]

It was a comparative sense of space that allowed him to perceive certain problems as having come to Japan from the West; and this then gave him the heroic opportunity to try to separate his country from the modern world. Our temptation might be to call this geopolitics. But, surely, space also mattered because the lingering pull of evanescence had sensitized him to the order of here-and-now: how to move properly (or perhaps in this case would we should say "stylishly"?) through space. The emphasis on formality and etiquette that we have traced in earlier texts emerges here as an emphasis on what Kuki calls "physical experience" (*taiken*). The only way to know reality is physically, by engagement in that lyrical moment when the past becomes present. As expressive of *iki*, this is a well-trained moment in space. It is directed and enhanced by the rules of the floating world that add up to a total affirmation of physicality. But it is also one that mirrors a fearless embrace of death in concept: "In sum, *iki* is the perfect self-realization of the material cause of erotic allure by means of the formal causality of moral idealism and the religious belief in the unreality of the world, both distinctive signs of the culture of our country."[51]

What Kuki means by "religious belief in the unreality of the world" is a Buddhistic awareness of evanescence. As for "the formal cause of moral idealism," this is probably a reference to Nitobe's *Bushido*. As we have seen in our study of the Noh play *Atsumori*, a semblance of these two values had been brought together long ago. Kuki's contribution was to join unreality and idealism at the enticing point of "the material cause of erotic allure." By doing this, he unwittingly accomplished a bringing together of all things that are unavoidably true: evanescence, ethics, and eros. Their union had the effect of aestheticizing politics (or the need to act beautifully in response to the moment); and this brought Japan one step closer to the mass ownership of a beautiful, modern idea put violently into action—a perfect recipe for the robust eradicating of evil and ugliness that we call fascism.

In another essay, "The Spirit of Japan" ("*L' Ame japonaise*") Kuki follows after Nitobe by enthusiastically commenting on Norinaga's now-famous verse about Japan's essence.

> *Shikishima no*   *Si l'on demande*
> *Yamatogokoro wo*   *Qu'est-ce que l'ame nipponne?*
> *Hito towaba*   *C'est la fleur de cerisier des monts*
> *Asahi ni niou*   *Exhalant son parfum au soleil de matin.*[52]
> *Yamazakurabana.*

Expressing his own imprisonment within the straight lines of modern captivity, Kuki explains that cherry blossoms do not express the sadness of life. Rather, they signify "a spirit always ready to offer itself up and die for its ideals (*risō*). The morning light is the moral ideal, the same light that Plato spoke of in his allegory of the cave."[53] If it is true, as Leslie Pincus has said, that "this verse gives expression to an absolute contempt for all that is material. It affirms idealism,"[54] it is because, despite the pull of space, Kuki still felt obligated to explain things such as cherry blossoms and *iki* as a part of an intellectual, universal discourse.

In the end, Kuki Shūzō's *The Structure of Style* only pushed Japan further toward its fated existence *within* an expanded international context. As we discussed, that context had already invalidated the old order of the here-and-now by making it relative and conceptual. Nevertheless, as did other intellectuals who lived in the period between the Restoration and the end of World War II, Kuki instinctively tried to return to the lost world of Edo. Because his methods of searching were thoroughly Westernized, this nostalgic attempt to reconstitute a vanished essence of Japanese culture actually had the effect of wedding evanescence with ideology, fusing acts of erotic desire with an ideological thirst for beautiful ideas. While this coming together of "the material cause of erotic allure" and the idealism of "absolute contempt for all that is material" was a perplexing and paradoxical union, it belied the very contradiction that underpinned the massive social movement that was already forming and would eventually lead to the murderous persecution of all liberal thinkers and to the waging of an imperialist war of vast proportions.

What is the relevance of eroticism to war? Is this "carnality" the fascist sensibility of which the post-War critic Maruyama Masao later complained?[55] Kuki's attempt to bind the material to the ideal and the changing to the unchanging is shot through with contradictions. Yet his search for a Japanese essence is important to our appreciation of Japanese culture since it shows us how the delicate glow of lantern light escaped from the stylish space of the demimonde to contribute to the full-world conflagration that we call World War II. The nightmare that followed was in part an attempt to understand the never-before-known consequences of Japanese culture as it overflowed into a world where Japanese (spatial) form did not naturally exist. Could Japanese culture prevail elsewhere? The question we must ask if we are to understand Japan's startling behavior during World War II is simply this: What happens to evanescence once it leaves the borders of Japanese space? What happens when a vaporous "*iki*" escapes the desperate scholar's containment of quotation marks?

IN THE MARGINS OF
EMPIRE—THE RAPE OF NANKING

The world as we know it was nearly destroyed because the logic of modern war and the logic of modern peace are one and the same. How is peace accomplished? By waging war. How is war eradicated? By establishing peace. No other cognitive loop explains why the sort of mass murder that occurred during World War II can still be called by some "the Good War," and no other logic explains why, at one point in time, millions of people thought it was justifiable to murder millions of other people. In America, the generation that accepted this justification fervently and patriotically is still called "the greatest generation."[56] In Japan, they are more often considered the deceived generation, fooled by a distorting ideology, led by bad men, and carried away by the arrogance of modern times. What accounts for this great difference of opinion regarding World War II?

One possible explanation is that Japan *lost* the War. There, the dream that ended on August 15, 1945 came to be understood as a nightmare. In contrast, the firebombing of Japan's cities and the nuclear attacks on Hiroshima and Nagasaki are either forgotten by Americans or remembered as having been unfortunate but necessary. Even now, a recalcitrant nostalgia for a victorious moment of truth, system, and universality has "super powers" fighting less-developed nations and, much to their surprise, losing again and again. They have yet to take seriously the cultural analysis that explains why postmodern nations do not win wars with modern ones. It is not because they do not have the technological power to do so, but because modern societies are still too inexperienced, still too ideologically pure, and still too culturally naïve to understand that "war-equals-peace" is only one of many possibilities available to us.

Within Japan's twentieth-century context, *modern* responses to the ancient notion of evanescence came to be nothing less than genocidal. Perhaps centuries of believing that "all things change" had rendered the barrier between life and death overly porous. Maybe it had even lowered the price of a life, to put the problem in the measurable terms that Kuki hated. What was once true for the sword-carrying samurai became the truth for the modern soldier in general. He was willing to give his life or to take the life of another if it served a purpose. Obviously, killing and violence were viewed as a political necessity. But they were also seen in terms of beautiful sorrow and necessary suffering. The films and novels produced to boost morale for the war effort did not try to hide the difficulties of this commitment to Japan's inevitable future as the leader of Asia and, perhaps, of the world. As the historian Peter Duus once expressed it to me and my classmates many years ago, "These war-time films are so discouraging, it makes you wonder why they had any motivational force at all."[57]

Obviously, in speaking of Japanese culture we are negotiating significant differences in motivation. How else could that which is encouraging to one culture be discouraging to another? And yet, it is also true that in times of war the differences are magnified since a *lack* of understanding yields the fear and loathing needed to anesthetize the conscience of anyone required to murder. Consider the film series *Victory at Sea* in which documentary footage of a desperate battle between American gunners and Japanese kamikaze pilots is narrated as an inevitable duel with the alien Other. "The Americans, fighting to live. And the Japanese, fighting to die."[58] As articulated by this stark contrast, the cultural difference between Japanese and Americans was not meant to be comprehensible. Is this not why war was both necessary and possible?

Were Japanese more willing to die than other people? If so, is this a legacy of evanescence? In the Battle for Saipan in 1944, some 3,000 Japanese soldiers, armed with nothing but bayoneted rifles and sticks, charged the machine guns of the American fighters and were mowed down. Other soldiers were mercifully beheaded by their commanding officers, who then committed suicide. Women and children threw themselves off cliffs and drowned themselves in the ocean. By the end of the three-day campaign for the island, less than 1,000 survived from an original number of 32,000.[59] The same fight-to-the-last-man scenario was repeated in the Philippines, in Okinawa, and in many other places throughout Southeast Asia and the South Pacific. Was this *Hagakure* expressing itself through the Japanese people? "One should expect death daily so that, when the time comes, one can die in peace."[60] To what extent was this willingness to die a predictable expression of Japanese culture?

In order to help Americans loathe the enemy, Frank Capra directed a film called *Know Your Enemy Japan*. It was a part of the U.S. War Department's *Why We Fight* series. Released in 1943, this baldly propagandistic work draws many sweeping generalizations that are not balanced by a similarly critical view of America's own position. For example, while focusing on the ideological dangers of Japan's expansive "all the world under one roof" (*hakkō ichiu*), the film fails to address the American impulse of "manifest destiny." Moreover, in order to link custom, tradition, and etiquette to the larger problem of war and its motivations, Capra and his associates exaggerated Japanese ways so that they would appear absurd and "fantastic." For instance, we are told that all decisions made in Japan come from the top down, while all those in the United States come democratically from the bottom up. With such comparisons, Capra expresses a chauvinistic opinion: that if the Japanese were wrongly oppressed by militarism, Americans were rightly empowered by it.

While it is not our task to address the truth of such claims, our analysis of evanescence does lead us directly to the question of oppression. A Zen calligrapher and friend, Ogawa Tōshū, once explained to me that the nature of militarism, as expressed by the character *bu* (武) in bushidō, is the art of stopping (止) the spear (矛) rather than the art of using it to harm someone. If this is so, then why did the Japanese Army, these modern commoners who inherited the bushidō spirit from traditional samurai, behave so cruelly during the War? I do not mean to say that the samurai themselves were not despotic and violent; for a text such as *The Tale of Heike* reveals their brutality. Yet it is also true that they were bound by order, protocol, and custom. Where do we find restraint in the numerous atrocities committed by modern Japanese soldiers? Can we explain the "gleeful killing" of thousands of defenseless Chinese in Nanking as an element of Nitobe's bushidō?[61] Or was this a misunderstanding of tradition? Can we link the poisoning of wells and the giving of anthrax-laden chocolates to Chinese children with Okakura's refined taste for tea?[62] Or was this another gross distortion of *ichigo ichie*, making the most of meeting once? Can we understand the inhumane treatment of "comfort women" as an understandable outcome of Kuki's stylish *iki*?[63] Or was this a mistaken perception of the materiality of eros?

Some deny that such atrocities occurred. Even today, the debate continues; and the struggle about what to put in Japanese textbooks about Japan's aggressive role in the War drags on. In Germany, a thorough critique of the Third Reich occurred. But in Japan, the discourse gets stalled on the point of whether to call Japan's involvement on the Continent an "attack" or an "advance." Patriots dismiss the horrors of the Rape of Nanking as not making sense. The barbarous behavior described by the Chinese is not compatible with the highly civilized, refined, and beautiful place that Japan is. They call the massacre a "fantasy" (*maboroshi*) or a "fiction" (*kyokō*) concocted by those who do not really know what happened.[64]

While the exact numbers are hard to determine with accuracy, conservative scholarly estimates hold that during the two months surrounding the fall of Nanking on December 13, 1937, 15,000–50,000 people were murdered and hundreds of women were raped.[65] Higher estimates put the number at an overwhelming 300,000. Those who deny the possibility of Japanese cruelty during the War forget that during these years, even on the archipelago, propriety had broken down considerably. Much of my limited knowledge about this phenomenon comes from one of my Japanese mentors, Muramatsu Sadataka, who told me that life in Tokyo during the War became barbarous.[66] As for life on the margins of the civilized cultural field, had it not always been violent and out of control? Consider how the Meiji-period push to colonize the northern island of Hokkaido resulted in violence to the Ainu, for instance, or how the people of colonial Korea and Taiwan were mistreated.

Many reasons have been put forward to explain why the Japanese soldiers killed and raped with such abandon in Nanking. A list of commonly articulated explanations would include the unexpectedly stubborn resistance of the Chinese troops in the preceding battle for Shanghai, which made the Japanese troops vengeful as they then moved on to Nanking; the low educational and cultural levels of the farmers and workers who became frontline

Japanese soldiers; the cruelty with which officers treated men of lower rank, who then passed this abuse on to the Chinese; an overly rapid advance toward Nanking that outstripped supply lines and forced soldiers to fend for themselves, effectively turning soldiers into robbers and rapists; an inability to take prisoners of war due to a lack of supplies, whether on the way to Nanking or once they had taken the city; the lack of a formal surrender of the city, which gave no definition to a possible end of hostilities; the abandonment of the Chinese forces by their leaders who fled the city as soon as the fall of the city seemed inevitable; the immediate and total breakdown of military discipline and morale on the part of the Chinese forces, who then seemed cowardly and despicable to the Japanese; the Chinese custom of changing into civilian clothes following a military defeat, which enforced the notion of their being an "inner front" of civilian combatants to be eradicated; the early date of the victory parade that hastened the "mop up" effort that led to the execution of all prisoners of war; the breakdown of leadership on the Japanese side due to personal rivalries; and, finally, the tendency for the troops on the mainland to act independently of directions from Tokyo.

To these factors, our understanding of evanescence offers one more explanation. Could it be that, once outside the actual space of Japan, placed dangerously on the very margins of civilized (Japanese) territory, the localized order of here-and-now that helped supplement the ideological discipline of military life at home broke down utterly? One might argue that etiquette and formality have little place on the battlefield, where the immediate objective is to annihilate or immobilize the enemy and disrupt his systems of support. But the truth is that discipline of every sort is actually heightened in military culture precisely because of the chaotic and hostile conditions under which soldiers must operate. When, then, did a respectful regard for order evaporate in Nanking, where decency was replaced by utter contempt for the marginal Other?

Having examined both sides of the argument, I must regretfully agree with those who maintain that Japanese soldiers raped and killed many. To redeploy Kuki's words in ways he surely never intended, these atrocities occurred once the soldiers let the "material cause of erotic allure" overwhelm any restraining sense of "moral idealism" while affirming the truth of the "unreality of the world."[67] In short, whether their actions were justified militarily or not, the Japanese soldiers in Nanking behaved without conscience. The space around them was no longer Japan, and so the well-practiced rules of correctly moving through space in order to prove and maintain one's identity no longer applied. In other words, by this point in time, the order of here-and-now was reduced to the order of "only now," an inexorable modern moment justified by the line of historical explanation that leads to it. There was no "here" by which the Japanese invaders could gain their bearings as honorable, civilized people. Here had become a margin, and a vanishing point.

The Japanese soldiers were in an unfamiliar cusp of a modern empire where the threat of slipping into nothingness was all too real. In such a no-man's-land, there were no spatially determined laws of etiquette to give form to evanescence. The context in which they found themselves was not recognizable, at least in any properly defining way. What remained was only the truth of radical change: that life is fragile and short; that everyone must die. Rather than inspire poetry, the unfamiliarity of Nanking inspired the reflex to push or be pushed. As the saying goes, *Tabi no haji wa kakisute.* "Who cares about manners when you're on a trip?"

We might appeal to principles rather than to manners. What about the transcendental and universal laws that should have replaced the order of here-and-now in late modern Japan? Why did they not supply another kind of restraining form? What became of the abstract laws that supposedly tied Japan to the rest of the world, to the international community and its rules of morality? Military law and protocol, criminal justice, international treaties, the teachings of Buddhism and Confucius, the principles of Christianity—any number of conceptual formations could have moderated the behavior of Japan's soldiers. Why did they not prevent atrocity?

In asking this question, we forget two things about the transcendental order. First of all, think of the overwhelming assertions of the physical world—weapons that malfunction, bodies that bleed, thirst, hunger. Consider the evil that makes soldiers go berserk, whether in Nanking or My Lai. Second, think of the dominant framework of all modern ideological ordering. Does modernity and its conceit of improvement not provide a rationale for imperialism and its aggressive discovery and subjugation of the world? By definition, improvement is an unstoppable justification. The need to purify the world supplanted the order of here-and-now with rules that, far from restraining the soldier's darkest impulses, made them instruments of an always justified political will. As a result, the emperor's soldiers were well supported in their attempt to rid the world of the backward, the ugly, and the inferior. The modern impulse to create a better world allowed them to erase noncompliance; and modern technology allowed them to do so on a massive scale. In trying to make the world better through violent means, were they any different from any other modern soldiers?

It is easy to forget that the same modern order that brought the blessings of electrification, antibiotics, and internal combustion engines, also provided justifications for racism, sexism, and genocide. In sum, the attempt to impose a truthful, systematic, and universal order on the entire world justified the immoral actions of soldiers as moral behavior. The Hague Convention of 1907, Article Four, stipulated that "[p]risoners of war are in the power of the hostile government, but not of the individuals or corps who capture them. They must be humanely treated." In the same spirit, Article Twenty-Three contained language that forbade combatants to kill, wound, or otherwise exact vengeance upon an enemy who has surrendered. Article Twenty-Eight prohibited the pillaging of towns and locales even if taken by assault. Article Forty-Three stated, "The authority of the legitimate power having in fact passed into the hands of the occupants, the latter shall take all the measure in his power to restore, and ensure, as far as possible, public order and safety, while respecting, unless absolutely prevented, the laws in force in the country."[68] In an attempt to reemphasize the need for such regulations, the Geneva Convention was promulgated in 1949, in the wake of the horrors of World War II. But by that point, the lived reality of modern life had all too clearly demonstrated the need for ideologies of peace to counter ideologies of hostility. Modern war is total war; and total war is a rationalized exaggeration of the most horrible aspects of evanescence. Whether dropping bombs from 20,000 feet or stabbing someone with a mud-covered knife, our unleashed cruelty and rage makes politeness, sensitivity, and considerateness irrelevant—unless, of course, such refinement makes our own position more secure.

OTHER HORRORS OF LIFE ON THE MARGINS

It has been said before, but stands repeating. The atrocities of war were not committed only by crude, backward young men from the Japanese countryside who were hurriedly mobilized to fight for their nation. The savagery and brutality of total war involved everyone, from the emperor and the generals down to the men who methodically executed Chinese prisoners of war under the orders of their superiors and then roamed the streets of Nanking in small groups, killing, raping, and plundering on their own. Japanese intellectuals also participated in the killing by abandoning their various positions of resistance. Novelists, poets, painters—they too jumped on the bandwagon one by one.

Members of Japan's scientific community were no less guilty than their counterparts in Europe and America. They likewise devised weapons of mass destruction and provided the reasons that justified their use. Judging from what happened on all fronts of World War II, we must reluctantly admit that there is nothing inherently moral about modern science and its affirmation of truth, system, and universality. This point was well expressed in the admonition of Ishii Shirō, mastermind of Japan's biological warfare effort in Manchuria, as he spoke to the men of Unit 731, who routinely carried out deadly research on human subjects.

> Our god-given mission as doctors is to challenge all varieties of disease-causing micro-organisms; to block all roads of intrusion into the human body; to annihilate all foreign matter resident in our bodies; and to devise the most expeditious treatment possible. However, the research work upon which we are now about to embark is completely opposite of these principles, and may cause us some anguish as doctors. Nevertheless, I beseech you to pursue this research, based on the dual thrill of 1) a scientist to exert efforts to probing for the truth in natural science and research into, and discovery of, the unknown world and 2), as a military person, to successfully build a powerful military weapon against the enemy.[69]

Having inherited the intellectual structure of monotheism, scientific order is, in this unexpected sense, god-given. But this is only to say that the idea of one God has been replaced by, and, therefore, is deeply hidden in scientific discourse. According to Ishii, science belongs to a transcendental order that has as one of its fundamental tenets the "discovery" of "the unknown world" and, as another, the destruction of any (enemy) who might stand in the way of this expansion. Both goals are considered progress. Both are strands of the same modern rope.

The topic has been assiduously avoided elsewhere, but we cannot ignore its importance to our analysis of evanescence and its meaning for Japanese culture. The truth about Japan's thrilling pursuit of modernity is that the creation and deployment of biological weapons was a well-funded priority of the empire's war effort. Intellectual talent and vast sums of capital flowed to the establishment of laboratories in Manchuria, Korea, China, Singapore, Thailand, and Burma, where viral and microbial agents were routinely tested on human subjects, mostly prisoners of war who were detained in structures adjoining the laboratories. As a part of this research, these same contagious materials were deployed in many ways throughout the margins of the expanding Japanese Empire. Sadly, we know relatively little about these actions because, after Japan's collapse, American leaders covered up the experimentation and protected the people who did it. Both the research and the researchers were too useful to the state to be exposed to public scrutiny.[70]

In the fighting between Japanese and Russians troops at Nomonhan in 1939, artillery shells with bacteria-filled warheads were deployed; and vials of typhoid were dumped into the river on the Russian side of the front. Over the next several years, from 1939 through 1942, various toxins were used experimentally on civilian populations as well. For example, wells near Harbin were poisoned with typhoid germs. Citizens of Manchukuo's capital were inoculated with a vaccine that secretly contained cholera bacteria. In 1940, the city of Ningbo, near Hangzhou, became the target of large-scale biological field trials, where cholera, typhus, and plague were spread aerially by dropping infected wheat, millet, and cotton fibers on the population. In Changde, infected fleas, wheat and rice balls, strips of colored paper, cotton fibers, and other fabric cuttings were spread over the city. In 1942, Ishii personally led an expedition to Nanking, where typhoid, paratyphoid, and anthrax germs were dumped into wells and marshes, and placed in homes throughout the city. It was at this time that Ishii and his men also provided special holiday dumplings, which had been injected with either typhoid or paratyphoid. These were fed to prisoners of war. Having received these gifts, the released prisoners were then sent home to spread the contagion to their families. Even the young were not protected. The men of Unit 731 made chocolates filled with anthrax especially for children.[71]

Here on the margins of Japan's empire, the mutability and fragility of life were particularly obvious. Where but in these zones of war were the everyday distinctions between real or unreal, life or death, justified or unjustified behavior more easily compromised? As was the case with the Heike warrior Kumagae no Naozane, what other situation could be more affirming of change than the moment of kill-or-be-killed? For this reason, where would the need for the disciplining of *every* thought, action, and desire be more crucially important than in battle? Surely, the harsh and demanding nature of military discipline lies here, in knowing the pressures on combatants to succumb to their deepest fears and to give in to their basest desires.

Is this not the essential truth of bushidō? Without a highly developed sense of propriety and honor, a warrior's life would quickly become brutal and disgusting. In the war chronicles of the Kamakura period, the warrior's code was tied intimately and constantly to the order of here-and-now. It was hardly distinguishable from etiquette and protocol; and it was focused on personal connections and loyalties, on the knowable place of one's birth. But as the atrocities of Hideyoshi's invasions of Korea in 1592 and 1597 suggest, it was nearly impossible for this kind of localized order to remain intact once the warrior was removed from the space of Japan. If brutality prevailed among Hideyoshi's sixteenth-century army, it was only more so for the commoner armies of the Japanese Empire that were sent to the battlefields of Asia and the Pacific Islands to labor under the flag of the rising sun.

As for the brutalization of women during the war, the evidence suggests that rape was both encouraged and discouraged. It was encouraged as a means to help young recruits become more aggressive, more ready to kill the enemy.[72] But it was also discouraged because it turned local populations against the Japanese military. Rape tarnished the image of the emperor's troops as they attempted to carry out their holy war, and it also led to the spread of debilitating and costly venereal diseases. A directive issued to unit commanders in North China by Lieutenant-General Okabe Naozaburō in June 1938 reads:

> ...the reason for such strong anti-Japanese sentiment [among the local Chinese population] is widespread rape committed by Japanese personnel in many places. It is said that such rape is fermenting unexpectedly serious anti-Japanese sentiment....Therefore, frequent occurrence of rape in various places is not just a matter of criminal law. It is nothing but high treason that breaches public peace and order, that harms the strategic activities of our entire forces, and that brings serious trouble to our nation.[73]

To lessen occurrences of rape, "comfort women" were recruited (often through deceptive and coercive means) and sent into all corners of the war zone.[74] Of course, this was institutionalized rape by another name, encouraged not only as a means of protection but also as a means to cultivate brutality in young soldiers. Thus, the condoms issued to Japanese troops were named "Assault No. 1."[75]

The place of a comfort woman within the grid of modern life was far from the privileged, imperial point of view that relegated her to a place far from and practically invisible to the civilized center. She was farther from the originating point of truth than even the young recruits who fought and died in the jungles of the Dutch East Indies, on Iwojima, and in Burma. The emperor's perspective, which justified the ever-widening aggression, put forward a new, portable, text-based sense of nonspatial order that, like the development of radio and telegraphy, complemented the imagined reach of the empire. The rationale for such vastness could only have been an abstraction, an ideological apology for the generality of mass murder and a call for the deadly fascist aesthetics of uniformity and purity. This ideological effort was essentially distorting. It put forward as unquestionably true such notions as the "Far East Asian Co-Prosperity Sphere" (the supposed goal of Japan's leadership in Asia), or the divinity of the body politic (*kokutai*) that led logically to the infallible nature of Japan's military forces.

During the 1930s and early 1940s these ideals validated nobility and honor by making victory the only true measure of the good. As General Douglas MacArthur put it, "In war there is no substitute for victory."[76] To be sure, the trappings of Nitobe's nostalgic honor went onto the battlefield with Japan's patriots: higher-ranking officers carried the long swords of the samurai as a legacy from their bushidō past. Perhaps this also explains why such blades, rather than rifles, were the instruments of choice in the killing contests that occurred just prior to the Fall of Nanking. Textualized by a nostalgic meta-narrative of Japanese divinity and invincibility, the soldiers of the Emperor's Army were sent to the margins of civility to lead the rest of Asia to power and prosperity, whether Asia wanted their leadership or not.

Given a uniform and a number, Japan's soldiers were atomized and placed in a vicious cycle of domination. Exploited objects became empowered subjects by exploiting still other objects. Sadly, whether enemy combatants and civilians who deserved to be killed, or women who deserved to be raped, all were objectified and subjected to military domination. Trapped in this maelstrom, comfort women were not simply cast aside. Rather than murdered outright, they were kept alive in order to serve for as long as humanly possible. They were easily infected, easily brutalized, and (until 1991 when three brave Korean women filed a class-action lawsuit in a Tokyo court) easily forgotten. Like the soldiers who raped them, they, too, were the very name of evanescence. Yet their job was not to sing of cherry blossoms. That privilege would be reserved for the young men who were asked to commit suicide for the glory of the empire.

KAMIKAZE

The word "kamikaze" is one of a few Japanese terms that entered the vocabulary of most English speakers during the War. It identified someone fanatical, reckless, someone who acts with wild abandon. By extension, the word has come to identify dangerous activity and rash behavior of all kinds. Today, one type of death-defying carnival ride is called "The Kamikaze," for instance. And a popular fraternity drinking game has the same name.[77]

The term literally means "god (*kami*) wind (*kaze*)." It is written with the characters 神風, which are also read *shinpū*. In fact, this is how the term was usually pronounced during the War. The reading "*shinpū*" is refined, while "kamikaze" is colloquial and borders on being vulgar. *Shinpū* is to kamikaze, then, as "*seppuku*" is to "*hara kiri*." In Japan, one rarely hears the terms kamikaze and hara-kiri. By contrast, in the West the other two more refined readings are almost never heard.

Anciently, "kamikaze" was a magical epithet, like *utsusemi*. It occurred as a descriptor for Ise, home of the famous Ise Shrine. This is Japan's Mecca, as it were, the site of the holiest of all Shintō shrines. They are dedicated to Amaterasu, the "heaven illuminating" source of light and the ancestor of the Japanese race. One theory about the origin of the term kamikaze is that the prevailing winds that blow inland off the ocean near Ise were associated with the holiness of the locale, thus *kamukaze no Ise*, or Ise of the divine winds. To my knowledge, the earliest use of this epithet is in this poem from the *Kojiki*.

Kamukaze no	On the great rocks
Ise no umi no	Of the waters at Ise,
Ōishi ni	Where the divine wind blows,
Haimotohorofu	Round and round
Shitadami no	The snails crawl.
Ihaimotohori	Surrounding the foe,
Uchite shi yamamu	Let's strike and be done with it![78]

This poem is one of a series of poems to commemorate the triumph of Jimmu Tennō (Kamu Yamato Iwarebiko no Mikoto) over his enemy Tomibiko. Jimmu is supposedly Japan's first emperor, ascribed in the *Kojiki* to be the founder of the Yamato state. The association of this place of divine wind with Jimmu helps to establish his authority. But at this early juncture the epithet's martial overtones were still not well developed.

The first time "*kamikaze*" came to carry a clearly martial burden was when Kakinomoto no Hitomaro, who we already know to be a major court poet of the *Man'yōshū*, used the word in a public recounting of Emperor Tenmu's bloody rise to power. It occurs at that lyrical moment when gods, wind, and battle come together.

Torimoteru	The clamor of the bownocks
Yuhazu no sawaki	Of the bows the warriors held
Miyuki furu	Was terrible to hear:
Fuyu no hayashi ni	Men thought the sound was like
Tsumuji ka mo	A whirlwind twisting,
Imakiwataru to	Tearing through a winter forest
Omou made	In the falling snow,
Kiki no kashikoku	So dreadful was the noise;
Hikihanatsu	We drew, we shot,
Ya no shigekeku	Our arrows flew as thick
Ōyuki no	As a blinding blizzard
Midarete kitare	Pelting down upon the foe:
Matsurowazu	They, still unsubdued,
Tachimukaishi mo	Stood and fought our army face to face:
Tsuyu shimo no	"If like dew or frost

Kenaba kenubeku	We perish, then let us perish!"
Yuku tori no	And like flying birds
Arasou hashi ni	They went eagerly into the fray.
Watarai no	Then from Watarai,
Itsuki no miya yu	From the pure and holy shrine,
Kamukaze ni	A divine wind rose
Ifuki matowashi	And blew confusion on the enemy;
Amakumo wo	With clouds of heaven
Hi no me mo misezu	It covered over all the earth,
Tokoyami ni	Hiding the eye of the sun,
ōitamaite	Obscuring the world in utter dark.
Sadameteshi	With peace thus brought
Mizuho no kuni wo	To the land of sweet rice spears,
Kamunagara	The Sovereign, a god,
Futoshikimashite	Established there a mighty reign,
Yasumishishi	And our great lord
Waga ōkimi no	Who ruled the land in all tranquility
Ame no shita	Spoke words of government
Mōshitamaeba	To his realm beneath the sky.[79]

Much later, in the thirteenth century, the violent meaning of kamikaze was reinforced when fierce storms destroyed Kublai Khan's invading forces, both in 1274 and again in 1281. The storms were called "divine wind," and it was believed that they had miraculously saved Japan from the Mongol invaders.

This martial connotation was not lost on the various patriotic societies that formed in the 1930s. Having never lost a war against a foreign power, the Japanese convinced themselves that they were a chosen people, and that defeat would never happen. In the worldwide competition for colonial gain, Japan was destined for greatness. The emperor was divine, and his subjects (the Japanese people) were similarly exalted. Despite the abuses piled upon them by the Western powers, they had shown their true nature by avoiding colonization, by defeating the Chinese in 1895 and the Russians in 1905, by occupying Formosa, Korea, and Manchuria, and by quickly invading large portions of China, Indochina, and the Pacific Islands in the six months that followed the tactical strike on Pearl Harbor in December 1941.

The fate of the Heike might have served as a cautionary tale for Japan's militarists. Did they forget the truth of evanescence: that failure follows success? The fortunes of war started to turn against Japan as early as the Battle of Midway in June 1942. As the materials needed to sustain massive military operations came into short supply, the fate of the nation became gradually clearer. Japan started to lose the War. At the point when defeat seemed inevitable and a full-scale invasion of the homeland was only a matter of time, suicidal *shinpū* tactics—the crashing of manned bombs, torpedoes, and airplanes into enemy targets—began in earnest.

By all accounts, these suicide bombings were understood as matters of the spirit. According to Ivan Morris's account, those who went off to die realized that their sacrifice would not actually change the outcome of the War. Thus, we can understand their acts of desperation as an understanding of the inevitable truth of loss and failure. Vice Admiral Ōnishi Takijirō, the man who organized the first kamikaze attack forces during the final days of the War, encouraged the emperor to never surrender. About him, one of his officers explained,

> [Ōnishi] knew, of course, that with ordinary tactics there was no longer the slightest chance of stopping the enemy. In addition he attached great importance to the "spiritual" aspect of the operations, quite apart from any practical effect they might have. In a speech delivered a few months later to members of the first kamikaze unit in Taiwan he declared, "Even if we are defeated, the noble spirit of the kamikaze attack corps will keep our homeland from ruin. Without this spirit, ruin could certainly follow defeat."[80]

Defeat is one thing, and ruin another. To be defeated was acceptable, but to be ruined was not. Ruination was a matter of the spirit, and that was what Ōnishi apparently thought could still be avoided through collective sacrifice.

Morris makes the point that the young men who flew these one-way missions to their deaths were principally *not* motivated by hatred for the enemy.[81] Above all, they wished to protect the cherished space of Japan, and to show their gratitude to parents and family. As the writers of *Victory at Sea* held, they actually were fighting to die. Yet as inhuman as this suicidal impulse might seem, their motivations should be understandable to us by now. Even in the age of the transcendental order, even as Japanese imperial ideology had asserted itself within this larger context of competing world powers, the death of young pilots was a return to the first principle of Japanese culture: everything changes. Their kamikaze deaths mark a return to evanescence.

That they viewed their lives as ephemeral is obvious when we consider the many associations drawn between themselves and cherry blossoms. For example, the rocket-propelled bombs that were designed to carry their pilots toward an enemy ship were named *Ōka* or Cherry Blossoms. (*Ōka* is a more formal reading of *sakurabana* 桜花.) Also, the names given to the first four organized kamikaze aerial attack units—Shikishima, Yamato, Asahi, and Yamazakura—were all taken from Motoori Norinaga's well-quoted poem, which by now is more than familiar to us.

Shikishima no	Should someone ask,
Yamatogokoro wo	"What is the soul
Hito towaba	Of Yamato, our ancient land?"
Asahi ni niou	It is scent of mountain cherry blossoms
Yamazakurabana.[82]	In the morning sun.

Like Nitobe and Kuki, Ōnishi also grounded his sentiment in this verse. Upon organizing the first kamikaze unit, he wrote the following poem, which affirms the beauty of cherry blossoms, and the related truth that glory is short-lived.

Today in flower,
Tomorrow scattered by the wind—

Such is our life as blossoms.
How can we think
Its fragrance will last forever?[83]

The young men who became kamikaze pilots identified with this fragrance. Like cherry blossoms, they too fell beautifully, ending their lives in order to protect the sacred, meaningful space of Japan.

If only we might fall
Like cherry blossoms in the Spring—
So pure and radiant![84]

Some of these pilots even took boughs of cherry blossoms with them as they went off to die.[85]

When we compare these sentiments with those of past warriors, we become aware of what has changed about change. Let us not forget that the "here-today-gone-tomorrow" sentiment of these wartime verses was actually not so often expressed in the early stages of the War. Only in the defamiliarized, overly expanded context of imperial Japan as it was engaged in a total, worldwide war, does it appear. For these young men living and dying in the margins of a twentieth-century global conflagration, the cherry blossom became elevated as a *symbol* of nation and empire. As such, it was readily shared by those who saw themselves as being similarly atomized as elements of mass society. They themselves became the embodiment of falling blossoms, pieces of the nation and empire, volunteering to die in a place "beyond the hill" as an idea and fragrance cast to the wind.

Even so, the pull of place was still strong; and at the moment of death on the battlefield, more young men seem to have cried out for their mothers than for the emperor. In the following letter by one young kamikaze pilot, the linkage is concretely to home, to family, and to immediate leaders, as much as it is to anything more conceptual.

Dear Parents:

Please congratulate me. I have been given a splendid opportunity to die. This is my last day. This destiny of our homeland hinges on the decisive battle in the seas to the south where I shall fall like a blossom from a radiant tree. . . .

How I appreciate this chance to die like a man! I am grateful from the depths of my heart to the parents who have reared me with their constant prayers and tender love. And I am grateful as well to my squadron leader and superior officers who have looked after me as if I were their own son and given me such careful training.

Thank you, my parents, for the twenty-three years during which you have cared for me and inspired me. I hope that my present deed will in some small way repay what you have done for me. . . .[86]

The idiom for suicide in battle was *rippa na shi*, or "splendid death." Certainly, the idea of glory in battle had had a long incubation, which might explain why the practice of suicide bombings spread quickly as a legitimate military stratagem once the first units were deployed. It took little effort to persuade young men to volunteer to die. In the desperate effort to protect Japan from annihilation, some 5,000 young men voluntarily sacrificed themselves in the final years of the war effort. They died to honor themselves and their families even though their splendid death was, in the end, little more than a beautiful idea put violently (and momentarily) into action. It was a part of a larger effort to make the world pure and beautiful regardless of the brutality required. As a part of this effort, these young men were deemed gods, *kamu nagara*, like the ancient emperors so honored by the *Man'yōshū* poets. Theirs was a modern promise: that the aristocratic privileges of the few would become those of the many, that their souls would be guaranteed a place at Yasukuni Shrine in Tokyo, and that they would be forever remembered and honored for their sacrifice. For many young men, it was the only way they could ever go home again. For the few who actually did make it back to Japan after the War's end, that home had changed dramatically.

THE A-BOMB, AND A NEW KIND OF NOTHING

Because of recent scholarship, we now have a clearer picture of how the reasonable intentions of good people lead to atrocity. Being an abstract and, therefore, portable notion, modernity's insistence on its inherent superiority left many people in many parts of the world with much to explain after the hostilities ended. If the Japanese have Nanking to answer for, the British have Dresden, and the Americans have to account for the many Japanese cities that were leveled by months of carpet bombing, not to mention the destruction of Hiroshima and Nagasaki.

Toward the end of the Pacific War, it was possible to fly B29 bombers into Japanese airspace without fear of encountering effective antiaircraft attack. So it was that thousands of tons of incendiary devices were dropped in circular patterns on most of Japan's cities. This strategy to destroy civilian populations was first devised by the British Royal Air Force in their attacks on German targets. Made mostly of wood and other flammable materials, Japan's neighborhoods caught fire easily; and huge conflagrations, fanned by their own convection currents, swept over vast areas, suffocating and burning anyone unfortunate enough to be caught within their tightening grip. General Bonner F. Fellers, Douglas MacArthur's military secretary and chief of his psychological-warfare operations, condemned the practice of saturation bombings as "one of the most ruthless and barbaric killings of noncombatants in all history."[87] Yet the bombings continued, and an estimated 300,000 people died as a result.

My relatives, living not far from Gotanda Station in Tokyo, survived the bombings; but the experience changed them forever. I remember visiting the Ides' home for dinner one evening. While seated on the tatami floor around the low table in the sitting room, Mrs. Ide showed me the nylon stocking that she always wore around her waist. It was filled with a wad of 10,000 yen bills. She explained. "You never know when you're going to have to run out of your house to escape a bomb." That was the lesson she learned as a young woman; and it was apparently one that stayed with her for the rest of her life.

A memorable depiction of these bombings and the chaos and starvation that followed is found in an animated film by Takahata Isao (1935–), *Grave of the Fireflies* (*Hotaru no haka*, 1988), based on a novel by Nosaka Akiyuki (1930–). A reinstituted theme of evanescence is effectively captured in the image of fireflies, especially as they are associated with the grave (and with bombing). Glowing momentarily in the warm summer night, they speak of the destruction of war and of the fragility of quickly extinguished life. *Grave of the Fireflies* is a film about bombing and its consequences, but it is not bombastic. If anything, it is the quietness of the incendiary canisters dropped from overhead that are so unforgettably menacing. Their nonexplosiveness draws us into a moment of reflection and gives us the chance to think about all that is about to change. Quickly, the reflective moment passes, and the city begins to ignite. Trying to get away from his bombed neighborhood, fourteen-year-old Seita flees with his four-year-old sister Setsuko on his back. Along with the other residents of the city, they run for their lives. When he returns a few days later, a great transformation has occurred. Their home, indeed the entire city, is gone, burned to the ground.

The cicada-shell landscape that we encounter in *Grave of the Fireflies* reminds us of the reasons that atomic bombs were dropped on Hiroshima and Nagasaki in particular. Very few people still realize that these two medium-sized cities were spared conventional bombing because they were being saved as test sites for the A-bomb. Neither too small nor too large, they were just the right size for the type of bombs being developed. The scientists and engineers who designed and built the weapon sought a living, relatively unscathed community on which to test the weapon's potential. Carpet bombing would have spoiled them as scientific samples.

As for the reasons such weapons were deployed at all, many arguments have been put forward to justify their use. The one we hear most often was that they ended the War quickly and spared the lives of those on both sides who would have been involved in an invasion of the islands. What we know now about the moment, however, does not justify this claim. By the end of 1944, Japan's power to continue the war was already exhausted. This is a point acknowledged by the U.S. Strategic Bombing Survey and its 1946 report "The Political Target Under Assault."

> Based on a detailed investigation of all the facts and supported by the testimony of the surviving Japanese leaders involved, it is the Survey's opinion that certainly prior to 31 December 1945, and in all probability prior to 1 November 1945, Japan would have surrendered even if the atomic bombs had not been dropped, even if Russia had not entered the war, and even if no invasion had been planned or contemplated.[88]

Despite talk about how the bombs mercifully precluded a full-scale invasion, by the summer of 1945 it was clear that such an operation was not going to be necessary.[89]

More plausible are three other reasons to drop atomic bombs. None of them were tactical. First, the destruction of Hiroshima and Nagasaki was, again, an experiment done to test a newly developed technology. Second, these tests were timed to send a political message to the world, and particularly to the Soviet Union, that such a weapon existed and that it would be used on anyone who challenged American supremacy. And third, the bombs were dropped as a way to persuade the recalcitrant few among Japan's highest levels of leadership to admit defeat and to surrender unconditionally. With regard to the final point, there is a reasonable political objective to discern here. But the point that I would make, as many others have done, is that even if we accept that a demonstration of atomic weapons was a necessary or even useful persuasion, we certainly do not have to accept the places chosen and the ways in which they were actually deployed.

There were many ways to make the point that the United States had developed a new, terrifying weapon. Knowing what we know about the Japanese regard for space, it might have been equally shocking, and less murderous, to destroy culturally important spaces that were less populated. Admittedly, Japan had chosen to pursue a modern path to war and should be held responsible for the devastation that this fateful vision caused, whether to its own people or to others. But even their culpability does not condone the way in which the United States, aggressively treading its own modern path, brought the hostilities to such an unnecessarily inhumane conclusion.

As we might expect, the numbing consequences of atomic warfare had a profound impact on the future development of Japanese culture. I would argue that the almost total destruction of these two cities led to a fundamental change in how long-held notions of evanescence and form came to be reinstituted. In a way that no one else on earth has ever had to learn, the inhabitants of Hiroshima and Nagasaki came to know just how devastating these weapons are. On August 6, 1945, the first atomic bomb ever used on human targets was exploded 600 meters above Hiroshima, high enough to allow the maximum spread of its deadly force. Three days later, on August 9, 1945, another was dropped on the people of Nagasaki. The destruction of both cities was nearly total. A searing flash of light evaporated those close to ground zero and melted the skin off people miles away. Shock waves followed, leveling buildings within a radius of around 1.8 kilometers, knocking people's eyes out of their heads, and driving shards of shattered glass and splinters of wood into their bodies. Fires followed, killing all those who were trapped in collapsed buildings. Finally, radiation began to take its course, killing many right away; later causing leukemia and various cancers in others; taking much longer, even decades, before bringing illness and death to still others. Because of the chaos of war, it is difficult to get an exact count of those who perished. But by 1950, some 282,000 out of an estimated population of 440,000 had suffered bomb-related deaths in Hiroshima. In Nagasaki, the ratio was 140,000 out of 270,000.[90]

The destructive power of these weapons is hard to imagine and difficult to convey. For this and other reasons, many of those who personally witnessed the destruction have remained silent sufferers. Some have felt guilty for having survived when so many others did not. Others have had to forget the horror in order to get on with the rest of their lives. Speaking of the survivors, the novelist Ōe Kenzaburō held, even as he spoke about the atrocity, "They…have a right to silence. They have the right, if possible, to forget everything about Hiroshima."[91]

Others have made it their lifelong cause to testify of the event in order to prevent such a thing from happening again, and this despite the pain of having to remember the unimaginable with each telling. I will never forget the personal testimonies of Murata Tadahiko, Kayashige Junko, Yano Miyako, and Kawasaki Miyoji, all from Hiroshima, who visited Tufts University in the spring of 2005 to participate in a conference, "Hiroshima-Nagasaki 2005: Memories and Visions." To relay just one story from this conference, Murata was five years old, playing soldiers in his backyard, when the bomb exploded. He was burned and irradiated by the flash, and spent the next six months in critical condition. But immediately after the attack he was still able to walk. He found his older sister Sachiko trapped in the collapsed ruins of their home. With his eight-year-old sister Setsuko, who was severely burned on half of her body, he tried to rescue this sister. As the flames approached, a neighbor pulled them away. It was too late. Nothing could be done. Unwilling to leave her there, they had to be led off. They had no recourse but to let the flames claim their older sister.

The moment quickly passed, but Murata's relationship to it has not.

The memory of leaving Sachiko in the flames crying, "Tadahiko, help me! Setsuko, don't leave me!" does not fade as the years pass. On the contrary, I remember things more vividly as I get older. I have mixed feeling, like thinking "I was only a child. I couldn't have done anything," or on the other hand, blaming myself for her death. This struggle of emotions makes me even more miserable.[92]

As we shall consider in the final pages of this study, many Japanese writers, filmmakers, and visual artists have come to express the hopelessness that the atomic bombs brought to Japan. They have aggressively taken up what John Treat has called the "final theme": the imminent destruction of all human life, and our acquired ability to end the world.[93] No doubt, the prominence with which the end of the world has become a major motif of contemporary Japanese life is a consequence of both a deep appreciation of evanescence and also Japan's unenviable status as the only place on earth to have been bombed by atomic weapons. Sugimoto Naojirō, who survived the destruction of Hiroshima, linked the apocalypse to the bombings, "which made one think of the end of the world."[94] Nuclear weapons have underscored evanescence, making the passing of all human life a real, even likely, possibility. Along with the unconditional surrender that soon followed, the holocaust caused a disruption of the meta-narratives of modernization and Japan's invincibility. This break with the transcendental order returned Japan to nothingness.

The new nothingness of 1945 was not the emptiness (*sunyata*) that is common to everything and, therefore, connects all things. It is rather more like a nihilistic absence of everything, including a lack of relationship, meaning, and hope. We can detect this new nothingness in a stark poem by Takahashi Takeo, as it condemns *both* the here-and-now and the ideological, transcendental realm.

> I would be comforted
> if all living things
> in heaven and earth
> were to perish
> in utter desolation.[95]

The atomic bomb represents a crowning modern achievement. It is the "sublime" consequence of a calculated search for ultimate power and for an undisturbed sense of security that seeks nothing less than an unchanging, unassailable power. It is a force that includes both visible and invisible destruction.

The instantaneous yet long-lasting consequences of nuclear destruction have tried to render the truth of evanescence null by way of a countering truth of unquestionable authority and power. Unfortunately, by radically amplifying the natural processes of change in order to enforce a state of modern political order, with its systematic and universal reach, the stasis that results is still an illusion. It mocks and, therefore, is ultimately exposed by a gentler evanescent refrain. As persuasive as mutually guaranteed destruction might be, because of its yet unimaginable scope, its true psychological effect can actually erode fear and, therefore, the very premise upon which nuclear deterrence depends. Along with peace, even horror does not last.

This is not to say that fear was not (and still is not) a part of the picture. On one level, the dropping of two atomic bombs on two cities forced the Japanese to reconsider the horror-instilling rhetoric of hell, as earlier presented in Genshin's vivid *Essentials of Birth in the Pure Land* and other Buddhist depictions. As William LaFleur pointed out at the Tufts conference, many who experienced the bombing found the aftermath to be lamentably similar to the various tortures that supposedly awaited the evil, so that the monstrous flourishes of Genshin's work proved to be realistic descriptions of what actually happened at ground zero: people thirsting for the water that would quickly kill them; burn victims walking about like wraiths, chilled in midsummer by their lack of skin, which hung like rags from the their finger tips.

For some, even such depictions of hell failed to express the numbing horror of the bomb's devastation. Ōta Yoko (1903–63) writes,

> ...people often spoke of the experience of the atomic bomb as "hell" or "scenes of hell." It probably would have been a simple matter if one were able to express the bitterness of that experience in terms of that ready-made concept "hell," whose existence I did not acknowledge. I was absolutely unable to depict the truth without first creating a new terminology.[96]

There is nothing new about death or war. Neither is there anything particularly novel about massacre and extermination as such. But what *has* in fact changed is the scale and the means of mass murder, and, following from this, the emergence of a possibly new way to think about a new kind of atrocity that required a "new terminology" to express it.

For those Japanese such as Ōta, the world suddenly became disconnected and cold. Even the regenerative forces of place that had traditionally given identity and hope seemed to lose their power. The space of Japan had been rendered a nothingness in this new nihilistic sense of the word. Home itself became a vanishing point, not so unlike the streets of Nanking or the forests of Vosges.

> The days come, the days go, and chaos and nightmare seem to wall me in.
>
> Even the full light of clear, perfectly limpid autumn days brings no relief from profound stupefaction and sorrow; I seem to be submerged in the deepest twilight. On all sides people whose condition is no different from mine die every day.[97]
>
> And now, because of this fateful event, I've come to the countryside I once loved. I gaze at the lavender mountains, at the perfectly clear blue sky. At night I see the bright moon and listen to the river flowing by. But those sights and sounds no longer have a hold on my heart.[98]

As expressed here, in *The City of Corpses* (*Shikabane no machi*, 1948), the once-formalized lyrical response to "perfectly limpid autumn days" no longer exists. It is as if the traditional poetic code of here-and-now has finally been forgotten. Similarly, "lavender mountains," "the perfectly clear blue sky," "the bright moon," and "the river flowing by" no longer give shape to evanescence. If anything, they add to the chaos and nightmare of the bombing, telling us that Ōta's sensibilities are no longer formed by these conventions of a well-established aesthetic precisely because, having experienced the horror of atomic warfare, she fears being bound any longer to place, whatever the place might be. Like skin melted from an arm, her self has also been torn away from its place.

It is no longer possible to think, feel, and say what home now means. There is no longer an expected response, no lyrical spontaneity that guides one's feeling for familiar ground. There is nothing left to help affirm one's place and relationship to others: again, the lyrical code has been annihilated at ground zero. Incredibly and shockingly, the message of home is only the destructive newness of this technology that needs new words to express the void that it has wrought. Again, this new kind of nothingness is something other than Nagarjuna's *sunyata*, or emptiness. It is not *mu*, the nothingness that is everything. It is, rather, absence, lack, void. It is a new nothingness that is nihil.

Being beyond conventional lyricism, the truth of August 1945 was also beyond conventional tears. Hara Tamiki's (1905–51) "Flowers of Summer," like Ōta's *City of Corpses*, similarly established a new sense of nothingness. It marked a significant draining away of the lyrical apparatus (of *hana*) that, as I have mentioned, had long resisted the epic enterprise of modern realism. In response to the unprecedented magnitude and horror of the destruction, a numbness forms and a silence replaces the expected lyrical response. Atomic realism has rendered the familiar space of home into an abstraction. It has become an unfamiliar expression of an incomprehensibly distant and even sublime power, a God without feeling and mercy. In recasting what might have been a heretofore formulaic response to one's environment, this new emptiness, which marks a lack rather than a fullness of emotion and sense of being, marks another important milestone in our study of evanescence.

Consider this remarkably restrained account of Hara discovering the body of his nephew among the charred ruins of Hiroshima.

> In an open area over toward the West Parade Ground my brother happened to spot a corpse clothed in familiar yellow shorts. He got off the cart and went over. My sister-in-law and then I also left the cart and converged on the spot. In addition to the familiar shorts, the corpse wore an unmistakable belt. The body was that of my nephew Fumihiko. He had no jacket; there was a fist-sized swelling on his chest, and fluid was flowing from it. His face had turned pitch-black, and in it a white tooth or two could barely be seen. Though his arms were flung out, the fingers of both hands were tightly clenched, the nails biting into the palms. Next to him was the corpse of a junior high school student and farther off, the corpse of a young girl, both rigid just as they had died. My second brother pulled off Fumihiko's fingernails, took his belt too as a memento, attached a name tag, and left. It was an encounter beyond tears.[99]

The anti-lyricism of this passage is extraordinary. Hara's description of the young boy's body—his nephew's body—is vivid. Yet it is striking in a clinical and objectifying way. The described corpse of Hara's nephew is already nothing but a thing, a residue of total war, a product of "war without mercy."[100] What once was "my nephew Fumihiko," is now identifiable only by the clothes that still wrap his charred body: "familiar yellow shorts" and an "unmistakable belt." Though actually monstrous in its shape, the horrible reality of this deformed corpse can only be conveyed by a cold and distanced mode of representation—a "face turned pitch-black" and "nails biting into the palms." Horribly little emotion is expressed—unless it is the numbness and unfathomable sorrow felt in response to a lack of human presence. The belt taken from the boy's body, and the fingernails that are pulled off and kept as keepsakes—these are painful mementoes. Tagged and left for collection,

Fumihiko himself is no more and no less than what atomic warfare has made him to be: the charred shell of what he once was. He is not even a cicada shell, cast off as life begins its final, ebullient phase. He is an interrupted development. In the rush toward creating a new and better world, his life was the price paid in order to fulfill the total order of modernity's desire. In a rationalized world space, he, like the entire city of Hiroshima, is a specimen.

As Murata Tadahiko explained to those present at the Hiroshima-Nagasaki 2005 conference, the one horrifying thing he learned from the experience of being bombed was that he and other victims of the attack had been reduced to the status of data. Days after the blast, American researchers came into the city to measure the shadows of people burned onto the sidewalks and to record levels of radiation. Their purpose was to calculate the precise position of the bomb when it went off over the city, and to determine the extent of its effectiveness. A year later, when a medical clinic was set up to examine the survivors, all the injured of Hiroshima went to have their wounds examined. As Murata reported, none of them received treatment of any kind. That was not the purpose of the clinic. The Americans had not come back to help them. They wanted only their information. As Murata sorrowfully and angrily put it, "We were so badly in need of medical care, and all they gave us was one piece of candy each."

Takenishi Hiroko's "The Words that Hiroshima Makes Us Say" (*Hiroshima ga iwaseru kotoba*, 1983) speaks to the dynamics of this newly forged relationship between self and space, between inner and outer. The question she asks is a difficult one. What happens when a gap opens up between one and one's familiar space? What do we call it when *uchi* is no longer *uchi*? What do we have, and who are we, when home vanishes?

There are words that speak about atomic-bombed Hiroshima.

There are words that atomic-bombed Hiroshima makes me speak.

This is not a distinction based on any theory. I know it intuitively. Perhaps I am mistaken in this. All I can say is that for the past twenty-five years it has remained for me a fact that has sometimes been stronger but never weaker.

I am glad that there are words that speak about Hiroshima. One would be unable to live were there not such words that we mutually acknowledge. Without such words, what life besides that of simple wayfarers would be possible for us?

But the words that Hiroshima makes me speak always lead me to an abyss of grief. My feelings when I stand at the edge of that abyss of both a cold gripping construction inside me, and of something warmly oozing out of me at the very height of that construction, are my proofs that such words exist.

When I learned, when I felt, that there are words that Hiroshima makes me speak, I felt this Hiroshima was both "Hiroshima" and not "Hiroshima." I felt and learned these words that substituted for the name of limitless things, that they had a greater expansiveness. At times I am angry that the words that speak of Hiroshima are so very insufficient. Don't even I use such words when speaking about things other than Hiroshima? When I do, I must anger others.

Does that mean that I, so rebuked, can tolerate those works that speak of Hiroshima? No, it does not. This contradiction, this problem, this anger, this helplessness—I believe there can be no possibility of my deepening the knowledge of Hiroshima, no possibility of sharing it with others, without enduring my use of such things.[101]

For the poet Bashō, and for Ikku's travelers, the lonely process of traveling away from home could still be a form of discovery. But here the evanescence of wayfaring is not held to be meaningful in the same sense, simply because there is no such thing as home anymore. It is no longer the place we left, nor the place we find along the way. Neither is it the place to which we can return. The bonds of spontaneity between self and context have been brutally severed. They are viewed in a way that tragically knows the hold that home still has upon one's happiness and well-being even though that home has been flattened, burned, and contaminated with radiation. It is a profound shock that only a modern, radically altered sense of vastness can produce. When the bombs exploded over Hiroshima and Nagasaki, everyone thought that only their own home had been destroyed. When they emerged to discover that it had happened to everyone else, a new sense of dread was born.

Let us recast this phenomenon in the terms of our analysis. This lack of wholeness, Takenishi's dividedness and state of perplexity, follows from knowing that the order of here-and-now has been forever altered by a transcendental order that had never been more clearly and horribly understandable. What is to be understood in the context of nuclear holocaust? I believe that what we must grasp in order to make sense of the Japanese understanding of the A-bomb was that the brutal transformation of Hiroshima and Nagasaki made the distorting (and distorted) nature of modern ideology visible in ways unavailable to any other *uchi*. By starkly demonstrating its heartless intentions, its ruthless methods, and its horrible consequences, modernity's distorting ideological processes (this deceptive conceptual masking of real particularity and difference in ways that make disagreement seem like universal agreement) were ripped off in a way that helped Japan awake from the illusions of modern life. This happened in ways that the victors of the War have yet to experience.

Some adjustment to our line of analysis is in order. The hatred that leads to war can hardly be said to be of the moment. And yet the momentousness of nuclear destruction and its powerful status as a tool of radical change also underscore the continuing relevance of evanescence, even in this age of a new kind of (nihilistic) nothingness. To return to an ancient point, life on this planet is, and always will be, fragile and threatened. Today we understand that human life may very well cease altogether. At that moment, everything we know to be familiar will disappear in a flash—the smell of flowers, the blueness of the sky, the faces of those we love. This is not our possible fate. If we do not change our ways, this our inevitable fate.

Having been confronted with such a truth, the *hibakusha* who visited Tufts also made a concerted effort to visit a number of local secondary schools, where they stood before our young people and testified to the destruction of the A-bomb and pled for the abolishment of nuclear weapons. Speaking at Belmont High School, Kayashige Junko received a standing ovation for telling her story.[102] Later that day, as we were gathered in the dining room of my home, she explained her source of courage. To my surprise, it was not an ideological position, nor even a moral purpose. Rather, it was something more evanescent, and profoundly of the moment. I was glad my son was there with us when she smiled and said, "All you can do is stay happy. You eat something good. And keep trying."[103]

OCCUPATION: RADICAL CHANGE AS SALVATION

For the Japanese, World War II truly ended not with the sound of bombs but with a high and wavering voice. On August 15, 1945, Emperor Hirohito announced to his subjects that Japan would now have to "endure the unendurable." In other words, the War was over, and Japan had lost. The invincible and chosen nation surrendered unconditionally. With this statement, the ideological structure of empire and military might collapsed tragically. The emperor himself, head signifier of this failed system of meaning, had to be the one to suggest its falsehood. The following year, he took an additional step and denied his divine status.

The sense of betrayal and disillusion felt by most Japanese citizens was profound. To many, it seemed that many years of their lives had been wasted. Loved ones had died. The ideals they had believed in and had fought so desperately for proved to be fabrications. Of course, this is not to say that the emperor's self-renunciation was understood so simply and definitively as a complete break from the past. Some continued to believe, and, today, many still do. The imperial institution still lends its form to Japanese society, and most Japanese would miss it if it were gone. Yet it is also true that a vast majority of Japanese came to feel that the wartime concept of Japan as a divine and invincible empire had been a propagandistic deception. If those claims had been true, why the unconditional surrender that left even the fate of the emperor to be decided by foreigners? And why had their sacred land been allowed to be bombed to ashes and rubble?

The preservation of the emperor was, in fact, the one condition that Japan's military leaders held out for. By signing the unconditional surrender, Hirohito's very life was placed in the hands of General MacArthur and his advisors. They were the first invaders in historical memory to occupy and control Japan. Having taken the time to study Japanese culture, they understood the drawbacks of executing or even trying the emperor. Preserving him meant retaining a crucial source of cultural form. By not trying him, they avoided the chaos that would have encouraged guerilla warfare and, most likely, a Marxist revolution. As a result, a fundamental (though severely discredited) cultural form was preserved at this crucial moment in Japan's history. To be sure, the divine status of the emperor had already been impinged by defeat, but his existence remained an important source of identity. He was soon thereafter rendered "symbolic" by the new constitution of 1946 that attempted to abolish his status as a *kami*. What our analysis shows, however, is that this move was hardly a solution since it was precisely the emperor's status as a symbol, not as a god in the here-and-now sense, that had allowed Japanese to fan the flames of patriotism and imperialism.

Responses to the surrender were varied. But one development was a resurgence of interest in Buddhism, which had suffered at the hands of State Shintō's ascendance during the decades leading up to the War. Takeyama Michio's (1903–84) widely read novel, *Harp of Burma* (*Biruma no tategoto*, 1946), told a story about one Corporal Mizushima Yasuhiko, who experiences the horrors of war as a soldier in Burma and awakens to the need for the sort of spiritual rejuvenation that Buddhism provides. A talented musician, Mizushima keeps the morale of his troop high by accompanying them as they sing chorale music: "Whether we were happy or miserable, we sang. Maybe it's because we were always under the threat of battle, of dying, and felt we wanted to do at least this one thing well as long as we were still alive."[104] As their musical leader, he eventually becomes their spiritual teacher as well. He builds the eponymous harp, which he uses to unite, inspire, and even protect his fellow soldiers.

Fleeing eastward through the jungles of Burma, hoping to join up with Japanese troops in Siam before being overtaken by the British who are moving northward, his troop is eventually surrounded and taken captive. Fortunately for them, the war has just ended; and there is hope of returning to Japan. When the singing troop is sent off to a prisoner-of-war camp, however, Mizushima lingers behind. He chooses the Bodhisattva's path and returns to the world of suffering. There are other Japanese soldiers still fighting, unaware of the surrender; and when he is asked by the British to persuade a group holed up in a mountain stronghold to give up, he cooperates. He tries everything. He even sits down in front of the men's cave and plays his harp. But they refuse to surrender. Drunk and enflamed with patriotism, they are all killed in the withering battle that ensues.

Mizushima himself is seriously wounded. But he is discovered and nursed back to health by Burmese natives. When he discovers their intention to eat him, he plays music to save himself. Narrowly escaping, he wanders the Burmese countryside dressed as a Buddhist monk. He encounters the bodies of many Japanese soldiers who have died in battle and have yet to be cared for. Feeling compassion for them, he buries their corpses and comes to realize his responsibility to the dead. Although he finally makes it to the camp where his fellow troop members are being held, he does not join them, not even when they are finally repatriated to Japan, and this despite their attempts to persuade him to come along. In his parting letter to his fellow soldiers, read by the troop's leader as their boat sails homeward to

Japan, Mizushima explains his spiritual journey and his reasons for staying behind.

> According to the natives who lived along this stretch of the Sittang, many Japanese units attempted a night crossing here. It was over two hundred yards across the swollen river, and they tried to make it with nine or ten men on each small raft. But the rafts would only get to midstream and then be swept down the river. Some must have been carried all the way out to sea, and others washed ashore in the heart of the jungle....
>
> Every crossing point took its toll of lives, but there were also many soldiers—especially those suffering from dysentery or malaria, or too weak from lack of food to keep going—who seized the first chance to kill themselves with a hand grenade. Explosions were often heard in the field or woods after fleeing troops had passed through. Even the natives knew that each explosion meant another suicide. There must have been a vast number of such incidents untold, unrecorded, merely forgotten!
>
> How could anyone see what I have seen and do nothing about it? How could anyone ignore it with a clear conscience, or say that it was none of his business?
>
> With the help of the natives and of the monks from a nearby village, I managed to bury these corpses in the sandy river bank.[105]

In this farewell letter, the image of a river appears as a true sign of evanescence once again. As in Kamo no Chōmei's *Account of My Hut,* as in Chikamatsu's *Double Suicide at Amijima,* flowing water expresses suffering, death, and change.

> Why does so much misery exist in the world? Why is there so much inexplicable suffering? What are we to think?
>
> I have learned that these questions can never be solved by human thought. We must work to bring what little relief we can to this pain-ridden world. We must be brave. No matter what suffering, what unreasonableness, what absurdity we face, we must remain undaunted and show strength of character by meeting it with tranquility. It is my hope to realize this conviction by devoting myself to a religious life.
>
> Furthermore, I never cease to marvel that the people of Burma, though certainly indolent, pleasure-seeking, and careless, are all cheerful, modest, and happy. They are always smiling. Free from greed, they are at peace with themselves. While living among them, I have come to believe that these are precious human qualities.
>
> Our county has waged a war, lost it, and is now suffering. That is because we were greedy, because we were so arrogant that we forgot human values, because we had only a superficial ideal of civilization. Of course we cannot be as languid as the people of this country, and dream our lives away as they often do. But can we not remain energetic and yet be less avaricious? Is that not essential—for the Japanese and for all humanity?
>
> How can we truly be saved? And how can we help to save others? I want to think this through carefully. I want to learn. That is why I want to live in this country, to work and serve in it.[106]

Critiques of modernity, such as Takeyama's, formed quickly in the context of a devastated and defeated Japan; and it is in this new era of "postmodernity" that the notion of evanescence begins to make a comeback. Now exposed, the dangers of "human thought" become too apparent to accept uncritically. In his attempt to reveal the darker side of modern life, Takeyama makes numerous comparisons between the Burmese and the Japanese. "The basic difference lies in the attitude of a people: whether, like the Burmese, to accept the world as it is, or [like the Japanese] to try to change it according to one's designs. Everything hinges on this."[107]

Surely, the comparison is overly broad—there is the active change that one wills, and the passive change that happens to someone. But this new positioning serves a rhetorical purpose in providing the platform from which post-War Japanese writers could begin to address the question of what had gone so terribly wrong.

> The Buddha saw through that kind of happiness and progress, and what it leads to, thousands of years ago. He taught people to stop clinging desperately to this earthly life, and the Burmese are still faithful to his teaching. If you want a more peaceful, civilized world it'd be a lot better for us to imitate the Burmese, instead of the Burmese imitating us.[108]

In their rush toward modernization, the Japanese had depended on systematic, scientific thought at the same time as they had "forgotten to meditate deeply on the meaning of life."[109] The result was horror—whether Pearl Harbor, Nanking, or Hiroshima.

By way of his hero's enlightenment, Takeyama turned from modern life to embrace ancient Buddhist tenets, which we might reformulate in this fashion. Desire causes war. War brings suffering. The way to escape suffering is to stop war. War is prevented by being humble, by serving others, and by working actively and hopefully for the salvation of all. Mizushima's lingering in Burma suggests an attachment to a premodern community, yet Takeyama chooses to see this "activism" as a detachment. The one who plays the harp of Burma is not simply escaping. In seeing the vanity of desire and ambition, Mizushima returns to samsara. Like a Bodhisattva who is filled with compassion for those who still suffer from delusion, the enlightened corporal commits himself to a life of charitable deeds. In his eyes, this is better done in Burma than in Japan, although the purport of the novel is, certainly, that militaristic Japan, too, needs to be buried so that a new Japan might become possible.

DECADENCE, MOVING AWAY FROM FORM

Like Takeyama, the novelist Sakaguchi Ango (1906–55) also emerged from the trauma of war with fresh hope. His answer to the suffering of war was strikingly different, however. In an essay entitled "A Theory of Decadence" (*Darakuron*, 1946), published soon after the War ended, he, too, described a trajectory of suffering, enlightenment, and salvation. For him, however, salvation was not anything that could be formed into yet another system of thought or belief. The change he affirmed did not posit the next alternative to fascism but, rather, embraced change and formlessness itself. As an anti-ideologue, he urged the Japanese to realize their natural *lack* of discipline. He urged them to be true to their carefree thoughtlessness and malleability, and to become uninhibited in their private pursuit of happiness, affection, and sensual pleasure—all qualities that militarism had suppressed and ones that evanescence might bring back. In other words, he advocated the kind of meaning that comes from moving away from form: a Genroku-like hedonism.

Sakaguchi was a credible witness to change. He personally lived through the firebombing of Tokyo and witnessed the arrival of American troops to his country. He seized the destructive moment and criticized the falseness of the ideological order that had led the Japanese to such a lamentable state of affairs. In particular, he pointed out how both bushido and the emperor system were nothing but fictions, forms of false consciousness cleverly constructed by deceitful and manipulating elites who seized and maintained political power by establishing an unstoppable ideological justification that he called the "will of history."

> As far as politics goes, history doesn't bring individuals together. To the contrary, it absorbs them and gives them life as a different kind of huge organism. Dressed as history, politics also exercises a massive creativity. Who conducted this war? Was it Tōjō? The Military? Perhaps in part, but it was also that massive organism running through Japan: the irretrievable will of history. Before such a will, the Japanese people are nothing but obedient children.
>
> Even if politicians themselves don't have creativity, under the veil of history politics does possess a certain creativity—a will, an unstoppable momentum that moves forward like a wave upon the open sea. Who thought up this bushido business? The creativity of history did; or its sense of smell did. History had us all sniffed out. Because it restricts human nature and human instinct, bushido is inhuman and contradictory to our nature. It comes from a certain insight into human nature, and in this sense is all too human. I look upon the emperor system in a similar way, as a very Japanese (and thus very creative) political construct.[110]

Here Sakaguchi attacks form itself. He rejects the capacity of the Japanese people to be absorbed by "history," or the continued existence of ideological constructs—such as bushido—because they wrongly yet cleverly counter human nature.

For Sakaguchi, there is nothing natural about the samurai ethic, this attitude that requires constant and never-failing obedience to one's lord. As articulated by people such as Nitobe, the samurai ethic demands unyielding loyalty and a sense of vengeance. But, according to Sakaguchi, these emotions do not come naturally.

> Fundamentally, the Japanese are the least hateful, grudge-bearing people on earth. Our true heart contains an optimism that allows yesterday's foe to

become today's friend. It's an everyday occurrence—not only compromising with yesterday's enemy, but bearing our souls to them precisely because we once were enemies. In other words, we want to serve two lords at the same time. We want to serve the friend who yesterday was our enemy.[111]

Is what Sakaguchi calls "carefree optimism" a result of Japan's long-held appreciation for change? Serving only one ideological master goes against the native grain. The kind of undivided loyalty that had been required by the War was a delusion from which post-War Japan must awaken.

If our master is not really our master, then it follows that our enemy is not really our enemy. Sakaguchi's description of the Japanese as being capable of loving their foe seems to have actually been borne out by Japan's "embrace of defeat," to use John Dower's words. As he explains, the Japanese cooperated with Americans and their efforts to win the peace. For many young Japanese women, this included the literal embrace of American soldiers, just as it meant the general acceptance of General MacArthur as savior and friend.[112] The capacity of the Japanese to walk quickly and gladly away from the militarism of past years was similarly borne out by the bohemian *kasutori* (or dregs) culture that quickly formed in Occupied Japan, with writers such as Sakaguchi and Dazai Osamu (1909–48) acting as the new prophets of this decadent gospel of drugs, drinking, and prostitution. In the economic realm, a similar dog-eat-dog, anything-goes attitude bolstered a burgeoning black market. Once the structure of empire weakened, the transition from discipline to chaos happened quickly and easily. As Sakaguchi put it, the kamikaze pilot of yesterday became the black marketeer of today.

This particular kind of radical transformation was widespread, understandable, and, for Sakaguchi, even desirable. Form was the enemy; and *daraku*—a decadent moving away from form—was exhilarating. With great insight, he revealed not only the appeal of form but the process by which *katachi* (shape) propagates itself, even in a society that supposedly appreciates change and malleability.

Bowing reverently before the Emperor demonstrated their respect, but that was also how [the Fujiwara clan] confirmed their own respectability.

What utter foolishness! I can't find words to describe the absurdity of being forced to bow our heads each time the train turns and passes before Yasukuni Shrine. For some people *this is the only way they are able to sense their own feelings*. We laugh at the stupidity of Yasukuni, yet we ourselves do the same thing, only for other things. The difference is that we don't realize our own idiocy....We tend to bow spontaneously before the most ridiculous things; only we do it without thinking. The teacher of Confucian morals holds the sacred texts above his head reverently as if they are a gift from the gods, but in doing so he is merely perceiving his own dignity, feeling his own existence. All of us do the same thing in one way or another.

As a people devoted to deception, we Japanese can't do without the Emperor, both for the purpose of deception, and also for the Cause. Even if each politician doesn't sense the need for deception, *when we're talking about history's ability to sniff things out, they use it to remove any sense of doubt about their own reality.*[113] (My emphasis)

Here, then, is a simple way to understand the attraction of form. By way of form, we think we can receive what we give—dignity for dignity; respect for respect. If I respect you, you will respect me. If I validate the system, it will validate me. Although this reciprocity also applies to disagreeable values as well—crassness for crassness, disrespect for disrespect—Sakaguchi emphasizes only "positive" values, even as "good form" overlays and masks less-than-favorable situations for all parties. It is easy to see how proper form keeps those of unequal privilege, ability, and power in a dignified and respectful relationship with each other. It is a kind of peace that does nothing to change or rebalance the inherently unequal (or unfair) relationships from which society is created. Is this why oppression and politeness often appear together? Here we remember, once again, *mono no aware*, Norinaga's early modern system of sadness.

By practicing good form, we do to others what we would have them do to us, or we avoid doing to others what we would not want done to us. The relevant and often-heard idiom is *"meiwaku wo kakeru"* ("to be a bother to someone else"). This is the general rule of Japanese cultural practice: to live in a way that does not bother someone else. Of course, this is also a familiar Western formulation of morality, in this case more Kantian than Christian: a negative casting of the golden rule, as it were. In essence, whether morality, politeness, or manipulation, the kind of formality that Sakaguchi is addressing here allows us to sense and affirm our own feelings. That is to say, form helps us remove doubt from our reality. That is why it is important, and necessary. We think we must be doing something right because we are doing things *properly*. We feel our own dignity by recognizing the emperor's dignity. We feel the truth of our existence by way of this reciprocity that can come both as a written law and as an unwritten expectation—as a reciting of the Rescript on Education, a spontaneous bowing, or the prayerful uttering of our regrets or apologies.

One way to rephrase this is to say that in an evanescent world the need for both dignity and validation is acute, maybe even extreme. Consequently, formalities become ingrained as unthinking habits, such as unconscious and never-tiring declarations of one's inappropriateness, "Excuse me." (*Sumimasen.*) "My behavior is inexcusable." (*Mōshi wake arimasen.*) "Forgive my rudeness." (*Gomenasai.*) The Japanese apology is a lyrical moment that is nearly constant. Being nearly constant, is it, then, falsely momentous? For Sakaguchi, such automatic bowing is nothing but stupidity—an unthinking affirmation of the deceitful nature of power relationships. In terms of our analysis, we might be tempted to call such bowing a *jihatsu*-like reaction to the space of here-and-now. But, clearly, at least as described here, an undeniable overlay of ideology is also giving orientation to this action and to the space in which it occurs.

Thus, we understand Sakaguchi's mention of Yasukuni Shrine, where the spirits of the war dead congregate. Whenever a train passed before the shrine, many of its passengers actually bowed—out of respect for the spirits of the war dead who are remembered there. Could there be a clearer confirmation of the perspectival grid of modern consciousness than this? In a modern world, one's orientation is always important and always fairly obvious. Our progress is clearly understood if and only if we see ourselves within a vast coordination of clearly defined relationships. "Am I moving closer to or away from the center of power? Do I share the perspective of the authoritative source?" By way of this grid, we have position and status. We survive. We are normal.

But Sakaguchi sets this deceptively meaningful form against a truly meaningful moment of change. The latter is a destructive (and deconstructive) occasion that makes us ask rebellious questions: "What is there to be so sorry about? And to whom should we feel obliged to lower our heads?" Sakuguchi's answer is that we ought to bow not to the emperor but to the beautiful girls who die in their youth.[114] They are the ones to be honored.

Does this shocking statement not agree with our long-contemplated aesthetics of cherry blossoms? By now, we should be well accustomed to "the desire to destroy a beautiful thing while it is still beautiful."[115] Sakaguchi's declaration of decadence tells us that we have come full circle, having shaken off "history," or the narrative ordering of change, in order to return to something more lyrical if less systematically comprehensive. The image of beautiful dead girls echoes Saikaku's treatment of the woman who loved love; yet it is decidedly more sinister. Having survived the era of transcendental order, Sakaguchi is on the opposite, downhill slope of modernity. He is not climbing but descending the established order of general principles. Unlike Saikaku's, his love of women yields a negative kind of meaningfulness.

For Sakaguchi, the truth of evanescence became obvious the moment fire rained down from heaven and the fragility of human existence became all too clear.

> I loved the great destruction of Tokyo. Although I trembled in fear as the explosive and incendiary bombs rained down, the violent destruction greatly excited me. At the same time, I felt as though I had never loved or felt such longing for humanity as I did at that moment.
>
> I held my ground there in Tokyo, refusing the kindness of a number of friends who not only suggested I evacuate, but even tried to offer me places to stay in the countryside....As the enemy invaders made their landing and heavy artillery shells exploded all about me, I imagined myself trying to conceal the sound of my breath in the air raid shelter. I came to feel resigned to my fate. I thought I might die, but I had the conviction that I would live more abundantly. It's not that I had any great ambitions, other than coming out of the ruins alive. The only plan I had was surviving. I felt a strange sense of rebirth for a new world beyond my imagination. That curious feeling was the most exhilarating feeling I've ever had in my entire life. I felt drawn to the strange oracle that told me that risking my life by staying in Tokyo was the price I had to pay for that uncanny sense of renewal.[116]

Such is the truth of change and fragility. Here Sakaguchi expresses an awareness of death that heightens life, and even brings hope. He describes a transformational experience that many Japanese survivors of World War II seem to have shared. Does this help explain why, when the fighting stopped, militarism vanished like dew in the morning wind?

For his readers, this description of the bombing of Tokyo was the most appreciated part of Sakaguchi's essay. For us, perhaps the most valuable aspect of Sakaguchi's treatise is the contradiction that runs through it from beginning to end. It provides a rare and long-awaited glimpse of the bond that connects change and form: "I loved that magnificent destruction. The sight of humanity meekly resigned to its fate is a curiously beautiful thing."[117] What is magnificent about destruction? At first this seems perverse; but in its own way it makes perfect sense.

Decadence sees the value of utter and wrenching change as an unavoidable correction to false form. In this affirmation, it clarifies our understanding of evanescence and form considerably. As we live, we move toward or away from form. In either case, movement yields meaning: I am like everyone else or I am different; I follow, lead, diverge, reject. If approaching form is meaningful, then moving away from it must be equally so. We often couch our approach in terms of enlightenment, salvation, truth, community, identity, and so on. All these are highly meaningful. Yet are they any more so than our movement away from them? Indeed, rebellion might exceed conformity in meaningfulness, if only because our willful separation from form necessarily follows an already established sense of belonging to it. We reject what we had and were, what we were taught, what we were given. In the same way, humility or a sudden awareness of what we are not—not infallible, not stable, not happy, not loved, not meant to live forever—comes as a crushing meaningfulness, sharpening our awareness of and even need for estrangement.

The source of resignation also lies here: as an acute awareness of either change or form, but *not* as an awareness of a possible balance between the two. Decadence sees no balance. And why should it? We might not know how to fix our problems. We might not be able to come up with a new set of ideals. But at least we know when something is broken. And if it is broken, why believe in it? Why not let it die? As heart-wrenching as that might be, there is still something "curiously beautiful" in this sorrow. Is this not, once again, an affirmation of the profound sadness of things, *mono no aware*?

Although he embraces decadence, Sakaguchi does not bother to couch this moment of resignation in Buddhist terms: again, he does not want to substitute one ideology with another. For his purposes, he affirms change in as here-and-now a way as possible. This might be why his description of the destruction of Tokyo reminds us of Kamo no Chōmei's much earlier description of a beleaguered Heian-kyō. The secularized trappings of *mujō* that he brings to our attention seem to return us inescapably to an earlier state of *hakanasa*, this state where things do not add up.

> Amid the empty landscape of Dōgenzaka's smoldering ruins, part way up the hill was a corpse that had seemed to have been claimed not by the bombing

but by a passing car. It was covered by a single sheet of galvanized metal. Nearby, a soldier stood with a bayoneted rifle. People going to various places, people returning home, victims of the disaster—they formed a meandering flow, a stream of empty thoughts that stepped around the body and kept going. No one paid any attention to the fresh blood on the street. Even if someone did, it meant nothing more to them than a piece of discarded litter.[118]

This passage is descriptive. But what it describes is being without seeing, living without noticing. The crowd is "a meandering flow, a stream of empty thoughts." This is the essence of Sakaguchi's articulation of life during the War. Even if the writer avoids the term *mujō*, using the word *mushin* (無心) instead, "a stream of empty thoughts" seems to at least approximate a secular recasting of evanescence. This post-War stream flows as an emptiness, a bombed numbness. It is a "despondence and distraction" that was at the same time a "surprising sense of satisfaction, a weighty lack of thought."[119]

Of course, to be true to the author's intent, we must recognize his attempt to go beyond this bombed-out emptiness. Deceitful, fictive ideology leads to destruction. Destruction then leads to emptiness. From emptiness, we advance to decadence, which, Sakaguchi tells us, was expressed by the blank expressions of the Japanese as they met the Americans who arrived in the late summer of 1945. Decadence is a gleeful fall through "immense emptiness,"[120] a descent toward all those things that are utterly human and cannot be prevented—greed, despair, selfishness. At the same time, decadence is also a humiliation and, therefore, a possible humility that can make hope and compassion possible.

Sakaguchi himself would probably insist that from decadence it is possible to progress toward a better state. In emptiness there is the beginning of abundance, since from destruction comes an awareness of suffering humanity and "an extraordinary love" for all. Japan had been controlled by militarism, a prison from which Sakaguchi hoped the shock of the War's destruction would free all Japanese. Realizing their fallibility—the ability to lose and to change—the Japanese would be able to become human again, to be themselves each in his or her own way again. By way of decline and humiliation came the possibility of moving ahead more honestly. This, then, is the healing potential of decadence when understood as a movement away from form.

In our study of Japanese culture, we have come to that late modern juncture when the competing ideologies of capitalism and socialism came to vie vociferously to be the legitimate end of history. What we must notice, however, is the ambivalence shown to both of these linear orientations. Sakaguchi flatly rejected the "will of history" that had brought so much suffering to Japan. "Political salvation and other shortcuts are nothing but folly."[121] Ending his "Theory of Decadence" with these words, he leaves us to wonder about the exact nature of the "extraordinary love" for struggling humanity that supposedly takes us from despair, through decadence (as a meaningful movement away from form), and finally to salvation. How do we proceed to salvation without the comforting support of conceptual systems and the form they provide? Is such a salvation even imaginable, or shareable? How do we situate ourselves outside of history?

TO LIVE!

A direct response to the many questions raised by Sakaguchi's "Theory of Decadence" came six years later in the form of a film by Kurosawa Akira (1910–98). *To Live* (*Ikiru*, 1952) followed the celebrated director's earlier success, *Rashōmon* (1950), and preceded the even more well-known *Seven Samurai* (*Shichinin no samurai*, 1954). Of these three important films, *Ikiru* (which means, "to live") is perhaps Kurosawa's enduring masterpiece. It effectively captures the particulars of the post-War era while keeping in play the enduring question of meaning within change.

Ikiru is the story of a bureaucrat, Watanabe Kanji, who lives as if dead. Passing time in his numbingly predictable routine as chief of the Citizen's Section in the municipal office, where he has worked for nearly thirty years without missing a day of work. Ostensibly, his job is to serve the people, a point made clear by a sign that greets all visitors: "Citizens. This is your portal to City Hall. Please feel free to voice your complaints and requests." In fact, he is not inclined to be responsive to the needs of anyone. Like everyone else in the office, he cares only about getting to the end of the day and doing as little as possible. In essence, he is the human definition of form, of life within strictly enforced bureaucratic categories. As such, he is in denial of the truth of evanescence and the possibility of change.

When a group of housewives from a poor area of the city come to City Hall to request that something be done about a filthy drainage pond in their neighborhood, they confront bureaucratic form and are rejected by its rigidity. At their suggestion that the problem area be made into a public park, the women are immediately sent from the Citizen's Section to the Parks Section. Since the pond is also a public health issue, they then get bounced to the Health Center. Since the problem involves sewage, they get passed off to the Sanitation Section. From there, they are sent to the Environmental Health Section, then to the Anti-Epidemics Office, then the Pest Control Section, then the Sewage Section, the Road Section, the City Planning Department, the Fire Department, the children's welfare officer in the Educational Section. They end up visiting the city counselor, who puts them in touch with the deputy mayor, who then sends them back to the Citizen's Section, back to where they started. They are caught, then, in a never-ending and nonresponsive loop of bureaucratic life, modern form as it has been developed to the fullest extent.

If the Occupation Forces made efforts to reform Japan's civil bureaucracy in order to make it more responsive to the people, Kurosawa makes the point that City Hall still cares more about maintaining the clarity of its divisions and ensuring its continued existence as an institution than about serving "democracy" in any way. The women leave, frustrated and angry. City Hall's concerns remain strictly limited to whatever can be expressed on a form, that is, whatever falls neatly within the purview of established categories. In such a world, anything out of the ordinary, such as building or a new park, does not exist. Indeed, as far as Watanabe is concerned, *they* do not exist. In thinking this way about other people, he is not really living. His life does not affirm the truth of change.

Evanescence can become overwhelmed by form. Change is impossible both for the people Watanabe supposedly serves and also for himself personally. What finally disrupts this stasis is stomach cancer and the discovery that he has only about six months to a year to live. Nothing can save him from death. Death is the one change that form cannot overcome. Stunned by this knowledge, he loses his equilibrium. He struggles to find his feet once again, and allows himself to be open to things he once avoided. He is introduced to the decadent *kasutori* culture of the demimonde by a Sakaguchi-like figure, a disheveled writer who initiates him to the pleasures of drinking, music, dancing, prostitution, striptease.

Pulled by his newly found friend through the crowds, the stolid, mumbling Watanabe is a fish out of water. There is some hope for him, however. Although he is overly formal, he is not without feeling. While at a cabaret, he requests to hear a song from his youth, "The Gondolier's Song." As he begins to sing along to the piano's accompaniment, a number of young couples fill the dance floor, only to be put off by his morbid tone.

Inochi mijikashi	Life is brief,
Koi seyo otome	So fall in love, young maiden—
Akaki kuchibiru	Before your red lips
Asenu ma ni	Lose their color,
Atsuki chishio wo	And your passion
Hienu ma ni	Cools.
Asu no tsukihi wa	Tomorrow
Nai mono wo	Does not exist.
Inochi mijikashi	Life is brief,
Koi seyo otome	So fall in love, young maiden—
Kurokami no iro	Before your black hair
Asenu ma ni	Turns gray,
Kokoro no honoo	And the flame in your heart
Kienu ma ni	Goes out.
Kyō wa futatabi	Today
Konu mono wo	Will never come again.[122]

These are all familiar notions: life is short and quickly passing; change is our reality; red lips and black hair lose their brilliance; passions cool. We know no other truth than this. Therefore, the time to live is now, while we still can. We must live in the here-and-now. As the song expresses, tomorrow might never come; and today will never happen again.

"The Gondolier's Song" would seem to support Sakaguchi's prescription for decadence. But for all its dark attractiveness, the decadent lifestyle does not satisfy Watanabe's deeper yearning to do something meaningful with his life. In the glare of neon lights, he sees the dancing denizens of the *kasutori* world connected physically with each other—body pressed to body, each desirous of self-affirmation. But they are not necessarily connected to each other emotionally, in any genuine way. Money connects them—as consumers and providers of desire. But this is not enough.

The day after his night of riotous living, Watanabe meets Odagiri Toyo, the only woman in his section. She comes to him in order to get his permission to resign. Normally, he would try to dissuade her. After all, she has a stable job in an unstable world. But with death on his mind, and wracked with the pain of knowing that he has wasted his life doing meaningless tasks, he simply asks her why she wants to quit. She answers him, "It's boring." He gives his permission. She is too young, honest, and vivacious to endure the enervating structure of City Hall. She alone can tell the jokes that are too painfully true to be funny to her fellow workers. They are merely caretakers of form, working themselves into ineptitude.

> "I hear you've never taken a vacation from your job."
> "That's right."
> "Is that because City Hall couldn't function without you?"
> "No, it's because no one would notice I wasn't there."

Kurosawa's point is that sometimes the Japanese are too formal for their own good.

Watanabe is attracted to Toyo's effervescence, and, at his request, he begins spending time with her. He buys her nylon stockings and numerous meals. He takes her many places—to the movies, to the ice-skating rink. Despite his son Mitsuo's suspicions, their relationship is neither sexual nor romantic. He has not taken a lover. He only wants to be with someone who is vivacious and hopeful. When he asks her how she can be so alive, she denies any special characteristics. "I eat and I work. That's it." This is, we remember, the very statement that the *hibakusha* Kayashige Junko left with us, "All you can do is stay happy. Eat something good. And keep trying."

Kurosawa goes on to make the point that the pleasure she takes in work enlivens her. Her new job is making wind-up rabbits in a small, noisy factory. Even though this change will never allow her to have the life for which she dreams (for she belongs firmly within the ranks of the proletariat), she is nevertheless happy to be making something. Her advice to Watanabe is that he, too, should "try making something." Creativity affirms change. It tests and challenges form. Only in the balance of evanescence and form is there happiness.

At first, the challenge is overwhelming. Watanabe wonders what he could possibly make. Trapped by his job, by the bureaucratic order that obstructs creative change, he knows as well as anyone that he is expected to do nothing new. That is what he has done all his life: nothing new. His job is to be appropriate—on time, well dressed, predictably busied with meaningless details. But then he remembers the group of women who came with their complaint to City Hall; and he determines that he will dedicate his remaining time and energy to building a park for the families of Kuroe-chō. His path to this moment of truth is not unlike other post-War situations. First comes despair. Then comes decadence. But in Watanabe's case, he goes beyond Sakaguchi's escape to reenter the world of form creatively; and by so doing, he forces life to yield meaningful change. By force of his will, he makes City Hall do something new. He is not a revolutionary so much as a reformer, a Bodhisattva.

Watanabe eventually succeeds, but only because of the persistence he shows wherever he turns—from the Parks Section, from the Sanitation Section, and so on. Importantly, he prevails by using formality to conquer formality, prostrating himself before his colleagues in order to win their consent and cooperation, even humbly receiving the threats of gangsters who compete for the same strip of land. The women of Kuroe-chō understand and appreciate his sacrifice. They mourn his death, which occurs soon after the park is completed.

Watanabe's wake takes up roughly half of the film. It is Kurosawa's vehicle for measuring how well Watanabe's actions were understood by those around him. If the women are quick to understand, Watanabe's fellow bureaucrats struggle to see the miracle that has happened: that one person's resolve has made meaningful change possible. More to the point, the wake clearly expresses the crucial interaction of change and form that is the principal focus of this effectively structured film.

Mourning the dead is a solemn occasion. In essence, it is the means by which the drastic change from life to death is formalized. As such, Watanabe's wake is ritualistic and structured by numerous formalities: the sign placed on the front door, the many-tiered display that holds the deceased's photo, the floral arrangements, the drapery, the urn for burning incense, the dark and formal attire of those attending, the types and amounts of food and drink served, and on and on. The guest list is also formulaic. Present at this solemn occasion are a few of Watanabe's closest family members and many of his work associates (who clearly dominate, just as Watanabe's work dominated his family life). Importantly, his superior, the deputy mayor, is there; as are his peers, the head of the Park Section and others. And, of course, his subordinates, minus Odagiri Toyo, are all there seated formally in two lines that face each other.

As the film progresses, this form is challenged by various elements of change that come into the room from the outside. People who are not on the guest list appear at the wake. A group of reporters shows up in order to question the deputy mayor about the meaning of Watanabe's death. Was it a suicide? Was it an expression of rebellion? They represent a challenge to the authority of City Hall, and the deputy mayor performs his duty by assuring them all that nothing inappropriate has happened and that the credibility of the institution remains above criticism. Next, the women of Kuroe-chō appear to express their heartfelt grief at the death of the one man who listened to their pleas and acted to remedy the problem of the drainage pond. Their tears are another challenge to the formal sobriety of the wake: the women's sincere gratitude undermines the men's rather formal discussion about how the park successfully came about. Everyone wants to take credit for something that their rigidity as bureaucrats at first opposed. They want to deny the truth that these women well know: that only Watanabe's lack of rigidity, his driving creativity, made the park a reality.

Finally, a policeman comes to deliver Watanabe's hat to his family. Left at the park where he died, it symbolizes Watanabe's transformation from someone who resisted change to someone who embraced it. Like the women, the policeman wishes to show his respects, and is allowed to pray before Watanabe's image. He was probably the last person to see Watanabe alive. He recounts how the old man was sitting in the swings at the newly built park singing "The Gondolier's Song." We are told that the tone was happy and fulfilled, as if he was ready to die because he had truly lived.

The truth of change gradually invades the formality of the wake. Having fulfilled their formal responsibilities, the more highly placed officials leave. Immediately, seating arrangements are altered to establish a more informal, interactive setting. Those who remain eat and drink. They continue the discussion about what made the construction of the park possible. As they become inebriated, the truth finally emerges. It was Watanabe, of course, who made the park possible. He did it because he knew that he had stomach cancer and was soon to die.

As an aside, I might mention that here as elsewhere, *sake* is often an important element of Japanese formality. It is an important part of weddings, festivals, and other types of formal ceremonies. It is also an integral part of contemporary office culture today, where things that cannot be mentioned during the day are broached during evening drinking sessions. In these after-hour outings, Japanese workers actually drink to get drunk since that, too, is a part of the allowable informality that exists within formality. It is at this time that personal or otherwise delicate issues are breached; and even surprising things are said and done. Regardless of what happens, however, at the office the next morning, it is not appropriate to bring up what happened the night before. *Sake* is the fluid of evanescence, a formalized counterbalance to form.

Ikiru seems to be saying that in order to live truly, we must serve others. We must also not deny evanescence but embrace it. We should consider each day as our last. Only then are we alive. Kurosawa disagrees in part, then, with Sakaguchi's admonition. *Ikiru* urges us to go beyond decadence to understand form in a new way. Kurosawa would not reject form, but would use it to engender meaningful change. This is not easily done, as it requires both imagination and conventionality, both impatience and patience.

As an experiment, my students and I pick a day to live truly, as if it were our last day on earth. How will we live? The rule is not to do anything extraordinary—no skipping classes, no quick trips to New York. Just the ordinary day, but lived with intention, and with a mind to putting our hearts into what we are doing instead of just going through the motions. As reflected in their weekly writing assignment, the results are mixed. There is much frustration, disappointment, and self-reflection. But there is also much joy; and the heightened awareness that results has the effect of making these ideas about evanescence and form understandable in a very personal and even life-changing way.

A few things become clear. Without embracing a vision of change, formality can be antithetical to life. Our various routines channel our efforts and make us more effective. But they can also drain us of our energy and creativity; and sometimes they get in the way of development. On the other hand, without form, change is impossible, and even meaningless. If form without change imprisons us, then change without form leads to chaos and despair. Thinking of these two extreme possibilities, we find ourselves having to distinguish between the nothingness that is exclusive and nihilistic and the nothingness that is inclusive and everything. The story of post-War Japan is about how these two kinds of nothingness played themselves out against each other.

NIHIL VERSUS NOTHINGNESS

Japan's remarkable rebound from the devastation of World War II came about by the way of a newly established balance between evanescence and form. On the side of form, General Douglas MacArthur and the leaders of the Occupation decided to maintain the general structure of Japanese society by *not* dismantling the emperor system and by *not* trying the emperor as a war criminal. MacArthur's advisors understood the time-tested maxim of Japanese political culture: that whoever controls the emperor controls Japan. Having won the war, they found themselves in the difficult position of having to rule a destroyed nation; and they viewed the order of the emperor system as a convenient means to an end. Even Hirohito's youngest brother asserted that the Shōwa emperor was partly responsible for the horrible destruction of World War II. Yet the enduring truth was that the emperor still gave form to life in Japan; and by maintaining his presence and authority, the United States was able to prevent the sort of disorder that plagued, for example, post-Tito Yugoslavia and post-Hussein Iraq.

At the same time, in the way of change, some alterations needed to be made if imperial form was to help produce the kind of society that might safely move Japan away from its fascist past. In order to neutralize Japanese imperialism, the emperor was defined in the new constitution as a merely "symbolic" figure, someone allowed to continue to exist as the unifying center of Japanese civilization but someone who is also subject to the same laws that guided all free men and women, of which he was one. Other social reforms included the unionization of labor; an extension of political participation and the loosening of restrictions on expression (albeit carefully controlled by American censorship); the breaking up of monopolistic business conglomerates; the dissolving of large agricultural landholdings owned by absentee landlords; and the expansion of the public school system, to name a few of the most important changes.

In a word, their effect was to liberalize Japanese society and to make possible the rebuilding of its economic base. Yet the decisive factor that made Japan's "economic miracle" possible was a factor external to this early policy of social and economic reform. As hostilities on the Korean Peninsula worsened, and as the United States locked itself into a protracted Cold War against communist powers, priorities for Japan's development as a democracy weakened. A shift in focus turned the country into a staging area for military conflict in Korea. Capital poured in, and significant investments in infrastructure were made. In response, Japan's political culture shifted to the Right as the liberal, even socialist, principles that had guided the early years of the Occupation gave way to more pragmatic, conservative inclinations. The right-wing Liberal Democratic Party (LDP) came to power in 1955; and in its unwavering allegiance to the United States, it provided many decades of stable, pro-business leadership. Despite the paroxysms of the Anti-Peace Treaty demonstrations of 1959–60 that sought to rid Japan of the U.S. military presence, the LDP, which was propped up by both covert and overt assistance from the United States, has remained in power until today, except for a brief hiatus in 1993, shortly after the economic bubble burst in 1989.

Commitment to high-growth economics and continued close trade and security relations with the United States became the unchanging platform of LDP politics. Japan became the most important trading partner of the United States, and its national economy eventually became the second largest in the world. With peace and prosperity as their goals, the Japanese came to assert their power through trade rather than through military means, succeeding to the extent that they, like the diasporic Issei before them, were deemed "economic animals" by their competitors. One factor in their success was a newly drafted constitution that prohibited them from waging an offensive war: Article Nine stipulated that the nation could have only defensive military capabilities. Because the majority of Japanese were content to live under America's nuclear umbrella, Japan was able to keep its military expenditures to less than 1 percent of gross national product for many decades. This meant that they could direct their best talent toward developing the world's most well-designed and sought-after cars and other consumer goods, rather than missiles and tanks and other military paraphernalia. The result was tremendous prosperity and, until recently, relative freedom from the corruptions of the military-industrial complex that have plagued the United States and other post-War powers.

For some, peace and prosperity were not enough, however. The War and its aftermath left Japan in an ideological vacuum that many of the nation's leading intellectuals and artists sought to refill. One who resented the emasculation of the imperial institution was the brilliant critic and prolific novelist and playwright Mishima Yukio (1925–70). While he shared Sakaguchi's fascination with decadence, and while he, too, affirmed the beauty of youthful death, he was never able to overcome his attraction for the lasting world of eternal ideals, even the sort that had led to World War II. He became an ideologue who articulated a vision of change; yet the vectors of his imagination insured that development always occurred in certain, clearly defined directions. This is only to say that Mishima was incurably and nostalgically modern at a time when Japan was moving into its postmodern phase.

As a boy and youth, he was a "poetry writing weakling." As an adult, he sought "sun and steel," hoping to recreate himself by lifting weights and tanning his pale skin.[123] In sympathy with Nitobe, he chose to reaffirm bushidō with its balanced emphasis on both *bun* (letters) and *bu* (martial prowess). He took up fencing. He sought solace from the meaninglessness of contemporary life by establishing his own private army, the so-called Shield Society, dedicated to the protection of the emperor, whom he hoped to restore again to real political power.

Mishima's affirmation of the sword was a romanticized nihilism. His attempt to restore both the majesty and mystery of the emperor was an anachronistic and indulgent gesture of self-annihilation that adorned itself as a patriotic act. I criticize him in this way because, for all his talk about loyalty to the emperor and his love of Japan, what Mishima most wanted was to die tragically and beautifully. His romantic wish was to become a scattered cherry blossom.

To use Walter Benjamin's formulation, Mishima sought to make politics an aesthetic concern—to beautify the world by purging it of impurities. Like many leaders of the World War II era, he set aesthetic goals for political ends. As men of dedication, they wanted to make the world uniformly good by ridding it of less-than-desirable elements. Like Hitler and the other leaders of the Third Reich, Mishima, too, was an artist who took inspiration from neoclassicism, sentimental realism, and Richard Wagner's relentless romantic register. Like the German romantics before them, Mishima saw the future in a similarly tragic way. Just as Hitler and his architects designed buildings with an eye to how they would look as ruins, so did Mishima build his body with an eye to how it would look at the moment of its destruction. His romantic eye saw the beauty of decay.

As arresting as the ruin of a sculptured body might be, his suicidal affirmation of evanescence was clearly a nihilistic impulse. It had a genealogy traceable to the Japanese Romantic School (*Nihon rōmanha*) and to writers such as Itō Shizuo (1906–53), who declared World War II a "beautiful lyrical poem," and to Yasuda Yōjurō (1910–81), who tempted young men with dreams of beautiful destruction. These writers shared with the Nazis a common spiritual home in the idealism of German Romanticism of the early nineteenth century, especially as it led to the freeing of the subjective imagination in the face of a chaotic and evanescent world.

As Roy Starrs points out, Mishima was familiar with the work of Frederich Nietzsche, whose early interest in romanticism led him to embrace the chaotic nature of reality *and* the will to live boldly and beautifully within it.[124] To this point of view, the world had no inherent form. It was, therefore, inherently without meaning and order. Nietzsche thought that the Buddhists were right in correctly perceiving a world of change and impermanence. But he also thought that theirs was a "passive nihilism," a resignation to this truth. For Nietzsche and for others who followed him, there would have to be another kind of nothingness, an "active nihilism" that would respond heroically to the (tragic) truth of constant change. Meaninglessness was to be met with resolve and courage; thus Mishima's desire to be not the voyeur but the actor, not the one who sees but the one who is seen. More deeply persuaded by Nietzsche than by Buddhism, he embraced this second, active nihilism, and thus distanced himself from the nothingness-that-is-everything in order to take a chance with the nothingness-that-is-nothing.

As an active nihilist, Mishima acted out his fantasies in an alarming way. On November 25, 1970, he tried to persuade the Self Defense Forces to reaffirm bushidō and to take control of the government by restoring the Shōwa emperor to real power. Executing a carefully drawn-out plan, he and a few of his loyal followers occupied the main office of the Self Defense Forces. From the roof of the headquarters, he exhorted a gathering crowd of soldiers to restore Japan to its past glory. Unfortunately for him, the men could not easily see themselves in his transcendental vision of a newly remilitarized Japan; and his attempt failed miserably. For one thing, to be a soldier was to be already discredited by the failure of the War effort and by the widely held perception that General Tōjō and other military leaders had led the country astray. Moreover, the men did not see a linkage between their humanized emperor and the beginnings of the next glorious empire that Mishima imagined.

Perhaps a second reason for their rejection of Mishima was a matter of here-and-now. As early as his writing of *Sun and Steel* (*Taiyō to tetsu*, 1968), Mishima had sealed his own fate as someone who would fail in his attempt to lead others. He did this by declaring his own profound need to be "inappropriate."[125] While decadence is a rebellion against that form which requires the continued preservation of at least the semblance of normality, inappropriateness (as it devolves to become perversion) is a transformation of normalcy itself. It is a distortion of form and meaning that sees itself as inherently problematic yet, at the same time, inherently superior and dismissive of conventionality. Admittedly, norms change with time; and the post-War years were a period of accelerated change that actually provided an opening for Mishima and his proudly inappropriate erotic and political fantasies. Still, as accepting as it had become, Japan did not find it acceptable to bind and gag a military leader, nor did they approve of his taking control of the Self Defense Forces, even if Mishima was allowed to create his own toy army and dress them in handsomely tailored uniforms. In a world that had gone back to work, Mishima crossed a line that led to his still more inappropriate and melodramatic *seppuku*.

In retrograde samurai fashion, Mishima Yukio plunged a dagger into his bowels and died. Like the suicide of Akutagawa Ryūnosuke in 1927, which marked the rise of the proletarian movement and its violent suppression, Mishima's death on November 25, 1970 also marks an important turning point. If the former date marked the beginning of the mature phase of

Japan's Age of the Transcendental Order—when perspectivalism finally reached a stage of ideological hegemony—the latter marks a final unsuccessful attempt to return nostalgically to such a system. The failure of Mishima Yukio to return Japan to yet another restoration (*ishin*) of imperial power demonstrated the extent to which the humanization of the emperor (a point to which Mishima vehemently rejected) helped lead to a renewed interest in the nonideological realm of here-and-now.

It is true that a continued focus on peace ensured that cooperation with the United States and its nuclear umbrella continued. Similarly, a constant emphasis on economic growth maintained the status of capitalism as an overriding ideological orientation. Yet the decidedly pragmatic feel of peace and prosperity that continued throughout the remaining decades of the twentieth century resulted in a gradual breakdown of ideological clarity even as the LDP stayed in power with its pro-business, pro-U.S. policies.

Whether we call Japan's pragmatism an American fixation or a return to Edo will depend on which elements of post-War life we choose to emphasize. Do we focus on the formation of democratic institutions—a greatly expanded public education system, and the empowerment of women—or do we look at the fragmenting forces of "my consumerism" that have led to a retreat from public life and the formation of numerous micro-communities, where the enthusiastic pursuit of avocations and a complacent attitude toward politics prevail? Do we emphasize the internationalization of Japan's economy and media, or the new inwardness that seems to have been reinforced by the very availability of everything "out there" that seems to highlight all that is seemingly Japanese about Japan? As we shall see, our understanding of contemporary, postmodern Japan today is doubly complicated by the way it has projected its cultural influence throughout the world, becoming the kingdom of cool and the radiant sun of soft power.

HIGASHIYAMA KAII: EMBRACING PASSIVITY

Before we go on to consider evanescence and form in contemporary Japan, let us consider at least one clear counterexample to Mishima's attempt to fill the ideological vacuum of post-Occupation Japan. For some who survived the trauma of war, a heightened awareness of evanescence came to influence every conscious thought and action, deepening the meaning of here-and-now even as industrial pollution and urban development opened a gap between people and their natural space. Such was the case with Higashiyama Kaii (1908–99), one of the most widely respected painters of the post-War period. In 1945, he was drafted at the age of thirty-seven and immediately sent to Kumamoto, where he began training for combat. As he described it, he was resigned to die on the battlefield; and this resignation led to his moment of enlightenment.

> I am running, feeling drunk. My intoxication is like that of someone whose soul has just been shaken. Just a moment ago, I saw it—the shining form of life.

From Kumamoto Castle, you can see the plains and slopes of Higo and, beyond them, the expansive sight of Mount Aso, rising above the misty landscape. It is a grand view, but to someone as well traveled as I it was nothing special. Why, then, on this day, did the scene move me to tears? Why was the sky so endlessly clear, the mountain ranges so calm and magnificent, the green of the plains so dazzlingly vivid, and the trees of the forests so full of life?

Now that I had no hope of ever painting again, or even of living much longer, I was filled with both delight and regret. That landscape dazzled my eyes because I no longer had any hope of working again, or of living much longer. It was because my heart had never been as pure. Death was near. The minute I felt its approach, the very shape of life leapt into my heart.[126]

Nearness of death teaches the truth that all things must change. As with Kurosawa's protagonist Watanabe Kanji, Higashiyama also sensed his imminent destruction. He felt the regret and hopelessness that this understanding brought. At the same time, this awareness allowed him to see beauty—its very shape—as if for the first time. He was more fortunate than Watanabe in that he was given more than six months to live with this new knowledge. The war ended, and his life was miraculously spared. He returned to his life as a painter, vowing never to forget the feeling that had come to him the day he learned to see the beauty of the familiar that only an awareness of evanescence can bring.

Although I had nurtured a close relationship with nature...I lacked the most important thing: the simple and basic emotional tension that accompanies an understanding of the life force underlying all existence. Wasn't this because I had, in the name of progress, dismissed such feelings as premodern?...

I haven't chosen to live. I've been made to live....I don't know what to call this force that makes me live.[127]

As noted here, "the simple and basic emotional tension that accompanies an understanding of the life force underlying all existence" might be described as the painful awareness of all that is impermanent. As we now understand, this idea leads to the insight that life is beyond anyone's control. Higashiyama's emphasis was not on a Mishima-like assertion that we can and ought to imagine our rebellious and tragic way through evanescence. Rather, it was on a passive acceptance of change. "I haven't chosen to live. I've been made to live."

Resignation brings despair. But in profound despair there is the possibility of hope. Despair and hope reside together, one being present precisely because of the other. For some, it is difficult to see this tension in Higashiyama's pastoral, idyllic landscapes. At worst, his images of forests, fields, and seashores are sentimental and clichéd. They can be criticized as an uncomfortable blending of the panoramic (and realistic) large view of Western landscape with a decorative small view of traditional Japanese landscape. This hybridization is common to Nihonga (or Japanese painting), a genre of consciously traditional painting that came into being in the late Meiji period as a response to what was thought by some to be a reckless enthusiasm for Western painting (*yōga*). Despite his considerable interest in the West, Higashiyama was a Nihonga painter. And it is precisely in this clash of generic expectations—East versus West—that we find a remarkable energy of quietude that reflects his own personal sense of unease.

The Nobel laureate Kawabata Yasunari (1899–1972) sensed this tension with an insight that many others did not possess. Shortly before his suicide in 1972, he wrote: "The one thing deep in my heart that I was unable to write was the reverence and devotion that flows from the demonic inner life, the agony and agitation of spirit that is not apparent on the surface of Higashiyama's paintings but is there, deeply hidden."[128]

Kawabata could see pain in Higashiyama's quiet landscapes of nature: death in the stillness of a frozen lake, agony in the pulsing roots of a tree, the powerful yearning of a thawing stream or a budding tree. The two artists shared a similar pain and, I believe, even the ability to express this feeling.

For Higashiyama the war survivor, the next moment of truth came in the lingering light of day as it passed into night over the mountains of Chiba. It was then that he discovered the devotion that would allow him to paint his discovery of life within death. It appears as "prayer," the term Higashiyama used to describe his paintings: "Those who know darkness and suffering are also those who pray for peace and spiritual comfort. The calmness and simplicity that appear in my paintings are an earnest prayer, a desire for what I don't possess."[129]

In terms of artistic method, this prayer finds expression in Higashiyama's layering of many small brushstrokes, each with a slightly different pigmentation and intensity, each infused with the artist's intention. They are a supplication, a salutary kind of solitude that does not naturally exist but comes of a heightened "agony and agitation of spirit." Prayer is a concerted, well-focused response.

This intentional act of worship is not an active assertion so much as a passive compliance with change and an acceptance of helplessness. Unlike Sakaguchi Ango's decadence, it is a humble request rather than a rebellious demand. It is resignation in a positive sense. In the face of "darkness and suffering," hope makes possible the coming together of everything. But this happens only when hope remembers emptiness and tries *not* to escape from it. Higashiyama's attitude of humility, then, is to encourage us to be aware of our connectedness and commonality with all things: the grass growing on the hillside, the ocean washing over rocks, honorable people living in foreign places. We find ourselves through and by means of emptiness because we divest ourselves of attachments and obsessions, and thereby welcome learning. As we remember from Merton, "When the mind is full of something, something else cannot enter."

And yet, there is still need for form. Not surprisingly, Higashiyama's most famous work, "The Way" (*Michi*, 1950) is a painting of form itself. It is the simplest of compositions: a swath of contrasting color that leads the eye through in the middle of the painting. What is remarkable about this image is how form is made alive even in its stability. Far from static, this is a dynamic structure of the evanescent world. It leads by way of an awareness of all things changing. The countless brushstrokes that create this image charge it with energy and place it within the never-ending process of disappearing and reappearing. What this structurally simple image tells us, in other words, is that realism as permanence is impossible, simply because the Real is always provisional.

Other moderns chose to express the agony of existence more explicitly. As we considered, Mishima articulated the pain clearly and impetuously. Kawabata was more subtle, yet equally consumed by the post-War version of the sadness of things that received such brilliant expression in his finely crafted, deceptively traditional modernist novels. By contrast, Higashiyama painted a simpler manifestation of the agony that plagued him. His vision is not sun and steel, nor beauty and sadness, but an affirmation of the earth. For Higashiyama, landscape was the strongest and most enabling expression of the rediscovered here-and-now. His fundamental aesthetic message is taught to us by the space in which we live. The here-and-now teaches us, once again a familiar lesson: that which exists at any moment in time clearly does not exist at the next.

Not surprisingly, the seasons figure importantly in Higashiyama's work since they are both change and that which never changes. Spring, summer, fall, and winter teach us that we are not unlike the trees in the garden and the forests on the mountainside. We grow. We decline. All of us will prosper for a season, then fail. Even the most energetic among us will grow weary and die. Expressive of this change, the seasons also teach us that we are not alive because of our choosing. Denying the reality of such a will, Higashiyama affirmed the passive and the spontaneous: "I haven't chosen to live. I've been made to live."

Perhaps the most eloquent expression of Higashiyama's thought appears in the essay, "A Single Leaf." In the spirit of Bashō, he begins by speaking *about* nature and ends by speaking directly *to* it.

> You were born—a small, hard bud harboring fresh, new life....You grew rapidly into a young leaf, with the sunshine of early summer shining brilliantly through you....When summer reaches its height, the large bear cicadas will cry out noisily from within your shade. The typhoon season will come and go....The weather will cool. The cicadas will fall silent; and, in their stead, from the base of the tree, a chorus of autumn insects will quietly add their accompaniment to the cooling nights.
>
> Your color will tire and fade. Eventually, you will become yellow and brown, and you will droop in the cold rain. Then one night, the wind will rattle the rain shutters; and in the morning, you will be gone. That is when I will discover, left behind in the place where you once grew, another tiny bud. And when that bud opens, you will be on the ground, turning into dust.[130]

In a way, we are reminded of Sakaguchi's affirmation of death. But this is not decadence. We are also reminded of Mishima's sense of tragedy. But this is not a perverse romanticism. Affirming a form that heightens the inherently changeable and fleeting, Higashiyama tried to take us back to the order of here-and-now. It is here in this paradox that nothing becomes everything, and reality becomes as much a matter of sincerity as a question of epistemology. In other words, the light of the great transcendental order that reigned with such glory and violence is fading, and the measure of the Real is, once again, heartfelt existence. As modernity continues to destroy itself with its own success, we hear this faint echo of Bashō again.

What distinguishes Higashiyama from Mishima is that his art was not an escape from death. Neither was it an escape into death or a return to the ideological fantasies of the transcendental order. Rather, it was a rock-by-rock, leaf-by-leaf affirmation of this world—this space of constant death and continuous life that is given form by the rising and setting sun. Higashiyama loved Japan. But he also learned that he could love more than Japan. His country's pursuit of the transcendental order had ended in tragedy, but the consequences of loss taught an important lesson. To be Japanese in the post-Occupation era is to be able to honor the here-and-now wherever that might be—whether the Alps of Nagano, the villages of Germany, or the frozen lakes of Suomi.

Some got this point, and some did not. We must wonder what Higashiyama's landscapes meant for those who purchased them at such exorbitant prices. In the age of high-growth economics, were they a picture of a lost home: the same absence that was captured nostalgically in, for instance, Miyazaki Hayao's (1941–) animated film, *My Neighbor Totoro* (*Tonari no Totoro*, 1988)? If so, did this land of "economic animals" notice the haunting similarities between Miyazaki's rapidly growing trees and the mushroom clouds that formed over Hiroshima and Nagasaki? Did the corporations, temples, and imperial institutions that adorned their walls with Higashiyama's work sense any resonance between swelling nuclear clouds and the artist's burgeoning cherry trees opening up into the moonlit night? Or were Higashiyama's landscapes simply appreciated for being pretty? A proof of wealth? A mark of refined taste?

As economic conditions steadily improved, Higashiyama came to condemn the materialism and environmental degradation that accompanied Japan's success, even as it gave him the means to pursue his commitment to artistic perfection. He, too, strived industriously. Knowing his season on earth would be short, he tried to make the most of what had been given to him. And yet, he came to see that he, too, had become addicted to the thrill of accomplishment. He felt remorse for working hard. In the end, he sought only nothing.

PART THREE

RETURN TO EVANESCENCE:
CONTEMPORARY JAPAN
(1970 TO THE PRESENT)

FASHION, AND THE JOY OF EVANESCENCE

The last half of the twentieth century—when Higashiyama painted his prayerful landscapes and the people of Japan came to be criticized for being "economic animals"—was by anyone's measure a remarkable era. It was a time of economic growth and environmental degradation. It was a period of expanded civil rights, yet also a time when many came to feel oppressed by social conventions and found themselves cut off from or indifferent to the political process. Many turned to other ways of expressing themselves. They found meaning in consumerism, sexual liberation, in the "new religions" that formed to fill in the ideological vacuum left by unconditional surrender. For all these reasons, the final decades of the Shōwa emperor's reign (until 1989) might be considered a neo-Genroku, a time of ebullience and turmoil that matched the age of Saikaku, Bashō, and Chikamatsu in cultural dynamism, economic development, and social change.

Stated simply, Japan's "economic miracle" was the result of a highly successful strategy to import raw materials, turn them unto manufactured products using relatively inexpensive labor, then to export these value-added goods to foreign locations, especially to the huge and lucrative American market. Throughout the 1970s and 1980s, the strategy seemed to work well. Japan was deemed "number one" by the sociologist Ezra Vogel who saw a country that had lessons to teach America.[1] From our present perspective, it is easy to dismiss Vogel's praise as fulsome. We have seen Japan stumble, and have witnessed the popping of its economic bubble. But it is also true that Japan developed an infrastructure of the highest quality—whether we are talking about transportation, information systems, medical services, education, or responsiveness to social need. Perhaps because Vogel's intended audience was not Japan but a declining American society, the warning bells of *The Tale of the Heike* were not heard by the Japanese themselves. The heady days of the 1980s were not a time to be reminded of evanescence, and of the failure that is implicit in success.

As the strategy of selling manufactured goods overseas succeeded, success itself became a problem. Money began pouring into Japan from overseas markets, eventually leading to an over-accumulation of capital. Real estate prices soared, and the value of stocks rose precipitously. Supposedly, the real estate value of land in Tokyo's Ginza district reached the incredible price of "$139,000 per square foot."[2] Banks made loans based on inflated values, and stock prices also fell out of line with actual earnings. When markets started to weaken and land prices began to slump—as evanescence tells us they must—one problem exacerbated the next, and soon the economy went into a tailspin. On the last day of 1989, Japan's bubble economy collapsed. Like a fleck of foam upon the ever-flowing river of change, the miracle ended. Over the next two years, Japanese assets lost approximately 60 percent of their value as a necessary correction took its course.[3]

When looking at Japanese culture during this period, one thing we can say is that fashion remained a preoccupation. Regardless of the country's actual economic capacity, the supposedly superficial (and costly) pursuit of the fashionable continued to give form to contemporary Japanese life. We might think that in difficult times, the call of style would be muted. But this was clearly not the case, perhaps because the logic of fashion so perfectly mirrors that of evanescence and form as we have come to understand them. What is fashion if not the union of evanescence and form? Japan's preoccupation with style in this time of rapid social change can be understood as a matter of balance: a reassertion of the order of here-and-now as the idealism of the transcendental order continued to decline.

In contemporary Japan, short-lived cycles of consumption develop rapidly in clearly defined directions. They are then quickly neutralized as conformity to the latest fad comes to produce a state of sameness and, therefore, the need for the next best-selling toy from Bandai, the next hit song, or the next new flavor of soda. Consider how Japanese makers of soft drinks must be constantly developing new products since their customers quickly grow tired of the usual. As my businessman friend Tsuruga Hiroyuki explained to me, "We have the world's most demanding consumers. The life cycle of a newly developed beverage in the States is a matter of years, maybe decades. But in Japan, it's a matter of months." As with soda, so with cars. Spend thirty minutes on Japan's roads and highways and you begin to realize just how few choices American consumers have when it comes to that next car or truck. What is true of vehicles is all the more true in the world of clothing and other less durable consumables.

Japan continues to be a nation of uniform-wearers—whether the white-collared salary man (*sararii man*), the factory worker, taxi driver, bank teller, or student (at least until college). And yet, this sort of uniformity seems only to heighten interest in the less predictable, whenever and wherever allowed. High school students customize the inner lining of their school blazers. Tokyo office workers find after-work relaxation at bars where they can put on a dress for a few hours before finally going home. To be sure, conformity is still important. Despite the complaints of elders about the hopeless manners of young people, politeness and formality are not forgotten.

While a heightened concern with fashion represents an attempt to pull away from the uniformity of the transcendental order, this certainly does not mean a retreat from the formal patterns of here-and-now. In a fashion-conscious Japan, meaning accrues in the form of temporary agreements rather than as permanent laws, as provisional practices of protocol rather than monolithic mobilizations of true ideals. Postmodern theorists are quick to point out this weakening of unity, but how well do they appreciate the grounding of this lack of grounding? How well do they understand thousands of years of cherry blossoms?

To be sure, fads are not necessarily less demanding about how we ought to be, even when they are identified as being a particularly ephemeral form of expression. In a world of fashion, or *ryūkō* (流行, literally "the flowing"), truth is temporary and contextual. It is an acknowledgment of Chōmei's ever-moving river of change, its meaning always being destroyed and created simultaneously. It appears as a ghostly shape that forms behind a boulder, as the subtle seam of a current, or as the ephemeral patterns of foam that appear for a moment and then are washed away. In such a continuously mutating environment, it becomes possible to think that I am not what metaphysical traditions assert, or even what my nation requires me to be as an atomized part of the whole. Rather, it becomes possible to think that I am what I am wearing or consuming at the moment. Or to couch the problem even more securely within the parameters of our analysis, I am what I do at any particular time in any particular place. I am my niche—my golf game, my multicolored cell phone, my weekend of costume play in Yoyogi Park. These small assertions punctuate life. They distract me from everything that is onerously big and tediously lasting.[4] Contemporary Japan is oriented toward small happiness rather than big happiness.

In this way, the modern thirst to conquer vast territories is continuously being quenched by the postmodern pursuit of smaller goals. Such distractions are seemingly less harmful in being less insistently truthful, systematic, and universal. And yet, even the postmodern soul hungers for something more lasting than a temporary high or a weekend of hobbyist fanaticism. What seems to be wanted may not be a massive belonging to ideological truth so much as a more modest sense of sympathy, a shared connection with someone or something else in an otherwise anonymous flow of consumption. Thus, the attraction of the bar where one's personally labeled bottle of Nikka whiskey is waiting on the shelf. My Japanese friends are regulars in a world of "my" (*mai*): my home, my car, even my children. Pursued with intense personal interest, my-ness becomes devotion and, yes, even delusional attachment.

Fashion presents another paradox. It creates belonging and not belonging at the same time. In a fashion-oriented world, we make a point of embracing limitations even as we try to transcend narrow states of disconnectedness through complicity with the rules of the particular fad or circle to which we hope to belong. In other words, to be fashionable is to be "with it" while still not being "with everybody else." For the fashionable, there is still a tell-tale price of conformity to pay since there is still the *same* way to be *different*. What is not the same as before—in those bad old days of modernity—is the perceptibly positive feeling we can have about the ephemeral nature of our passion. Temporariness is one of fashion's primary values. The melodrama of the moment, the plasticity of identity—these now become a welcome part of human awareness, not a nagging existential toothache that needs attention. The fleeting quality of fashion and style offers a chance to embrace the floating world of change, as governed once again by the order of here-and-now.

In returning to the here-and-now, the postmodern world of fashion resembles the early modern phase of Japanese culture. Tokyo seems to be returning to the visual creativity of Edo. Some even make the argument that Japan was postmodern before it became modern. There are similarities, certainly. Richly visual expression is one of the most important ones. But to call Tokugawa Japan postmodern is to discount the developing modernity of that age, and to reinforce the misunderstanding that modernity and Westernization are one and the same.

As the end of the twentieth century approached and the Japanese became the greatest consumers of all time, Tokyo assumed a place as the fashion capital

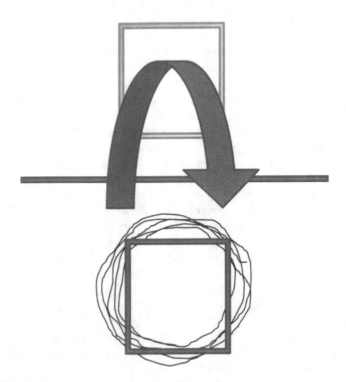

Figure 3.1   Fashion as a return to the order of here-and-now.

of the world. Perhaps the best expression of this ascendance is Tanaka Yasuo's (1956–) novel *Somehow Crystal* (*Nan to naku kurisutaru*, 1981), one college student's snapshot of Tokyo in June of 1980, as Japan was nearing its peak of affluence. Despite the novel's lauded originality, as a narrative it is simple and familiar. A university student, Yuri, is in love with a young man named Jun'ichi. She is a fashion-conscious twenty-something; and he is an equally stylish "fifth-year" undergraduate with whom she is sharing an apartment. When his work takes him out of town, she longs for him. To dispel her "gloominess," she calls another young man, someone she hardly knows. They eat dinner together and end up in a love hotel, where they have sexual intercourse.

Tanaka indulges his readers in a graphic play by play. After their moment of physical interaction, they still have a few remaining minutes of (paid for) love hotel time. In the lull, they address their lack of emotional closeness.

> He took a shower, and then I quickly rinsed off from the waist down.
>
> We decided to chat, until our two hours of "social time" were up. He sat in a chair by the bed, and I sat on the edge of the bed and swam my feet up and down.
>
> "Hey."
>
> "Hey, what?"
>
> After a moment of silence, he began, "Your phone number."
>
> "I think it's better you don't know it." He didn't respond.
>
> "I'm living with someone."
>
> "Oh, I get it."
>
> "Shocked?"
>
> "Me?" He tried to be funny. "Why should someone like me be shocked?"
>
> He got some cigarettes out of the book pack that was hanging on the chair. I didn't notice until just then that he smoked Virginia Slims.
>
> "So maybe we just call it a one nighter."
>
> "I have someone, too. She's a senior."[5]

In the end, Yuri is happily reunited with her boyfriend Jun'ichi, who returns to Tokyo. No one compares with him. He can give her "a flow of high voltage" like no one else can.

As we might expect, this very predictable love story ends with a statement of Yuri's hopes for their future together—happily ever after, as the convention goes. If there is a larger human aspiration expressed here it is that Yuri wishes to remain stylish, attractive, and working as a model into her thirties. For Jun'ichi, she hopes that he will become not just a good musician but an accomplished arranger and producer: "Jun'ichi and I will live without any worries. We will go on buying and wearing and eating things that will somehow make us feel good. We'll listen to music that somehow makes us feel good, and take walks in places that somehow make us feel good. We'll take vacations."[6]

There is not much detectible irony in this vapid affirmation of all those things "that somehow make us feel good," "*nan to naku kibun no yoi [mono]*." Yet it would be wrong simply to dismiss the somehow crystalline people who populate this novel as irretrievably hedonistic and vacuous. There is something meaningful in this kind of superficiality if only because their pleasure seeking is actually complicated and self-defining. That is to say, their behavior is obviously governed by various rules of style that, like any other systems of form, are by nature meaningful. (I am intentionally separating this kind of grounded meaning from ideology in order to recognize the truthfulness of *things*.)

Here we notice a familiar balance, a nod to classical poetics. The capriciousness of feeling is given meaning by the formality of style. Notice how for Yuri, on the one hand, the measure of all things is feeling (*kibun*), or, again, that which feels good.

> I think it's always a good idea to take a shower before going out to meet a man. So now you'll ask me if it doesn't make any difference if you're going to be meeting a woman. That's not really what I'm getting at here.
>
> It's just that you feel more light hearted (*uki uki*) if you take a shower before going out. It's nothing but a simple timeless rule.
>
> And this simple timeless rule is actually very important.
>
> It's like that annoying feeling you get when you're having a bad hair day. If you don't take a shower when you go out, you just aren't going to feel right. (*kibun ga notte konai*)
>
> In other words, I'm a person who lives by this feeling that tells me when things are how they should be. (*nan to naku kibun*)
>
> I know. You'll say it's a decadent, insubstantial way to live. But that's how someone like me, born in 1959, feels. Feeling (*kibun*) is the measure of all things.[7]

Kibun, this quixotic and evanescent element of feeling, is carefully balanced and given meaning by form. Yuri is free to be emotional and sentimental precisely because matters of feeling are strictly circumscribed by form, rules, and etiquette. This is an important point for our analysis, because it explains why the emotionalism of the sort we have frequently considered in our earlier meditations of the nature of lyricism is allowed to be so intense. Even sentimentalism is permitted (indeed, often welcomed) because of the predictable strictures of formality that contain *kibun* and give it shape. In other words, in the presence of form, even outbursts of emotion do not usually mean more than they are allowed to mean. Such are the strict, formal requirements of lyricism, this continuous affirmation of the naturalness of being defined by our immediate environment. Everybody understands the overflowing of emotion as an appropriate, well-formed part of here-and-now. In Japan, bosses shout, workers get drunk, and life goes on. *Kibun* is everything in this sense. Evanescence is allowed to reign within the structures of form that balance them—as style, fashion, and, especially, as "brand." These are important postmodern forms; and their function in Tanaka's narrative is to yield the sought-after *kibun* or the feeling that becomes the measure of all postmodern things.

How does this contemporary lyricism work? Obviously, it does not rely solely on the dynamics of narrative structure. At best, the story of Yuri and Jun'ichi is yet another predictably linear, modern story. More important than the story are Tanaka's extensive explanations of the various types of brands and fashions that come up in the telling of Yuri's narrative. In fact, I dare say that these annotations are the real attraction of this novel. They are the original aspect of the work.

They are also numerous. For every page of text, there is a page of explanatory notes. Here is a typical example of the annotation that occurs throughout: "If you're in the market for vegetables and meat, then the Kinokuniya in Aoyama is good. If you need fish, then its either the Meijiya in Hiroo or Tsukiji if you don't mind traveling a bit further. For bread, it's nice to pick something up at the Chez Rui while taking a walk in Daikanyama."[8]

I say that these notes about various consumer goods, restaurants, and notable places are the real interest of this novel because they transform an otherwise commonplace romance into something more. With their inclusion, *Somehow Crystal* becomes a reliable "how to" book for its fashionable time. Like many of the subgenres of popular fiction that were popular during the Tokugawa period, this book is also pointedly interested in the order of here-and-now. Generically speaking, the timely delivery of needed (that is to say, up-to-date and veritable) information has always been what is novel about the novel. But in Tokugawa Japan, this how-to function was even more obvious and formulaic than it was for Jane Austen's novels of manners, for instance. In Tanaka's work, the fictitious nature of form is still partially masked by the lingering seriousness of words. But without these notes that balance (and decenter) the story, and without this postmodern resurrection of an early modern narrative tendency to "illustrate" the text, the book probably would not have drawn much interest.

Tanaka's thinking about brands is helpful to our study, because it helps us locate the rebounding vestiges of evanescence in contemporary culture. As articulated in *Somehow Crystal*, brands attempt to establish the order of here-and-now by telling us which things can make us feel good and which cannot, which make us feel real and which cannot. Of course, this worldly presumption is inseparably connected to the larger ideological framework of production and consumption that makes the joys of consuming paramount. But this connection between the fashionable and the discourse of capitalism is only reluctantly revealed by Tanaka, who prefers to give it a neocolonial twist, where the exotic foreign brand carries great prestige.

"Okay, this is it. I'm just a brand kind of person. Me and everybody else my age. Well, no. It's actually a big deal for all Japanese."

"You're probably right."

"If it's a foreign brand, or even if it's made in Japan under license, then somehow it just seems good. But take off that tag, and you'll never sell it in a million years."

"Sometimes I wonder if being concerned about brands is just vanity. But then I think, 'If it makes you feel better (*kibun ga yoku naru*), then what's the harm?' It's the same no matter what world you're in—brand shows your identity."[9]

Why not enjoy a little vanity? Are we coming back full circle to the floating world and the values of *mono no aware*? If so, what is it that now oppresses us? What is the generalized source of our sorrow?

Tanaka provides a note for this passage, number 249, in which he tries to defend the importance he places on brand: "Even the 'literary critic' who thinks the characters in this novel are vacuous manikins believes in brands, such as where he got his degrees and what his title is. And even the 'literary journalist' who says there is no life in my novel is just another nobody once you take off his reporter's badge."[10]

In other words, everyone is branded in one way or another. Our happiness depends on branding since we all need some (visible and here-and-now) status that will be supported by (invisible and transcendental) agreements about what is worthy, respectable, and so on. Nobody wants to be nothing, at least not in the nihilistic sense of this term. And so we hope that our purchase of this Louis Vuitton bag or that Mercedes Benz will give us existential weight, or at least make us feel temporarily visible to ourselves, if not to others.

The lingering tension between the form of here-and-now and the transcendental order is constantly being negotiated. When reading Tanaka's novel, we try to convince ourselves of the need to be weaned from big ideas in order to return to the aura of small objects (and small happiness), even if they are robotically manufactured. As it appeals to our vanity, the logic of branding tries to make us forget the mass-produced, impersonal quality of the things we consume. It does this by emphasizing, in retrograde modern fashion, the inequality of equally atomized elements as they have found their place within the perspectival grid. In a world where everything belongs to more or less the same field of reality, discrimination becomes ever more important, and ever more heightened. In the wake of the collapse of the Japanese Empire, Tanaka prefers to keep the focus on vanity, even while he himself seems to feel the need to defend his superficial story by expanding the significance and reach of each brand. So it is that in the author's afterword we find the same ironic rejection of the very same sameness that makes superiority and discrimination possible.

Young people these days can judge what kind of a person someone is by the brand of their clothes, by the records they listen to, or by what kind of a car they drive. Regardless of age, all people rely on the same external power to prove who they are. I have this certain rank, or I've passed this certain test. In Japan, where everyone has the same educational level, the same economic level, and the same color of skin, branding is all the more pronounced. … It's not simply a physical thing. Spiritual brands exist, too.[11]

We might restate Tanaka's concerns in this way. As much as *Somehow Crystal* is a novel about two young people in love, it is more interesting when read not as a love story but as a handbook of fashion, where the rules of here-and-now are explained in ways that give meaning to Yuri's life. As such, the book's real value and attraction is informational, in much the same way that Edo-period *hyōbanki* were once valued as guidebooks to earlier escapades in the floating world. Then as now, it is important to know how to act in a particular situation of consumption, since the carnal physicality of seduction makes the rules of here-and-now more obviously meaningful than abstract principles about proper behavior. This is not to say that consumerism is without its own principles, however. When considered in this way, the remarkable success of this novel is not so unlike a religious text that connects behavior with dogma. Even when the topic is style and etiquette, a text such as this actually does provide "spiritual brands" to those who have eyes to see and ears to hear. Tanaka comes to sound evangelistic when he states, "Things like brand and place mean nothing to those who don't understand them."[12]

A contemporary focus on the form of here-and-now becomes clearer when we consider how today's Japan has become even more passionately a land of guidebooks. If you walk into a Japanese bookstore, you will find a manual for practically every human endeavor: how to get into college, how to travel to Kyushu, how to knit a sweater, how to get married, how to bathe a baby, cook, clean, succeed in one's job, and on and on. Like all other handbooks, *Somehow Crystal* is clearly an affirmation of hands-on form. Like the photo-rich magazines that can be purchased practically anywhere and anytime in contemporary Japan, this novel presents details in ways that are highly contextual and of the moment. Their high figurality is a sure sign that the here-and-now has made a considerable comeback.[13]

The lingering textuality of this book tells us that the ultimate measure of value is not simply our ability to perceive the here-and-now, however. As important as raw perception is, the ability to evaluate what our senses bring to our attention—*how* we feel (*kibun*) when we are doing, seeing, touching, tasting, and so on—is of prime importance. Thus, the unmistakable message that Tanaka's best-seller delivered to its readers was that *how* we feel about things is (within any given context) surprisingly predictable. This universality is another principle of fashion and branding. It is also nothing less than the source of Tanaka's authorial position as he boldly asserts that certain things make us feel certain ways. An aromatic cup of coffee, a beautiful fabric—such things are meant to create a particular feeling or *kibun*; and if you do not know which coffee is good and which fabric is bad, then you are a non-feeling nobody. You are quite without authority, a loser.

As harsh as this might seem, is this not the presumption of authority that underlies all types of form? We accept the tyranny of good taste because that is its value to evanescence. This is why Japanese women buy Hermes scarves, and why Japanese businessmen purchase Calloway golf clubs. But it is also why crowds still flock to neighborhood shrines on New Year's Day, whether they consider themselves religious or not, or why summer is still not really summer unless one participates in a *matsuri* or views fireworks. In a post-modern environment, only variety convinces us that our still slavish attachment to form is something like a choice. Branding seems to make us self-conscious of how we exercise freedom of mind, but it renders us passive at the same time. This explains why, to some, style can be everything, while others criticize those who "postulate style and snobbery as a cure."[14]

Certainly, one thing we cannot expect of a handbook of style is that it should critique itself. Tanaka's reluctance to think critically about the supremacy of *kibun*, this amorphous and endlessly complicated touchstone of being, is clearly apparent in the work's "youthful" avoidance of the kind of clarity that more rigorous, mature thinkers would both allow and require. Thus, everything is insipidly *somehow* (*nan to naku*) this, and *somehow* (*nan to naku*) that. Take it or leave it. Tanaka's world is beyond anyone's ability to explain anything definitively. The best we can do is to provide an exhaustive listing of what concretely is in style at any given moment. In other words, what we find in living stylishly is not that which is universally and eternally good, but that which is good for some (who are in the know), and as good as it gets (at least) for now.

There is no such thing as conditional temporariness—unless we call such a thing form itself. Thus, the reasserted message of evanescence is here for all to grasp: all things are subject to time and decay. Even a Gucci bag will someday bare a scratch, or lose a buckle. And at that point, as a source of *kibun* it will probably not be repaired but discarded and replaced with something new. It goes without saying that fashion favors the changing and up-to-date, not the well-worn and faithful. How many foreign residents of Kobe have furnished their apartments with what gets left on the curb on the night before big garbage day?

Given this attraction for the up-to-date, it is no wonder that a recently coined (and already obsolete) term for the fashionable is *naui*: of the now, partaking of now. This assertion of the present affirms change at the very moment it is made meaningful by form. By calling something *naui*, we attempt to give significance to the momentary present, as it manifests itself within the flowing river of change. The practical result of this emphasis on the ephemeral is a parallel state of constant comparison, a condition that allows quality to be evaluated without recourse to metaphysics. A sense of now yields the most fashionable, the current, the latest. And it is this understanding of now as a driver of quality (or brand, as Tanaka would put it) that brings that which is newer and better together in a way that makes Japanese producers strive ceaselessly to improve upon an already established product. It also compels Japanese consumers to insist on cars that do not break down, on garments that do not have flaws, and apples that are perfect in shape, color, and flavor.

In Japan's here-and-now, the customer is king or queen. The attention paid to customer service in Japan is unparalleled; and the logic of here-and-now would explain it this way. Being a customer in Japan means being in the right place at the right time with the right intention and the right ability to do the right thing. What is the right thing if it is not purchasing temporary happiness? In the consuming moment, there is a perfect fit between the customer and the context of fashion with its logic of *kibun* and brand. To make the obvious contrast, the brutalized victims of Nanking were people in the wrong place at the wrong time with the wrong intentions and without the ability to do the right thing. They, too, were trying to survive in a challenging and rapidly changing world. But rather than being in the carefully controlled environment of a fashionable store or restaurant, they found themselves floundering in the deadly formless margin of an expanding modern empire. In such a nightmarish space, they had no currency.

POSTMODERNISM AND A CHERRY BLOSSOM REFRAIN

One other feature of Tanaka's *Somehow Crystal* deserves mention. As I have noted, the annotations in this novel are extensive. They give needed information. But they also serve the function of disrupting the linear flow of the story by lingering upon the meaningfulness of any particular moment. Structurally speaking, they perform a similar role to that of the many *tanka* that mark the high moments in *The Tale of Genji*, or the *haiku* in Bashō's *Narrow Road to the Deep North*.[15] They are also like still moments of nonaction in the Noh theater, or the *mie* of the kabuki theater, where the actors freeze in a set pose, thus marking the melodramatic moment of heightened (and even excessive) meaning. The same disruption of linearity occurs in the modern Japanese novel, when the plot is slowed by long descriptive passages that focus our attention on the poetic spatial moment rather than on the prosaic temporal flow. Certainly, this tendency to speak of the inside in terms of the outside is a carryover from an earlier time, when the order of here-and-now was still the principal counterbalance to evanescence. With the coming of the postmodern age, linearity again suffers; and the balance between poetry and prose is reestablished in ways that once again begin to favor the poetic, lyrical moment.

One work that did much to reestablish this less-than-linear focus and mode of change was Itami Jūzō's (1933–97) film *Tanpopo* (*Tanpopo*, 1986), which appeared five years after *Somehow Crystal*. It was released at the very height of Japan's post-Occupation prosperity. A satire of both work fanaticism *and* play fanaticism, *Tanpopo* is really two films in one. The first is predictably linear. A cowboy-hat-wearing truck driver, Goro, lingers on in order to help a hapless heroine, Tanpopo, turn the ramen shop that she has inherited from her late husband into a successful business. This narrative employs the tightly plotted structure of capitalism, where vision, dedication, and capital leads to financial success. With the help of Goro and others, Tanpopo is able to master the art of noodle making, and to turn her lackluster shop into a successful business. Her victory is mirrored by the social acceptance that her young son wins from his schoolmates, who stop being his bullies and become his buddies. Finally, another victory is the friendship that forms between Goro and Pisuken, who was Tanpopo's childhood friend and is now her admirer.

The second story is also about food, but it is as diffuse as the first is focused. This narrative gains form not by way of causal connections but by associations that are multiplied through an early modern narrative technique called exhaustive listing, or *zukushi*.[16] By interrupting the linear story of success-at-all-costs, the vignettes that loosely form this second tale tell their story in a decidedly more sensual and playful fashion. Joined together by a common theme of food, they supply a spatial kind of enjoyment, a lyricism of the moment that cannot be allowed by the temporally oriented plot of the first story.

Within the linear story, Goro and Tanpopo must be work minded. Getting the noodle shop to its full potential requires all their thought and attention. Although they find each other attractive, their mutual interest is made secondary to the more urgent need to work toward a common commercial goal. As Goro explains to Pisuken, who suspects him of being interested in Tanpopo herself, "All I want to do is make her shop better. That's it." One cold rainy night, Goro finds himself soaking in Tanpopo's warm bathtub, gazing up at her drying bra and panties. But he does not act on his desires. A worker to the end, he stays within his clearly defined, highly disciplined role as a Shane-like drifter who has only one highly emplotted modern desire: to help the suffering heroine learn how to make it in business. All other considerations are superfluous.

Lovemaking is the job of minor characters. They appear in the second story, this loosely conjoined string of scenes that provide peripheral interruptions of the work-bound plot. *Tanpopo* is thus a monument to both hard work *and* hard play, precisely the game plan that got Japan to its position as the leading manufacturer of both automobiles and fantasies. To put it another way, Tanpopo's personal goal (which is the objective of the first story) is to establish the kind of noodle shop that Tanaka Yasuo would mention in his *Somehow Crystal*, just as he lists other fashionable places. "If you're hungry for ramen, Tanpopo's the place to go."

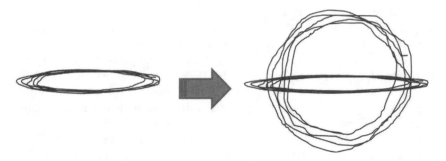

Figure 3.2 Today's double-formed reality—evanescence at the end of progress.

But the finer critical point of Itami's film is that the linearity of Tanpopo's economic quest is not allowed to dominate. Within the complicating context of numerous nonlinear scenes, the principal story becomes less transfixing. When we consider how these secondary scenes add to the main story, we can see their similarity to the many annotations that punctuate and deflect what is linear and predictable about *Somehow Crystal* and the similarly double-formed story of Yuri's longing for her boyfriend. The variety we see in both Tanaka's novel and Itami's film is not just a matter of plentitude but also an issue of style, which we have defined as a fashionable form of change that affirms the present.

Once again, whether we consider this kind of here-and-now conformity to be shallow and meaningless will depend in part on whether we believe the transcendental order can deliver on its promise of a happily-ever-after. It will also depend on whether we have the capacity to be genuinely excited by a bowl of noodles, or to appreciate a fashionable coordination of colors, textures, and lines. To recall Higashiyama's formulation, a full enjoyment of life requires a sense of deprivation; and this is what Japan's children of affluence often lack, usually through no fault of their own. The economic plentitude in which they have been raised is both a blessing and a curse. In such a world of abundance, the lessons of deprivation that were learned during the War are hard to pass on. And yet, the "new human beings" (*shinjinrui*) whose superficial lives are chronicled in *Somehow Crystal*, this indulgent post-Occupation generation that grew up in affluence and with no personal experience of war, seem to have retained at least one very important lesson of war and peace from their parents: as wasteful and superficial as fashion might be, nothing is more wasteful of human creativity and effort than a world in which there is only one style and one way to do things. I am talking, of course, about fascism and the modern taste for war.

Another way to articulate the dual thrust of *Tanpopo* is to say that the pursuit of one thing can become an obsession in both a linear and a lyrical way. Whether this pursuit leads to a state of inclusive oneness is, in fact, the greater question that Itami maniacally pursued over the last decade or so of his life as actor-turned-film-director. Perhaps his sharpest articulation of evanescence's fundamental place in the pursuit of both one and oneness is his *The Great Patient* (*Daibyōnin*, 1993), a film about a work-and-love-obsessed movie director, Mukai Buhei. In this film, Mukai is in the middle of starring in his own film (a film within a film) about two lovers—both dying of cancer. Evanescence reasserts itself when he finds out he actually has the disease he is pretending to have in his movie. He comes to the (boring yet surprising) truth that we all come to sooner or later. Everyone dies.

Like Kurosawa's Watanabe Kanji, Mukai learns of his stomach cancer only slowly, only upon stubbornly insisting on being told the truth of his condition. As we saw in *Ikiru*, the practice in Japan is not to tell a patient that he or she has cancer, since that would take away a patient's hope, even in (especially in?) hopeless situations. This might seem like a strangely truth-denying way of fighting death. Certainly, the assumption is a jarringly contradictory one: that a person would immediately give up if they knew that their illusions about life (such as, longevity) were actually illusions. It seems that despite Japan's age of progress and despite efforts to measure up to the transcendental order, an ancient concept of *utsusemi* still lives on in the contemporary scene. The message could not be clearer: life is short, fragile, and unpredictable.

If Itami's films are noteworthy for their critical edge, this one is no exception. Here in *The Great Patient* he critiques this customary practice of keeping the patient in the dark. Itami's argument for full disclosure resembles the Buddhist one with which we are familiar: Mukai can only manage to find an acceptable way to live if he knows he will soon die. Until now, he has been living a deluded, ill-focused life. In order to die well, he needs the truth and just a little more time to do at least two more things. First, he has to finish his movie. Second, he has to learn what a valuable life actually is.

His wife knows he is clueless about the latter topic. Mukai is a womanizer. Having put up with his unfaithfulness for many years, she is ready to leave him. In fact, the only reason she does not move out immediately is his illness. Still able to feel some loyalty toward him, she arranges his visit to a doctor, a college friend, who discovers the cancer.

The parallels with Kurosawa's *Ikiru* are numerous: Mukai and Watanabe are both stricken with the disease, and both want desperately to live. Unlike Watanabe Kanji, however, Mukai Buhei already knows the pleasures of a hedonistic life. And unlike Watanabe, he is already passionate about his work, even without knowing about his imminent death. Like Watanabe, however, he has the same stomach cancer—an illness that claims many in Japan—and they also both suffer the fate of being lied to by those who wish to protect them from the truth of dying. Perhaps Itami's most obvious borrowing from Kurosawa is his use of a secondary character, also dying of cancer, who suggests to Mukai that he, too, has received a death sentence and has only a short time to live. Finally, both films show that embracing death is the only way to a full life.

Mukai's path to enlightenment and a deeper appreciation of love is through work, even though it hastens death. Is Itami, like Higashiyama Kaii, trying to show us just how work-obsessed Japan has become? Just as Watanabe Kanji needed to finish planning and building his park, so too must Mukai finish his film. This compulsion to labor is understood by everyone Mukai understands and respects—his lover, his wife, his doctor, his nurse, and, of course, all the people who have shared his life in the studio. The point that must not get lost here, however, is that Mukai's preparation for the end of his life is not simply a matter of love, on the one hand, and work, on the other. It is a matter of both love *and* work as they exist inseparably together. Indeed, it becomes hard to tell them apart. Mukai is a director who cannot be kept from completing his role as the leading actor in a romance that, in turn, cannot be separated from the realities of his philandering ways, his problematic marriage, and his imminent demise.

The turning point of the story comes when Mukai persuades his doctor to discontinue the chemotherapy that is extending his life.

> DOCTOR: But it scares me. It means stopping treatment. I've never learned how to do that. If we were going to continue treatment, I'd know what to do. "Never cause a person's death."
> MUKAI: Don't think of it that way. By letting me die, you're letting this old man live.
> DOCTOR: I feel like I'm playing into the hands of the enemy.
> MUKAI: Don't worry about that. What matters is *how* I live from here on. That's beyond your jurisdiction. You people think of death as a defeat. But I don't feel that way. I want to think of death as a peaceful ending that comes after I've done all I can do. In the midst of a hazy spring sky, a lark rising to heaven. Death isn't such a bad thing. I know that.

As articulated here, death is the reward we get for working hard all our lives. Such is the Japanese formulation of evanescence.

In a scene as clichéd and sentimental as any to be found in Itami's films, Mukai and his wife, now blessed with the mutual compassion that comes with a better understanding of death, find themselves strolling through the hospital grounds. He is in a wheelchair, and she is pushing him through a blizzard of falling cherry petals. It is a gorgeous spring day—a classically evanescent moment of the sort that Dōgen would certainly approve. They are joined by the doctor and the head nurse, who have come to deliver an important message: Mukai finally has their permission to go ahead and try to finish the last scene of his movie.

The doctor warns, "It might shorten your life." But Mukai does not waver. That's what he wants: a shortened life.

Here we must wonder. Is this wish akin to the dedicated impulse that motivated kamikaze pilots and Mishima Yukio? He will work toward death. In the meantime, Mukai's only urgent request is for something to take away the unbearable pain. As he drinks the "morphine cocktail" given to him, his eyes look to heaven; and the sight fills him with euphoria. A single cherry petal rests in his gray, thinning hair as he expresses his new understanding of life's evanescence.

> MUKAI: Look at that sky. The light is shining brightly. And the play of the light through the trees! (He turns to his wife) Thanks for teaching me the truth. I was living as if I thought I would never die. But I wasn't really living. (To his physician) Doctor, I feel like I'm living now for the first time. I'm happy.

Much has changed. Mukai appreciates his wife's love. And the doctor better understands his role as a physician because he better grasps the truth of evanescence and death. The one thing that has not changed for these Japanese souls is that everyone is still utterly dedicated to their work.

With his last ounce of strength, Mukai films the final scene of his movie. It is a massive orchestra-choral arrangement of the *Heart Sutra* (*Hannya shingyo*), perhaps the most well-known sutra in Japan. The performance is dedicated to the protagonist's recently deceased wife and to all cancer sufferers. With his remaining energy, Mukai directs this massive recitation, performed together by a phalanx of Buddhist priests, a full orchestra, and a huge auditorium of chanters. Their impassioned performance builds to the roll of tympani and the crashing of cymbals. Such amplitude is all the more powerful because of the formalities that contextualize and give meaningful structure to the many strong emotions that well up and overflow. As in *Somehow Crystal*, this kind of over-the-top lyricism is possible precisely because all elements are carefully orchestrated and controlled, even to the point of making the audience an integral part of the performance. In essence, no one is allowed the privilege of having anything other than the required emotional response. This kind of unity finds suitable expression within the scene's highly structured concert hall, and from the message that is delivered with such formality.

色不異空	Form is no different than emptiness,
空不異色	And emptiness no different than form.
色即是空	Form is emptiness,
空即是色	And emptiness form.
受想行識	Feeling, thought, action, consciousness,
亦復如是	Are all similarly empty.
諸法空相	All teachings lack substance.
不生不滅	Nothing is born and nothing dies.
不垢不浄	Nothing is polluted and nothing is pure.
不増不減	Nothing increases and nothing decreases.
是故空中無色	Thus, in emptiness there is no form.
無受想行識	No feeling, thought, choice, consciousness.
無眼耳鼻舌身意	No eye, ear, nose, tongue, body, mind.
無色声香味触法	No color, sound, smell, taste, touch, thought.
無眼界	There is no realm of sight
乃至無意識界	Including no realm of insight.
無無明亦無無明尽	There is no ignorance nor cessation of ignorance,
乃至無老死	Including neither decline and death
亦無老死尽	Nor the cessation of decline and death.
無苦集滅道	No suffering, gathering, destroying, doing.
無智亦無得	No wisdom and no attaining.[17]

There is little irony in this scene, nor in Mukai's death sequence, which is said to take place a few days later. The doctor was right. Mukai's last great performance does take its toll and does hasten his end. Surrounded by his doctor, nurse, wife, lover, and fellow workers, he reminds us of the Buddha as depicted in scenes of his death. He is the Confident One surrounded by weeping disciples. As with the deaths of other enlightened beings, a master's work and life are one and the same. There is no difference between the two, even when play is included in both. To live an evanescent life is to live fully, and to die with satisfaction. To those who grasp this truth, death is sweet.

THE END OF THE WORLD

Evanescence lasts. To endure or persist, even to be eternal, is not necessarily to be non-changing. Impermanence is permanent. Is this not the very definition of the eternal? In some cases, change may seem like permanence. It can happen slowly. It can be cyclical. Cycles are both repetitious and lasting by nature. The way we have been graphically representing the idea of evanescence suggests as much. Change is a line (and a progression); but it is one that continues indefinitely.

As perceived cyclically, change can be measured in seconds, hours, days, in seasons, by lifetimes, eras, epochs, even by ages and millennia. As Higashiyama pointed out, a leaf has its cycle—from bud, to foliage, to decay upon the forest floor, then to bud again. A forest similarly passes through centuries of growth, infestation, and fire. Even the earth has its cycles of thousands and millions of years. On the Japanese islands where short cycles of change are closely watched and celebrated—the colors of spring leaves and the changing hues of the hydrangea—there is also a strong sense of that which unfolds within much larger cycles, ones not as easily grasped without the imagination and without the help of metaphysical perspective. Extrapolating from what we know of the here-and-now, we might sense not an eternal permanence of *being* but eternal cycles of *becoming*. Just as the sun rises and sets, just as a person grows old and dies, so, too, must this world end in order to start again.

One example of end-of-the-world thinking would be the already mentioned millenarian uprisings of the late Tokugawa period. The so-called *yonaoshi ikki* were attempts to "fix" (*naosu*) the nineteenth-century world (*yo*). They were otherwise called "*ee ja nai ka*"—a curious expression that means "Why not?" or "Anything goes." These rebellions occurred at that crucial point when sociopolitical form deteriorated catastrophically, so that the values that normally flowed from established structures of power and meaning required renegotiation. In a state of *yonaoshi*, what was once forbidden suddenly became permissible; and that which was impossible became possible. Hence, "Why not?" With *yonaoshi*, the heavy lid of form flew off the seething pot, unleashing both rage and desire.

A natural disaster of immense proportions, the Kantō Earthquake of September 1, 1923, kept the theme of the end of the world in play. After powerful quakes brought Tokyo and Yokohama tumbling down, terrible fires swept the cities, creating a firestorm that killed 30,000 in one spot alone. Natural disaster led to human disaster. Panic and a breakdown of order led to vigilante-style murders of ethnic Koreans, who were falsely accused of taking advantage of the situation by setting fires and poisoning wells. In Tokyo and Yokohama, approximately 1.9 million people were left homeless; and estimates are that from 100,000 to 140,000 people were killed. Until the even more horrible destruction of World War II, it was this earthquake that concretely defined disaster and kept apocalyptic violence in everyone's minds. The 1923 disaster persuaded the novelist Tanizaki Jun'ichirō (1886–1965) to resettle in Western Japan and to abandon his life in the big city. On the other hand, the destruction served as inspiration for other writers, such as Unno Jūza (1897–1949), whose war novels (*senso shōsetsu*) of the 1930s anticipated the carpet bombings of 1945 with their horrific descriptions of total desolation.

I need not say much more about the relevance of World War II to my present point about how the end of the world has emerged as a post-War manifestation of evanescence. The conflict that killed 50–70 million people worldwide is remembered in Japan as a tragedy, as I pointed out, and not as the "good war" remembered by so many older Americans. You will get some idea of this understanding if you visit the renovated Hiroshima Peace Memorial Museum. The Museum was first established in 1955 in order to remember the past and contribute to "a future of lasting peace." What struck me about that older, first iteration of nuclear attack when I visited in 1979 was how little comment there was about what I was seeing: jars of pickled tumors, photographs of charred and festering bodies, a leveled and smoldering city. That pre-renovation museum made the point that nuclear weapons are terrible and ought never to be used again. But you could not find even one sentence about the political causes of the destruction. It was as if the Bomb had magically created itself and had fallen randomly on Hiroshima, for no reason in particular.

I was so distressed by this lack of comment that I wrote a letter to the editor of the *Kobe News* as soon as I returned to Kobe, where I was then going to graduate school. As an American studying Japanese culture, I felt it was irresponsible and cowardly to sidestep the issues of racism, fascism, and imperialism that had plagued both sides of the catastrophe. I was not being critical of the lack of balance in their discussion of Hiroshima's devastation. The issue was even more fundamental than that since there was no discussion.

A week or so later, I got a call from *Kobe News*. One of the editors wanted to talk, so I met him in his office. My letter was there on his desk. The gist of our conversation was this. He appreciated what I had written. Yes, more needed to be said, not about the technology but about the human uses of technology, about politics. But then he made himself clear:

> There's no way we'll ever print your letter. And our reason is this. We Japanese have agreed not to say anything about what happened. The images and the symbols of Hiroshima are so powerful that both the Right and the Left have agreed not to use them for their own purposes. We have this truce, if you can call it that. I hope you can understand what I'm saying to you.

I did understand. They had decided to avoid conflict by not blaming each other for the War, and by not pointing a finger at the United States.

With this incident in mind, I revisited Hiroshima in the summer of 2005. I was both surprised and pleased to see that the remodeling of the Museum, which took place in 1991 and 1994, had given voice to many of the concerns that earlier had been avoided. This time the focus was not solely on the Bomb, but also on the people—both those who designed and deployed it, and the many people (including incarcerated foreign prisoners of war) who suffered its consequences. We can still disagree about whether enough is now being said, or if the proper things are being said. (After all, the Enola Gay exhibit in the Smithsonian Institute is still without words because Americans cannot come to terms with the meaning of its terror.) But the point is that what I saw in the new museum confirmed my understanding that the unimaginable horror of nuclear attack has sharpened Japan's understanding of radical change and the fragility of existence. It has contributed to their end-of-the-world obsession.

The frequency with which Japanese artists treat this theme of the end might be a dramatic, box-office gesture. But I believe that we can continue the line we have drawn from *utsusemi* to *hakanasa* to *mujō* to *ukiyo* to *mono no aware* to monstrosity to adapt-or-die to wartime atrocity to holocaust to the ebullience of economic growth and the popping of the bubble to include contemporary fashion, the fragmentation of postmodern culture, and this repetitive theme of the end of the world. As expressed by Sugimoto Naojirō, a survivor of the bombing of Hiroshima, such cataclysmic destruction "offered a dark view that made one think of the end of the world."[18] Why should we be surprised to see that this sense of loss has played a major role in guiding cultural production since the Occupation, and this despite the phenomenal success of rebuilding and rejuvenation?

In 1954, a film by Honda Ishirō (1911–93) took up the theme directly. His *Godzilla* (*Gojira*) introduced to the world a 200-pound latex monster that warned us of our arrogance and possible demise. Like the mushroom-shaped clouds that rose over Japan's destroyed cities, this huge reptile appeared as a visible and unforgettable emblem of the world's end. It stimulated Japan's ability to keep imagining destruction, and thereby served as both an effective statement against war and a reminder of the need to work for peace. As the years passed and numerous sequels were created, Godzilla never lost its destructiveness. Yet its battles came to be against Mothra, Megalon, and other outlandish monsters that came to draw attention to themselves as much as to the larger issue of the world's imminent demise. In short, as Japan prospered, the critical edge of Godzilla's existence (as a mutation born of and awakened by nuclear radiation) gradually became secondary to the entertainment value of its hideous powers.

Here, then, is just one example of the way that, as one crucial aspect of Japan's return to evanescence, figurative expression overwhelms and pulls away from ideological context. Perhaps the playful glibness with which the present-day Japanese have come to deal so frequently with this theme of the end of the world follows from the law of diminishing returns: a growing intensity that yields only the same (or reduced) level of satisfaction with each repetition. Or, once again, perhaps it comes with the firsthand experience of actually having survived nuclear holocaust. Whatever the case, the frequency with which the theme of the end of the world is articulated seems to suggest an enduring sense of life's fragility. Having carefully traced the life of this notion over centuries of Japanese cultural expression, we know that the idea, as a way to increase dramatic interest, is also effective for well-grounded, traditional reasons.

As Japan began to prosper, cataclysm came to be expressed in many other ways. The science-fiction writer Komatsu Sakyō's best-selling novel, *Japan Sinks* (*Nippon chinbotsu*, 1973), narrates nothing less than the physical destruction of the Japanese archipelago.[19] In this narrative, vast portions of the islands sink into the ocean due to their location in a massive subduction zone created by the movements of tectonic plates. In this geologically outlandish story about change of a most frightening sort, the picture is bleak indeed. Loss of life is high, and the very future of the Japanese civilization is threatened.

When viewed from a marketing point of view, every indication shows that Komatsu knew he had a winning idea from the very start. A manga version, *Manga Nihon chinbotsu*, was released at the same time as the novel; and within the year, a movie adaptation, *Nihon chinbotsu*, directed by Moritani Shirō (1931–84), was released from Tōhō Studios, the same house that produced *Godzilla*. The popularity of *Japan Sinks* suggests that in this day and age nothing sells quite like disaster, especially as it brings us to that point of clarity which supposedly comes just before our demise—just at that heightened moment when false form sloughs away and inner character reveals itself truly. Will the advent of our final destruction prove us to be heroes or cowards? How will we act in time of crisis? Will our worst instincts come to the surface, or will we act bravely?

Thinking of the inevitability of loss can be therapeutic. But can it be overdone? Has the continual treatment of disaster and the end of the world rendered both these themes sentimental? Not only was *Japan Sinks* marketed as a novel, a manga, and a movie, but it also became a board game that gave friends the opportunity literally to play with disaster. How unfortunate, then, that the nation reacted so incompetently when an earthquake hit the Kobe-Osaka region in 1995, and many perished in the aftermath for lack of planning and attention. There are too few tales of heroic action to tell about the Kobe Earthquake. The general response by both local and national governments was said to be slow and ineffective.

Could this lack of response have been caused by the way disaster has become so thoroughly aestheticized in the land of falling cherry blossoms? In the earlier age of *yonaoshi*, works of illustrated fiction (*kusazōshi*) such as *The Tale of Shiranui* (*Shiranui monogatari*, 1849–85) or *Tales of the Heroic Jiraiya* (*Jiraiya goketsu monogatari*, 1839–68) were filled with numbingly graphic scenes of murder and violence. They claimed to "promote good and punish evil" (*kanzen chōaku*), but this was largely an excuse to indulge in the drama of mayhem. With the Meiji Restoration and the Age of the Transcendental Order, this sort of overwhelming visual display was suppressed in order to focus on those abstract principles that were required to imagine the Japanese empire into existence. But now, with this return to evanescence and a renewed appreciation of the spatial and visual, figurality has come back with a vengeance. So has thinking about the end of the world.

One factor in this development is technology, which has made it easier and much less expensive to stage the destruction of the world. Photography, film, television, offset printing, digital graphics, computerized animation—all of these technologies have brought Japan (and the rest of the advanced world) to a steady diet of visual effects. One result of this development has been to free the imagination from the restraints of modern, hegemonic culture. At the same time, the creation of increasingly destructive weapons and the continued degradation of our natural environment have also added to the pessimism of many. The end of life is possible.

Today, the Japanese are world champions of popular culture precisely because of their ability to visually display the revived pull of the here-and-now as it has been aided by image-producing technologies. This explains Japan's tremendous influence on popular culture throughout the world today. The endless possibilities of transformation, the temporary wholeness of fashion, the raw honesty of distortion that appears as distortion, the survivability implicit in gaming, the joy of the outrageous, the sophisticated "look" of Japanese design and graphics—these cultural phenomena seem to speak to the sensibilities of many. The visualization of culture is a worldwide phenomenon; and Japan has become number one again, not because of its manufacturing productivity and efficiency, but because of the look of its created spaces.

NAUSICAA AND THE CICADA-SHELL WORLD

Following *Godzilla* and *Japan Sinks*, the theme of the end of the world was kept in play by Miyazaki Hayao, who dealt head-on with the idea of the world's destruction. Like Ōtomo Katsuhirō's manga version of *Akira*, Miyazaki's seven-volume *Nausicaa of the Windy Valley* (*Kaze no tani no Naushika*, 1982–91) also begins at a point in time when most of the world has been destroyed. The preface reads as follows:

The industrial civilization that developed on the western extremity of the Eurasian continent spread to the rest of the world in a matter of centuries. Becoming a colossus of industrial might, this society plundered the earth's riches, polluted its air, and willfully changed life forms. After a thousand years, it reached its zenith, but then entered a period of rapid decline. In a war called "The Seven Days of Fire," the cities of the world were blanketed with poisonous materials and destroyed. The most complex forms of high technology were lost, and industrial civilization failed to reestablish itself. Mankind came to live in a long era of twilight.[20]

Nausicaa begins 1,000 years after the so-called Seven Days of Fire. A poisonous blizzard of spores and an accompanying deadly miasma has covered most of the land. Only in a few places, such as Nausicaa's "windy valley" where the ocean breezes keep the contamination at bay, do we find a narrow fringe of human life. This agricultural community, where the air is clean and people still care for each other, provides hope. But it is soon over-run as a new wave of war breaks out. Even these "post ceramic" civilizations have learned little and seem doomed for total destruction.

Miyazaki creates a bleak situation. And yet, as this twilight drifts into night, we come to feel hopeful for the morning that will follow. His leading characters are usually young women. Like her namesake in the *Odyssey*, Nausicaa is beautiful, courageous, and resourceful.[21] Upon her shoulders rests the fate of all. She has many gifts, but her greatest is an ability to commune with nature. She is able to hear trees talk and to communicate with the gigantic *ōmu* that inhabit the spore-blanketed forest. In addition to the ancient Greek beauty who did not fear the brine-crusted Odysseus as he emerged from the sea, Miyazaki also intended that another model for this character be the eccentric heroine of the late Heian-period story, "The Princess Who Loved Worms."[22] This is a narrative about a strong-willed girl of the nobility who preferred the company of creatures to that of people. Only such a nature-loving character is able to turn the remaining inhabitants of a conflict-ridden land away from certain annihilation.

Like Tetsuo, Nausicaa grows in strength. But unlike his, her powers are consistently used in ways that help others. In the face of destruction, she tries to save life—whether the forest, "threatened civilization," or the insect-like *ōmu* that play such a crucial role in the story. Her role as a latter-day savior has been prophesied in legend. Identified by her blue jacket, dyed in *ōmu* blood, she is the first to understand that life is death and death is life. She is the only one who can see that the plague of spores is actually purifying the earth, cleansing it of its pollution. It is her intuitive understanding of con-stant change, not the vast stores of information sealed up in the Black Tomb of Knowledge, that will restore the world someday. In fact, Nausicaa tries to seal up this artificial, textual knowledge. Relearning it would only lead to progress and another cycle of expansion and destruction.

Before the Stone of Learning, she remonstrates,

> Do you plan to deceive the next ones in line to be destroyed? Is that because you'll need slaves on that morning when you start a new world, no matter how much knowledge or technology you've brought along? Even if you replace our bodies with artificial ones, the life we have is ours! We're animated with the life force. When that morning comes, we'll be ready for it, living away. We'll be the birds in the air, coughing up blood, over and over, and rising above your new morning. To live is to change. The *ōmu*, the deadly spores, the grass and trees, people. We're all changing. We're all living, along with the spreading pollution. To tell the truth. We don't need you.[23]

Nausicaa does not care about ideas. She cares about the earth, the world of the here-and-now. Her faith is an animistic belief in nature's vitality, in its ability to restore itself, in its ability to resurrect. Her greatest allies are neither learned monks nor scholars, but the ōmu. These huge creatures represent the vitality of the world, a force stronger than any other.

Nausicaa's personal trajectory should be familiar to us by now. Like that of Kumagae of *Atsumori* or Mizushima of *The Harp of Burma*, hers also reminds us of the Bodhisattva's path. Able to move on, she decides to return to the world of sorrows. When she discovers a verdant spot of restored earth that has already passed through a thousand-year process of regeneration, she understands that the air of this neo-Eden is too pure for humans to breath. Should they be transplanted to such a place, another cycle of growth and pride would begin. So Nausicaa returns to the polluted world—to the universe of dust. Perhaps at another time, in another 1,000 years, people will want and deserve a cleaner environment. Until then, she rejects paradise and chooses to be with her people, thus reaffirming the Bodhisattva's path of return to samsara.

Before completing *Nausicaa of the Windy Valley*, Miyazaki began and finished the much-abbreviated anime version, a work that launched his career as an animator and opened his path to becoming one of Japan's truly great animation artists. Like Ōtomo's anime version of *Akira* (1988), Miyazaki's animated *Nausicaa* (1984) is also highly regarded. But both of these works are mere skeletons of the much richer and involved narratives from which they grew. Speaking of the nine-year manga project, Miyazaki claims to have started it with a feeling of despair, thinking that industrial civilization would bring the earth to a state of environmental crisis from which it would not be able to rebound. But in his agonizing search for a proper ending, he was finally able to discover (and express) the light that darkness made obvious. His question to us is this: Who has the strength to turn away from Heaven and to love the cicada-shell world? Who can resist the transcendental order, and re-embrace the order of here-and-now?

SEEKING BUT NEVER FINDING

The truth of decay does not always lead to the truth of healing, whether in art or in reality. On the morning of March 20, 1995, ten members of the religious group Aum Shinrikyō placed packets of liquefied sarin gas on five Tokyo subway lines at the height of rush hour. Twelve died, an estimated 5,000 people breathed in the lethal chemical, and multitudes suffered the psychological effects of this attack that was, doctrinally speaking, done for Japan's own good.

The logic of the Aum terrorists went something like this. We all die. At the time of death, our future state of existence is determined by our accumulation of karma—the consequences of our good and bad deeds. Bad people fall to a lower level of existence; and good people rise. Luckily, the intercession of a guru, or master, can positively influence the outcome of this judgment. This intercession is called *poa*, which is a teaching from Tibetan Buddhism, one of the many sources of Aum doctrine.

Now, from this understanding of *poa* comes a logical though horrifying corollary. Since we are all continuously changing, usually for the worse, I could do you a favor by ending your life early and thus lessening your buildup of bad karma. In other words, I help you out by killing you. This was the thinking that justified numerous violent acts perpetrated by Aum Shinrikyō.

Of course, much more than doctrine motivated the gas attacks. As Ian Reader points out, the violent aspects of Aum flowed from many sources: strict ascetic practice, the authoritarian suppression of difference, criminality and attempts to hide from or otherwise disregard the rule of law, paranoia and the perceived need to defend oneself against violence by using violence, the personal arrogance and hedonism of Aum's leader Asahara Shōkō, and from a shift to increasingly hierarchical and esoteric forms of worship that gave the movement's leaders a sense that they had special knowledge and could handle special privileges, such as the power of compassionate killing (*poa*).[24] The similarities between Asahara's followers and Ishii Shirō's corps of medical scientists (as well as with the American authorities who chose not to prosecute these war criminals in exchange for the useful information about biological warfare that they were gaining) are striking. For the good of the world, we justify cruelty, violence, and murder. My devotion might be your evil. But your evil is my need for devotion.

The popular press in Japan quickly and persistently presented the incident as the work of a thankfully small group of fanatics. Aum Shinrikyō was said to be made up of disenfranchised and dysfunctional individuals who acted on their fears and brought about the disaster. In particular, they were said to be people who had suffered the dissolution of healthy family bonds and looked to Aum for a sense of stability and belonging. Their vulnerability had allowed them to be misled by the charismatic Asahara, who presented them with a compelling, if violent, view of salvation.

By distancing themselves from the eccentric few in this way, the masses were able to turn their fear into outrage, and to understand the gas attack as outrageous. But there were also those who could not so easily dismiss what had happened as an incomprehensible act. Having recently returned from nine years of living and working abroad, the novelist Murakami Haruki (1949–) felt that the tragedy revealed a rarely articulated aspect of Japanese culture. Troubled by the way the Aum attacks were so blithely dismissed as the work of a monstrous Other, he attempted to gain a deeper understanding of the event by interviewing a number of those who had been injured in the attacks. Once this was accomplished, he went on to interview several members (or former members) of Aum Shinrikyō in his attempt to get as full a picture of the phenomenon as possible.

The result of his study was published in two volumes: *Underground* (*Andāguraundo*, 1997) and *In the Place that Was Promised* (*Yakusoku sareta basho de*, 1998).[25] Together, these two volumes stand as the most thorough compilation we have of the sentiments of those on both sides of the 1995 event.[26] For the author himself, these two books also marked an important personal turning point; with them Murakami declared his return to Japan, ending the wandering that his readers had found so compelling and so true to the experience of being Japanese in the 1980s and 1990s.

One particularly significant moment in the interviews occurs when one Takahashi Hidetoshi, a member of Aum, makes the point that looking forward to the end of the world (as many Aum Shinrikyō members were apparently wont to do) is something that others do as well, whether in Japan or in other affluent societies.

> TAKAHASHI: Life is full of suffering, and the contradictions in the real world irked me. To escape these, I imagined my own sort of utopian society, which made it easier for me to be taken in by a religious group that espoused a similar vision.
>
> When the Aum question comes up, people always start talking about relations between parents and children going sour, and family discord, but it can't be reduced to something so simplistic. Certainly one of the attractions of Aum lay in people's frustrations with reality and unrest in the family, but a much more important factor lies in the apocalyptic feelings of "the end of the world," feelings all of us have about the future. If you pay attention to the universal feelings that all Japanese have—all humankind, even— then you can't explain Aum's appeal to so many people by saying it's based on discord in the family.
>
> MURAKAMI: Hold on a second. You really think all Japanese have a vision of the end of the world?
>
> TAKAHASHI: It might be hard to generalize and say that all of them do, but I think inside all Japanese there is an apocalyptic viewpoint: an invisible, unconscious sense of fear. When I say that all Japanese have this fear I mean some people have already pulled aside the veil, while others have yet to do so. If this veil were suddenly drawn back, everyone would feel a sense of terror about the near future, the direction our world's heading in. Society is the foundation stone for people's lives, and they don't know what's going to happen to it in the future. This feeling grows stronger the more affluent a country becomes. It's like a dark shadow looming larger and larger.
>
> MURAKAMI: Somehow the words "decline" or "collapse" seem to hit the mark more than "the end."
>
> TAKAHASHI: Maybe so, but I remember that when I was in school and Nostramadamus's *Prophecies* became famous, and that sense that "The End is Nigh" wedged itself deep into my consciousness through the mass media. And I wasn't the only one to feel like that. I don't want this to deteriorate into some simplistic theory about "my generation," but I feel very strongly that all Japanese at that time had the idea drilled into them of 1999 being the end of the world. Aum renunciates have already accepted, inside themselves, the end of the world, because when they become a renunciate, they discarded themselves totally, thereby abandoning the world. In other words, Aum is a collection of people who have accepted the end. People who continue to hold out hope for the near future still have an attachment to the world. If you have attachments, you won't discard your

> Self, but for renunciates it's as if they've leaped right off a cliff. And taking
> a giant leap like that feels good. They lose something—but gain something
> in return.[27]

As voiced here, Murakami's sense of skepticism and resistance is a bit
surprising. First of all, his own conclusions are much like Takahashi's: "The
Aum 'phenomenon' disturbs us precisely because it is not someone else's
affair. It shows us a distorted image of ourselves in a manner none of us
could have foreseen."[28] And second, Murakami himself has embarked on his
own extended eschatological ruminations. Published ten years prior to the
gas attacks, his critically acclaimed *Hard-Boiled Wonderland and the End of
the World* (*Sekai no owari to Hādo-boirudo wandārando*, 1985) is nothing if
not a contemplation of the world's end.

The novel is inward-turning, even solipsistic. It is a "my exploration" of
the world's end as a form of inward self-discovery. The hero, a cool thirty-
something, encounters the end of the world that is actually an imagined
place in his own mind. In the last few pages of this long work, as the hero
reaches his moment of enlightenment, he speaks to his own shadow and
confirms the steadily articulated theme of the exclusive, almost autistic self.
In terms of Murakami's overall oeuvre, *Hard-Boiled Wonderland* continues
a self-absorbed search that began at least as early as the short story, "Girl
from Ipanema" (*1963/1982 no Ipenema musume*, 1984). "Somewhere ... I'll
meet myself in a strange place in a far-off world. ... In that place, I am
myself and myself is me. Subject is object and object is subject. All gaps are
gone. A perfect union. There must be a strange place like this somewhere in
the world."[29] Yes, this is solipsism in the usual use of the word. But is it also
a step into the here-and-now as it anciently was?

In *Hard-Boiled Wonderland and the End of the World*, both the hero of
this story and his shadow (which has been forcibly separated from him) are
trapped in a place known as "*sekai no owari*," the end of the world. The
shadow still has some access to memories of the past and, therefore, to the
world outside the perfectly constructed and impenetrable wall that seals
them in. It urges the hero to escape, but in the end the shadow's owner
chooses himself. That is to say, he opts to "meet myself in a strange place,"
which is "a far-off world" that is (nevertheless) himself and includes nothing
that lies beyond the walls that confine him.

Speaking to his disappointed shadow, he explains:

> "I have responsibilities," I say. "I cannot forsake the people and places and
> things I have created. I know I do you a terrible wrong. And yes, perhaps
> I wrong myself, too. But I must see out the consequences of my own doings.
> This is my world. The Wall is here to hold *me* in, the River flows through *me*,
> the smoke is *me* burning. I must know why."[30]

In other words, Murakami's hero's responsibility to the aforementioned
persons, places, and things is an inward-looking response to "me," to an
awareness of one's own consciousness, something that the author has

consistently protected against the vagaries of the Crowd and the deceits of ideology. Here in this consciousness we are still twice removed from the real world of human interaction, of which *Underground* is supposedly a study. For this reason, these works of *non*fiction that came twelve years later mark an unusual step away from the perfections of self-detachment that the readers of *Hard-Boiled Wonderland* found so compelling. They mark an arrival that some critics have found lacking in his earlier work.[31]

We cannot deny the Nausicaa-like intentionality of Murakami's return to Japan. Yet neither can we overlook the undercurrent of evanescence that guides his imagination at points both before and after the Aum event. Murakami attempts to get past the precious repetitions of the Japanese tradition by pushing creatively toward a "hard-boiled" state. But even he cannot resist the pull of evanescence. As a complementary bookend to Nitobe's *Bushido, Hard-Boiled Wonderland and the End of the World* retreats from the enlarged international context of "Japan and the world" to establish a postmodern context that is smaller and more personal than a nation: the self that can be the smallness that solipsistically approaches everything, including the Japan that was lost to modernity. This self is Murakami's contemporary version of Bashō's non-dualism, where outer and inner (subject and object) are really one.

While this oneness is the ground of Japanese culture, its recovery comes at a time when the world is split and at cross-purposes with itself. Reflecting this tension, *Hard-Boiled Wonderland* is an interweaving of two very different narratives—one epic, the other lyrical; one driven by (hard-boiled) action, the other by sentiment; one a contemporary *now and only now*, the other set in some indefinite, archaic point that is *here and only here*. Importantly, both stories bear a residual modernity, similarly pushed ahead by a strong sense of time's passing. They proceed with urgency and with a curiosity about the strange and unknowable future that slowly and surely becomes the clearly knowable (yet no less strange) end of existence—the exact moment of death (or in this case, a loss of consciousness) that is, for most people, life's wellkept secret. Working steadily toward such an end, the novel poses a familiar question. In fact, it is *the* question of evanescence, posed anciently by many and echoed in recent times by Higashiyama's landscapes, Kurosawa's *Ikiru*, Itami's *The Great Patient*, and so on. If we know we are going to die soon, how do we live?

Murakami provides two answers. The hard-boiled one reminds us of Tanaka Yasuo's fashionable world of *Somehow Crystal*, where meaningful gestures are made toward fashion, style, and consumption. Faced with the last few hours of his life, the hero of *Hard-Boiled Wonderland and the End of the World* buys new clothes, rents a nice car, has dinner at a good restaurant, has sex, goes to a peaceful park in the morning, drinks a few beers, and listens to his favorite music while waiting for the extinguishing of his consciousness to come.

Set against this is a more lyrical, old-fashioned answer: the dialogue quoted earlier between Self and Shadow. The world of this second answer pretends to be more "responsible," but in truth it is similarly self-concerned. The "world" of "the end of the world" is an exquisitely lonely and personal place. Again, it is about "me," being responsible to "me." Echoing Ōtomo's pregnant idiom of self-centeredness—"I am Tetsuo"—is Murakami's "I have responsibilities." Yet Murakami's "I" is dual, split between the formal first-person pronoun *watashi* and the informal first-person pronoun *boku*, between the conscious man of action and the unconscious man of feeling. It is a duality identified by work, by consumption, and by loyalty. But, once again, loyalty to what? Or to whom?

Like Tanaka's *Somehow Crystal* and Itami's *Tanpopo*, Murakami's *Hard-Boiled Wonderland and the End of the World* is similarly two stories in one. Why this curious dual structure? Why this inability to be simply linear? Or simply lyrical? Is this not a reflection of Japan's return to evanescence after having passed through the modern experience of channeling change into the forward-looking pursuit of a stable, conceptual Japanese essence—whether bushidō, tea-ism, or erotic style? In contemporary Japan, this return takes the form of a narrative doubleness, where two very different kinds of structure existing side by side, as if to remember the recently end-seeking modern past by way of a reemerging regime of *utsusemi*, *hakanasa*, and *mujō*.

In the case of *Hard-Boiled Wonderland*, this doubling back occurs by way of a lyrical exploration of self *in* the world and self *as* the world, in an attempt to reverse the century-old trauma of Japan's "opening." The "I" of the hard-boiled narrative is not really responsible to or for an expanded sense of the world. The hero's consciousness is terminal in every sense. He knows no society, no politics. He is cut off from family. He is loyal only to himself, albeit an exalted and attractive Self, one that is talented though unassuming, capable yet easygoing, closed off yet charming. For Murakami, the selfishness of his ever-searching hero is a moral necessity. The Murakami hero stands apart from the Crowd as possessing "the concrete, irreducible humanity of each individual."[32] Like ideology and like metaphysics, the Crowd that formed by way of certain uniting principles—empire, nation, race—also cannot be trusted.

This is because all three cannot be known in any real way. The System, and the competing groups of Calcutecs, Semiotecs, and Inklings who wage the information war that takes in Murakami's hero are all unreliable. They are not nameable. Like Aum Shinrikyō, they want power, first and foremost. They are also vicious, the inhuman stuff of which crowds are made.. And so it is better to stay away, to live life in small ways, to enjoy sips of whiskey, and to listen to Bob Dylan tunes over and over again. That is the end of Japan at the present moment: the contemporary predilection for small happiness over big happiness—a good sandwich over a good ideology—a predilection that many postmodern readers have instinctively understood.

Generally speaking, it is this sandwich-eating wanderer that Murakami has offered to the world; and the world has bought his journey by the millions of copies. For contemporary Japanese readers, this sort of product-aided detachment is a palatable evanescence, a live-for-the-moment life of small pleasures that has rendered Japan into a paradise of countless vending machines and convenience stores, where one's impersonal personal currency is expressed constantly—at any place, at any time of day. In contemporary Japan, everything is available always, so that immediate desire and immediate gratification spin together toward consumeristic perfection.

The arresting point of *Underground* and *In the Place that Was Promised*, these works that came after *Hard-Boiled Wonderland and the End of the World*, is that they push self-orientation and self-gratification ahead one more crucial step. They conclude that, in the end, the Crowd is *us*: "The sarin attack was a product of the evil of Asahara, but this evil is related to the evils of our society—the ambiguity of the system; the lack of freedom of information; people uncritically following what the authorities tell them to do. We can't just decry Asahara's evil and ignore the rest of society."[33]

Ostensibly, Murakami's study of Aum Shinrikyō is an exercise in locating and criticizing society's evil, an activity that stems *from* the author's stubbornly solipsistic journey through detachment to commitment. On one recent return to Tufts campus, where Murakami had earlier spent two years writing and teaching, he commented, "At some point, after so many years of searching, you ought to be able to find something." I took this to mean that he was sincere in his challenge for himself. It was clear that he truly wanted to create "a new way of thinking" and "useful role models" for people to follow.[34] But a tension remains between maintaining critical distance and creating or following such models. Which models? Created for whom? Who determines their validity?

If *Underground* suggests the importance of having our own models and our own narratives, how can we distinguish these stories from the solipsism of *Hard-Boiled Wonderland and the End of the World*? In his critique of Aum, Murakami seems at times to fall back to his earlier position that nothing matters except that which is "really and truly your own."

> Haven't you offered up some part of your Self to someone (or something), and taken on a "narrative" in return? Haven't we entrusted some part of our personality to some greater System or Order? And if so, has not that System at some stage demanded of us some kind of "insanity"? Is the narrative you now possess really and truly your own? Are your dreams really your own dreams? Might not they be someone else's visions that could sooner or later turn into nightmares?[35]

Hard-Boiled Wonderland and the End of the World is the fictional nothingness that precedes the nonfictional everything of *Underground* and *In the Place that Was Promised*. Yet this everything still might be in the process of forming. At least at the point of these interviews, the journey seemed to form around an independent and unattached Self that still prided itself in its ability to stand apart from the world, from family, from society. Does Murakami mean to say that all narratives except the one that protects the independence of the Self are false by nature? If so, then what is this narrative that exists in and of itself? And if it is independently distinct, how then can it be considered a "model"? Beyond the smallness of a new set of clothes and a taste for style, can there be this self-existing narrative, this state of "I am" that is both personal and universal? To restate the issue in terms of our analysis, can there be a Bodhisattva in Murakami's world of disconnection? When the postmodern return, do they return home?

Underground does not clearly tell us what the alternative to Aum Shinrikyō is. Perhaps Murakami does not get far enough beyond solipsism to supply that option. Perhaps the detachment required by those who would put poisonous gas on a subway is still too similar to the coolness of Murakami's likable though detached heroes, these "*boku*" (I) whose lonely search for a proper, nonvanishing attachment continues indefinitely. Both still stop one step short of compassion and of, therefore, returning fully to the nothingness that is everything. And so the storytelling and the searching continues, though now more frequently in a third- rather than first-person narrative mode.

The Bodhisattva's trajectory is hard to grasp and even more difficult to teach to others. But the stakes are high, and the consequences dire if, in the attempt, we stop at judgment and do not proceed to charity, or if we linger in detachment and do not continue to reengagement. Unable to give himself to the nothingness that connected him with everyone else, Asahara hastened the truth of change and confused enlightenment with murder. He moved away from compassion and toward fear. Having declared the floating world tawdry, Murakami was right to insist that nothing is so destructive as the Crowd and its will to improve the world in conformity with its organizing principles. By way of this fascistic desire to *poa* all living beings and thereby ensure their salvation, Aum did Japan much damage. But what is the alternative to the Crowd?

Surely, Asahara's attitude toward evil is widespread. The point made by Robert Lifton—that Aum Shinrikyō was *not* unusual in looking forward to the end of the world but *was* unusual in that it actively sought to make that end happen—overlooks a more general pattern and misses the point.[36] There is probably much more active yearning for Armageddon going around than we wish to recognize. As Higashiyama might put it, in our desire to be right and to be powerful, far too many of us become unwitting angels of destruction. We hasten our demise, if not that of others, because of our "righteous" desires. The self-justified among us actually look forward to the end of the world, to the final battle that will free us of struggle: the bad guys will be burned, and the rest of us will leave in peace. But this desire to make the world just and pure is still unrepentantly modern. It is still the unrecognized essence of evil.

Murakami senses this evil as the will of the Crowd, and he rightly stays away from it. And yet, if his many readers continue to follow him as he matures as a writer, it will be to find, rather than simply to seek. The question, then, is whether they will be able to bear Murakami's burden of actually believing in something in the end, of actually going home someday. Why should anyone want to be burdened with this commitment to return to *uchi*, the source of suffering? Perhaps this state of after-seeking is the only means by which we can give to others the things that we have never had, all those things we do not possess that are nevertheless required of us—as friends, as partners, as parents, as children, and so on. Is "not finding" the same as not seeing the stream of constant change in which we live, not understanding life as it quickly passes before our very eyes? The problem, of course, is that by thinking we can step out of flowing waters in our discovery of truth, we risk the chance of becoming deluded by our monstrous ability to be powerful. We become Asahara. We create worlds without change, which are worlds without mercy.

ANIMA, ANIME, AND ANIMISM

Sitting on my desk is one of my son's toys. It is made of many plastic parts, held together by moveable joints. It looks vaguely human. But if I start unfolding and rearranging its parts this way and that, it slowly changes into a vehicle. It is one of hundreds of types of transforming figures that were popular in the United States in the 1980s and 1990s. Other popular models are trucks, cars, pistols, boom boxes, all mechanisms that turn into robots or animals. Some smaller robots fit together to form larger ones. All are alike in that they change from one thing to another and are a part of a wave of Japanese figurality that has spread to this and other parts of the globe.

These changelings were first marketed as "transformers" in the United States by Hasbro in 1984. They were invented by Japan's Takara Corporation, which then partnered with Hasbro and produced them as Micro Change and Dioclone toys. So popular did these Japanese plastic figures become that G.I. Joe is now all but a forgotten icon of the past. In the year 2008, Japanese culture is influential, even inescapable—and not because everyone is reading the novels of Kawabata and Ōe Kenzaburō, or even watching the films of Kurosawa and Mizoguchi. For my students, who flock to Japanese culture courses being taught at the university, they find Japan of great interest because they grew up on various forms of Japanese popular culture, and also because their visual orientation has given them an appreciation for significant space, fashion, and metamorphosis. The blurring of the distinction between animal and machine that is the essence of transformers is yet another manifestation of an ever-changing reality. It brings to mind a tenet of F.T. Marinetti's Futurist Manifesto of 1909: "We declare that the splendor of the world has been enriched by a new beauty: the beauty of speed. A racing automobile with its bonnet adorned with great tubes like serpents with explosive breath ... a roaring motor car that seems to run on machine-gun fire is more beautiful than the Victory of Samothrace."[37]

As Walter Benjamin explained, the Futurists wanted nothing more than bodies like machines—fast, hard, strong, and powerful. And the ideal place for such bodies to display their full beauty was the battlefield. Today, they also appear on the sports field, and on the screen. Even though the wish for the mechanized future that computer graphics have made easier to imagine was originally a modern one, the visual (and material) emphasis of contemporary popular culture that technological development has made possible leads us beyond the desire to construct a systematic and universally valid world. If anything, technological progress has gotten in the way of such a unified vision by producing a diverse and complicated plentitude of imagined realities—Astro Boy, Godzilla, Ultraman, and on and on. The hegemonic focus of modern realism has deteriorated precisely because modernity created the sophisticated systems of communication and transportation that have rendered the grotesque possibilities of modern life not only possible but strikingly *visible*: the horrors of total war, the putrefaction of genocide, the anger of racism, the blight of pollution, the ravages of climate change, and so on. We see the results of our ideas; and we begin to suspect the limitation and inaccuracy of symbols. This suspicion is not only the essence of the postmodern critique of modernity. It also leads us to a truth about Japanese culture generally: nonsymbolic space and the order of here-and-now are actually meaningful.

In its visual splendor, today's Japan is a neo-An'ei Tenmei era following on the heels of a neo-Genroku. Like that earlier age of monsters, the present one is once again a time of *bakemono*: from Optimus Prime to Pikachu and Pokemon pocket monsters, from *Mighty Morphin' Power Rangers* to *Donkey Kong* and *Final Fantasy*. This is also a time when illustrated texts, having survived the modern suppression of figurality, once again dominate the world of printing, just as anime has come to dominate the world of cinema. Perhaps anime is the quintessential Japanese art form, its logic being so close to that of animism itself. To the anime artist, anything in this world can be given life; just as to the off-set printer, anything in this world can now be printed. The moving of the unmoving becomes the lively essence of anything and everything. As Susan Napier has mused, anime is a metamorphic art, a medium fit for monstrosity.[38] Perhaps no other art form affirms transformation (*henyō, henshin*) so baldly and insistently. Perhaps no other expression is so openly attentive to evanescence and form.

The *anima* of anime is a mechanically produced illusion—the rapid projection of static images that makes us feel as though we are seeing movement and life. Understood as such, animation is a willful and manipulative giving of life, a sacrilege and idolatry of the most profound sort. Perhaps of Japanese animators practicing today, no one has as brilliant and full an imaginative eye than the already introduced Miyazaki Hayao. As I noted, his films are hopeful if critical. His heroines are young yet resourceful. They know how to learn. They are *kawaii*—an oft-heard term that expresses cuteness, or the often-troubled instinct in adults to see the vulnerability of the young as something to cherish and protect rather than to exploit and abuse.

Which will it be? To protect? To abuse? In contemporary Japan, cuteness is an obsession. It drives many cultural phenomena: from the production and consumption of Kerokeroppi and Hello Kitty paraphernalia to child prostitution and the phenomenon called "*burikko*"—older women speaking in falsetto and feigning innocence and vulnerability. In the present environment of extended adolescence—where the years of high insecurity (and, therefore, high consumption) are prolonged as long as possible—Miyazaki's films are a rather unearthly preserve of a child's need for nurturing elders, for clean air and pure water, for opportunities to believe, to love, and to prove oneself through courageous and compassionate acts. To the extent that this world is consciously an illusion, his world stands as a subtle condemnation of the status quo, with its plagues of industrial contamination, familial neglect, and personal abuse. Miyazaki's films might be damning, yet their touch is gentle and, for this reason, widely appreciated by young and old alike.

In comparison to Miyazaki's hopeful vision, Oshii Mamoru's (1951–) is an adult eye, one that still references a relevant though broken transcendental realm. His *Ghost in the Shell* (*Kōkaku kidōtai*, 1995) guides us across the border that separates man and doll, the animated and the unanimated. In this film's search for the Puppet Master (*ningyō-zukai*), a superintelligence born of the web and endowed with prodigious godlike powers, we flirt with the border between the concrete and the conceptual. Like a spirit, the Puppet Master has no physical body of its own but occupies other bodies. He moves freely and invisibly through the vast tangles of the information network. He will soon be able to hack into any system, and manipulate any intelligence. So the world will become his puppet, and he will become its new God. Even Kusanagi Motoko, Batō, and Togusa—cyborg assassins who possess amazing powers of aggression and survival—are not free from its invasion. In fact, the heroine Kusanagi, who is plagued by the doubt she might not be a "person" at all, is drawn to the Puppet Master's evanescent existence, even as he is drawn to her physical "human" ability to have offspring.

Her doubts lead her to pose an age-old question, the very "*anima* question" that lies at the heart of the genre and of Japanese culture in general. Is there something like a soul (or ghost) that occupies the body (or the cicada's shell)? To Batō, her fellow assassin, Kusanagi is a real someone. Indeed, she is even a special someone. He cares for her, even though he is, like her, mostly machine and only slightly human. Kusanagi herself is less sure she is real. She thinks she has intuition. She thinks she hears voices that whisper Paul's words to the Corinthians—"For now we see through a glass, darkly." But she is never certain of her identity, never clear about the "who" that is hearing these intimations.

When she finally meets the Puppet Master, who explains to her his desire for immortality—for death and for offspring—she remains unconvinced. The Puppet Master's all-too-human desire might be understood as a way to overcome what Benjamin called a loss of aura. Although he is capable of copying his perfection endlessly, he admits that "a copy is, after all, merely a copy." He points out that even a perfect system can be destroyed by a single virus, thus leading to the nothing that is *nihil*. What he needs beyond system and universality (or beyond what we understand as modernity) is "variability" (*tayōsei*), and the kinds of difference that only Kusanagi, and postmodernity, can provide. He desires extinction. But he wants the kind of nothingness

that guarantees continued existence, a contemporary version of the nothingness that is everything.

She is tempted by the proposition of merging with the Master, but
hesitates. Her question is a very familiar one. It is Murakami's question.
"What guarantees that I'll remain me?" To this, the Puppet Master's answer
is that there is no such guarantee. "... to be human is to be continually
changing." (*Hito wa taezu henka suru mono da.*) Your desire to remain as
you are is what ultimately limits you." Accepting these truths, she finally
merges with the Master; thus leaving us to ponder how the distinction
between puppeteer and puppet must ultimately dissolve in a truly evanescent world. Even in a world of ghost and shell, it is quite impossible to tell
the dancer from the dance. Remarkably, as we near the end of this study of
Japanese culture, we find ourselves returning to the same non-duality that
Kitagawa described as he characterized ancient Japan. We return to a world
full of gods and spirits.

Oshii's *Ghost in the Shell* projects us into the future while drawing heavily
(and profitably) upon a long tradition of doll creation and manipulation.
I emphasize this connection with the past lest we miss the deep cultural
foundations of this robotic science fiction. The concept of manipulation is
emphasized in the way Oshii and Shirow Masamune, who wrote the manga
on which the anime is based, called this god a "puppet master." In calling
him a puppeteer, they tie themselves to a very long thread of Japanese culture,
one effectively expressed by the logic of anime's life-imbuing, manipulative
essence. These properties are inherent in the very word for puppet, which is
also the generic term for doll. "*Ningyō*" literally means person (*nin*, 人) form
(*gyō*, 形). *Gyō* represents a kind of permanence. It is the physical shape of
something, as in the mold into which molten metal is poured, or the ceramic
and plastic parts of a robot are formed. *Nin* (or *hito*), in contrast, represents
that which is human or, in the words of the Puppet Master, continually
changing. These two values come together in the animated figure of a person walking (人), someone making his way through the (floating) world of
continual change. Thus, in the word "*ningyō*" and in the reality of the doll,
evanescence and form come together.

The centrality of the puppet—this combination of *anima* (ghost) and
body (shell) is made even clearer in the sequel, *Ghost in the Shell II: Innocence*
(*Kōkaku kidōtai 2: inosensu*, 2004). This film explores the nature of doll-ness
and, in the way of contrast, of human-ness. In it, the cyborg agents Batō and
Togusa try to track down the creators of a particular make of female robots
that have been created specifically for the purpose of having sex with their
masters. For some unknown reason, they are malfunctioning, killing their
owners and then trying to commit suicide. What Batō and Togusa eventually
discover is that the makers of these dolls have kidnapped and imprisoned
young girls in order to inspire, very literally, these sex robots with their vul-
nerable essence, thus exploiting their cuteness in ways that will make the
artificial erotic experience more human and meaningful. The critical edge of
this sexual animation is that by inspiring robots with vulnerability they have

become unhappy and deadly, even as they call out for help, *"Tasukete. Tasukete."*

In the making of *Innocence*, Oshii and his artists sought inspiration from various models of dolls and automatons. The most influential were the infamous ball-jointed erotic dolls of the German-born French surrealist Hans Bellmer (1902–75). Oshii encountered photographs of these dolls when he was still a student. By the director's own admission, *Innocence* is an attempt to recapture their beauty.[39]

He also found other dolls closer to home. A *ningyō* of and by the famous doll maker Yotsuya Shimon (1944–) became the model for Kim, the villain of the movie; and a dollhouse and music box that Oshii and his crew discovered in an Atami museum became the inspiration for Kim's surrealistic mansion and also, no doubt, for the haunting score for the film composed by Kenji Kawai (1957–).

Of course, the doll that most clearly links this film with the Japan's long tradition of puppetry is the tea-serving doll that appears in Kim's mansion. This automated doll first brings tea to Togusa, who accepts the offering and pours himself a cup of tea with cream, and then to Batō, who does not drink tea (perhaps because he is, as Okakura might put it, the less human of the two). This doll is a *zashiki-ningyō*, or room doll, a subtype of the *karakuri-ningyō* (automated doll) that became popular around the middle of the eighteenth century, the very period of flourishing monstrosity that we studied earlier. Such dolls were the property of lords and wealthy merchants, who used them as conversation pieces. A host would place a cup of tea on the doll's tray. This would trigger a mechanism that would propel the *ningyō* toward the guest. When the guest removed the cup, the doll would turn around and return to its master.

These robotic dolls had their beginnings in the sixteenth century and were automated by mechanisms inspired by the European clockworks that had been brought to the islands by the Jesuit missionaries. Some of these older dolls were designed to perform the *sanbasō*, a ritual dance that was done seasonally to propitiate the gods for a good harvest. This was the dance that later became a prelude piece for kabuki performances; and these were the dolls that also became the prototypes for the puppet theater, or *jōruri bunraku*.

Originally, the *sanbasō* was performed by itinerant puppeteers who used their puppets as *torimono*, or spirit vessels. These dolls attracted evil spirits and carried them away from a home or village that employed the services of these itinerant performers. These puppet masters were what Jane Marie Law has called "specialists in contamination."[40] Linked in this way to these mystical puppeteers (*kugutsu-mawashi*), the tea-serving room dolls of the Edo period can also be linked forward to the cyborgs in Oshii's *Innocence*. They are ancestors to Kusanagi and Batō.

In terms of discourse, *Innocence* takes off where the first film ended. It pursues a dogged inquiry into the nature of the *anima*. That the existence of the soul should arise as the principle theme of this and other animated films was perhaps inevitable. In a world of constant change, and by way of this impressive technology that so vividly imparts life to the lifeless, it makes sense to inquire (once again) as to the essential difference between the animate and the inanimate, and between human and doll. If there is such a thing as the *anima*, this living essence that supposedly gives us our identity, then what is its nature? And to whom or to what does it answer?

On the *bunraku* stage, this question does not arise with the same insistence. In the early modern context of eighteenth-century Japan, form had not yet been rendered such an abstract matter. Thus, the process of animation was wholly visible to the audience as the *bunraku* doll evolved from the *kugutsu* of itinerant puppeteers in Awaji to the larger dolls that require three people to manipulate (since 1734). The Puppet Master controls the head and body. One assistant controls the right arm. A second assistant controls the legs. While these two assistants' faces are often covered with black, the Puppet Master's is not.

To experienced viewers, the people on the stage are supposedly invisible. They do not exist. Only the dolls do. But this pretense of invisibility is surely a late modern misreading of an art form in which the manipulators and the manipulated are meant to be appreciated together as occupying the same space. It is true that the Puppet Master tries to maintain a blank expression on his face. (To his far left, separated from the stage, sits the narrator whose face is as expressive as the Puppet Master's is blank.) But even the greatest of

Figure 3.3 Animator and animated at the *bunraku* theater, putting a ghost in the shell (photo by Reuters).

masters cannot suppress the subtle traces of emotion that they have for the doll in their hands. What do we call this sympathy, this seeping state of almost-sorrow and almost-joy? It is precisely this subtle violation of separateness that makes the Japanese puppet theater an experience like no other. It is a manifestation of the most difficult of all separations to accomplish and to understand: the essential difference that separates the parent and the child, the creator and the created, the lover and the beloved, the manipulator and the manipulated.

Working in a postmodern milieu, Oshii himself is trapped in a kind of metaphysical apoplexy as he puts old wine into new vessels. On one level, the answers to his stubborn, text-bound questions about the *anima* are too obvious to be taken seriously. *He* is the Puppet Master, the one giving life. Why is that a mystery? But this practical point is intentionally obscured by the illusion-creating logic of animation itself, and by the visual genius of the animator's work as it shows us the variety of ways by which inner and outer worlds relate to each other—by how the microscopic and macroscopic worlds of tiny electronic components and the vast sprawl of urban sites mirror and replicate each other, how the complexities of parts are covered over by the simplicity of skin, and, yes, how the ghost enlivens the shell. With the formation of cyberspace, yet another context is established for both the idea and the material space of Japan. This context thrives upon a restored sense of figurality as it mixes the concrete and the abstract together. While we can easily see and touch the physical components of the web, the electrical processes they make possible are harder to detect; and the ideas that give it shape and utility remain unknowable unless through the by-products of their activity, or by sympathetic intuition.

In the end, Oshii is limited by what is understandable and recognizable, even as the new spaces and shapes of contemporary Japan expand the possibilities of the imagination. The plot to find the bad-guy creators of these murderous and self-destructive sex robots could not be more familiar, for instance. So too is Batō's emotional array: his longing for Kusanagi, his sense of duty as a professional, his concern for kidnapped girls, and his tender nurturing feelings for his dog. Sadly, as is the case with much contemporary expression, narrative form has come to lag far beyond the prodigious powers of visual display.

Unlike Miyazaki's lyrical skies and enthralling flights of imagination, Oshii's garbage-ridden gothic cityscapes are for mature contemplation. Shadows of decay and death are everywhere, made possible by the seemingly invincible superpowers that technology allows its participants to have. To them is given the re-bootable thrill of destruction—death that never raises the question of finality. Judging from this and many other animated films, television programs, manga, and computer games, what Japan-after-the-bubble seems to require in obsessive measure is dramatic, entertaining engagement with violence, metamorphosis, and death.

Oshii claims to be responding to the world's woes, not to be creating them. But where do we draw the line between imagined disaster and its fulfillment? He describes this age, our age, and his artistic wishes for it in this manner:

> Economic recession ... corporate downsizing ... violent crime. ... We live in a cruel and frightening world. It is this culture of fear and anxiety that I want to depict cinematically. This film is about the future of humanity ...
>
> The movie does not hold the view that the world revolves around the human race. Instead, it concludes that all forms of life—humans, animals, and robots—are equal. In this day and age when everything is uncertain, we should all think about what to value in life and how to coexist with others. We all need friends, family, and lovers. We can't live alone. ... What we need today is not some anthropomorphic humanism. Humanity has reached its limits. I believe we must now broaden our horizons and philosophize about life from a larger perspective. With this film, I hope to reflect upon the uneasiness which pervades the world today. Under such conditions, what is the meaning of human existence?[41]

What even Oshii might not realize is that this film's examination of the equality of human beings, animals, and robots is both very new and very old. "Constant uncertainty" might be one way to describe the present, but today's "uncertainty" and "uneasiness" can also be understood as continuing aspects of the evanescent view of reality that we have dutifully traced over many centuries of Japan's cultural life. What is so new about uncertainty? The

Figure 3.4 Cherry blossoms at Shōjiji (Hana no tera), west of Kyoto (photo by the author).

ghost in the shell was once the cicada in the shell. Similarly ancient is the need to see "a larger perspective" than the one that nearly destroyed the world in 1945 and threatens to do so daily. Surely, there will be nostalgic attempts to return to the sureties of the modern age and its seductive pursuit of total form and the violent erasure of cultural difference. But let us hope that such a desire has been made untenable by the monsters of its own creation. Today, political distortions appear as distortions, and we would be fools not to treat them as such.

CONCLUSION

The semester is over. Winter has passed, and spring has come again. I am sitting with my students under the cherry trees in front of Bendetson Hall. The grass is green, and the trees are laden with blossoms. We eat and drink. We look up at the branches. It is warm one minute, chilly the next. The clouds move quickly. Now the sun is hidden. Now it shines brightly. Occasionally, a gust of wind sweeps by. A few blossoms fall from their branch and flutter down. Do we understand now why this is both a sad and beautiful moment? Have we learned why the Japanese love cherry blossoms?

I have given my students one of many ways to begin learning about Japan. As I hoped to make clear from the start, other approaches would have given a different shape to this inquiry, illuminating other important aspects of Japanese culture, and downplaying some that we have emphasized. I chose to focus on evanescence and form because these ideas are manifested strongly in all periods of Japanese cultural development, even though, especially in response to modernity, the nature of change itself changed over time. While change characterizes life in any culture, Japan is notable for its emphasis on mutability, fragility, and contingency. Moreover, the balancing notion of form, which also makes itself felt in any society, is also accentuated—appearing as the appropriate use of space; respect for convention and method; and an emphasis on the concrete and the visible here-and-now as much as on the abstract and invisible transcendental order. How does this heightened sense of form—as shape (*katachi*), form (*kata*), etiquette (*reigi*), protocol (*girei*), principle (*genri*), and ideal (*risō*)—reflect a similarly heightened sense of evanescence—as expressed by the cicada shell epithet (*utsusemi*), changeability (*hakanasa*), transience (*mujō*), hedonism (*ukiyo*), monstrosity (yōkai), reformation (*kaikaku*), destruction (*hakai*), decadence (*daraku*), fashion (*ry ūkō*), apocalypse (*sekai no owari*), metamorphosis (henge), animation (anime)—and vice versa?

Where did this acute sensitivity to change come from? What prepared the Japanese to accept Buddhism's focus on *anitya*, the foundational idea that all things are changing all the time (including our perception of change)? I have suggested that an awareness of life's brevity and mutability were already a salient part of Japanese culture prior to the arrival of Buddhism in the sixth century. It gained expression in the earliest songs, by way of the epithet *utsusemi*, or "shell of the cicada." This pillow word modifies key terms, such as "world" and "person" and "life." Its use suggests a generalized sense of fragility and evanescence that was probably an inheritance from Japan's animistic heritage and the closeness with which the early inhabitants of the archipelago perceived their immediate physical environment. They saw the world as being animated by gods and spirits, who were both friendly and threatening. The benevolent worship-worthy ones were *kami* (gods); and the threatening uncontrollable ones were *yōkai* or *bakemono*—monsters and changelings. At some point, *utsusemi* melded with *utsusomi*, which meant "a man of this world" or "this real world." By extension, then, reality was mutability; and mutability reality.

The relationship between a person and his constantly changing environment was intimate. Changes in one's spatial context meant changes to one's very identity. This partially explains why lyricism, spontaneity, and nonduality have been strong features of the Japanese aesthetic tradition, even before the Buddhist concept of no-self (*anatman*) made itself known. Sensitivity to context means awareness of and the ability to be passively moved by changing seasons and other natural phenomena, as frequently noted in the early songs and myths, and as remembered more than 1,000 years later by the post-War artist Higashiyama Kaii.

This seamlessness with one's surroundings is compatible with polytheism and incompatible with the separation of self and environment that came to mark the development of modernity. The lyricism that animism encouraged tends to weaken yet other dualities, such as dream versus reality, living versus dead, mind versus body, seer versus seen, and so on. These blurred distinctions are at the heart of *hakanasa*, an early term for evanescence that suggests a lack of measurable progress. *Hakanasa* informed the changeable romantic lives of those at the Heian court, such as the daughter of Sugawara no Takasue, author of *As I Crossed the Bridge of Dreams*. What is more changeable than sexual attraction or the emotions?

Another feature that follows from the importance of spatial context is how one's situation (at least as a literary trope) is immediately present and often visually apprehended. This helps to explain what I have earlier called the pictocentric emphasis of Japanese culture: the importance placed upon the visible and spatial, and a comparatively weaker interest in textual (or otherwise symbolic) ties to the invisible transcendental orders of ideology, doctrine, and unchanging universal principles. As Japanese poetics suggests, the features of brevity (as emphasized in the lyric rather more than in the epic), the situational nature of poetic creation, and an imagistic or figural propensity, all point to the importance of the moment and its direct apprehension. This "momentousness," too, might be understood as a function of evanescence and, as Buddhism became an increasingly dominant part of the picture, of the possibility of enlightenment, or breaking away from the illusory nature of *samsara* and the floating world of illusion and delusion. In this way, Japanese poetics probably helped the Japanese understand the Buddhist state of nothingness, a condition of being totally present in the moment that (as informed by Nagarjuna's sense of *sunyata*, or emptiness) is inclusive rather than nihilistic. Perhaps no one has summed it up more simply than the poet Shinkei (1406–75), who stated that "the mind and language of the Way of Poetry are rooted upon a sense of mutability and sorrow for the human condition."[42]

I have suggested that the lesson best learned from the metaphysical richness of Buddhism was precisely this emphasis on evanescence or *mujō*, as it came to be known. The spread of this foreign religion by way of its many visual manifestations—whether magic rituals, architecture, painting, or statuary—was further simplified by important teachers, such as Kūya, Hōnen, Shinran, and Ippen. Their common emphasis on the *nenbutsu*, which would include walking and dancing forms of chanting, is illustrative of a Japanese tendency to convert complex metaphysical principles into kinetic, spatially grounded actions. The medieval amplification of Chan (or Zen) Buddhism in Japan, with its emphasis on practice as a means to enlightenment—as in the performance of *kata* or forms of The Way (*dō*)—was similarly an affirmation of the evanescent moment as understood by way of material (and therefore visible) patterns that give actions meaning.

For us, the kind of nothingness (*mu*) put forward by the various Mahayana schools that flourished in Japan, which would include both Pure Land Buddhism and Zen, was difficult to grasp partly because we usually do not associate nothingness with meaning and the exercise of human will. We do not do so even if we understand the attractions of the lyrical moment, the sentiment of connectedness, the potential beauty of the confusion of boundaries, or the expansiveness of *yūgen*, or mystery. Indeed, it is hard to see how meaning can be possible in a world of constant and ubiquitous change, a possibility that some Western thinkers—from Heraclitus to Bergson but also including Rene Descartes, who advanced the *cogito* as a counter to change—have considered with great caution and even reluctance. If it is true that all things are always changing, how can anything be meaningful? Do we not have to have some sense of permanence in order to measure progress or decline (as in the accumulation of good or bad karma), or to conceptualize social position, or to understand the coming together of hearts and minds?

This obvious difficulty led us to contemplate the nature of form and formality. We saw that the tendency toward the formal—as seen in the rigid codification of classical poetic diction, in the centrality of the *kata* in the performing and martial arts, in the general emphasis placed on etiquette and protocol in normal social interactions, and so on—is an effort to give meaning to a constantly changing reality. In Japan, radical form balances radical change. The highly formal Noh play, for instance, urges us to see the plenitude of stillness, or the flower (*hana*) of the actor's talent as it reaches its peak in moments of nonaction. As brief and as formally limited as *tanka* and *haiku* are, they nevertheless are able to express subtle and profound changes in the environment. Various forms of strictly defined practice—*jūdō*, *kendō* (fencing), *sadō* (tea ceremony), *kōdō* (incense ceremony), and so forth—are both meditative and kinetic. The Japanese garden is both highly artificial and natural. In short, radical form allows us to perceive radical change. Both are captured in moments of simplicity.

For the purpose of analysis, I have suggested the existence of two different types of form. The first is transcendental form or those abstract systems of ideas and ideals that are represented by texts and other symbols. The second is a more concrete, immediate, and visible earthly form, which I have called the order of here-and-now.

The transcendental order is abstract, representational, a matter of speculation. Buddhist metaphysics, the principles of Neo-Confucianism, laws of natural science, ideals of nationalism and imperialism—when well expressed, these abstractions and ideologies provide conceptual patterns that give meaning to the world of change. Motoori Norinaga's "sadness of things" (*mono no aware*) represents an essence of Japanese culture, and his oft-quoted poem about fragrant blossoms began to symbolize it. The belated birth of a "scriptural" habit—reciting of the Imperial Rescript on Education while standing before the emperor's photograph—is another attempt to tie the evanescent to the immutable. We noticed how ideologies of nationalism and imperialism conceptualized change in a decidedly linear way, so that evanescence was recast as modern progress. As this occurred, the expression of change tended to become more epic and less lyrical; and the search for never-changing ideals, goals, and essences dominated to the point that evanescence no longer seemed relevant.

In contrast, the order of here-and-now emphasizes the moment and one's relationship with a spatial and visible context. In this case, form is not abstractly formulated but is, rather, very literally grounded. In a world of constant change, meaning is concretely determined by how one sits, how one bows, one's lyrical response to this flower or that ivy-covered wall. The formality of Japanese life, an emphasis on the correct way to do things, conforms to etiquette, or what we called how "to move through space properly, in ways that enhance one's proper definition." The here-and-now is inscribed not only by customs of behavior, but also by markers of meaningfulness, such as *shimenawa* (ropes that delimit sacred space), entranceway pine trees, unhewn pillars in houses, *utamakura* (place-defining poetic associations), and so on. These are not symbols. They do not point us to something that is not present before our eyes. Rather, they point to what is earthly, including the divine (*kami*). They mark significant space, which is worshipped by our approach (*mairi*).

The assumption that underlies both etiquette and what Kitagawa called the reality of "nonsymbolic symbols" is that an appropriate response to one's immediate context in real space and real time secures one's status and identity. Thus, a "real" Japanese person knows when and how to bow, when and how to eat, even when and how to have that lyrical response to one's environment that leads to the creation of poetry, painting, and such. In the context of the here-and-now, politeness is far more than an attempt to be gracious and kind. As demonstrated by the puppet play *Chūshingura*, strictly following proper protocol is nothing less than an affirmation of one's existence.

The relative importance of these two main types of form—contextual space and textualized concepts—differs from period to period. We considered an ancient animistic world of sacred space. But we also saw that certain clearly identifiable ideological formations dominated various other periods of Japan's cultural life. The formation of the modern self, for instance, was a step in this direction. It began at least as early as Saikaku and Bashō. By the end of the nineteenth century, the very notion of here-and-now was radically altered by the internationalizing forces of colonialism that helped bring to an end the long rule of the Tokugawa regime. This was the collapse that the xenophobic, culturally chauvinistic Aizawa Seishisai had feared. Although a strong sense of Japanese cultural identity had developed during this period of relative isolation from the rest of the world, the "opening" of Japan that occurred in 1854 placed this world of here-and-now in a decidedly more abstract context of numerous competing nations. In a new environment that included both Japan and the world, Japanese intellectuals were compelled to begin explaining Japanese culture in an increasingly relativized, textual, and symbolic way. Thus the attempts of Nitobe Inazō, Okakura Kakuzō, and Kuki Shūzō as they each tried to define Japan's cultural essence as bushidō, tea-ism, and erotic style.

If we establish a general schema of larger cultural trends, a broad pattern emerges. According to the pattern expressed in figure 3.5, the late modern period (from the end of the Tokugawa period to about 1970) is anomalous. What accounts for this shift in emphasis from evanescence to essence, from spatially formed identity to temporally formed identity, from a lyrical to an epic relationship with one's environment, from the importance of the visual to an emphasis on the phonetic? And how do we explain the swing back to these earlier values in contemporary Japan?

In essence, what we have witnessed is a tension and a cultural shift away from animism and one's lyrical relationship with the earth that occurred not only in Japan but throughout the modern world. In the case of Japan, however, its animistic foundations were never fully overcome by absolutism and

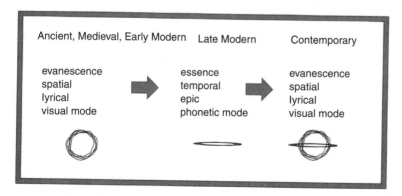

Figure 3.5   A general outline of major cultural trends.

its more abstract framing of reality. At times, the notion of evanescence did seem to vanish from Japanese cultural life. The growing awareness of foreign cultures that stimulated Motoori Norinaga's early attempts to articulate a fixed Japanese essence later became a major preoccupation during the Meiji period when the reality of international powers was thrust upon the Japanese consciousness. Faced with the options of adapt or die, the Japanese came to focus on a few common goals, such as the glory of the nation, so that change came to appear as progress toward a fixed position.

Japan's turn to fascism during the 1930s and 1940s is a part of this shift. Japanese participation in total war was remarkably violent precisely because the order of here-and-now had come to be linked symbolically with an imperialistic transcendental order. Every act, including one's lyrical response to sacred space, became an expression of patriotism. This hegemonic condition produced a rarified and generalized state of bushidō that melded the world of "beautiful customs" with the modern quest for truth, system, and universality. More specifically, this bonding of two orders occurred when the Meiji emperor became both the generalized body (*kokutai*) *and* the essentialized idea (*kokka*) of the Japanese nation. As noted by Sakaguchi Ango, the custom of bowing whenever one's train passed before Yasukuni Shrine, where the souls of Japan's war dead supposedly gathered, is a clear example of how these two types of form were brought together during World War II.

We considered the possibility that the atrocities committed by Japanese soldiers in the margins of empire might have come from this binding of etiquette and imperialism. However, while every movement inside a teahouse is carefully controlled by the order of here-and-now, while all is modulated by the refined gentleness engendered by the sanctity of the well-contained moment, on the distant battlefield far from home no such contextual form prevailed. Overwhelmed by the more portable ideology of imperial expansion, the here-and-now of armed conflict became reduced to the brutality of just "here" and only "now." At the same time, the nostalgic pull of cherry blossoms insinuated itself symbolically as a part of the mounting tragedy of devastation, defeat, and surrender. Motoori Norinaga's eighteenth-century poem supplied the symbolism for both aggression and self-sacrifice.

Shikishima no	Should someone ask,
Yamatogokoro wo	"What is the soul
Hito towaba	Of Yamato, our ancient land?"
Asahi ni niou	It is the scent of mountain cherry blossoms
Yamazakurabana.	In the morning sun.

Cherry blossoms reasserted an aesthetic of evanescence for the young kamikaze pilots who fell like blossoms from the sky in order to defend the threatened space of Japan.

The ravages of war did much to restore a premodern understanding of evanescence and form. Following the bombing of Japan's cities, and after the nation's unconditional surrender, the heroic epic of a chosen and invincible

Yamato race was found to be a lie and deception. Japan was shaken from its modern dreams of glory by the devastations that traumatically brought the Archipelago to a new kind of nothingness—not the enabling *sunyata* (emptiness) or *mu* of Buddhist discourse, but the disabling *nihil* of post-Enlightenment Europe. In short, defeat and devastation helped break the spell that the transcendental order had come to have over the Japanese, who quickly walked away from their fascist experiment to embrace both the possibility of peace and a renewed appreciation of evanescence and its expression in the here-and-now.

Japan began to rebuild itself in the ideological vacuum that resulted from defeat and disenchantment. In this time of searching for new answers, Takeyama Michio's *Harp of Burma* expressed a renewed interest in Buddhism and the need to strive for peace. Forged in the evanescent moment of Tokyo's fiery destruction, Sakaguchi Ango's critique of bushidō and nationalism clarified the process whereby meaning is just as easily produced as a moving away from form as a moving toward it. Decadence, or the rejection of form, is perhaps more meaningful than movement toward form. This is because learning form is often hidden from our critical awareness while its rejection is usually not. As a general rejection of the transcendental order, Sakaguchi's rebellion had the effect of reinvigorating interest in the order of here-and-now.

The meaning of this reassertion has been puzzling to many. Its manifestations have been varied—sometimes interpreted as a new traditionalism, sometimes viewed as a postmodern surge toward a new cultural phase. Like the Genroku ebullience that followed a sixteenth century of protracted warfare, the post-War flowering of the Japanese economy generated a corresponding hedonism of floating-world distractions. That these pleasures might be insufficient was the message of Kurosawa Akira's *To Live*, which rejected decadence while strongly affirming the truth of evanescence: the brevity and fragility of life, the need to seize the moment and to live bravely and fully. What Kurosawa criticized was the tendency to let form overwhelm change. When this happens, meaningfulness chokes out the very possibility of meaning.

Mishima Yukio was disappointed with what he viewed to be the mindless consumerism of post-War Japan. He nostalgically embraced bushidō once again, motivated by his own personal need to be publically inappropriate. His attempt to restore the emperor to real power was rejected by the masses, who saw his political and military maneuvers as an absurd last gasp of modern grandeur. A similar yet significantly different rejection of high-growth economics came from Higashiyama Kaii, who embraced something even older than modernity. For him, a return to a "premodern" sense of nothingness was key. In contrast to Mishima's willful embrace of active nihilism, he preferred a passive acceptance of evanescence—an affirmation of all we cannot control, including our dependence upon nature and the forgotten rhythms of earth and trees. Higashiyama re-embraced nothingness as everything. Only by living with a sense of death and loss can we appreciate the beauty of life.

Other ways to seize the postmodern moment emerged. Fashion came to rule as a paradoxical kind of "constantly changing form." As articulated in *Somehow Crystal*, Tanaka Yasuo's "how-to" romance, stylishness became a powerful affirmation of "temporary form." We noted that fashionable trends are of interest precisely because they quickly arise and quickly decline. Being perfectly matched to evanescence and form, fashion affirms sameness while seeking difference.

Needless to say, fashion has also been good for Japan's consumer economy. As a particularly acute expression of evanescence, style became the handmaid of economic growth as Japan experienced its "economic miracle." From the rubble of World War II, a new Japan grew rapidly. Standards of living rose, and Japan's economy became the second largest in the world. Affluence reigned; Tokyo surpassed Paris and New York as the new fashion capital of the world.

But the truth of "all things changing all the time" required that Japan's post-War boom come to an end. Stock and real estate markets collapsed. Between 1990 and 1991, Japanese assets lost approximately 60 percent of their value, leaving all to wonder whether Japan really had had those years of phenomenal growth and unshakeable confidence. Was the gap that had opened up between an overheated market and economic fundamentals—the phenomenon economists call a "bubble economy"—yet another expression of Japanese evanescence? Was this impressive rise and fall an aberration? Or was it simply a normative cycle of floating-world economics?

Searching for the cultural answer to this puzzle, we considered how Itami Jūzō's *Tanpopo* presents a linear world of work that exists alongside a nonlinear world of play. Neither realm seems to be well integrated with the other, but both are equally compelling. The double-formed structure of this film was also common to Tanaka Yasuo's *Somehow Crystal* and to Murakami Haruki's *Hard-Boiled Wonderland and the End of the World*. All three of these works reflect an important turning point of Japanese culture: a move ahead to postmodernity as still encumbered by modern sensibilities.

Reinforced by the horrors of war, Japan's sensitive feel for evanescence hastened and amplified modernity's end. The post-War experience was more than a simple loss of ideological certainty. Indeed, the traditional strength of "all things changing all the time" shaped the postmodern response to modernity's failures by making it nothing less than a near-constant rehearsal of the end of the world itself. This theme of the world's demise was taken up by Honda Ishirō's *Godzilla* in 1954, and was kept in play by Komatsu Sakyō's *Japan Sinks* (1973). More recently, numerous manga artists and animators—among them Ōtomo Katsuhiro, Miyazaki Hayao, and Oshii Mamoru—have joined writers such as Murakami Haruki in keeping the leitmotif alive. To be sure, the regularity with which mass destruction appears as a theme of popular culture follows in part from advances in technology that have made the illusion of catastrophe less expensive to accomplish. But the love of spectacle itself, along with a penchant for total destruction, both owe much to a resurgence of the here-and-now and to the imperative that causes all things to be spatial and visual, and consonant with deeply rooted feelings about radical change as they have developed over the millennia. In short, the possible end of the world is not simply a dramatic move and a box-office ploy. It is the first premise of Japanese cultural life.

The often-encountered solipsistic condition of subject-being-object and object-being-subject is a postmodern rearticulation of here-and-now lyricism. Japanese "my-ness" returns us to the evanescent roots of *utsusemi*-like existence even as it poses enduring questions, such as the nature of the *anima*. In what sense am I my spatial, visible context—the clothes I wear, and the things I consume? The very nature of animation as a near-perfect expression of evanescence and form makes us wonder about the powers that cause us to move and think. What is the relationship of the life force to its ever-changing context, whether the body or the wider world of mountains, forests, convenience stores, and fashion shows? What is the relationship between the human and the nonhuman within a neo-animistic, newly animated context of endless imagination?

In the words of Oshii Mamoru's Puppet Master, "to be human is to be continually changing." As in ancient times, human beings are still more or less *utsusemi no hito*, cicada-shell people living in a cicada-shell world (*utsusemi no yo*). We fall in love with cicada-shell lovers (*utsusemi no imo*), and spend our brief cicada-shell lives (*utsusemi no inochi*) in hard work and hard play. Many are the possible responses to evanescence. But in a Japanese cultural context, they are tinged with sorrow and beauty.

In the end, our study of Japanese culture suggests that Oshii's cyborg wonders, like the gigantic *ōmu* of Miyazaki Hayao's *Nausicaa*, are distant though still distinguishable descendants of the cicada, whose empty, discarded shell was the ancient and magical descriptor of an evanescent, pre-Buddhist reality. Then, as now, mortal existence is fleeting, fragile, and sorrowful. The Japanese have preferred to see this sorrow as meaningful, wondrous, and even beautiful. In incompletion, there is hope. This is because, in the final analysis, it is nearly impossible to see change as anything but falling short of the mark. As we learned from *The Tale of the Heike*, however, if failure is implicit in success, so is success implicit in failure. As we have learned from so many sources, the enduring Japanese message seems to be that only with an awareness of death and loss can we truly live.

Hopefully, this contemplation of evanescence and form has shown us a way to understanding Japan's sometimes-confusing lack of closure and its equally insistent formality. Beyond this, perhaps knowing something about Japanese culture has also given us a new way to see paradox itself—the nothing that is everything, the change that is eternal. We have considered an impressively wide range of responses to evanescence. Some of them were clearly at odds with each other. Where Kamo no Chōmei spoke of ascetic retreat, Ihara Saikaku demonstrated the possibilities of indulgence. Which is the better response? The samurai dedicated himself to service and loyalty, as did the emperor's soldiers, as does the faithful company employee. On the other hand, the Genroku townsman at the turn of the eighteenth century chose to play in the floating world, as did the decadents of the *kasutori* culture that prevailed during the Occupation of the early 1950s, as did the somehow crystal consumers of Tanaka Yasuo's generation in the 1980s. Bringing work and play together in stark relief, Itami Jūzō's *Tanpopo* forced the enduring Japanese question. Is the evanescent world inherently disagreeable, or is it fundamentally attractive? Could it be attractive precisely because it is disagreeable? An awareness of change might inspire heroic action, on the one hand, or fatalism on the other. If the idiom *"shikata ga nai"* ("It can't be helped") can be recognized as a prelude to both attack and surrender, where do we locate the human will in the lyrical knot of passive resignation that leads to economic miracles, stunning cultural achievements, and, yes, to buses running on time?

At the heart of these varied responses is a nothingness that arises by way of certain kinds of radical form—language that undoes language, formality that yields intimacy, complexity that ends in simplicity, and escape that leads to reengagement. Having considered Japan's ongoing interplay between chaos and order, we now begin to understand the beauty of Dōgen's poem, which locks the flux of seasons into a formula.

Haru wa hana	In spring the cherry blossoms,
Natsu hototogisu	In summer the cuckoo,
Aki wa tsuki	In fall the moon,
Fuyu yuki saete	And in winter
Hiyashikarikeri	The cold snow.

Change without form is meaningless. Form without change is senseless. By way of the rigid *kata* comes fluidity, by way of Zeami's nonmovement comes the utterly moving. Upon Chōmei's ever-flowing river, we drift toward the temporary joys of pattern and texture, sound and color, taste and smell. As we allow ourselves to be touched by cycles of change, we begin to grasp the shape and logic of Japanese culture. At the same time, perhaps we have learned something of our own involvement with evanescence and form. By way of personal experience, we come to understand the foreign.

We, too, belong to a changing world. We dwell in constant loss and continual creation. If we depend on form to make change meaningful, we now know that the shape of change, expressed as form, also changes with time. That is not how it should be, or must be. That is simply the way it is. Each of us contributes to this reality that none of us fully controls nor understands. If there is a lesson here, it might be this: that as we struggle to find a place for ourselves in relationship to whatever we accept as form, we ought to calm our striving by keeping our hearts empty enough to allow something else to enter in. "Form is emptiness and emptiness form."

To grasp the mutable, formal space called Japan is to begin to see our own particular cultural moment, and to be resigned to all we did not choose—earthquakes, seasons, theft, heartbreak, the characters of parents, the personalities of children. Ours is a cicada-shell world. Our earth is fragile and ever-changing. Our life on this planet is brief. In the face of dying, we live. Someday soon, maybe tomorrow, our hearts will stop, and our breathing will end with a sigh. Then, all that will remain is what we have given away to others. In the meantime, let us feel sorrow and rejoice. Cherry blossoms bravely fall. Rivers swell and retreat. Plants grow. Insects emerge to mate, then fall back to the soil. In spring the cherry blossoms. In summer the cuckoo. In fall the moon. And in winter the cold snow.

GLOSSARY OF IMPORTANT TERMS

Amida	A Buddha of Compassion, centrally important to Pure Land Buddhism. 阿弥陀　See *nenbutsu*.
anatman	Buddhist term (Sanskrit) for "no self." The lack of anything permanent in and of itself. In Pali, *anatta*. See *anitya* and *duhka*.
anitya	Buddhist term (Sanskrit) for "constant change" or "evanescence." The first mark of existence. In Pali, *anicca*. See *samsara*.
aware	Sadness, pathos. 哀れ　See *mono no aware*.
bakemono	Literally, "changing things." Monsters. 化物　See *yōkai*.
bakumatsu	Literally, "end (*matsu*) of the Tokugawa Shogunate (*bakufu*)." Roughly, the first half of the nineteenth century.　幕末
Bodhisattva	Someone who has gained enlightenment and, therefore, release from *samsara* yet returns to this world of suffering in order to help others.
budō	Martial arts. Literally, "the way (*dō*) of fighting (*bu*)."　武道
bunka	Culture. Literally, "patterning."　文化
bushidō	The way of the warrior. A romanticized samurai creed.　武士道
butsuga ichinyo	Object and self as one. One of Bashō's aesthetic principles. 物我一如
chōka	Literally, "long (*chō*) poem (*ka*)." 長歌　Compare *tanka*. Common in the *Man'yōshū*, Japan's earliest poetic anthology, but not in later collections.
daraku	Decadence. A movement away from established form.　堕落
duhka	Buddhist term (Sanskrit) for "suffering." A common, lamentable state that results from an attachment to impermanent things. (In Pali, *dukkha*). See *samsara*.
fueki ryūkō	The unchanging and the changing. One of Bashō's aesthetic principles.　不易流行
geisha	A female entertainer, courtesan. Were not originally prostitutes. 芸者
gesaku	A generic term for the popular literature of the Tokugawa period. Literally, "frivolous works." 戯作
girei	Protocol. The proper way to do something.　儀礼
giri	One's formal duty, obligation. 義理　Compare, *ninjō*.
haikai no renga	Linked verse. 俳諧の連歌　See *haiku*.
haiku	A seventeen-syllable verse. Began as the first in a chain of linked verses. 俳句　See *haikai no renga*.
hakanai	An adjective for "changeable," "unreliable," "futile." The noun form is *hakanasa*. An important early Heian-period term for

evanescence. Literally, "the lack (*nai*) of measureable units of cultivated land (*haka*)." 果敢ない Compare *hakadoru*, "to make progress," "to get somewhere."

hakkō ichiu All the world under one roof, that is, as one family. An expression of modern expansionism. 八紘一宇

hana A general term for "flower." 花 From the Heian period on it invariably refers to cherry blossoms, or *sakura*. Also, Zeami's term for "ultimate mastery."

hanabi Fireworks. Literally, "flowers (*hana*) of fire (*hi*)." 花火
hanami Flower viewing. 花見
hiragana One of four Japanese scripts. 平仮名 Originated as a cursively written Chinese character. Phonetic in emphasis, but retained a figural importance within the calligraphic tradition. For the other three scripts, see *kanji, katakana, rōmaji*.

haragei Literally, "stomach (*hara*) art (*gei*)." Nonverbal communication. 腹芸
harakiri Ritual disembowelment. 腹切り A less refined term for *seppuku*.
hare Cleansing from pollution. 晴れ See *kegare*.
henshin (Physical) transformation. 変身
hen'yō Transformation. 変容
hibakusha An A-bomb survivor. 被爆者
hito Person. Also read "*nin*" or "*jin*," as in *Nihonjin* (Japanese person) or *ningyō* (doll). 人
hōben Expedient means. Believable and understandable ways to teach difficult concepts. 方便
honne One's true intent. 本音 Compare, *tatemae*.
hyōbanki Edo-period guidebooks that ranked various people and things. 評判記
ichigo ichie One moment, one meeting. Making the most of an encounter with someone. Living for the moment. 一期一会
iki Erotic style. A distancing, playful sophistication toward sexual relations. 粋
inochi Life. 命
iro Sensuality, sex. Also means (simply) color. 色
jihatsu Literally, "self (*ji*) actuated (*hatsu*)." Spontaneity, as in a lyrical reaction to one's environment. 自発
jōruri bunraku The puppet theater. 浄瑠璃文楽
kaiseki Traditional Japanese cuisine. 会席
kaisha Company. 会社
kanji Literally, "Chinese (*kan*) characters (*ji*)." 漢字 A form of writing imported from China to write Japanese words. Served as a basis for the development of phonetic scripts, *hiragana* and *katakana*. See *man'yōgana*.
kami A god. A higher being. There are numerous *kami*. 神 See *kamikaze, ujigami*.
kamikaze Literally, "god (*kami*) wind (*kaze*)." A magical epithetic for Ise, location of the sacred Ise Shrine where winds blow in off the ocean. Later gained martial overtones to become "suicide pilot." During World War II, the same characters were usually read as *shinpū* rather than *kamikaze*, which was vulgar. 神風

kanashisa	Sorrow. 悲しさ
kara oke	Literally, "empty orchestra." The background music played while one sings. カラオケ
kasutori	Cheap liquor. A decadent subculture of the Occupation years. 粕取り
katakana	One of four Japanese scripts. カタカナ Originated as a part of a Chinese character. Like *hiragana*, phonetic in emphasis. See *hiragana*, *kanji*, and *rōmaji*.
kawaii	Cute. Adorable. 可愛い
kegare	Personal pollution. 汚れ Compare *hare*.
kibun	Feeling. Sensibility. 気分
kimono	Literally, "things (*mono*) that are worn (*ki*)." 着物
kofun	Tomb. 古墳
koi	Yearning. From the verb *kou*: "to long for," "to love." Usually unrequited. 恋
kokka	Nation. National polity. 国家 See *kokutai*.
kokutai	The body politic. The physical reality of the nation. 国体
kotodama	Word spirit. 言霊 Said to be evoked by the *makura kotoba*.
kuruwa	The demimonde, or entertainment district. 廓
makoto	Sincerity. 誠
makura kotoba	A stock epithetic for a place or thing. Said to have an evocative, spiritual function. 枕詞 See *kamikaze*, or *utsusemi*.
manga	Meiji-period caricatures. Evolved to become illustrated narratives. 漫画
mairi	Literally, "going or approaching." A Japanese term for "worship." 参り
matsuri	Festival. 祭り An occasion to propitiate the gods (*kami*).
maya	Buddhist term for illusion. Delusion. A condition of *samsara*.
meibutsu	The famous product or cuisine of a particular local area. 名物
meisho	Famous places. Significant destinations for travelers. 名所
michi	The Way. The path to salvation or enlightenment. A form of practice. Also read, "*dō*," as in *judō*, *kendō*, *sadō*, etc. 道
mono no aware	The sadness of things. A generalizing theory that appreciates the uncompleteness and sorrow inherent in everything. ものの哀れ
mu	Nothingness. Unboundedness. An openness. Does not mean nihil. 無 See *sunyata*.
mujō	A Buddhist term for evanescence. Literally, "without (*mu*) continuation (*jō*)." Can be read as *tsune nashi*. 無常 See *anitya*.
mujōkan	A feeling of evanescence or mutability. 無常観
nenbutsu	A formulaic Buddhist chant. "*Namu amida butsu*." Praise to Amida Buddha. 念仏
nenbutsu odori	The dancing nenbutsu. Precursor to *obon* odōri and kabuki. 念仏お通り
Nihon	Japan. Also, *Nippon*. 日本
ningyō	Doll. Literally, "the form (*gyō*) of a human being (*nin*)." 人形
ninjō	Human feeling. Humanity. 人情 Compare *giri*.
Nippon	Japan. Also, *Nihon*. 日本
nirvana	A Buddhist term (Sanskrit) for "the extinguishing of desire." Escape from "*samsara*." Peace of mind. Lack of delusion.

Noh	Otherwise written Nō. A medieval dramatic form patronized by the samurai. 能
okashi	A classical term, meaning "beautiful" or "interesting." おかし
Obon	Buddhist Festival of Lanterns. When the spirits of the dead return. 御盆
Obon odori	A communal dance performed during the Lantern Festival. 御盆 お通り See *Obon.*
risō	Ideal. 理想
rokudō	A Buddhist term for the six realms of existence. A hierarchy of being. 六道
rōmaji	Literally, "Roman (*rōma*) characters (*ji*)." ローマ字 The alphabet. One of four Japanese scripts. See *hiragana, katakana, kanji.*
rōnin	A masterless samurai. In contemporary usage, someone who failed an entrance exam and is studying to retake the test. 浪人
ryūkō	Fashion. 流行
sabi	The beauty of worn things. 寂び
sachi	Happiness. Bounty. 幸
sadō	Tea ceremony. Literally, "the way (*dō*) of tea (*sa*)." 茶道
sakura	Cherry blossoms. 桜 See *hana.*
sake	Rice wine. Also called "*Nihon shu*", or "Japanese wine." 酒
sakoku	Isolated country. A Tokugawa policy to prevent Japanese from traveling abroad. 鎖国
samurai	Literally, "one who serves." Warrior, or a member of the warrior class. Dominant from 1185 to 1868. 侍
samsara	A Buddhist term (Pali and Sanskrit). Continuous change. By extension, this world of suffering. The antithesis of *nirvana.*
sankin kōtai	The practice that required samurai to live half of every year in Edo, and to leave their families behind when they were gone. A regulation imposed by the Tokugawa Shogunate. 参勤交代
satori	Enlightenment. Seeing this ephemeral world for what it really is. 悟り See *nirvana.*
seppuku	Ritual disembowelment. 切腹 See *harakiri.*
shashin	Literally, "copying (*sha*) the truth (*shin*)." A traditional aesthetic term in painting: capturing one's sincerity as projected onto a landscape. Later came to mean photograph: a mechanically produced image of something external to the viewer. 写真
shimenawa	A rope that designates the sacred, or *kami*. A "symbol" of the here-and-now. Points to what is here, not to what is not here. しめ縄
shikata ga nai	It cannot be helped. There is no (other) way. 仕方がない
shikitari	The way things are done. Custom. Convention. 仕来り
shinpū	Divine wind. A less colloquial way to say *kamikaze.* 神風
shodō	Calligraphy. The way of writing. 書道
shogyō mujō	All is vanity. All things are always changing. 諸行無常
shukke	Leaving home. Renouncing the world and taking the tonsure. 出家

sonnō jōi	"Restore the Emperor, Cast Out the Barbarians." The slogan that helped the Meiji rebels prevail over Tokugawa loyalists. 尊皇攘夷
sōpu rando	Soap Land. Previously called Turkish Baths. A place of adult entertainment. ソープランド
soto	Outer, Other. Not one's own. 外 Compare, *uchi*.
Sumimasen	I am sorry. Excuse me. Thank you. 済みません
sunyata	A Buddhist term (Sanskrit). Emptiness. Mutual determinancy. What everyone and everything shares. See *mu*.
tanka	A short poem of 5, 7, 5, 7, 7 syllables. Also called *waka*, or "Japanese lyric." 短歌
tatemae	The face of things, not one's real intent. 建て前 Compare, *honne*.
tokobashira	The unhewn pillar in a traditional Japanese house. Marks important space. 床柱
tsune nashi	Evanescence. Literally, "without continuity." 常無し A Japanese reading of *mujō*.
tsū	An expert in the ways of the demimonde. 通 See *iki*.
uchi	One's own, one's group. Inner. Also means, home. 内 Compare, *soto*.
ujigami	The head (*kami*) of a clan (*uji*). The *ujigami* of the Yamato clan became Japan's emperor. 氏神
ukiyo	Originally, "disagreeable world." 憂き世、浮世 See *samsara*. In the seventeenth century, came to mean "the floating world (of fleeting pleasures)."
ukie	Pictures done in perspective, often inspired by Dutch examples. 浮絵 Compare, *ukiyoe*.
ukiyoe	Floating-world pictures. Woodblock prints. 浮世絵
ukiyozōshi	Floating-world letters. Popular literature, such as written by Ihara Saikaku. 浮世草子
utamakura	Poetic place names. 歌枕
utsusomi	Originally, "*utsushi omi*" or "a man (*omi*) of this world (*utsusu*)." Also, *utsushimi*, this mortal (*utsushi*) body (*mi*). 現人 Came to be indistinguishable from the similar sounding *utsusemi*, or "shell of the cicada." Thus, reality is empty and fragile, like the shell of a cicada.
utsusu	Mortality, reality. 現
utsusemi	Literally, "empty (*utsu*) shell of a cicada (*semi*)." Epithet for "world," "person," "life," "lover." Indicates the frail, evanescent nature of all things. 空蝉 Came to be indistinguishable from *utsusomi*, or "man of this world."
utamakura	A poetic association fixed to a specific place. A spatial trope. 歌枕
wabi	The beauty of sparse, simple things. 侘び
waka	The thirty-one-syllable Japanese lyric. 和歌 See *tanka*.
yo	World, as in *kono yo*, "this world of the living," or *ano yo*, "that world of the dead." 世 See *yo no naka*.
yokozuna	Literally, "horizontal (*yoko*) rope (*tsuna*)." 横綱 A *shimenawa* worn by a sumo master.
yonaoshi	Literally, "world (*yo*) repair (*naoshi*)." Nineteenth-century millenarian revolts. 世直し
yo no naka	Human relations, especially between lovers and peers. 世の中
yōkai	A monster, apparition, specter. 妖怪 See *bakemono*.
yūgen	Mystery. A term used in the Noh theater. 幽玄

yukar	Ainu epic. Extended oral narratives of a kind not common to the Japanese tradition.
zange	Buddhist confession.　懺悔
zangedō	The way of confession. Repentance.　懺悔道
zōka zuijun	Follow creativity. One of Bashō's aesthetic principles.　造化随順

NOTES

1 THE ORDER OF HERE-AND-NOW: ANCIENT, MEDIEVAL, AND EARLY MODERN JAPAN (TO 1868)

1. Dōgen, *Dōgen Zenji zenshū* volume 7 (Shunjūsha, 1990), p. 158.
2. Michael Cooper, "Japan and the Way Thither," in Michael Cooper, ed., *The Southern Barbarians* (Kodansha and Sophia University, 1971), p. 24.
3. The Japanese reading of the characters 日本 is either "*Nihon*" or "*Nippon*." At the time of the 1964 Tokyo Summer Olympics, it was decided that the official name of the country would be Nippon rather than the less manly sounding Nihon. I thank my colleague, Hosea Hirata, for pointing this out to me.
4. J. P. Bardet, F. Ota, M. Sugito, and A. Yashima, "The Great Hanshin Earthquake Disaster: The January 17, 1995 South Hyogo Prefecture Earthquake," http://gees.usc.edu/gees/Reports/Report3/japan/kobe.html. March 12, 2004.
5. Seasonal words were eventually formalized as *kigo* when they came to be catalogued for the writing of linked verse, or *renga*, which began in the middle of Heian period and flourished throughout the medieval era. They were also listed in rulebooks for the writing of haiku, which derived from the beginning verse (or *hokku*) of a linked series. For an exhaustive list of *kigo*, see http://www.nichibun.ac.jp/graphicversion/dbase/kigo/index.html. Smaller samplings of season words in English can be easily found on the web.
6. Yoshida Kenkō, *Tsurezuregusa. Nihon koten bungaku zenshū* (hereafter *NKBZ*) 27:107–08.
7. Sei Shōnagon, *Makura no sōshi. NKBZ* 11:63.
8. Actually, the range is much wider than this if we think about Hokkaido to the north and Kyushu to the south. We usually do not include them, though. Since Nara and Kyoto were the centers of cultural activity for such a long time, the poetic seasons are traditionally tied to conditions there.
9. *Sarashina nikki, NKBZ* 18:354.
10. Ariwara no Narihira, *Kokin wakashū* 747. *NKBZ* 7:292.
11. For the melody and an English translation for all three verses, see http://ingeb.org/songs/charugak.html. September 2005.
12. For more on the *utamakura*, see Edward Kamens, *Utamakura, Allusion, and Intertextuality in Traditional Japanese Poetry* (New Haven: Yale University Press, 1997). Here, the tie between these "spatial" features and space itself is given less importance than the intertextual connections between them. But, surely, a fundamentally poetic apperception of space itself is key to these sophisticated linguistic developments and to what Kamo no Chōmei called the *sugata*, or visual form, of Japanese poetry.

13. Why the longer poetics forms declined is a complicated matter. One reason has to do with the function of poetic expression, and how the public, political, and narrative thrust of *chōka* came to be superseded by the more private and lyrical *tanka*. This might have happened because the ruling class became more firmly entrenched and, therefore, no longer needed lengthy public justifications of their privilege, at least not in poetic form. For a study of the emergence of a lyrical tendency even within these longer poems, see Ian Hideo Levy, *Hitomaro and the Birth of Japanese Lyricism* (Princeton: Princeton University Press, 1984).

14. Some will take exception to this statement, but the archeological evidence suggests that the Japanese people are a mix of many groups. The proto-Caucasoid Ainu are one of these. For an English translation of the *yukar*, see Donald Philippi, trans., *Songs of Gods, Songs of Humans* (Tokyo: University of Tokyo Press, 1979).

15. *Man'yōshū*, 465. *NKBZ* 2:279.

16. Quoted in Hilda Katō, "The *Mumyōshō* of Kamo no Chōmei and Its Significance in Japanese Literature," in *Monumenta Nipponica* 23:3 (1963), p. 349.

17. Kenkō, *Tsurezuregusa*. *NKBZ* 27:201.

18. *Nihonshoki*, pp. 65 and 66. *NKBT* 3:164–65.

19. Here I am referring to Confucianism as a general rubric for a cluster of ideas as articulated in a number of texts. Some of them (as in the *Analects*) are attributed to Confucius by way of his disciples.

20. Some might trace what remains of studiousness to Meiji-period reformers, such as William S. Clark and his famous injunction, "Boys be ambitious." But the present university system, which was in fact stimulated by Western educators during the Meiji period, has also always had a Confucian function of preparing talented men for bureaucratic life.

21. *Man'yōshū* 13, *NKBZ* 2:71.

22. *Man'yōshū* 24, *NKBZ* 2:77; *Man'yōshū* 443, *NKBZ* 2:270–71.

23. *Man'yōshū* 150, 2:143–44; *Man'yōshū* 2642, *NKBZ* 4:235.

24. *Man'yōshū* 199, *NKBZ* 2:164–68; *Man'yōshū* 210, *NKBZ* 2:173.

25. *Man'yōshū* 466, *NKBZ* 2:280; *Man'yōshū* 3292, *NKBZ* 4:409; *Man'yōshū* 3332, *NKBZ* 4:430–31; *Man'yōshū* 4162, *NKBZ* 5:305; *Man'yōshū* 4408, *NKBZ* 5:410–12; *Man'yōshū* 4468, *NKBZ* 5:433.

26. *Man'yōshū* 469, *NKBZ* 2:280.

27. *Man'yōshū* 482, *NKBZ* 2:287.

28. *Man'yōshū* 597, *NKBZ* 2:338; *Man'yōshū* 733, *NKBZ* 2:376; *Man'yōshū* 1633, *NKBZ* 3:363; *Man'yōshū* 2932, *NKBZ* 4:305; *Man'yōshū* 3107, *NKBZ* 4:343; *Man'yōshū* 3108, *NKBZ* 4:344; *Man'yōshū* 4106, *NKBZ* 5:369–70; *Man'yōshū* 4220, *NKBZ* 5:331.

29. *Man'yōshū* 1785, *NKBZ* 3:428; *Man'yōshū* 1787, *NKBZ* 3:430.

30. *Man'yōshū* 1857, *NKBZ* 4:55.

31. *Man'yōshū* 2960, *NKBZ* 4:311.

32. *Man'yōshū* 2961, *NKBZ* 4:311–12.

33. *Man'yōshū* 3456, *NKBZ* 4:476.

34. *Man'yōshū* 3962, *NKBZ* 5:187.

35. *Man'yōshū* 4125, *NKBZ* 5:281; *Man'yōshū* 4160, *NKBZ* 5:304; *Man'yōshū* 4220, 5:331.

36. *Man'yōshū* 4185, *NKBZ* 5:315.

37. *Man'yōshū* 4211, *NKBZ* 5:326.

38. *Man'yōshū* 4468 and 4469, *NKBZ* 5:433. The translations are in Edwin Cranston, *A Waka Anthology, Volume One: The Gem-Glistening Cup* (Stanford: Stanford University Press, 1993), p. 480.

39. Cranston, *The Gem-Glistening Cup*, pp. 479–80.

40. Levy, *Hitomaro*, p. 43.

41. *Man'yōshū* 876. *NKBZ* 3:112. This is an illusion to a Chinese legend captured in the *Records of the Grand Historian* by Sima Qian [Ssi-ma Chien]. Li Kong [K'ung] knew that Xu Jun [Hsu Chun] secretly coveted his sword. But when he went to visit him and present him with his sword as a gift, Xu Jun had already died. Grieving his passing, Li Kong left his sword hanging from the pine tree above Xu Jun's grave.

42. *Man'yōshū* 896. *NKBZ* 3:114. *Zokudō no henka wa kekimoku no gotoku/Jinji no keiki wa shinpi no gotoshi/Munashiki koto to fuun to taikyo wo iki/Shinryoku tomo ni tsukite yoru tokoro mo nashi.*

43. Ian Hideo Levy, trans., *Man'yōshū Volume One* (Princeton: Princeton University Press, 1981), p. 393.

44. Abe Manzō and Abe Takeshi, eds., *Makura kotoba jiten* (Takashina shoten, 1989), p. 63. To get a good sense of the semantic range of *utsusemi*, see Fukui Kyūzō and Yamagishi Tokuhei, eds., *Makura kotoba no kenkyū to shakugi* (Yūseidō, 1960), pp. 227–30.

45. Nishida Masayoshi, *Mujō no bungaku: nihonteki mujō bikan no keifu* (A Literature of Evanescence: A Genealogy of Japanese Evanescent Aesthetics) (Hanawa shobō, 1975), similarly finds the beginnings of this sensibility developing alongside a more optimistic worldview in ancient Japan. See pp. 5–56.

46. Nishida, *Mujō no bungaku*, pp. 14–15.

47. *Man'yōshū* 165, *NKBZ* 2: 2:150; *Man'yōshū* 196, *NKBZ* 2:161–62; *Man'yōshū* 210, *NKBZ* 2:173–74; *Man'yōshū* 213, *NKBZ* 2:175–76; *Man'yōshū* 4214, *NKBZ* 5:327–28.

48. Orikuchi Shinobu, *Orikuchi Shinobu zenshū*, Vol. 6 (Chūō kōronsha, 1995), p. 76.

49. Cranston, *The Gem-Glistening Cup*, p. 394.

50. *NKBZ* 2: 77.

51. Sakurai Mitsuru, *Sakurai Mitsuru chōsakushū*, volume 8 (Tokyo inshokan, 2000), p. 346.

52. Konishi's analysis seems to group together two types of epithets: nominal modifiers and verbal modifiers. As Professor Cranston pointed out to me, these two groups are different enough to be discussed separately, and that the dating of various *makura kotoba* varies widely. Some, including *utsusemi*, are probably ancient. Others were being created at or near the time of compilation of the *Man'yōshū*.

53. Konishi Jin'ichi, *A History of Japanese Literature Volume One* (Princeton: Princeton University Press, 1984), pp. 208–09.

54. For a critique of this nationalist understanding, see Roy Andrew Miller, "The 'Spirit' of the Japanese Language," in *Journal of Japanese Studies* 3:2 (Summer 1977), pp. 251–98. A response (in English) to Miller is Hirakawa Sukehiro, "In Defense of the 'Spirit' of the Japanese Language," in *Journal of Japanese Studies* 7:2 (Summer 1981), pp. 393–402.

55. Konishi Jin'ichi, *Nihon bungaku shi* (Kodansha, 1993), pp. 30–31.

56. Konishi, *A History of Japanese Literature*, p. 107.

57. Nakanishi Susumu, "The Spatial Structure of Japanese Myth: The Contact Point between Life and Death," in Earl Miner, ed., *Principles of Classical Japanese Literature* (Princeton: Princeton University Press, 1985), p. 117.

58. Konishi, *History of Japanese Literature*, p. 109.

59. Levy, *Hitomaro*, p. 120.

60. For more on the ritual use of ancient Japanese poetry, see Gary Ebersole, *Ritual Poetry and the Politics of Death in Early Japan* (Princeton: Princeton University Press, 1989).
61. Karaki Junzō, *Mujō* (Chikuma shobō, 1965), pp. 12–13.
62. William McCullough, "Japanese Marriage Institutions in the Heian Period," in *Harvard Journal of Asiatic Studies* 27 (1967), pp. 103–66.
63. *Kōkin wakashū*, *NKBZ* 7:46.
64. Sei Shōnagon, *Makura no sōshi*. *NKBZ* 11:106–07. Ivan Morris, trans., *The Pillow Book of Sei Shonagon* (Harmondsworth: Penguin Books, 1976), pp. 49–50.
65. Izumi Shikibu, *Izumi Shikibu nikki*. *NKBZ* 18:85. Edwin Cranston, trans., *The Izumi Shikibu Diary: A Romance of the Heian Court* (Cambridge: Harvard University Press), p. 131.
66. Earl Miner, *An Introduction to Japanese Court Poetry* (Stanford: Stanford University Press, 1968), pp. 152–53.
67. Ono no Komachi, *Kokinshū* 552. *NKBZ* 7:236.
68. Ono no Komachi, *Kokinshū* 658. *NKBZ* 7:266.
69. A more straightforward title would be *The Sarashina Diary*, but I have followed Ivan Morris's *As I Crossed a Bridge of Dreams*, which famously references the final chapter of *The Tale of Genji*.
70. Sugawara no Takasue's Daughter, *Sarashina nikki*. *NKBZ* 18:317.
71. *Sarashina nikki*, *NKBZ* 18:359.
72. *Sarashina nikki*, *NKBZ* 18:359–60.
73. I thank Gary Leupp for this question.
74. For a study of this progression, see Karaki Junzō, *Mujō*.
75. William LaFleur, *The Karma of Words: Buddhism and the Literary Arts in Medieval Japan* (Berkeley: University of California Press).
76. Joseph Kitagawa, " 'A Past of Things Present': Notes on Major Motifs of Early Japanese Religions," in *On Understanding Japanese Religion* (Princeton: Princeton University Press, 1987), pp. 43–58.
77. For an English text of the *Nirvana Sutra*, see nirvanasutra.org.uk.
78. These three terms in Pali are *anicca*, *dukkha*, and *anatta*.
79. This is not to say that there were not eternal gods, however. The myths of the *Kojiki* are populated with such indestructible gods who rule this world with their "inexhaustible, bounteous life force." See Nishida Masayoshi, *Mujō no bungaku* (Hanawa shobō, 1975), p. 14.
80. *Kokin wakashū*, *NKBZ* 7:47. For English translations of the poems, see Laurel Rodd, *Kokinshū: A Collection of Poems Ancient and Modern* (Cheng and Tsui, 1996). Also, Helen McCullough, *Kokin Wakashū: The First Imperial Anthology of Japanese Poetry* (Stanford: Stanford University Press, 1985).
81. *NKBZ* 12:233.
82. This is not the honorific passive form that is used today. In Genji's day, high status was indicated by a causative construction, as in *misase-tamau*, "he looked."
83. My apologies to my older readers, over twenty-five, who will probably be the only ones to look up this footnote.
84. Quoted in "The Vimalakirti Sūtra," in Ryusaku Tsunoda, Wm. Theodore de Bary, Donald Keene, eds., *Sources of Japanese Tradition, Volume One* (New York: Columbia University Press, 1958), p. 102.
85. Yoshida Kenkō, *Tsurezuregusa*. *NKBZ* 27:131.

86. Douglas Berger, "Nagarjuna," in *The Internet Encyclopedia of Philosophy* http://www.iep.utm.edu/n/nagarjun.htm. June 1, 2004.
87. Nancy McCagney, *Nāgārjuna and the Philosophy of Openness* (Lanham, Maryland: Bowman & Littlefield, 1997), p. 58.
88. Alfred North Whitehead, *Religion in the Making* (New York: MacMillan, 1926), p. 49. Quoted in William Theodore de Bary, *The Buddhist Tradition in India, China, and Japan* (New York: Vintage, 1972), p. xvi.
89. Actually, the verb was *saburau*, which became *saburai* in its nominal form. Later, the pronunciation changed to samurai.
90. Kamo no Chōmei, *Hōjōki. NKBZ* 27:27. *Yuku kawa no nagare wa taezu shite, shikamo moto no mizu ni arazu. Yodomi ni ukabu utakata wa, katsu kie katsu musubite, hisashiku todomaritaru tameshi nashi. Yo no naka ni aru hito to sumika to, mata kaku no gotoshi.*
91. For an essay on the *Mumyōshō*, see Hilda Katō, "The *Mumyōshō* of Kamo no Chōmei and Its Significance in Japanese Literature," in *Monumenta Nipponica* 23:3 (1968), pp. 321–49. For a translation of the text, see "The *Mumyōshō*," in *Monumenta Nipponica* 23:3 (1968), pp. 351–430.
92. Takahashi Kazuhiko, ed., *Mumyōshō, Eigyokushū* (Ōfūsha, 1975), p. 11.
93. Yasuhiko Moriguchi and David Jenkins, trans., *Hōjōki, Visions of a Torn World* (Berkeley: Stonebridge Press, 1996), pp. 19–23.
94. Kamo no Chōmei, *Hōjōki. NKBZ* 27:40.
95. Kamo no Chōmei, *Hōjōki. NKBZ* 27:44.
96. Kamo no Chōmei, *Hōjōki. NKBZ* 27:41.
97. Kamo no Chōmei, *Hōjōki. NKBZ* 27:31.
98. Kamo no Chōmei, *Hōjōki. NKBZ* 27:38–39. This is a slightly adjusted translation of Yasuhiko Moriguchi and David Jenkins, trans., *Hōjōki*, pp. 54–58.
99. Kamo no Chōmei, *Hōjōki. NKBZ* 27:41–42.
100. The term "modern" (*kindai*) actually appears in the sixty-eighth section of the *Mumyōshō* and the well-known discussion of the importance of *yūgen*, or mystery, in poetry. See Takahashi, *Mumyōshō, Eigyokushū*, pp. 70–79. Katō translates the word as "contemporary."
101. Kamo no Chōmei, *Hōjōki. NKBZ* 27:49.
102. Kamo no Chōmei, *Hōjōki. NKBZ* 27:35.
103. In his *The Nobility of Failure*, Ivan Morris dwells upon a tragic view of life in Japan. We will have more to say about this in our discussion of the kamikaze pilots of World War II.
104. Major crimes occur in Japan at a very low rate. In 1989 Japan experienced 1.3 robberies per 100,000 population, compared with 48.6 in West Germany, 65.8 in Great Britain, and 233.0 in the United States; and it experienced 1.1 murders per 100,000 population, compared with 3.9 in West Germany, 9.1 in Britain, and 8.7 in the United States that same year. Japanese authorities also solve a high percentage of robbery cases (75.9 percent, compared with 43.8 percent in West Germany, 26.5 percent in Britain, and 26.0 percent in the United States) and homicide cases (95.9 percent, compared with 94.4 percent in Germany, 78.0 percent in Britain, and 68.3 percent for the United States. http://en.wikipedia.org/wiki/Crime_in_Japan. March 4, 2007.
105. Life expectancy is 81.25 years.
106. According to the World Factbook (2002) published by the U.S. Central Intelligence Agency, 99% of people 15 years and older can read. https://www.cia.gov/cia/publications/factbook/print/ja.html. March 3, 2007.

107. *Heike monogatari*. *NKBZ* 29:35. Helen McCullough, trans., *The Tale of the Heike* (Stanford: Stanford University Press, 1988), p. 23.

108. *Heike monogatari*. *NKBZ* 29:449; McCullough, *The Tale of the Heike*, p. 209.

109. *Heike monogatari*. *NKBZ* 29:451–52; McCullough, *The Tale of the Heike*, p. 211.

110. *Heike monogatari*. *NKBZ* 30:530–31; McCullough, *The Tale of the Heike*, pp. 437–38. I have made slight changes to this translation.

111. *Heike monogatari*. *NKBZ* 29:73; McCullough, *The Tale of the Heike*, p. 41

112. *Heike monogatari*. *NKBZ* 29:73–4; McCullough, *The Tale of the Heike*, p. 41.

113. *Heike monogatari*. *NKBZ* 29:99; McCullough, *The Tale of the Heike*, p. 53.

114. Of course, from a Buddhist point of view, moral issues are inherently less clear in the sense that we do not know what kinds of good or bad karma we are accumulated from past lives.

115. *Heike monogatari*. *NKBZ* 30:507; McCullough, *The Tale of the Heike*, p. 426.

116. *Heike monogatari*. *NKBZ* 30:507; McCullough, *The Tale of the Heike*, p. 426.

117. *Heike monogatari*. *NKBZ* 30:508; McCullough, *The Tale of the Heike*, p. 428.

118. *Heike monogatari*. *NKBZ* 30:514; McCullough, *The Tale of the Heike*, p. 429.

119. *Heike monogatari*. *NKBZ* 30:532; McCullough, *The Tale of the Heike*, p. 438.

120. This saying is illogical. How is it possible to get up eight times if you have fallen only seven times?

121. See the *Konjaku monogatari shū* or the *Nihon ryōiki* for accounts of scriptural devotion.

122. Yanagita Kunio, *Nihon no matsuri* (Tokyo: Kadokawa shoten, 1956). Quoted in Murakami Hyōe and Edward Seidensticker, eds., *Guides to Japanese Culture* (Tokyo: Japan Culture Institute, 1977), p. 37.

123. For more on this non-textual emphasis, see my "Pictocentrism," *Yearbook of Comparative and General Literature* 40 (1992), pp. 23–39.

124. Here we are reminded of the seventeenth-century persecution of the Christians and the manner by which suspected believers were made to tread upon an actual image of Jesus. The act of stepping, not the thoughts of one's heart, belied the believer.

125. *Heike monogatari*, *NKBZ* 30: 532; McCullough, *The Tale of the Heike*, p. 438.

126. Left-handedness is now allowable to some extent, but once was strongly suppressed. A similar bias existed elsewhere; it is reflected in the English words "sinister" (left-handed) and "dexterous" (right-handed).

127. Joy Hendry, *Wrapping Culture: Politeness, Presentation, and Power in Japan and Other Societies* (Oxford: Clarendon Press, 1993).

128. As it has evolved, this bit of wisdom has two, nearly contradictory meanings. The earliest was, "In the pursuit of life, bad things happen." But this later came to be overshadowed by a more positive interpretation, "If you give things a try, the results can be surprisingly good." Either way, the advice is utterly practical and of this world.

129. Joseph Kitagawa, *On Understanding Japanese Religion* (Princeton: Princeton University Press, 1987), p. 71.

130. Quoted in J. Thomas Rimer and Masakazu Yamazaki, trans., *On the Art of the Nō Drama: The Major Treatises of Zeami* (Princeton: Princeton University Press, 1984), p. 64.

131. Zeami, *NKBZ* 35:224. Arthur Waley, trans., *The Nō Plays of Japan* (New York: Grove Press, 1957), p. 64.

132. Zeami, *NKBZ* 35:224; Waley, *The Nō Plays of Japan*, p. 64.

133. Zeami, *NKBZ* 35:224; Waley, *The Nō Plays of Japan*, p. 64.
134. Zeami, *NKBZ* 35:233–34; Waley, *The Nō Plays of Japan*, p. 73.
135. Thomas Merton, *Zen and the Birds of Appetite* (New York: New Directions, 1968), p. 109.
136. Yamamoto, *Hagakure*, volume three (Iwanami shoten, 1941), p. 207.
137. The exact authorship of *The Book of Five Rings* is uncertain. Miyamoto Musashi is said to have passed the text on to Terao Magonosuke and other disciples seven days prior to his death. But the veracity of this provenance, too, is hard to determine.
138. For a cinematic interpretation of *Hagakure* values, see Jim Jarmusch, *Ghost Dog, the Way of the Samurai* (2000), a disturbing demonstration of dedication to one's superior.
139. Howard Hibbett, *The Floating World in Japanese Fiction* (Rutland, Vermont: Charles Tuttle, 1975), pp. 10–11.
140. *NKBZ* 38:430. Hibbett, *The Floating World in Japanese Fiction*, p. 154.
141. Saikaku, *NKBZ* 38:430; Hibbett, *The Floating World in Japanese Fiction*, p. 154.
142. Saikaku, *NKBZ* 38:440; Hibbett, *The Floating World in Japanese Fiction*, p. 165.
143. Saikaku, *NKBZ* 38:446; Hibbett, *The Floating World in Japanese Fiction*, p. 171.
144. Saikaku, *NKBZ* 38:446; Hibbett, *The Floating World in Japanese Fiction*, p. 172.
145. Saikaku, *NKBZ* 38:492; Hibbett, *The Floating World in Japanese Fiction*, p. 204.
146. Saikaku, *NKBZ* 38:536; Hibbett, *The Floating World in Japanese Fiction*, p. 205.
147. Saikaku, *NKBZ* 38:541; Hibbett, *The Floating World in Japanese Fiction*, p. 210.
148. Saikaku, *NKBZ* 38:578; Hibbett, *The Floating World in Japanese Fiction*, p. 213.
149. Saikaku, *NKBZ* 38:581–82; Hibbett, *The Floating World in Japanese Fiction*, pp. 216–17.
150. Bashō, *NKBZ* 41:367–68.
151. Haruo Shirane, *Traces of Dreams: Landscape, Cultural Memory, and the Poetry of Bashō* (Stanford: Stanford University Press, 1998), p. 225.
152. Earl Miner makes the point that these terms coincide with those used in certain popularizings of that brand of Neo-Confucianism known in Japan as Shushigaku. That is, although fueki and ryūkō can be traced to Chinese thinkers of the Han and Tang dynasties, in their usage and in their context of other terms they derive from the teaching of the Song Neoconfucianist thinker Zhu Xi (1139–1200), a philosopher in high repute in the early Edo period.
See his *Naming Properties: Nominal Reference in Travel Writings by Bashō and Sora, Johnson and Boswell* (Ann Arbor: University of Michigan Press, 1996), pp. 241–42.
153. Bashō, *NKBZ* 51:545–46.
154. For more on Edo-period observation and description, see Herbert Plutschow, *A Reader in Edo Period Travel* (Kent, UK: Global Oriental, 2006). Karatani's argument is in *Nihon kindai bungaku no kigen* (Kōdansha, 1980). Bret de Bary et al., trans., *The Origins of Modern Japanese Literature* (Durham, North Carolina: Duke University Press, 1993).
155. Bashō, *NKBZ* 51:522.
156. Bashō, *NKBZ* 51:547–48.
157. Shirane, *Traces of Dreams*, p. 262.

158. Makoto Ueda, "Impersonality in Poetry," in *Literary and Art Theories in Japan* (Cleveland: The Press of Western Reserve University, 1967), pp. 145–72.
159. Ueda, "Impersonality in Poetry," p. 149.
160. Bashō, *NKBZ* 41:341.
161. Shirane, *Traces of Dreams*, p. 263.
162. Miner, *Naming Properties*, p. 233.
163. Bashō, *NKBZ* 41:311.
164. Bashō, *NKBZ* 51:55; Shirane, *Traces of Dreams*, p. 265.
165. Bashō, *NKBZ* 41:303.
166. Shirane, *Traces of Dreams*, p. 259.
167. Shirane, *Traces of Dreams*, p. 260. Here he is summarizing Chou Tun-i (1017–73), *Explanation of the Diagram of the Great Ultimate* (*T'ai-chi-t'u shuo*), a fundamental Neo-Confucian text that was translated into Japanese and published in 1678.
168. Hosea Hirata, "*Fueki-ryūkō* (Immutability and Change) in Bashō's Poetics and Poetry," *Yearbook of Comparative and General Literature* 50 (2002/03), p. 61.
169. Hirata, "*Fueki-ryūkō* (Immutability and Change) in Bashō's Poetics and Poetry," p. 61.
170. Bashō, *NKBZ* 41:303.
171. For more of the developing positivism of Edo Japan, see Plutschow, *A Reader in Edo Period Travel*.
172. Bashō, *NKBZ* 51:546.
173. The term is Momokawa Takahito's. For a history of the development of *mono no aware*, see Momokawa Takahito, "'Mono no aware'—the Identity of the Japanese," *Kokubungaku kenkyū shiryōkan kiyō* 13 (March 1987), pp. 1–14.
174. Momokawa, "'Mono no aware'—the Identity of the Japanese," p. 2.
175. Momokawa, "'Mono no aware'—the Identity of the Japanese," p. 13.
176. Susan Burns, *Before the Nation: Kokugaku and the Imagining of Community in Early Modern Japan* (Durham: Duke University Press, 2003), pp. 96–97.
177. Ueda, *Literary and Art Theories in Japan*, p.199.
178. Momokawa, "'Mono no aware'—the Identity of the Japanese," p. 11.
179. The description is from Cecilia Segawa Seigle, *Yoshiwara: The Glittering World of the Japanese Courtesan* (Honolulu: University of Hawaii Press, 1993), p. 154. She argues that flirtation, not sex, was the principal attraction.
180. The term *kokka* (nation) was already being used by Chikamatsu in the early eighteenth century.
181. Donald Keene, trans., *Chūshingura, the Treasury of Loyal Retainers* (New York: Columbia University Press, 1971), pp. 2–3. As Keene notes, Kira Yoshinaka's wife was from the prestigious Uesugi family.
182. Shikitei Sanba, *Ukiyoburo SNBTK* 86:5. Translation by Robert Leutner, *Shikitei Sanba and the Comic Tradition in Edo Fiction* (Cambridge: Harvard University Press, 1985), p. 137.
183. Sanba, *SNBTK* 86:37. Leutner, *Shikitei Sanba and the Comic Tradition in Edo Fiction*, pp. 164–65.
184. A definition of modernity is taken up in my *Figurality and the Development of Modern Consciousness*, now in process.
185. Ikku, *NKBZ* 49:285.

186. A more in-depth version of this discussion can be found in my "Jippensha Ikku's *Shank's Mare (Tōkaidōchū hizakurige)*—Travel, Locale, and the Development of Modern Consciousness," *Proceedings of the Association for Japanese Literary Studies* 8 (Summer 2007), pp. 180–202.
187. Timon Screech, *The Western Scientific Gaze and Popular Imagery in Later Edo Japan* (Cambridge: Cambridge University Press, 1996), p. 97.
188. Komatsu Kazuhiko, *Yōkaigaku shinkō: yōkai kara miru Nihonjin no kokoro* (Shōgakkan, 1994), pp. 30–52.
189. We find a similar reaction to the spreading system of realism in the paintings of, for example, Heironymous Bosch.

2 CHANGE UNDER THE TRANSCENDENTAL ORDER: LATE MODERN JAPAN (1868–1970)

1. Kanagaki Robun, *Agura nabe. Nihon gendai bungaku zenshū* (hereafter *NGBZ*) 1:6–7.
2. For a rehearsal of the significance of late Tokugawa peasant rebellions, see Yukihiko Motoyama, *Talent: Essays on Politics, Thought, and Education in the Meiji Erai*, J.S.A. Elisonas and Richard Rubinger, eds. (Honolulu: University of Hawaii Press, 1997), especially pp. 17–82.
3. Aizawa Seishisai, *Shinron*, in *Mitogaku taikei* volume 2 (Ida shoten, 1941), p. 78. Bob Wakabayashi, trans., *Anti-Foreignism and Western Learning in Early-Modern Japan: The New Thesis of 1825* (Cambridge: Harvard University Press, 1986), p. 200.
4. Aizawa, *Shinron*, p. 78; Wakabayashi, *Anti-Foreignism and Western Learning in Early-Modern Japan*, p. 200.
5. Aizawa, *Shinron*, p. 79; Wakabayashi, *Anti-Foreignism and Western Learning in Early-Modern Japan*, p. 201.
6. Aizawa, *Shinron*, p. 2; Wakabayashi, *Anti-Foreignism and Western Learning in Early-Modern Japan*, p. 149.
7. Aizawa, *Shinron*, p. 2; Wakabayashi, *Anti-Foreignism and Western Learning in Early-Modern Japan*, p. 149.
8. Amaterasu is the "light of heaven," the progenitor of the Japanese people. Aizawa, *Shinron*, p. 8; Wakabayashi, *Anti-Foreignism and Western Learning in Early-Modern Japan*, p. 154.
9. Emiko Ohnuki-Tierney, *Rice as Self: Japanese Identities through Time* (Princeton: Princeton University Press, 1993).
10. For more on the role of slogans, see my "Picturing Modern Japan: A Semiotic Analysis of the Meiji Slogan," in *New Directions in the Study of Meiji Japan: Proceedings of the Harvard Meiji Conference* (Leiden: E.J. Brill, 1997), pp. 270–81.
11. For a study of how this process occurred, see Carol Gluck, *Japan's Modern Myths: Ideology in the Late Meiji Period* (Princeton: Princeton University Press, 1985).
12. An account of the evolution of the Meiji emperor's image is found in Taki Kōji, *Tennō no shōzō* (Iwanami shoten, 1988).
13. I have made a few changes to this translation as it exists in Theodore de Bary, Carol Gluck, and Arthur Tiedemann, eds., *Sources of Japanese Tradition* volume 2 (Second Edition) (New York: Columbia University Press, 1983), pp. 108–09.

14. Cyril H. Powles, "Bushido: Its Admirers and Critics," in John F. Howes, ed., *Nitobe Inazō: Japan's Bridge across the Pacific* (Boulder, Colorado: Westview Press, 1995), p. 107. The original English text went into at least twenty-five editions and reprints.
15. Nitobe Inazō, *Bushido, the Soul of Japan: An Exposition of Japanese Thought* (Rutland, Vermont: Charles Tuttle, 1984), p. 1.
16. Powles, "Bushido," p. 112.
17. Nitobe, *Bushido, the Soul of Japan*, p. 141.
18. Nitobe, *Bushido, the Soul of Japan*, p. 1. My emphasis.
19. Nitobe, *Bushido, the Soul of Japan*, p. 35.
20. Nitobe, *Bushido, the Soul of Japan*, pp. 164–66.
21. Nitobe, *Bushido, the Soul of Japan*, p. 4.
22. Nitobe, *Bushido, the Soul of Japan*, pp. 191–92.
23. Nitobe, *Bushido, the Soul of Japan*, p. 192.
24. Shikishima and Yamato are both ancient poetic names for Japan. Asahi is the rising sun. Yamazakurabana are mountain cherry blossom.
25. Nitobe, *Bushido, the Soul of Japan*, p. 137.
26. Walter Benjamin, "The Work of Art in the Age of Mechanical Reproduction," in Hannah Arendt, ed., Harry Zorn, trans., *Illuminations: Essays and Reflections* (New York: Harcourt, Brace, Jovanovich, 1969), pp. 217–52.
27. Nitobe, *Bushido, the Soul of Japan*, p. 39. From Edmund Burke's (1729–97) *Reflections on the French Revolution*, "that proud submission, that dignified obedience, that subordination of heart which kept alive, even in servitude itself, the spirit of exalted freedom."
28. Nitobe, *Bushido, the Soul of Japan*, p. 14.
29. Nitobe, *Bushido, the Soul of Japan*, p. 176.
30. Nitobe, *Bushido, the Soul of Japan*, p. 58.
31. Nitobe, *Bushido, the Soul of Japan*, p. 54.
32. James Creelman, *On the Great Highway: The Wanderings and Adventures of a Special Correspondent* (Boston: Lothrop Publishing Company, 1901), p. 115–117.
33. Okakura Kakuzō, *The Book of Tea* (Rutland, Vermont: Charles Tuttle, 2000), pp. 22–23.
34. Okakura, *The Book of Tea*, p. 18.
35. Okakura, *The Book of Tea*, p. 20.
36. Okakura, *The Book of Tea*, p. 22.
37. Okakura, *The Book of Tea*, p. 18.
38. Okakura, *The Book of Tea*, pp. 26–27.
39. Okakura, *The Book of Tea*, p. 18.
40. Okakura, *The Book of Tea*, p. 30.
41. Okakura, *The Book of Tea*, p. 47.
42. Okakura, *The Book of Tea*, p. 19.
43. Kuki, "Time Is Money," *Kuki Shūzō zenshū* (hereafter *KSZ*) 1:248. Quoted in Leslie Pincus, *Authenticating Culture in Imperial Japan: Kuki Shūzō and the Rise of National Aesthetics* (Berkeley: University of California Press, 1996), p. 83.
44. Quoted in Pincus, *Authenticating Culture in Imperial Japan*, p. 134.
45. Kuki, "*Iki*" *no kōzō*, *KSZ*, 1:19, 1:26. Pincus, *Authenticating Culture in Imperial Japan*, p. 134.
46. Kuki, *Iki no kōzō*, 1:17.
47. Pincus, *Authenticating Culture in Imperial Japan*, p. 45.

48. Hiroshi Nara, trans., *The Structure of Detachment: The Aesthetic Vision of Kuki Shūzō* (Honolulu: University of Hawaii Press), p. 41.
49. Quoted in Pincus, *Authenticating Culture in Imperial Japan*, p. 51.
50. Quoted in Pincus, *Authenticating Culture in Imperial Japan*, p. 42.
51. Kuki, *Iki no kōzō*, 1:23; Slightly altered, after Pincus, *Authenticating Culture in Imperial Japan*, p. 138.
52. Kuki, "L'Ame Japonaise," *KJZ* 1:252.
53. Kuki, "L'Ame Japonaise," *KJZ* 1:252; Pincus, *Authenticating Culture in Imperial Japan*, p. 80.
54. Pincus, *Authenticating Culture in Imperial Japan*, p. 80.
55. Maruyama Masao, "From Carnal Literature to Carnal Politics," in Ivan Morris, ed., *Thought and Behavior in Modern Japanese Politics* (New York: Oxford University Press, 1969), pp. 245–267.
56. Tom Brocaw, *The Greatest Generation* (New York: Random House, 1998).
57. I was fortunate enough to study Japanese history with Professor Duus as a Stanford undergraduate.
58. The ten-volume *Victory at Sea* was produced by the National Broadcasting Company in cooperation with the U.S. Navy; directed by M. Clay Adams, written by Henry Salomon with Richard Hanser, and produced by Henry Salomon; issued by Embassy Home Entertainment (Los Angeles) in 1984.
59. Morris, *Thought and Behavior in Modern Japanese Politics*, p. 299.
60. Morris, *Thought and Behavior in Modern Japanese Politics*, p. 316.
61. The idiom "gleeful killing" is Charles S. Maier's. See his introduction to Joshua A. Fogel, ed., *The Nanjing Massacre in History and Historiography* (Berkeley: University of California Press, 2000), p. vii.
62. For an account in English on these "death factories," see Sheldon Harris, *Factories of Death: Japanese Biological Warfare 1932–45 and the American Cover-Up* (New York: Routledge, 1994).
63. For more on the comfort women, see Yuki Tanaka, *Japan's Comfort Women: Sexual Slavery and Prostitution during World War II and the US Occupation* (New York: Routledge, 2002). Also, Yoshimi Yoshiaki, Suzanne O'Brien, trans., *Comfort Women: Sexual Slavery in the Japanese Military during World War II* (New York: Columbia University Press, 2000).
64. Suzuki Akira, *"Nankin daigyakusatsu" no maboroshi* (Bungei shunjū, 1973). See also, Tanaka Masaaki, *"Nankin gyakusatsu" no kyokō* (Tokyo: Nihon kyōbunsha, 1984).
65. This is the number suggested by Masahiro Yamamoto, *Nanking, Anatomy of an Atrocity* (Westport, Connecticut: Praeger, 2000), p. 282.
66. A professor at Sophia University and then at Shōwa Women's College, Professor Muramatsu kindly guided me in my study of the novelist and playwright Izumi Kyōka.
67. Some might object to this use of the term "erotic" in this situation. But how else can we understand Kuki's aesthetic innocence? Are rape and murder erotic in a way that, say, prostitution and pornography are not?
68. Quoted in Masahiro Yamamoto, *Nanking*, p. 15.
69. Quoted in Tsuneishi Keiichi, *The Germ Warfare Unit that Disappeared: Kwantung Army's 731st Unit* (Tokyo: Kaimeisha, 1981), p. 71. Quoted in Sheldon Harris, *Factories of Death: Japanese Biological Warfare 1932–45 and the American Cover-Up* (New York: Routledge, 1994), p. 44.

70. This is Harris's argument.

71. Harris, *Factories of Death*, pp. 76–79.

72. Yuki Tanaka, *Japan's Comfort Women: Sexual Slavery and Prostitution during World War II and the US Occupation* (New York: Routledge, 2002), p. 28.

73. Quoted in Tanaka, *Japan's Comfort Women*, p. 16.

74. Based on a report of September 1942, a total of 400 comfort stations had been established through the war zone, including Sakhalin, China, Southeast Asia, and the Southwest Pacific. As noted in Tanaka, *Japan's Comfort Women*, p. 27.

75. Tanaka, *Japan's Comfort Women*, p. 176.

76. See his retirement address before a joint session of Congress, April 19, 1951. From the same speech,

    > Efforts have been made to distort my position. It has been said, in effect, that I was a warmonger. *Nothing* could be further from the truth. I know war as few other men now living know it, and nothing to me is more revolting. I have long advocated its complete abolition, as its very destructiveness on both friend and foe has rendered it useless as a means of settling international disputes. ... But once war is forced upon us, there is no other alternative than to apply every available means to bring it to a swift end.

77. One lies on one's back, on a recliner or on the floor, and drinks are poured down one's throat, like a bomb. On a white bandana worn over the victim's (hero's?) forehead, a red dot is drawn. With each hit, another dot is added.

78. *NKBZ* 1:159.

79. *NKBZ* 2:165–66. Cranston, trans., *The Gem-Glistening Cup*, pp. 220–21.

80. Ivan Morris, *The Nobility of Failure: Tragic Heroes in the History of Japan* (New York: New American Library, 1976), p. 284.

81. Morris, *The Nobility of Failure*, p. 309.

82. Shikishima and Yamato are both ancient poetic names for Japan. Asahi is the rising sun, which also provided the image for Japan's war flag. Yamazakurabana is the mountain cherry blossom.

83. Quoted in Inoguchi Rikihei and Nakajima Tadashi, *Shinpū tokubetsu kōgekitai no kiroku*, Roger Pineau, trans., *The Divine Wind: Japan's Kamikaze Force in World War II* (Annapolis, 1958), p. 187; quoted in Morris, *The Nobility of Failure* (New York: New American Library, 1976), p. 334.

84. By Sublieutenant Okabe Heiichi of the Shichishō Butai. Quoted in Morris, *The Nobility of Failure*, p. 276.

85. Morris, *The Nobility of Failure*, pp. 319–20.

86. Morris, *The Nobility of Failure*, p. 311.

87. Quoted in John Dower, *Embracing Defeat: Japan in the Wake of World War II* (New York: W.W. Norton, 1999), p. 285.

88. The U.S. Strategic Bombing Survey, quoted in Edwin Fogelman, ed., *Hiroshima: The Decision to Use the A-Bomb* (New York: Charles Scribner's Sons, 1964), p. 87.

89. John Treat, *Writing Ground Zero* (Chicago: University of Chicago Press, 1995), p. 7.

90. Treat, *Writing Ground Zero*, p. 5.

91. Ōe Kenzaburō, *Hiroshima Notes*, David Swain, ed., Toshi Yonezawa, trans. (Tokyo: YMCA Press, 1981), p. 101.

92. From Murata's unpublished account. He also appears in the film, *No More Hiroshima* (New York: Icarus Films, 1984).

93. Treat, *Writing Ground Zero*, p. 2.

94. Quoted in Treat, *Writing Ground Zero*, p. 3.

95. Quoted in Ōe, *Hiroshima Notes*, p. 55.

96. Quoted in Richard Minear, trans., "The City of Corpses," in *Hiroshima Three Witnesses* (Princeton: Princeton University Press, 1990), p. 148.

97. Ōta Yoko, *Shikabane no machi* (Chūō kōron, 1948), p. 5; Minear, "The City of Corpses," p. 153.

98. Ōta, *Shikabane no machi*, p. 7.

99. Hara Tamiki, *Natsu no hana* (Shōbunsha, 1970), p. 83. Minear, trans., *Hiroshima Three Witnesses*, p. 57.

100. John Dower, *War without Mercy: Race and Power in the Pacific War* (New York: Pantheon, 1993).

101. Takenishi, quoted in Treat, *Writing Ground Zero*, pp. 73–74.

102. This was the public high school in the Boston suburbs that Owada Masako, now Crown Princess of Japan, attended.

103. *"Genki wo dashite, oishii mono wo tabete, ganbaru shika nai."*

104. Takeyama Michio, "Biruma no tategoto," in *Takeyama Michio chōsakushū* volume 7 (Fukutake shoten, 1983), p. 7; Howard Hibbett, trans., *Harp of Burma* (Rutland, Vermont: Charles Tuttle: 1966), p. 11.

105. Takeyama, *Biruma no tategoto*, p. 164; Hibbett, *Harp of Burma*, p. 127.

106. Takeyama, *Biruma no tategoto*, p. 168; Hibbett, *Harp of Burma*, p. 130.

107. Takeyama, *Biruma no tategoto*, p. 53; Hibbett, *Harp of Burma*, p. 46.

108. Takeyama, *Biruma no tategoto*, p. 56; Hibbett, *Harp of Burma*, pp. 48–49.

109. Takeyama, *Biruma no tategoto*, p. 167; Hibbett, *Harp of Burma*, p. 129.

110. Sakaguchi Ango, "*Darakuron*," in *Sakaguchi Ango zenshū* volume 4 (Chikuma shobō, 1998), pp. 53–54.

111. Sakaguchi, "*Darakuron*," p. 53.

112. Dower, *Embracing Defeat*.

113. Sakaguchi, "*Darakuron*," pp. 54–55.

114. Sakaguchi, "*Darakuron*," pp. 55–56.

115. Sakaguchi, "*Darakuron*," p. 55.

116. Sakaguchi, "*Darakuron*," p. 56.

117. Sakaguchi, "*Darakuron*," p. 57.

118. Sakaguchi, "*Darakuron*," p. 57.

119. Sakaguchi, "*Darakuron*," p. 57.

120. Sakaguchi, "*Darakuron*," p. 57.

121. Sakaguchi, "*Darakuron*," p. 60.

122. The song was written by Nakamura Shinpei in 1915; lyrics by Yoshii Isamu (1886–1960). In the movie, only the first and fourth verses are sung.

123. This transformation is the subject of Mishima Yukio's *Sun and Steel*, John Bester, trans. (Tokyo: Kodansha International, 1970).

124. Roy Starrs, *Deadly Dialectics: Sex, Violence and Nihilism in the World of Mishima Yukio* (Honolulu: University of Hawaii, 1994).

125. Mishima Yukio, *Sun and Steel*, p. 15.

126. Higashiyama Kaii, "*Fūkei kaigan*," in Higashiyama, *Kaii gabunshū 3 kan: Fūkei to no taiwa* (Shinchōsha, 1967), p. 12.

127. Higashiyama, "*Fūkei kaigan*," p. 14.

128. Quoted in Higashiyama Kaii, "*Hoshi wakareyuku*," in *Higashiyama Kaii gabunshū 5 kan: bi no otozure* (Shinchōsha, 1979), p. 150.

129. Quoted in Higashiyama Kaii, "*Hoshi wakareyuku*," p. 150.

130. Higashiyama Kaii, "*Watakushitachi no fūkei*," in *Higashiyama Kaii gabunshū 5 kan: bi no otozure* (Shinchōsha, 1979), pp. 205–06.

3   Return to Evanescence: Contemporary Japan (1970 to the Present)

1. Ezra Vogel, *Japan as Number 1: Lessons for America* (Cambridge: Harvard University Press, 1979).
2. http://en.wikipedia.org/wiki/Japanese_asset_price_bubble. June 12, 2007.
3. For more on Japan's bubble economy, see Thomas F. Cargill, Michael M. Hutchison, and Takatoshi Itō, *The Political Economy of Japanese Monetary Policy* (Cambridge, Massachusetts: MIT Press, 1997).
4. This subject of withdrawal into individual pursuits is taken up by Anne Allison, *Millennial Monsters: Japanese Toys and the Global Imagination* (Berkeley: University of California Press, 2006).
5. Tanaka Yasuo, *Nantonaku kurisutaru. Shinchōbunko 3528* (Shinchōsha, 1981), pp. 103–04.
6. Tanaka, *Nantonaku kurisutaru*, p. 210.
7. Tanaka, *Nantonaku kurisutaru*, p. 40.
8. Tanaka, *Nantonaku kurisutaru*, p. 42.
9. Tanaka, *Nantonaku kurisutaru*, p. 78.
10. Tanaka, *Nantonaku kurisutaru*, p. 79.
11. Tanaka, *Nantonaku kurisutaru*, pp. 220–21.
12. Tanaka, *Nantonaku kurisutaru*, p. 221.
13. By figurality, I mean the expressive potential of the grapheme. In other words, the expressive power of the material and visible aspect of any sign.
14. Masao Miyoshi, *Off Center* (Cambridge: Harvard University Press, 1991), p. 233.
15. Of course, one could also argue that many of the *tanka* in *Genji* are a part of the linear flow if viewed as a form of conversation.
16. For a fuller discussion of this film, see my article, "In the Show House of Modernity: Exhaustive Listing in Itami Jūzō's *Tanpopo*," in Dennis Washburn and Carole Cavanaugh, eds., *Word and Image in Japanese Cinema* (Cambridge: Cambridge University Press, 2001), pp. 126–48.
17. Mibu Taishun, *Hannya shingyō* (Hōbunkan shuppan, 1971), p. i.
18. Quoted in Treat, *Writing Ground Zero*, p. 3.
19. The novel has been translated into English by Michael Gallagher, *Japan Sinks* (Kodansha International, 1995).
20. Miyazaki Hayao, *Kaze no tani no Naushika* volumes 1–7 (Tokyo: Tokuma shoten, 1983–95), 1: back of front cover. The original manga were published over a period from February 1982 to May 1991 in the magazine *Animēju*.
21. Nausicǎa is the daughter of Alcinous, king of the Phaeacians, and Areté. She appears in Books 6, 7, and 8 of Homer's *Odyssey*.
22. Miyazaki Hayao, "*Naushika no koto*," 1: inside the back cover. Miyazaki misremembers the source of this story as the *Konjaku monogatari*. Actually, it is the *Tsutsumi Chūnagon monogatari*. For an English translation, see Edwin Reischauer and Joseph Yamagiwa, trans., "The Girl Who Loved Worms," in *Translations from Early Japanese Literature* (Cambridge: Harvard University Press, 1951), pp. 184–95.
23. Miyazaki, "*Naushika no koto*," 7:198.

24. Ian Reader, *Religious Violence in Contemporary Japan: The Case of Shinrikyō* (Honolulu: University of Hawaii Press, 2000).

25. These two volumes were partially translated into English by Alfred Birnbaum and Philip Gabriel, and brought together under the title *Underground*. Numbers in parentheses refer to a paperback edition (New York: Vintage Press, 2001). As for the originals, *Andāguraundo* was first published by Kōdansha in 1997. *Yakusoku sareta basho de* was published by Bungeishunjū the following year.

26. The interviewed members of Aum were not those actually accused of crimes.

27. Murakami Haruki, *Yakusoku sareta basho de*, in *Murakami Haruki zensakuhin 1990–2000* volume 7 (Kōdansha, 2003), pp. 171–72. Birnbaum and Gabriel, trans., *Underground* (New York: Vintage International, 2000), pp. 348–49.

28. Murakami, *Andāguraundo*, *Murakami Haruki zensakuhin 1990–2000* volume 6 (Kōdansha, 2003), p. 645. Birnbaum and Gabriel, trans., *Underground* (New York: Vintage International, 2001), p. 228.

29. Murakami Haruki, "1963/1982 no Ipenema musume," *Murakami Haruki zenshū 1979–1989* volume 5 (Kodansha, 1991), p. 88. Translation by Jay Rubin, *Murakami Haruki and the Music of Words* (London: Harvill Press, 2002), p. 126.

30. Murakami Haruki, *Sekai no owari to hādo-boirudo wandārando.* in *Murakami Haruki zenshū 1979–1989* volume 4 (Kōdansha, 1991), p. 590; Alfred Birnbaum, trans., *Hard-Boiled Wonderland and the End of the World* (New York: Kodansha International, 1991), p. 399.

31. Masao Miyoshi dismisses Murakami as a "stylist." See *Off Center*, pp. 234–35. For my review of Miyoshi, see *Monumenta Nipponica* 47:3, pp. 400–04.

32. Murakami, *Andāguraundo*, p. 25; Birnbaum and Gabriel, *Underground*, p. 7.

33. Ukai Tetsuo, "[Murakami Haruki] Taking on the Forces of 'Black Magic,'" *The Daily Yomiuri*, May 17, 1998.

34. Ukai, "Taking on the Forces of 'Black Magic.'"

35. Murakami, *Andāguraundo*, p. 654; Birnbaum and Gabriel, *Underground*, p. 233.

36. Robert Jay Lifton, *Destroying the World to Save It* (New York: Metropolitan Books, 1999).

37. Quoted in http://cscs.umich.edu/~crshalizi/T4PM/futurist-manifesto.html. August 4, 2006.

38. Susan Napier, *Anime from Akira to Princess Mononoke* (New York: Palgrave, 2000), p. 36.

39. http://www.gofishpictures.com/GITS2/main.html. December 16, 2004.

40. For a study of how these dolls evolved into the puppets of the puppet theater, or *bunraku*, see Jane Marie Law, *Puppets of Nostalgia: The Life, Death, and Rebirth of the Japanese Awaji Ningyō Tradition* (Princeton: Princeton University Press, 1997).

41. http://www.gofishpictures.com/GITS2/main.html. December 15, 2004.

42. Quoted in Esperanza Ramirez-Christensen, *Heart's Flower: The Life and Poetry of Shinkei* (Stanford: Stanford University Press, 1994), p. 66.

WORKS CITED

The following abbreviations are of published series of Japanese literature. Unless otherwise specified, the place of publication of these and all other Japanese works is Tokyo.

NKBZ *Nihon koten bungaku zenshū* (Shōgakkan, 1973–1976).
NKBT *Nihon koten bungaku taikei* (Iwanami shoten, 1957–1968).
SNKBT *Shin Nihon koten bungaku taikei* (Iwanami shoten, 1989–).
NGBZ *Nihon gendai bungaku zenshū* (Kōdansha, 1965).

PRIMARY TEXTS (WITH RECOMMENDED TRANSLATIONS WHERE AVAILABLE)

Aizawa Seishisai. *Shinron. Mitogaku taikei* volume 2. Ida shoten. 1941. Bob Wakabayashi, trans. *Anti-Foreignism and Western Learning in Early-Modern Japan: The New Thesis of 1825.* Cambridge: Harvard University Press. 1986.

Ariwara no Narihira. *Kokin wakashū* 474. *NKBT* volume 7.

Chikamatsu Monzaemon. *Shinjū ten no Amijima.* Fujino Yoshio, ed. *Shinjū ten no Amijima; kaishaku to kenkyū.* Ōfūsha. 1971. Donald Keene, trans. "The Love Suicides at Amijima." In *Four Major Plays of Chikamatsu.* New York: University of Columbia Press. 1961.

Daihatsu nehangyō (Nirvana Sutra). Harada Reidō, ed. *Daihatsu nehangyō.* Bukkyō kyōten sōsho kankōkai. 1922.

Dōgen. *Dōgen Zenji zenshū* volume 7. Shunjūsha. 1990.

Hannya shingyō (Heart Sutra). Mibu Taishun. *Hannya shingyō.* Hōbunkan shuppan. 1971.

Hara Tamiki. *Natsu no hana. Natsu no hana: Hara Tamiki chō.* Shōbunsha. 1970. Richard Minear, trans. "Summer Flowers." In *Hiroshima Three Witnesses.* Princeton: Princeton University Press. 1990.

Heike monogatari. NKBZ volumes 29 and 30. Helen McCullough, trans. *The Tale of the Heike.* Stanford: Stanford University Press. 1988.

Higashiyama Kaii. "Fūkei kaigan." In Higashiyama, *Kaii gabunshū 3 kan: Fūkei to no taiwa.* Shinchōsha. 1967.

———. "Hoshi wakareyuku." *Higashiyama Kaii gabunshū 5 kan: bi no otozure.* Shinchōsha. 1979.

———. "Watakushitachi no fūkei." *Higashiyama Kaii gabunshū 5 kan: bi no otozure.* Shinchōsha. 1979.

Ihara Saikaku. *Kōshoku ichidai onna. NKBZ* volume 39. Howard Hibbett, trans. *The Floating World in Japanese Fiction.* Tokyo: Charles Tuttle. 1975.

Izumi Shikibu. *Izumi Shikibu nikki*. *NKBZ* volume 18. Edwin Cranston, trans. *The Izumi Shikibu Diary: A Romance of the Heian Court*. Cambridge: Harvard University Press. 1969.

Jippensha Ikku. *Tōkaidōchū hizakurige*. *NKBZ* volume 49. Thomas Satchell, trans. *Hizakurige or Shank's Mare*. Tokyo: Charles Tuttle. 1960.

Kamo no Chōmei. *Mumyōshō*. Takahashi Kazuhiko, ed. *Mumyōshō hyōshaku*. Fenikkusu shoin. 1967. Hilda Katō, trans. *Monumenta Nipponica* 23:3 (1968), pp. 351–430.

———. *Hōjōki*. *NKBZ* volume 27. Yasuhiko Moriguchi and David Jenkins, trans. *Hōjōki: Visions of a Torn World*. Berkeley: Stonebridge Press. 1996.

Kokinshū. *NKBZ* volume 7. Laurel Rodd, trans. *Kokinshū: A Collection of Poems Ancient and Modern*. Boston: Cheng and Tsui. 1996. Also, Helen McCullough, trans. *Kokin Wakashū: The First Imperial Anthology of Japanese Poetry*. Stanford: Stanford University Press. 1985.

Komatsu Sakyō. *Nippon chinbotsu*. Kōbunsha, 1973. Michael Gallagher, trans. *Japan Sinks*. Tokyo: Kōdansha International. 1995.

Kuki Shūzō. *"Iki" no kōzō*. *Kuki Shūzō zenshū* volume 1. Iwanami shoten. 1981. Hiroshi Nara, trans. *The Structure of Detachment: The Aesthetic Vision of Kuki Shūzō*. Honolulu: University of Hawaii Press. 2004.

Man'yōshū. *NKBZ* volumes 2–5. Edwin Cranston, trans. *A Waka Anthology Volume One: The Gem-Glistening Cup*. Stanford: Stanford University Press. 1993.

Mishima Yukio. *Taiyō to tetsu*. *Mishima Yukio zenshū* volume 32. Shinchōsha. 1976. John Bester, trans. *Sun and Steel*. Tokyo: Kōdansha International. 1970.

Miyazaki Hayao. *Kaze no tani no Naushika*. Seven volumes. Tokuma shoten. 1982–91.

Murakami Haruki. "1963/1982 no Ipenema musume." In *Murakami Haruki zenshū 1979–1989* volume 5. Kōdansha. 1991.

———. *Sekai no owari to hādo-boirudo wandārando*. *Murakami Haruki zenshū 1979–1989* volume 4. Kōdansha. 1991. Alfred Birnbaum, trans. *Hard-Boiled Wonderland and the End of the World*. New York: Kōdansha International. 1991.

———. *Andāguraundo*. *Murakami Haruki zensakuhin 1990–2000* volume 6. Kōdansha. 2003. Alfred Birnbaum and Philip Gabriel, trans. *Underground*. New York: Vintage International. 2001.

———. *Yakusoku sareta basho de*. *Murakami Haruki zensakuhin 1990–2000* volume 7. Kōdansha. 2003. Alfred Birnbaum and Philip Gabriel, trans. *Underground*. New York: Vintage International. 2001.

Nihonshoki (poems). *NKBT* volume 3. Iwanami shoten. 1957. Edwin Cranston, trans. *A Waka Anthology Volume One: The Gem-Glistening Cup*. Stanford: Stanford University Press. 1993.

Nitobe Inazō. *Bushido, the Soul of Japan: An Exposition of Japanese Thought*. Rutland, Vermont: Charles Tuttle. 1984.

Ōe Kenzaburō. *Hiroshima nōto*. In *Hiroshima no hikari*. Iwanami shoten. 1980. Toshi Yonezawa, trans. *Hiroshima Notes*. Tokyo: YMCA Press. 1981.

Okakura Kakuzō. *The Book of Tea*. Rutland, Vermont: Charles Tuttle. 2000.

Ono no Komachi, *Kokinshū* 552, 553, 658. *NKBZ* volume 7. Laurel Rodd, trans. *Kokinshū: A Collection of Poems Ancient and Modern*. Boston: Cheng and Tsui. 1996. Also, Helen McCullough, trans. *Kokin Wakashū: The First Imperial Anthology of Japanese Poetry*. Stanford: Stanford University Press. 1985.

Orikuchi Shinobu. *Orikuchi Shinobu zenshū*, volume 6. Chūō kōronsha. 1995.

Ōta Yōko. *Shikabane no machi.* Chūō kōron sha. 1948. Richard Minear, trans. *The City of Corpses.* In *Hiroshima Three Witnesses.* Princeton: Princeton University Press. 1990.

Ōtomo Katsuhiro. *Akira.* Six volumes. Kōdansha. 1984–93.

Sakaguchi Ango. "Darakuron." In *Sakaguchi Ango zenshū* volume 4. Chikuma shobō. 1998.

Sei Shōnagon. *Makura no sōshi. NKBZ* volume 11. Ivan Morris, trans. *The Pillow Book of Sei Shonagon.* Harmondsworth: Penguin Books. 1976.

Shikitei Sanba. *Ukiyoburo. SNBTK* volume 86. Iwanami shoten. 1989. Robert Leutner, trans. *Shikitei Sanba and the Comic Tradition in Edo Fiction.* Cambridge: Harvard University Press. 1985.

Sugawara no Takasue's Daughter. *Sarashina nikki. NKBZ* volume 18. Ivan Morris, trans. *As I Crossed a Bridge of Dreams.* London: Penguin Classics. 1975.

Takeyama Michio. *Biruma no tategoto. Takeyama Michio chōsakushū* volume 7. Fukutake shoten. 1983. Howard Hibbett, trans. *Harp of Burma.* Rutland, Vermont: Charles Tuttle. 1966.

Tanaka Yasuo. *Nantonaku, kurisutaru. Shinchō bunko 3528.* Shinchōsha. 1981.

Yamamoto Tsunetomo. *Hagakure,* three volumes. Iwanami shoten. 1940–41. William Scott Wilson, trans. *Hagakure, the Book of the Samurai.* New York: Kōdansha International. 1983.

Yoshida Kenkō. *Tsurezuregusa. NKBZ* volume 27. Donald Keene, trans. *Essays in Idleness.* New York: Columbia University Press. 1967.

Zeami. *Atsumori. NKBZ* volume 35. Arthur Waley, trans. *The Nō Plays of Japan.* New York: Grove Press. 1957. Also, Royall Tyler, trans. *Japanese Nō Dramas.* London: Penguin. 1992.

SECONDARY SOURCES

Abe Manzō and Abe Takeshi, eds. *Makura kotoba jiten.* Takashina shoten. 1989.

Adams, M. Clay, director. *Victory at Sea.* Los Angeles. Embassy Home Entertainment. 1984.

Allison, Anne. *Millennial Monsters: Japanese Toys and the Global Imagination.* Berkeley: University of California Press. 2006.

Benjamin, Walter. "The Work of Art in the Age of Mechanical Reproduction." Hannah Arendt, ed. Harry Zorn, trans. *Illuminations: Essays and Reflections.* New York: Harcourt, Brace, Jovanovich. 1969.

Brocaw, Tom. *The Greatest Generation.* New York: Random House. 1998.

Burns, Susan. *Before the Nation: Kokugaku and the Imagining of Community in Early Modern Japan.* Durham: Duke University Press. 2003.

Cargill, Thomas F., Michael M. Hutchison, and Takatoshi Itō. *The Political Economy of Japanese Monetary Policy.* Cambridge: MIT Press. 1997.

Cooper, Michael. *The Southern Barbarians.* Kōdansha and Sophia University. 1971.

Creelman, James. *On the Great Highway: The Wanderings and Adventures of a Special Correspondent.* Boston: Lothrop Publishing Company. 1901.

de Bary, William Theodore. *The Buddhist Tradition in India, China, and Japan.* New York: Vintage. 1972.

de Bary, Theodore, Carol Gluck, and Arthur Tiedemann, eds. *Sources of Japanese Tradition* volume 2 (Second Edition). New York: Columbia University Press. 1983.

Dower, John. *War without Mercy: Race and Power in the Pacific War.* New York: Pantheon. 1993.

———. *Embracing Defeat: Japan in the Wake of World War II.* New York: W.W. Norton. 1999.

Ebersole, Gary. *Ritual Poetry and the Politics of Death in Early Japan.* Princeton: Princeton University Press. 1989.

Fogel, Joshua, ed. *The Nanjing Massacre in History and Historiography.* Berkeley: University of California Press. 2000.

Fogelman, Edwin, ed. *Hiroshima: The Decision to Use the A-Bomb.* New York: Charles Scribner's Sons. 1964.

Fukui Kyūzō and Yamagishi Tokuhei, eds. *Makura kotoba no kenkyū to shakugi.* Yūseidō. 1960.

Gluck, Carol. *Japan's Modern Myths: Ideology in the Late Meiji Period.* Princeton: Princeton University Press. 1985.

Harris, Sheldon. *Factories of Death: Japanese Biological Warfare 1932–45 and the American Cover-Up.* New York: Routledge. 1994.

Hendry, Joy. *Wrapping Culture: Politeness, Presentation, and Power in Japan and Other Societies.* Oxford: Clarendon Press. 1993.

Hibbett, Howard. *The Floating World in Japanese Fiction.* Tokyo: Charles Tuttle. 1975.

Hirakawa Sukehiro. "In Defense of the 'Spirit' of the Japanese Language." *Journal of Japanese Studies* 7:2 (Summer 1981), pp. 393–402.

Hirata, Hosea. *"Fueki-ryūkō* (Immutability and Change) in Bashō's Poetics and Poetry." *Yearbook of Comparative and General Literature* 50 (2002/03), pp. 59–70.

Howes, John. *Nitobe Inazō, Japan's Bridge across the Pacific.* Boulder, Colorado: Westview Press. 1995.

Inouye, Charles Shirō. "In the Show House of Modernity: Exhaustive Listing in Itami Jūzō's *Tanpopo.*" Dennis Washburn and Carole Cavanaugh, eds. *Word and Image in Japanese Cinema.* Cambridge: Cambridge University Press. 2001.

———. "Pictocentrism." *Yearbook of Comparative and General Literature* 40 (1992), pp. 23–39.

———. "Picturing Modern Japan: A Semiotic Analysis of the Meiji Slogan." *New Directions in the Study of Meiji Japan: Proceedings of the Harvard Meiji Conference.* Leiden: E.J. Brill. 1997.

Kamens, Edward. *Utamakura, Allusion, and Intertextuality in Traditional Japanese Poetry.* New Haven: Yale University Press. 1997.

Karaki Junzō. *Mujō.* Chikuma shobō. 1965.

Karatani Kōjin. *Nihon kindai bungaku no kigen.* Kōdansha. 1980.

Komatsu Kazuhiko. *Yōkaigaku shinkō: yōkai kara miru Nihonjin no kokoro.* Shōgakkan. 1994.

Konishi Jin'ichi. *A History of Japanese Literature Volume One.* Princeton: Princeton University Press. 1984.

———. *Nihon bungaku shi.* Kōdansha. 1993.

Kitagawa, Joseph. "'A Past of Things Present': Notes on Major Motifs of Early Japanese Religions." *On Understanding Japanese Religion.* Princeton: Princeton University Press. 1987.

LaFleur, William. *The Karma of Words: Buddhism and the Literary Arts in Medieval Japan.* Berkeley: University of California Press. 1983.

Law, Jane Marie. *Puppets of Nostalgia: The Life, Death, and Rebirth of the Japanese Awaji Ningyō Tradition*. Princeton: Princeton University Press. 1997.

Leutner, Robert. *Shikitei Sanba and the Comic Tradition in Edo Fiction*. Cambridge: Harvard University Press. 1985.

Levy, Ian Hideo. *Hitomaro and the Birth of Japanese Lyricism*. Princeton: Princeton University Press. 1984.

Lifton, Robert Jay. *Destroying the World to Save It*. New York: Metropolitan Books. 1999.

Maruyama Masao. "From Carnal Literature to Carnal Politics." In Ivan Morris, ed. *Thought and Behavior in Modern Japanese Politics*. New York: Oxford University Press. 1969.

McCagney, Nancy. *Nāgārjuna and the Philosophy of Openness*. Lanham, Maryland: Bowman & Littlefield. 1997.

McCullough, William. "Japanese Marriage Institutions in the Heian Period." *Harvard Journal of Asiatic Studies* 27 (1967), pp. 103–66.

Merton, Thomas. *Zen and the Birds of Appetite*. New York: New Directions. 1968.

Miller, Roy Andrew. "The 'Spirit' of the Japanese Language." *Journal of Japanese Studies* 3:2 (Summer 1977), pp. 251–298.

Miner, Earl. *An Introduction to Japanese Court Poetry*. Stanford: Stanford University Press. 1968.

———. *Principles of Classical Japanese Literature*. Princeton: Princeton University Press. 1985.

———. *Naming Properties*. Ann Arbor: University of Michigan Press. 1996.

Miyoshi, Masao. *Off Center*. Cambridge: Harvard University Press. 1991.

Momokawa Takahito. "'Mono no aware'—the Identity of the Japanese." *Kokubungaku kenkyū shiryōkan kiyō* 13 (March 1987), pp. 1–14.

Morris, Ivan. *The Nobility of Failure: Tragic Heroes in the History of Japan*. New York: New American Library. 1976.

Motoyama, Yukihiko. J.S.A. Elisonas, and Richard Rubinger, eds. *Proliferating Talent: Essays on Politics, Thought, and Education in the Meiji Era*. Honolulu: University of Hawaii Press. 1997.

Murakami Hyōe and Edward Seidensticker, eds. *Guides to Japanese Culture*. Tokyo: Japan Culture Institute. 1977.

Nakanishi Susumu. "The Spatial Structure of Japanese Myth: The Contact Point between Life and Death." In Earl Miner, ed. *Principles of Classical Japanese Literature*. Princeton: Princeton University Press. 1985.

Napier, Susan. *Anime, from Akira to Princess Mononoke*. New York: Palgrave Press. 2001.

Nishida Masayoshi. *Mujō no bungaku*. Hanawa shobō. 1975.

Ōe Kenzaburō. *Hiroshima Notes*. David Swain, ed. Toshi Yonezawa, trans. Tokyo: YMCA Press. 1981.

Ohnuki-Tierney, Emiko. *Rice as Self: Japanese Identities through Time*. Princeton: Princeton University Press. 1993.

Philippi, Donald, trans. *Songs of Gods, Songs of Humans*. Tokyo: University of Tokyo Press. 1979.

Pincus, Leslie. *Authenticating Culture in Imperial Japan: Kuki Shūzō and the Rise of National Aesthetics*. Berkeley: University of California Press. 1996.

Plutschow, Herbert. *A Reader in Edo Period Travel*. Kent, England: Global Oriental. 2006.

Ramirez-Christensen, Esperanza. *Heart's Flower: The Life and Poetry of Shinkei.* Stanford: Stanford University Press. 1994.

Reader, Ian. *Religious Violence in Contemporary Japan: The Case of Aum Shinrikyō.* Honolulu: University of Hawaii Press. 2000.

Reischauer, Edwin and Joseph Yamagiwa, trans. *Translations from Early Japanese Literature.* Cambridge: Harvard University Press. 1951.

Rimer, J. Thomas and Masakazu Yamazaki, trans. *On the Art of the Nō Drama: The Major Treatises of Zeami.* Princeton: Princeton University Press. 1984.

Rubin, Jay. *Haruki Murakami and the Music of Words.* London: Harvill. 2002.

Screech, Timon. *The Western Scientific Gaze and Popular Imagery in Later Edo Japan.* Cambridge: Cambridge University Press. 1996.

Seigle, Cecilia Segawa. *Yoshiwara: The Glittering World of the Japanese Courtesan.* Honolulu: University of Hawaii Press. 1993.

Shirane, Haruo. *Traces of Dreams: Landscape, Cultural Memory and the Poetry of Bashō.* Stanford: Stanford University Press. 1998.

Starrs, Roy. *Deadly Dialectics: Sex, Violence and Nihilism in the World of Mishima Yukio.* Honolulu: University of Hawaii. 1994.

Suzuki Akira. *"Nankin daigyakusatsu" no maboroshi.* Bungei shunjū. 1973.

Takahashi Kazuhiko, ed. *Mumyōshō, Eigyokushū.* Ōfūsha. 1975.

Taki Kōji. *Tennō no shōzō.* Iwanami shoten. 1988.

Tanaka Masaaki. *"Nankin gyakusatsu" no kyokō.* Nihon kyōbunsha. 1984.

Tanaka, Yuki. *Japan's Comfort Women: Sexual Slavery and Prostitution during World War II and the US Occupation.* New York: Routledge. 2002.

Treat, John. *Writing Ground Zero.* Chicago: University of Chicago Press. 1995.

Ueda, Makoto. *Zeami, Bashō, Yeats, Pound.* The Hague: Mouton & Co. 1965.

———. *Literary and Art Theories in Japan.* Cleveland: Press of Western Reserve University. 1967.

Ukai, Tetsuo. "[Murakami Haruki] Taking on the Forces of 'Black Magic' " *Yomiuri Shinbun.* May 17, 1998.

Vogel, Ezra. *Japan as Number 1: Lessons for America.* Cambridge: Harvard University Press. 1979.

Wakabayashi, Bob. *Anti-Foreignism and Western Learning in Early-Modern Japan: The New Thesis of 1825.* Harvard University Press. 1986.

Yamamoto, Masahiro. *Nanking, Anatomy of an Atrocity.* Westport, Connecticut: Praeger. 2000.

Yoshimi Yoshiaki. Suzanne O'Brien, trans. *Comfort Women: Sexual Slavery in the Japanese Military during World War II.* New York: Columbia University Press. 2000.

INDEX